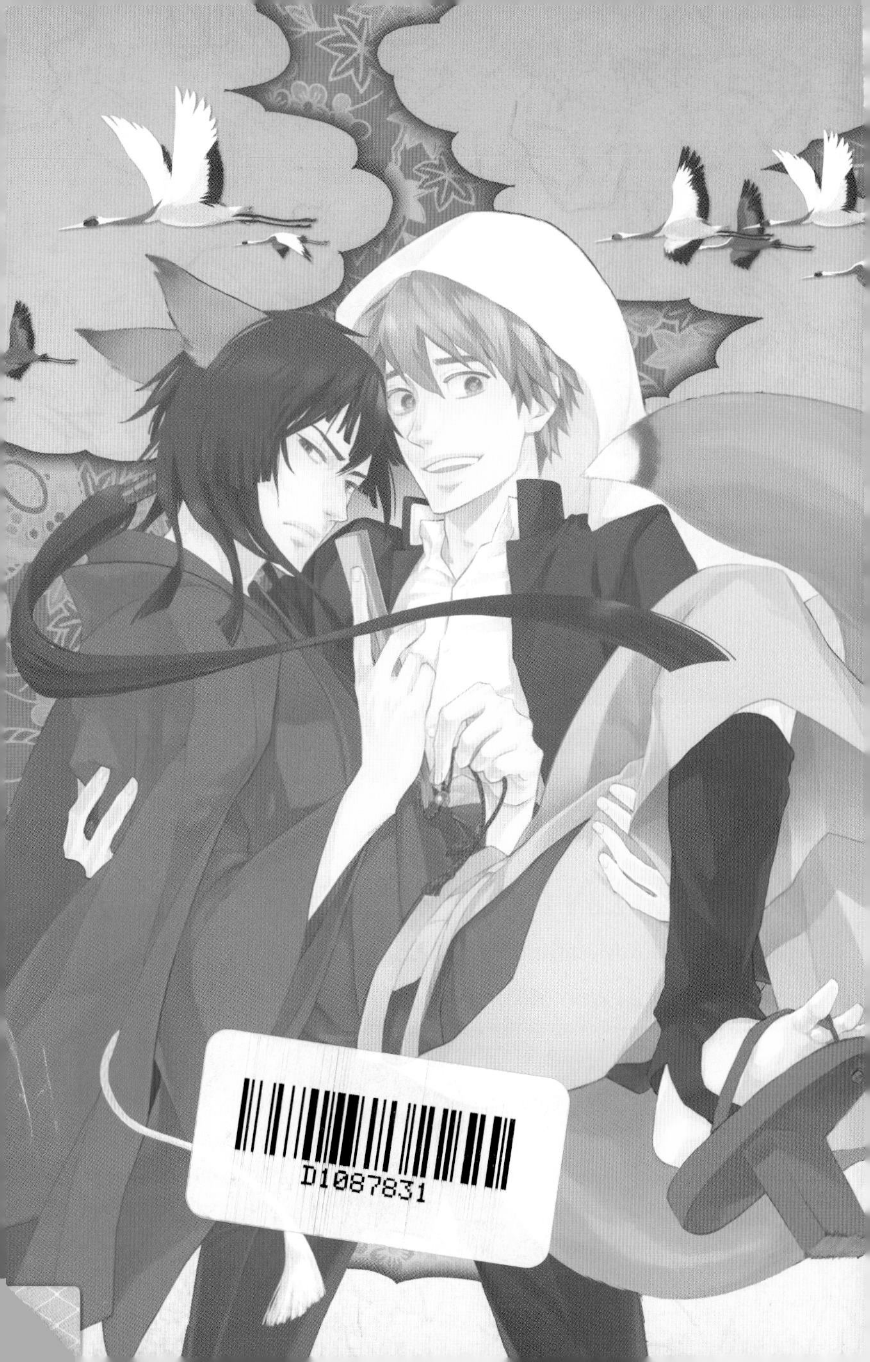

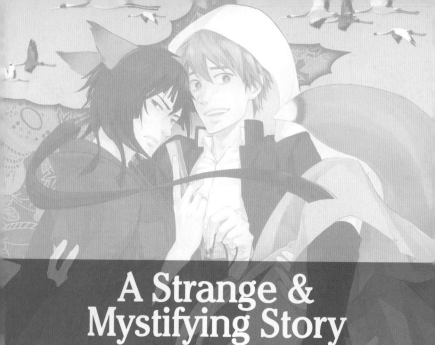

A Strange & Mystifying Story

Story and Art by **Tsuta Suzuki**　　　volume **4**

CONTENTS

SUBLIME

SuBLime Manga Edition

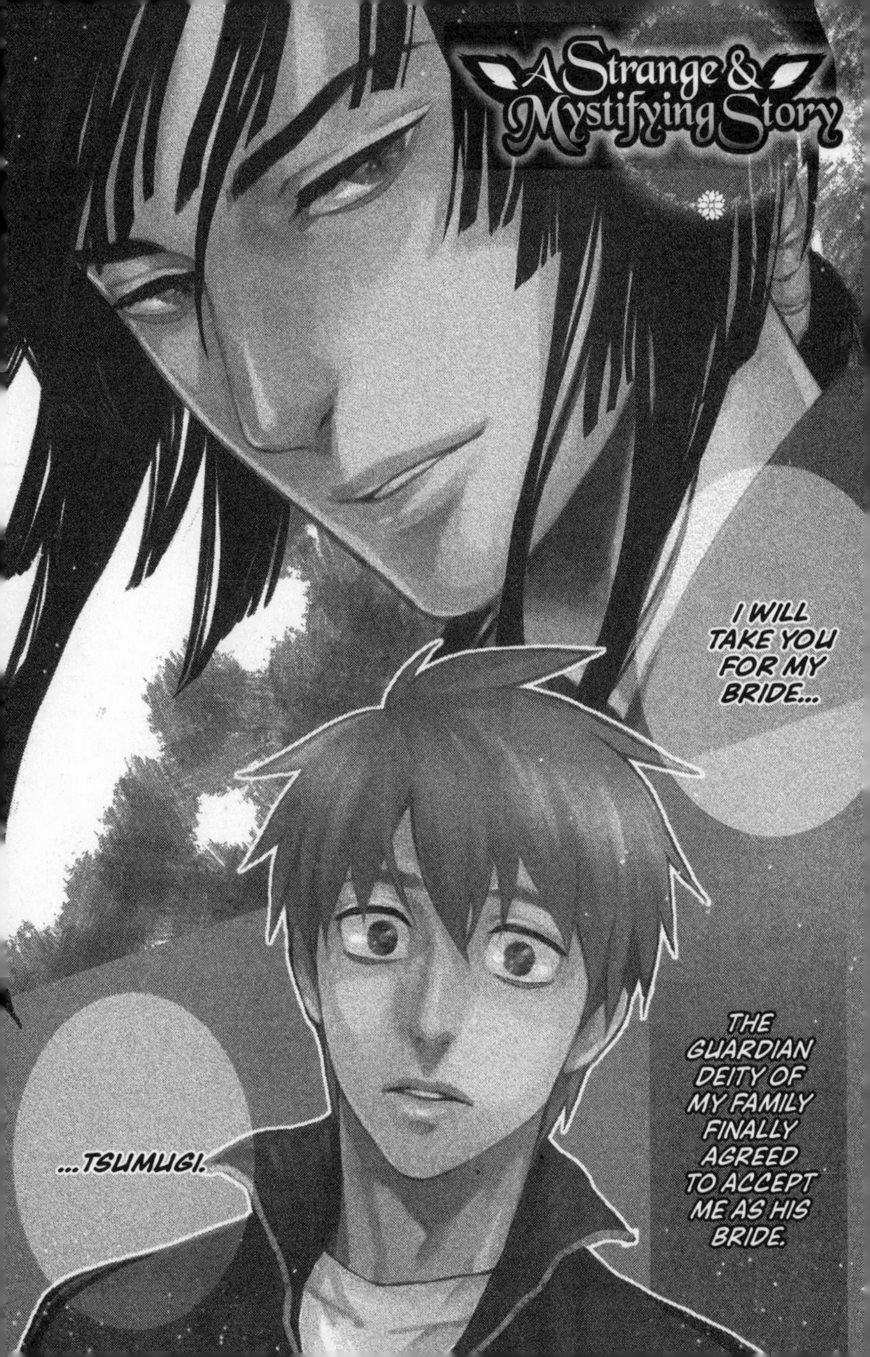
A Strange & Mystifying Story
I WILL TAKE YOU FOR MY BRIDE...
...TSUMUGI.
THE GUARDIAN DEITY OF MY FAMILY FINALLY AGREED TO ACCEPT ME AS HIS BRIDE.

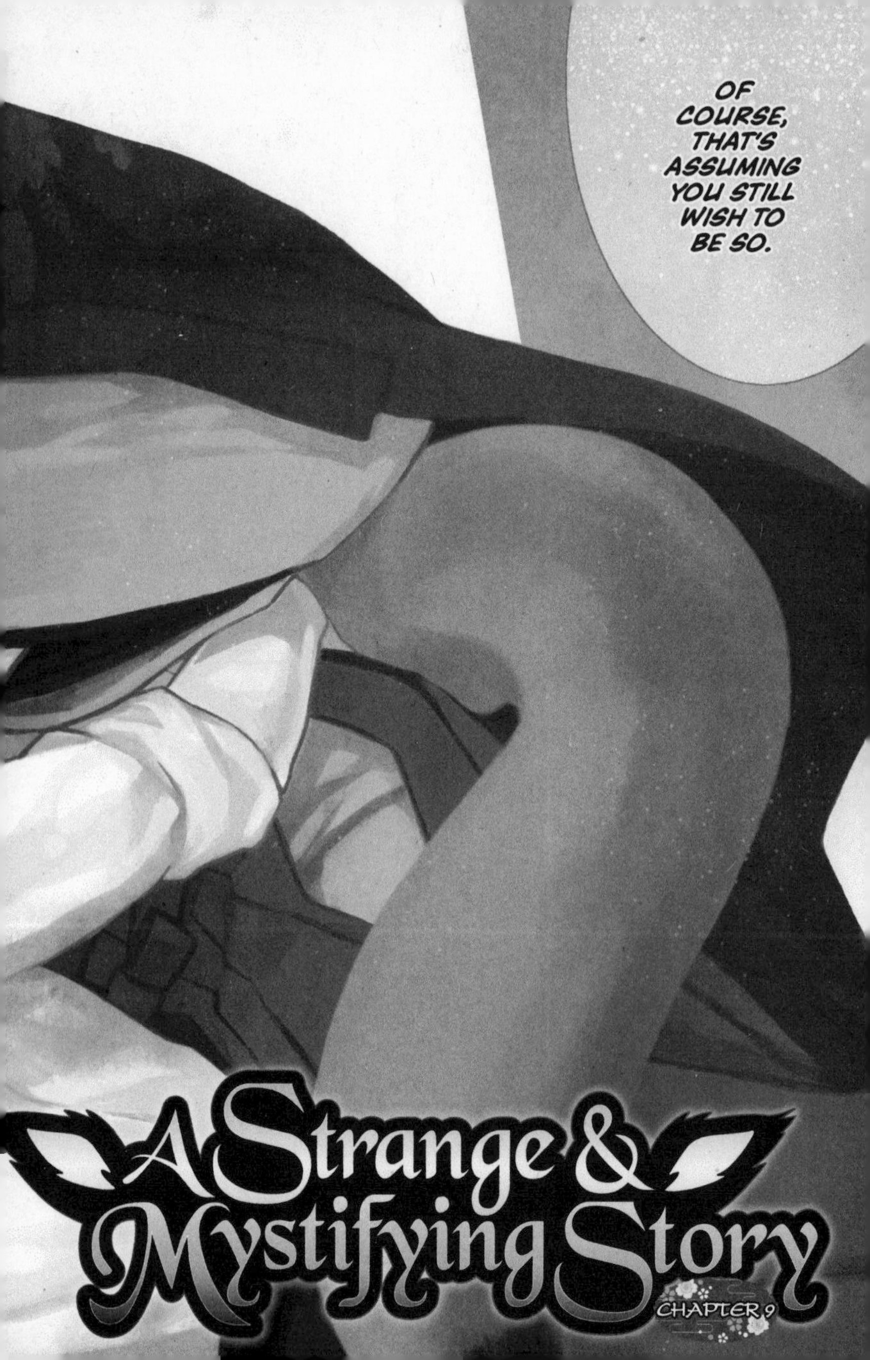
OF COURSE, THAT'S ASSUMING YOU STILL WISH TO BE SO.
A Strange & Mystifying Story
CHAPTER 9

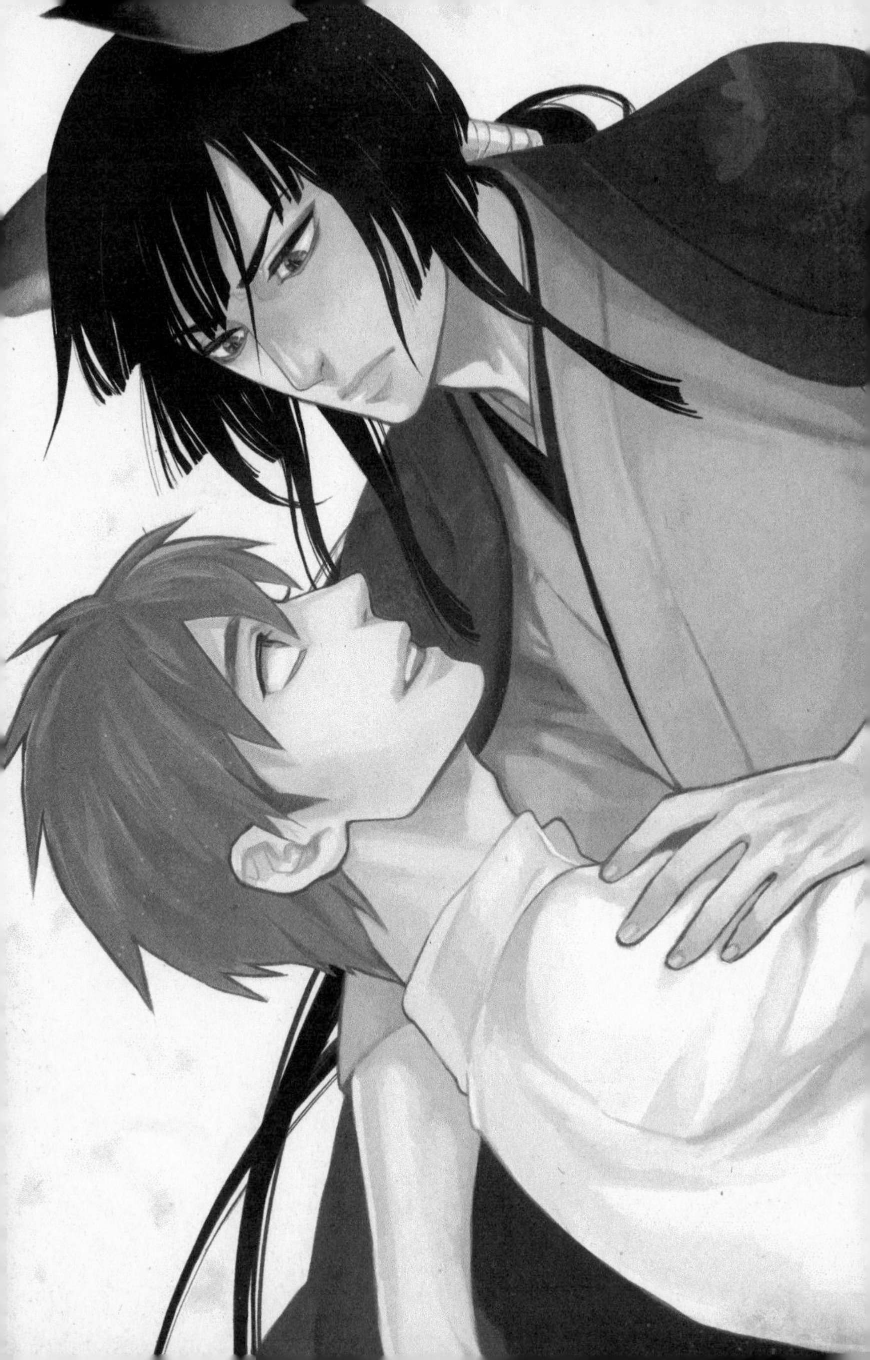

A Strange & Mystifying Story

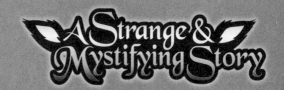

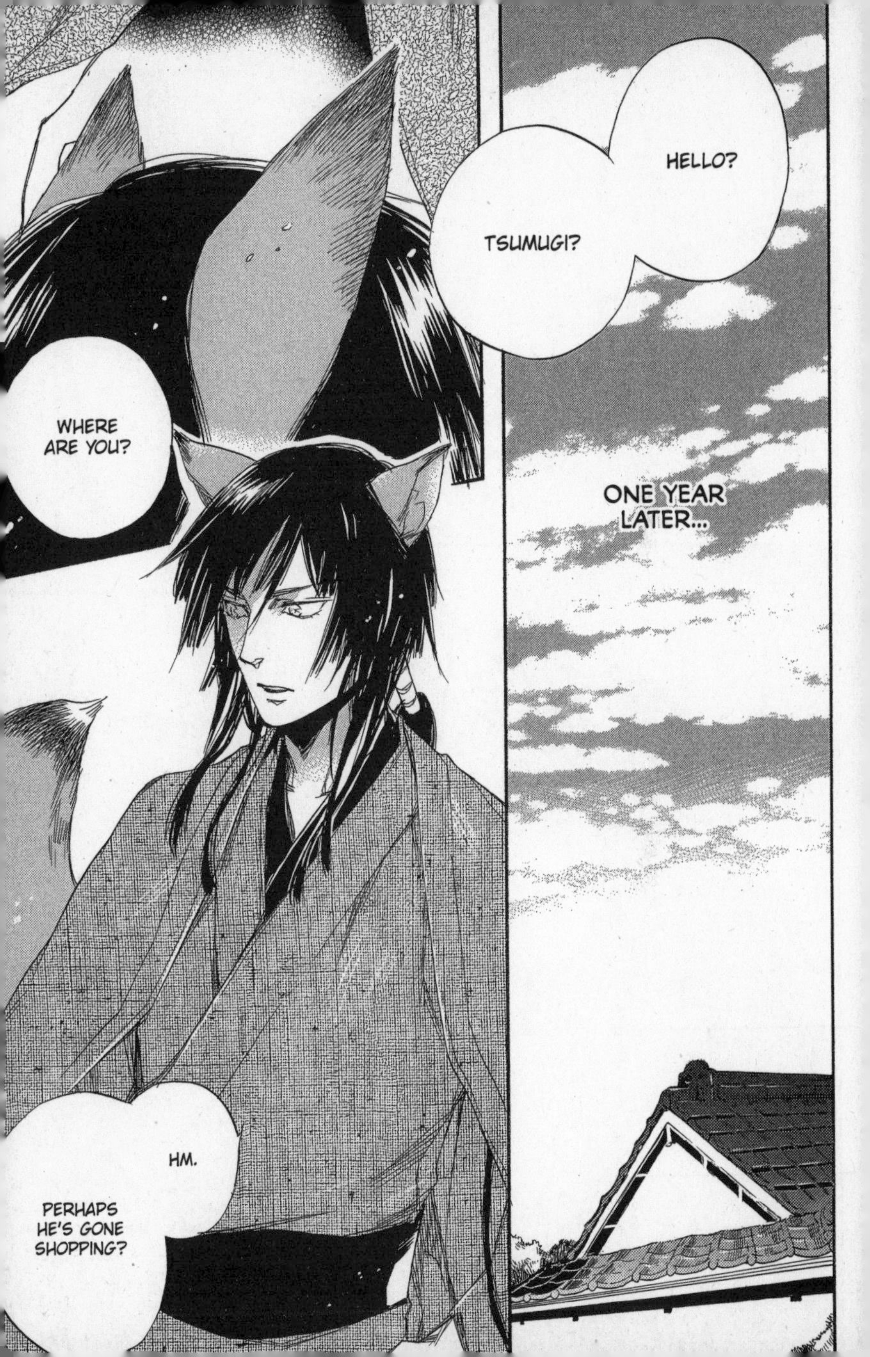
HELLO?
TSUMUGI?
ONE YEAR LATER...
WHERE ARE YOU?
HM.
PERHAPS HE'S GONE SHOPPING?

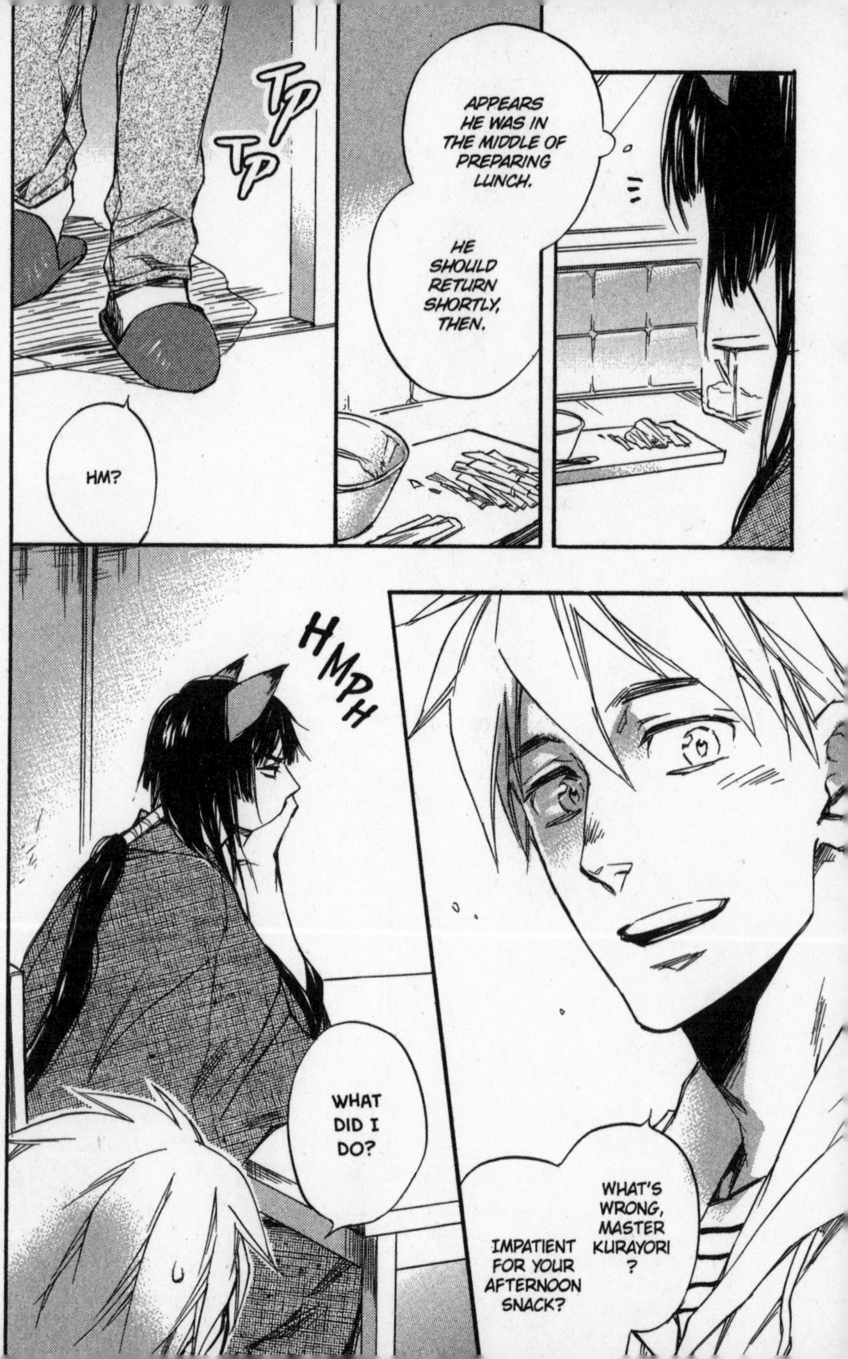
APPEARS HE WAS IN THE MIDDLE OF PREPARING LUNCH.
HE SHOULD RETURN SHORTLY, THEN.
TP TP
HM?
WHAT'S WRONG, MASTER KURAYORI?
IMPATIENT FOR YOUR AFTERNOON SNACK?
HMPH
WHAT DID I DO?

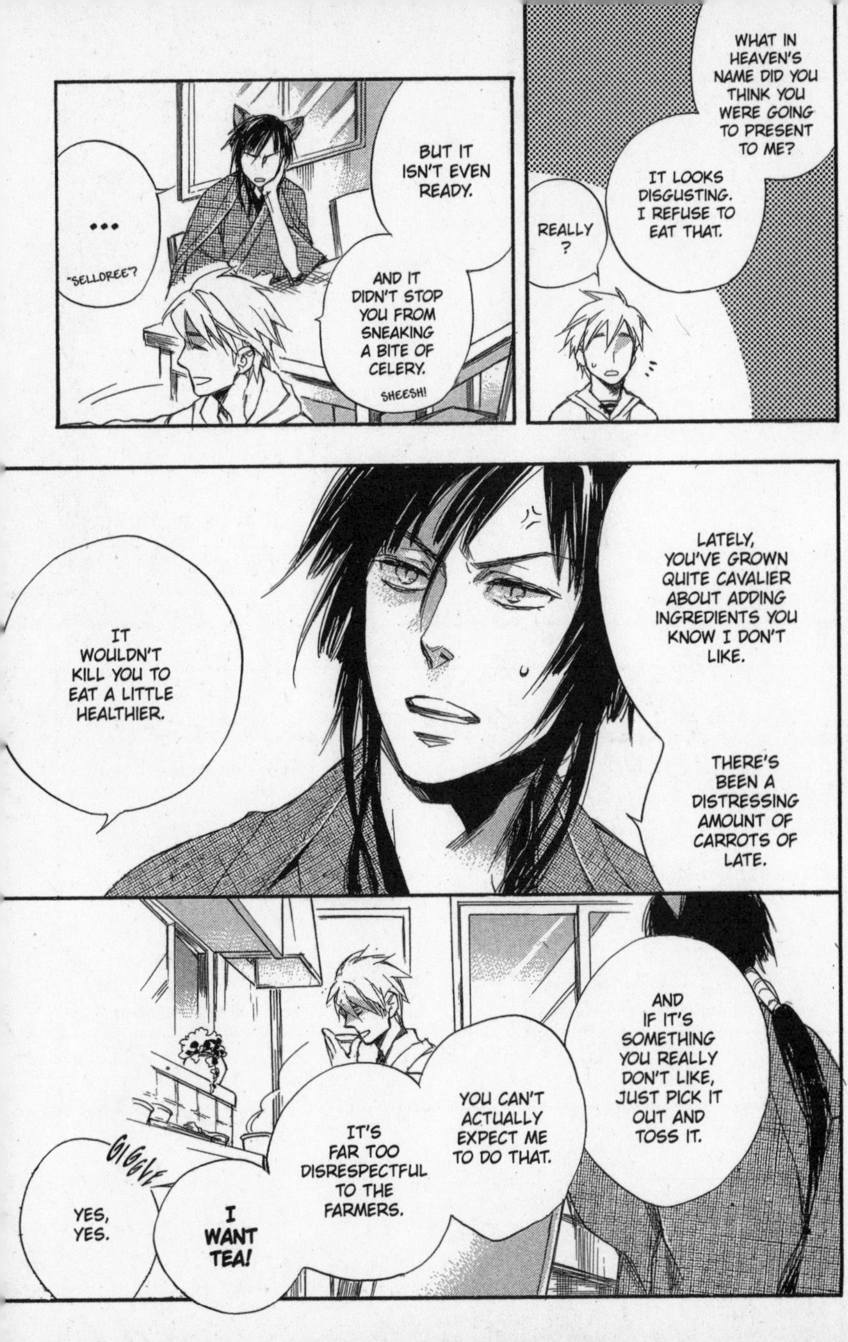
WHAT IN HEAVEN'S NAME DID YOU THINK YOU WERE GOING TO PRESENT TO ME?
IT LOOKS DISGUSTING. I REFUSE TO EAT THAT.
REALLY?
BUT IT ISN'T EVEN READY.
AND IT DIDN'T STOP YOU FROM SNEAKING A BITE OF CELERY.
SHEESH!
...
"SELLOREE"?
LATELY, YOU'VE GROWN QUITE CAVALIER ABOUT ADDING INGREDIENTS YOU KNOW I DON'T LIKE.
THERE'S BEEN A DISTRESSING AMOUNT OF CARROTS OF LATE.
IT WOULDN'T KILL YOU TO EAT A LITTLE HEALTHIER.
AND IF IT'S SOMETHING YOU REALLY DON'T LIKE, JUST PICK IT OUT AND TOSS IT.
YOU CAN'T ACTUALLY EXPECT ME TO DO THAT.
IT'S FAR TOO DISRESPECTFUL TO THE FARMERS.
I WANT TEA!
GIGGLE
YES, YES.

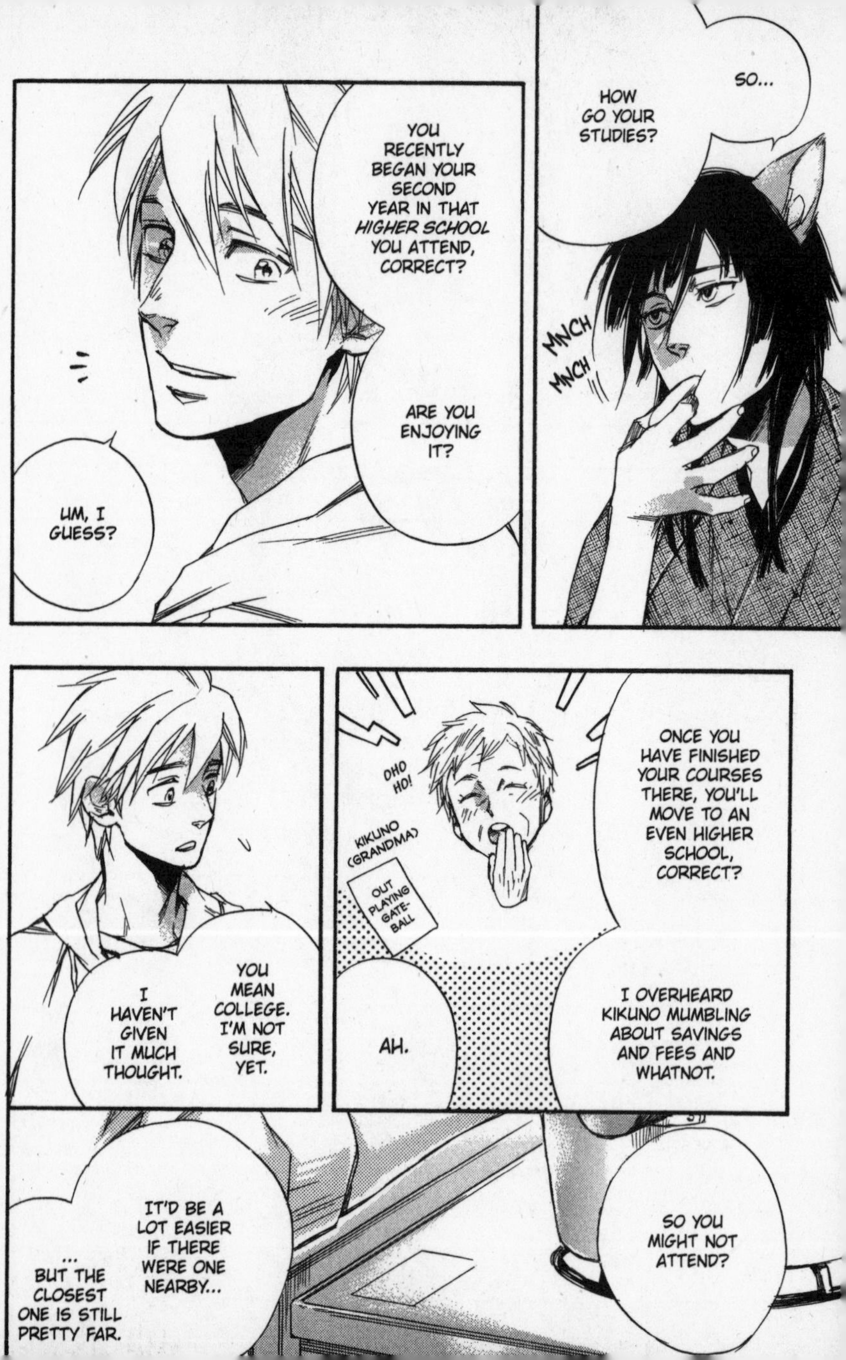
SO...
HOW GO YOUR STUDIES?
MNCH MNCH
YOU RECENTLY BEGAN YOUR SECOND YEAR IN THAT *HIGHER SCHOOL* YOU ATTEND, CORRECT?
ARE YOU ENJOYING IT?
UM, I GUESS?
ONCE YOU HAVE FINISHED YOUR COURSES THERE, YOU'LL MOVE TO AN EVEN HIGHER SCHOOL, CORRECT?
OHO HO!
KIKUNO (GRANDMA)
OUT PLAYING GATE-BALL
I OVERHEARD KIKUNO MUMBLING ABOUT SAVINGS AND FEES AND WHATNOT.
AH.
YOU MEAN COLLEGE. I'M NOT SURE, YET.
I HAVEN'T GIVEN IT MUCH THOUGHT.
SO YOU MIGHT NOT ATTEND?
IT'D BE A LOT EASIER IF THERE WERE ONE NEARBY...
... BUT THE CLOSEST ONE IS STILL PRETTY FAR.

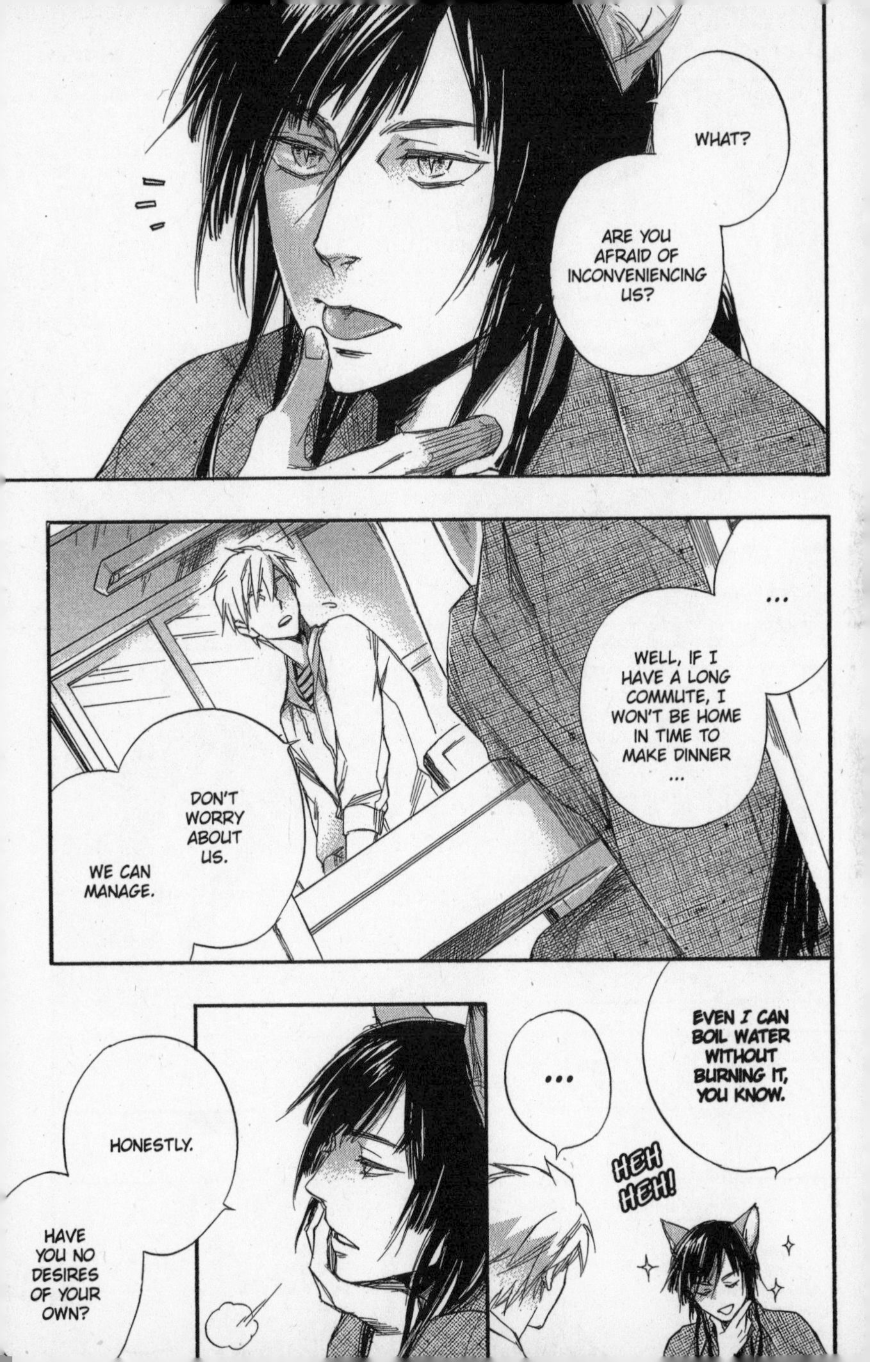
WHAT?
ARE YOU AFRAID OF INCONVENIENCING US?
...
WELL, IF I HAVE A LONG COMMUTE, I WON'T BE HOME IN TIME TO MAKE DINNER ...
DON'T WORRY ABOUT US.
WE CAN MANAGE.
EVEN I CAN BOIL WATER WITHOUT BURNING IT, YOU KNOW.
HEH HEH!
...
HONESTLY.
HAVE YOU NO DESIRES OF YOUR OWN?

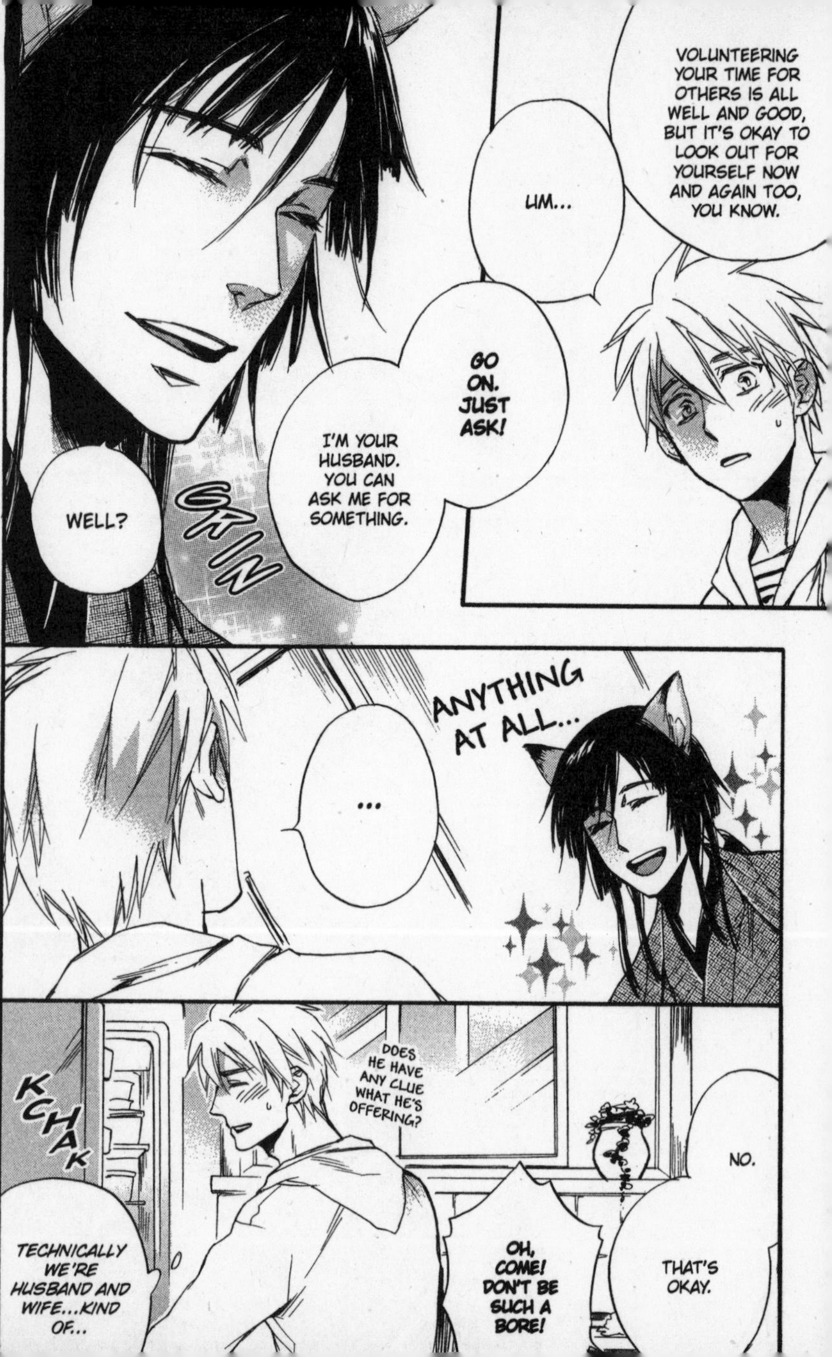
VOLUNTEERING YOUR TIME FOR OTHERS IS ALL WELL AND GOOD, BUT IT'S OKAY TO LOOK OUT FOR YOURSELF NOW AND AGAIN TOO, YOU KNOW.
UM...
GO ON. JUST ASK!
I'M YOUR HUSBAND. YOU CAN ASK ME FOR SOMETHING.
GRIN
WELL?
ANYTHING AT ALL...
...
NO.
THAT'S OKAY.
OH, COME! DON'T BE SUCH A BORE!
DOES HE HAVE ANY CLUE WHAT HE'S OFFERING?
KCHAK
TECHNICALLY WE'RE HUSBAND AND WIFE...KIND OF...

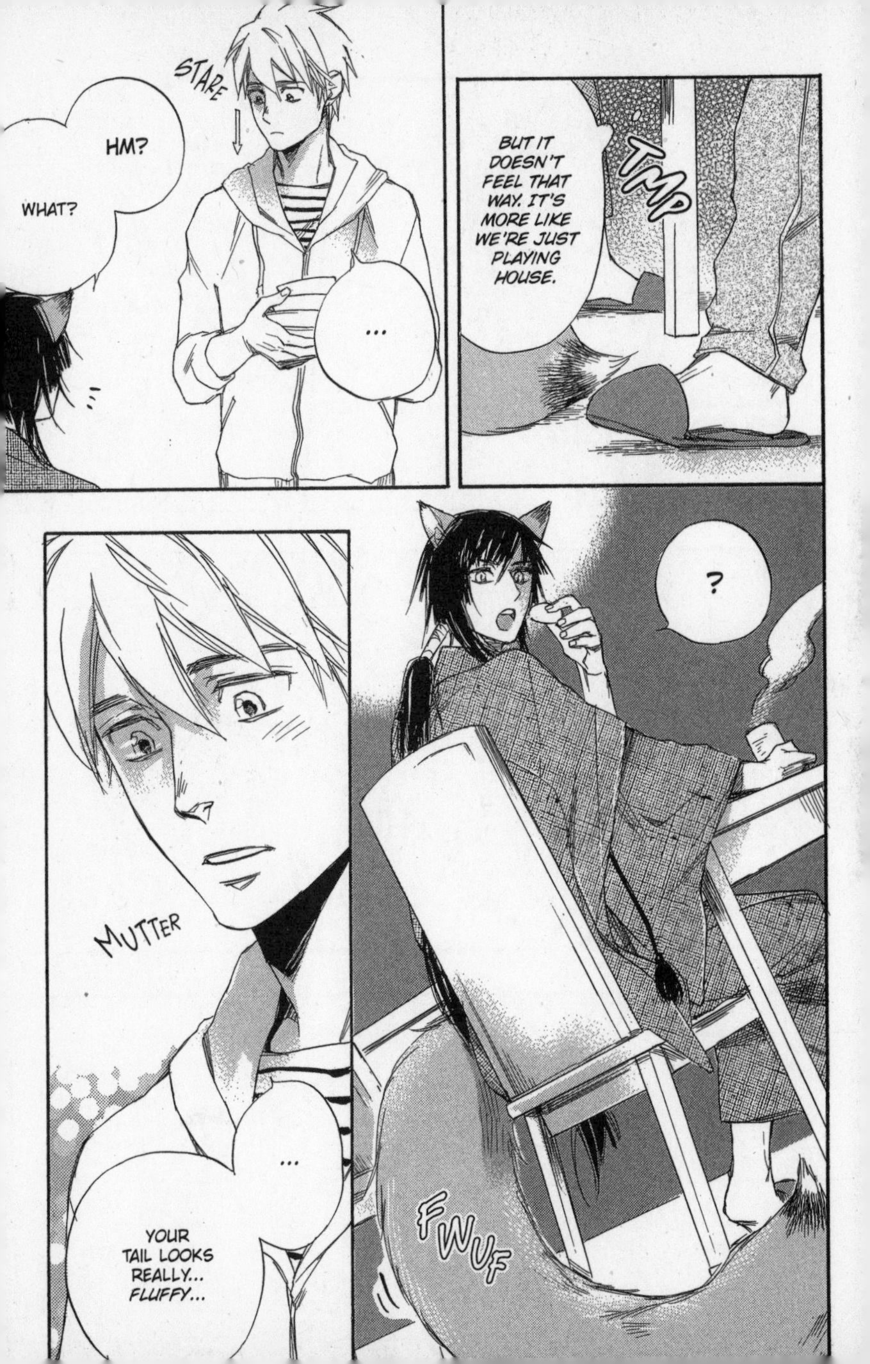
BUT IT DOESN'T FEEL THAT WAY. IT'S MORE LIKE WE'RE JUST PLAYING HOUSE.
TMP
STARE
HM?
WHAT?
...
?
FWUF
MUTTER
...
YOUR TAIL LOOKS REALLY... FLUFFY...

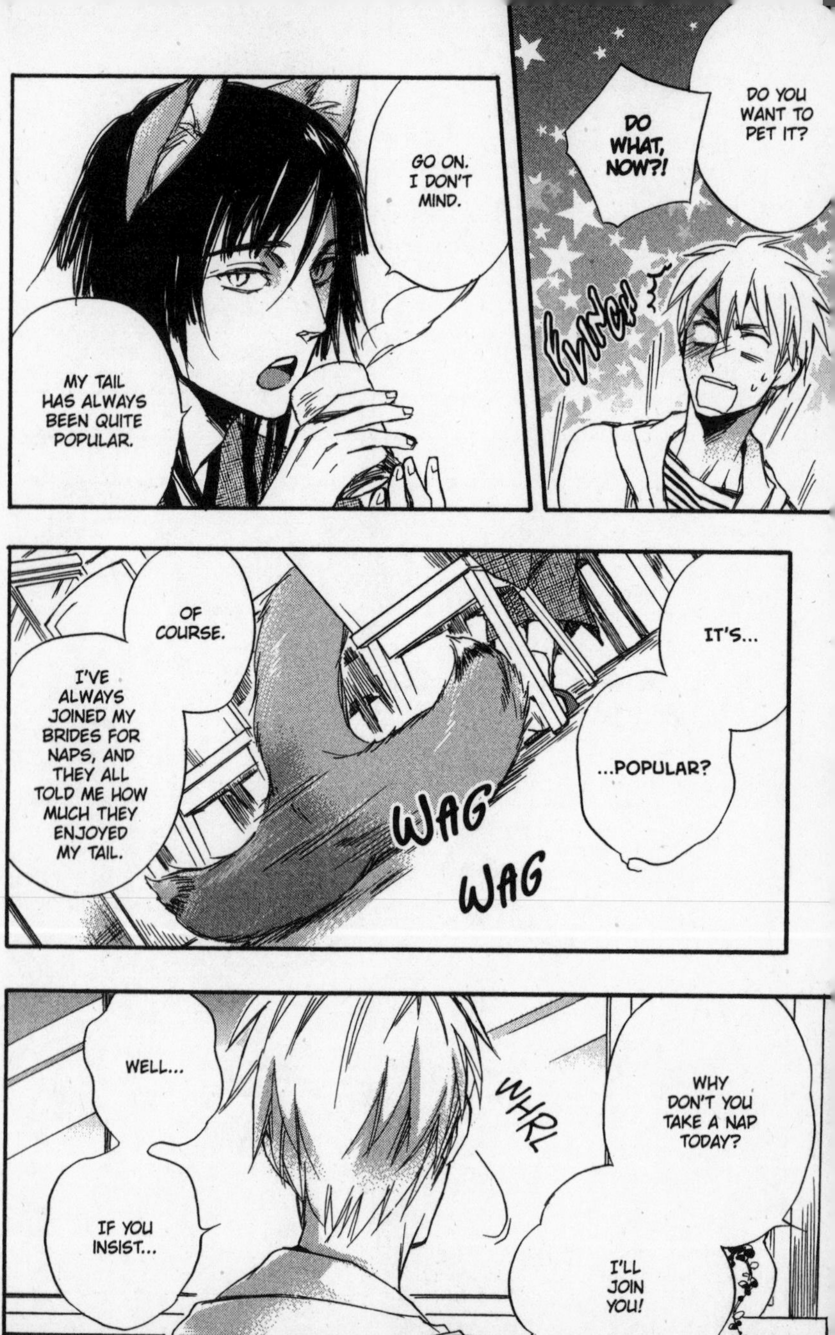
DO YOU WANT TO PET IT?
DO WHAT, NOW?!
GO ON. I DON'T MIND.
MY TAIL HAS ALWAYS BEEN QUITE POPULAR.
IT'S...
...POPULAR?
OF COURSE.
I'VE ALWAYS JOINED MY BRIDES FOR NAPS, AND THEY ALL TOLD ME HOW MUCH THEY ENJOYED MY TAIL.
WAG
WAG
WHY DON'T YOU TAKE A NAP TODAY?
I'LL JOIN YOU!
WHRL
WELL...
IF YOU INSIST...

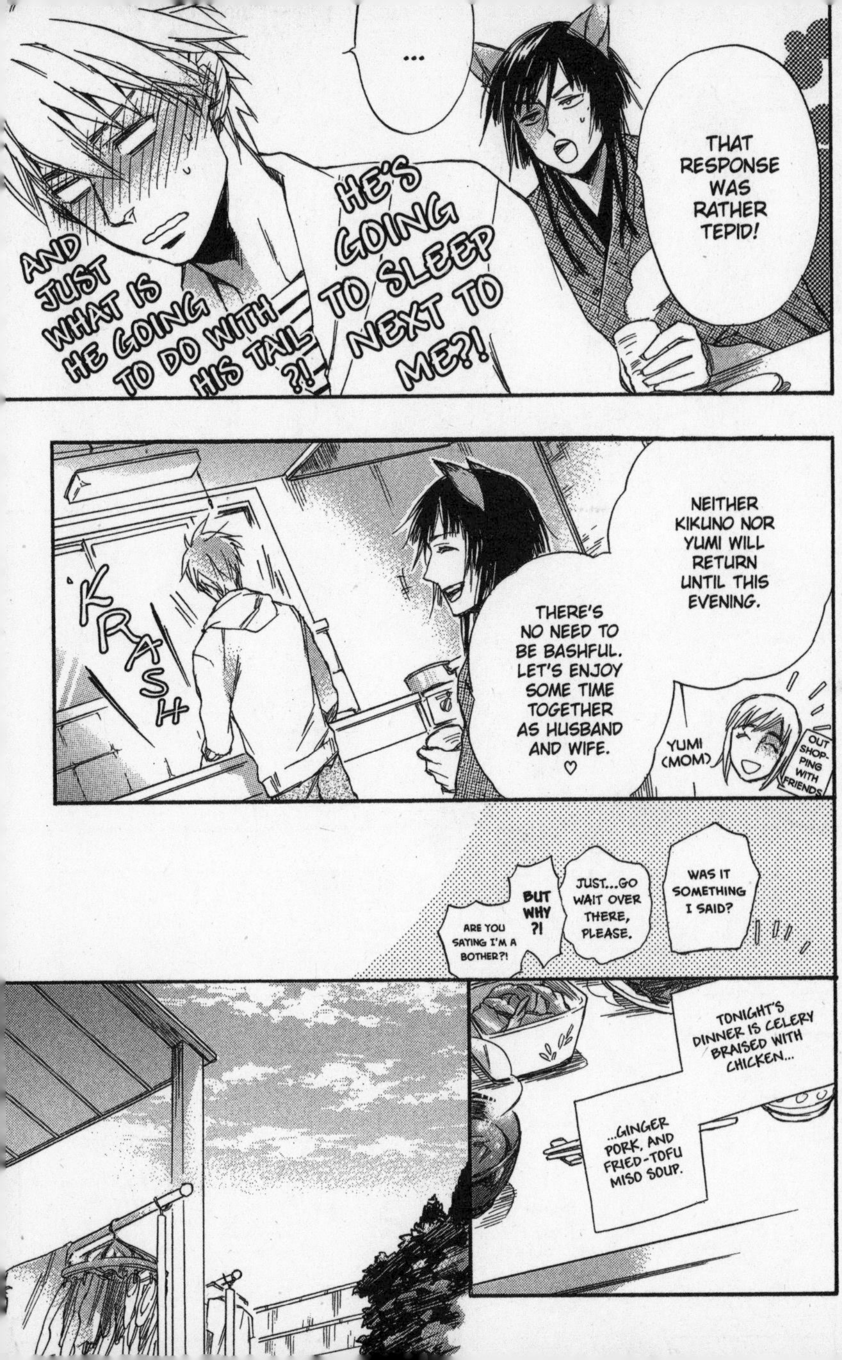
THAT RESPONSE WAS RATHER TEPID!
...
HE'S GOING TO SLEEP NEXT TO ME?!
AND JUST WHAT IS HE GOING TO DO WITH HIS TAIL?!
NEITHER KIKUNO NOR YUMI WILL RETURN UNTIL THIS EVENING.
YUMI (MOM)
OUT SHOPPING WITH FRIENDS
THERE'S NO NEED TO BE BASHFUL. LET'S ENJOY SOME TIME TOGETHER AS HUSBAND AND WIFE. ♡
KRASH
WAS IT SOMETHING I SAID?
JUST...GO WAIT OVER THERE, PLEASE.
BUT WHY?!
ARE YOU SAYING I'M A BOTHER?!
TONIGHT'S DINNER IS CELERY BRAISED WITH CHICKEN...
...GINGER PORK, AND FRIED-TOFU MISO SOUP.

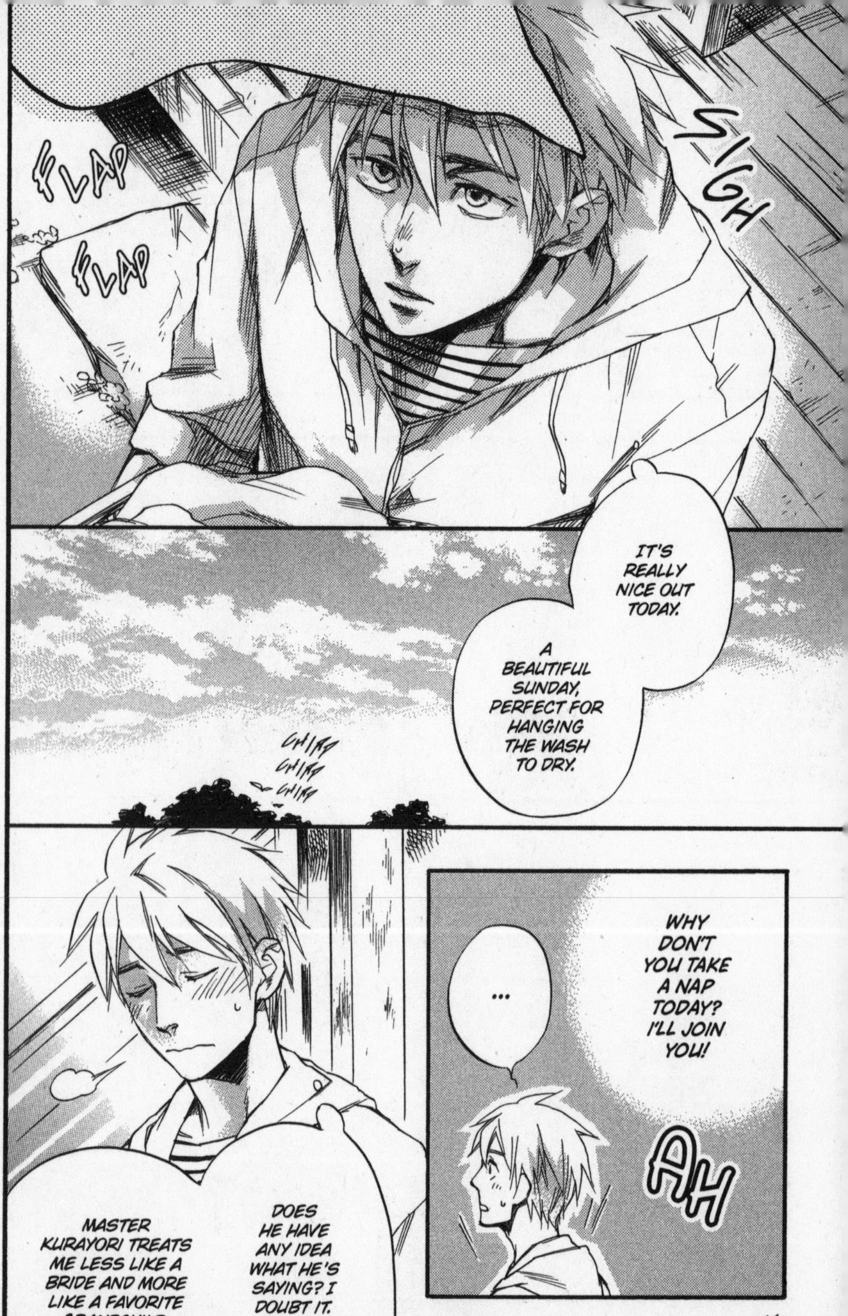
SIGH
FLAP
FLAP
IT'S REALLY NICE OUT TODAY.
A BEAUTIFUL SUNDAY, PERFECT FOR HANGING THE WASH TO DRY.
CHIRP
CHIRP
CHIRP
WHY DON'T YOU TAKE A NAP TODAY? I'LL JOIN YOU!
...
AH
DOES HE HAVE ANY IDEA WHAT HE'S SAYING? I DOUBT IT.
MASTER KURAYORI TREATS ME LESS LIKE A BRIDE AND MORE LIKE A FAVORITE GRANDCHILD.

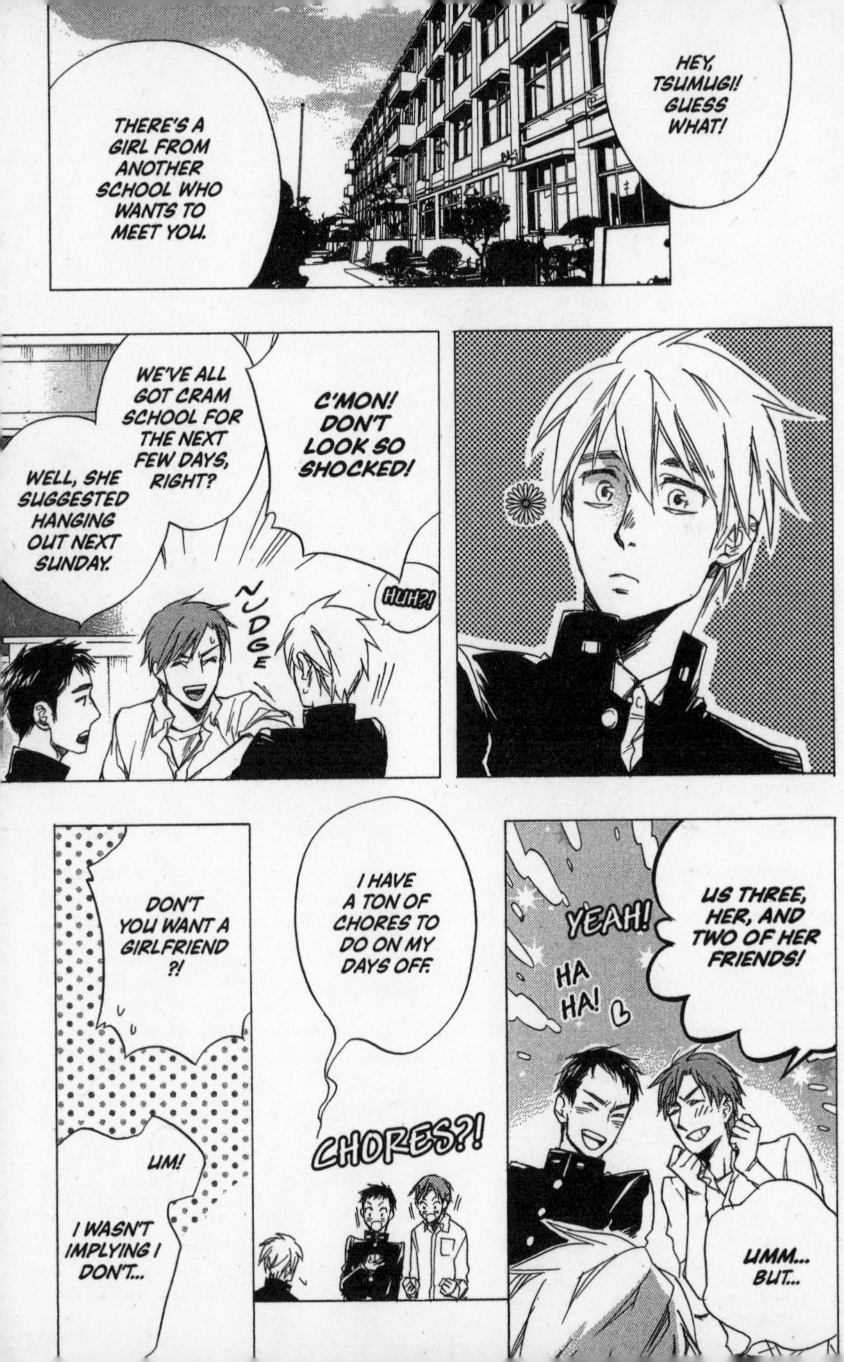
HEY, TSUMUGI! GUESS WHAT!
THERE'S A GIRL FROM ANOTHER SCHOOL WHO WANTS TO MEET YOU.
C'MON! DON'T LOOK SO SHOCKED!
WE'VE ALL GOT CRAM SCHOOL FOR THE NEXT FEW DAYS, RIGHT?
WELL, SHE SUGGESTED HANGING OUT NEXT SUNDAY.
NUDGE
HUH?!
US THREE, HER, AND TWO OF HER FRIENDS!
YEAH!
HA HA!
UMM... BUT...
I HAVE A TON OF CHORES TO DO ON MY DAYS OFF.
CHORES?!
DON'T YOU WANT A GIRLFRIEND ?!
UM!
I WASN'T IMPLYING I DON'T...

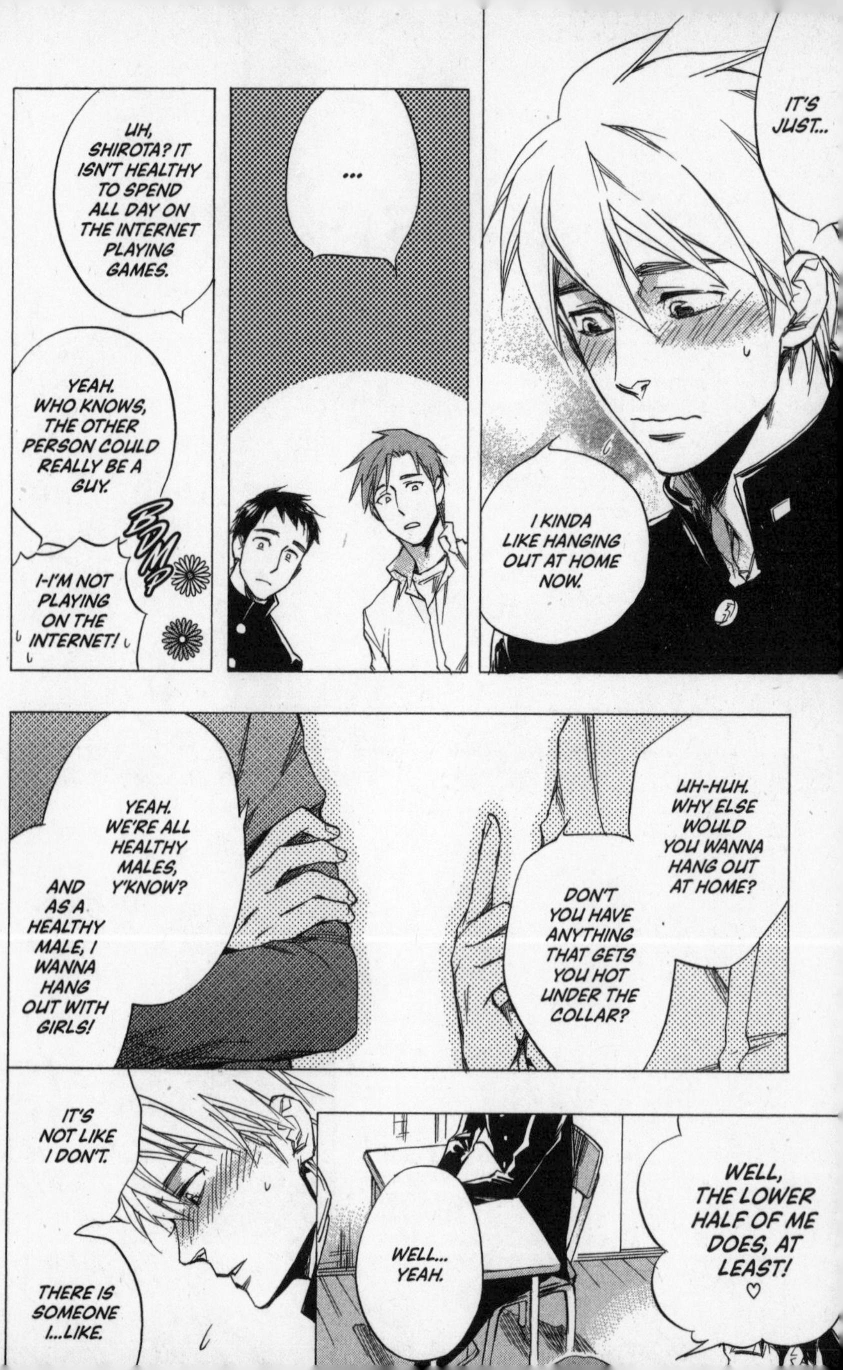
IT'S JUST...
I KINDA LIKE HANGING OUT AT HOME NOW.
...
UH, SHIROTA? IT ISN'T HEALTHY TO SPEND ALL DAY ON THE INTERNET PLAYING GAMES.
YEAH. WHO KNOWS, THE OTHER PERSON COULD REALLY BE A GUY.
I-I'M NOT PLAYING ON THE INTERNET!
UH-HUH. WHY ELSE WOULD YOU WANNA HANG OUT AT HOME?
DON'T YOU HAVE ANYTHING THAT GETS YOU HOT UNDER THE COLLAR?
YEAH. WE'RE ALL HEALTHY MALES, Y'KNOW?
AND AS A HEALTHY MALE, I WANNA HANG OUT WITH GIRLS!
WELL, THE LOWER HALF OF ME DOES, AT LEAST! ♡
WELL... YEAH.
IT'S NOT LIKE I DON'T.
THERE IS SOMEONE I...LIKE.

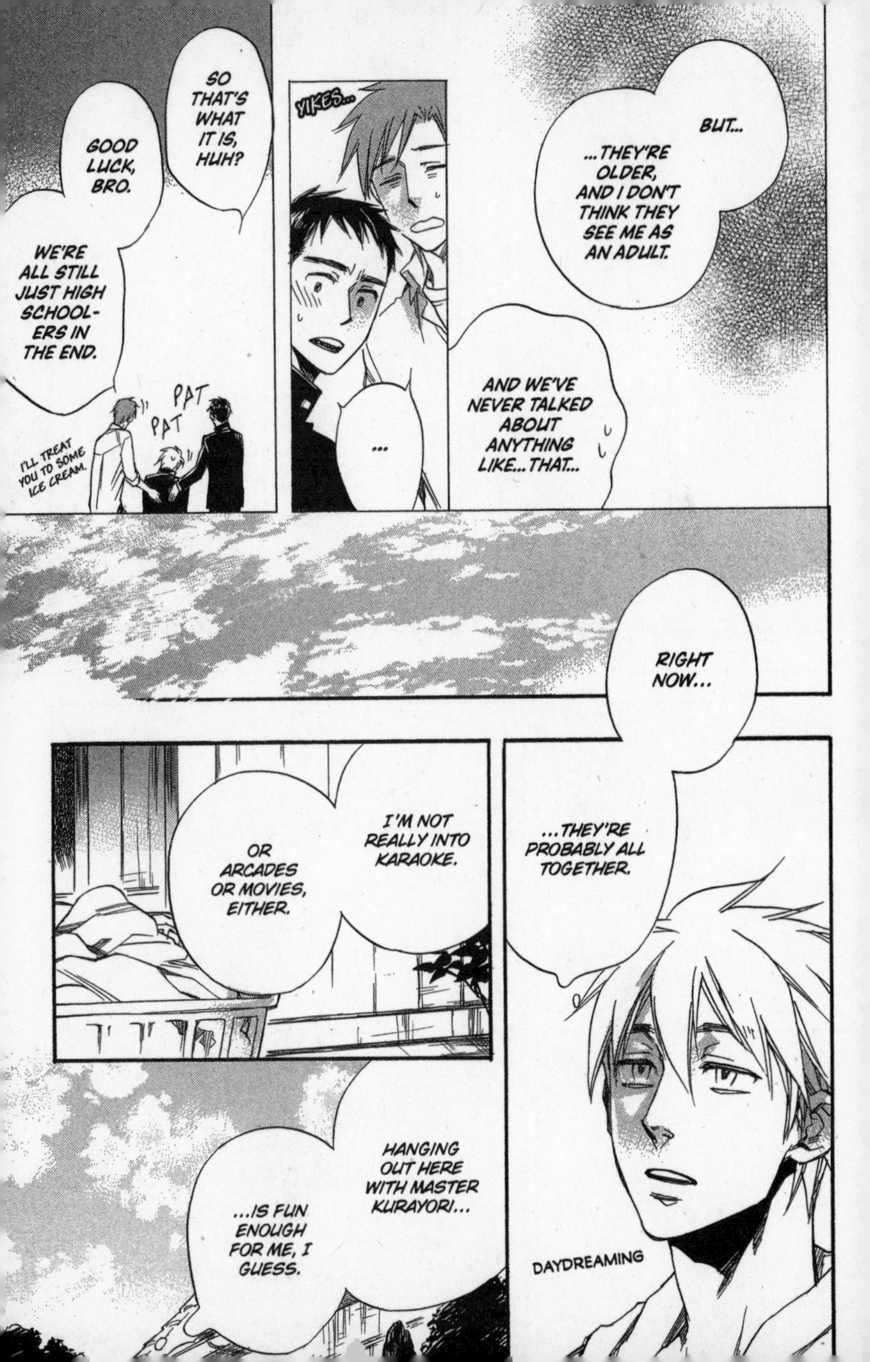
BUT...
...THEY'RE OLDER, AND I DON'T THINK THEY SEE ME AS AN ADULT.
AND WE'VE NEVER TALKED ABOUT ANYTHING LIKE...THAT...
YIKES...
...
SO THAT'S WHAT IT IS, HUH?
GOOD LUCK, BRO.
WE'RE ALL STILL JUST HIGH SCHOOLERS IN THE END.
PAT
PAT
I'LL TREAT YOU TO SOME ICE CREAM.
RIGHT NOW...
...THEY'RE PROBABLY ALL TOGETHER.
DAYDREAMING
I'M NOT REALLY INTO KARAOKE.
OR ARCADES OR MOVIES, EITHER.
HANGING OUT HERE WITH MASTER KURAYORI...
...IS FUN ENOUGH FOR ME, I GUESS.

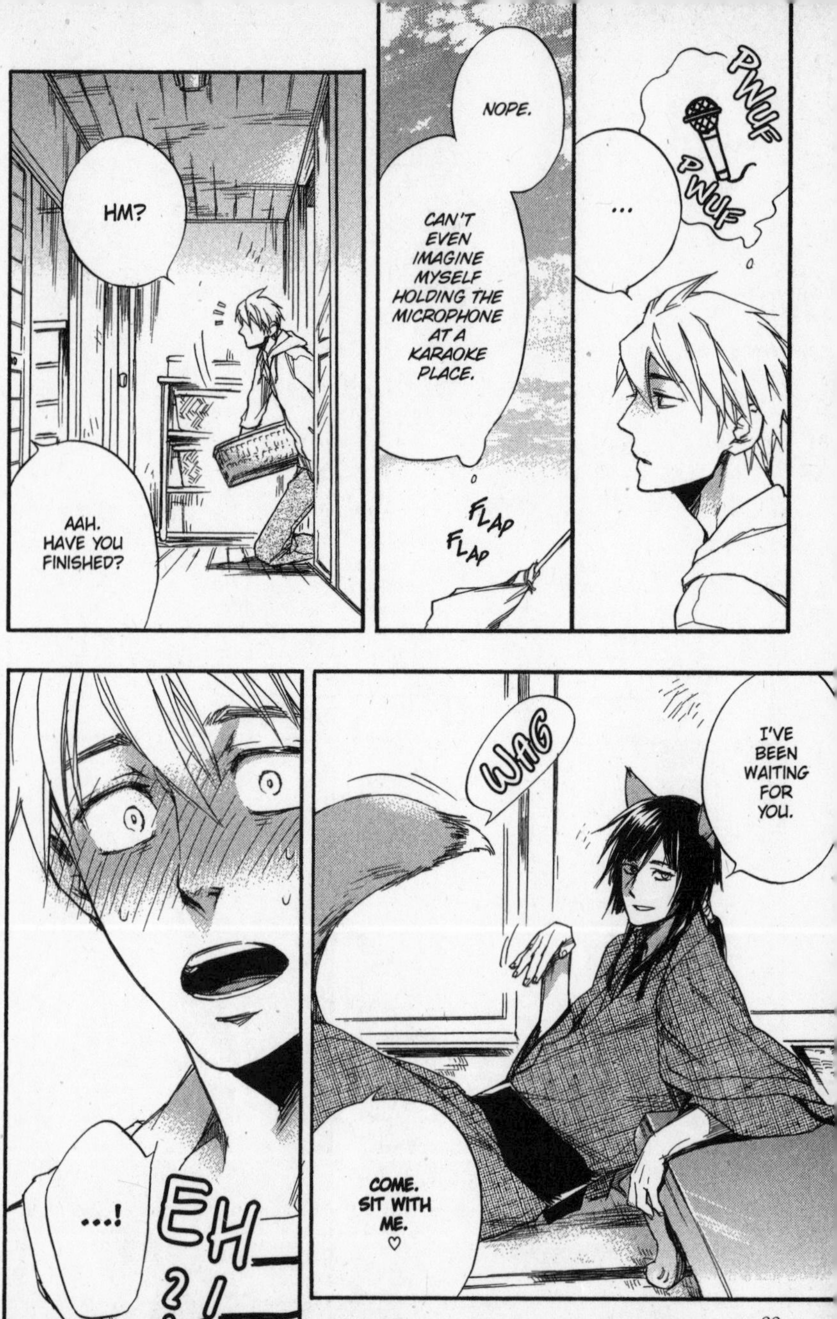
PWUF PWUF
...
NOPE.
CAN'T EVEN IMAGINE MYSELF HOLDING THE MICROPHONE AT A KARAOKE PLACE.
FLAP FLAP
HM?
AAH. HAVE YOU FINISHED?
I'VE BEEN WAITING FOR YOU.
WAG
COME. SIT WITH ME. ♡
...!
EH?!

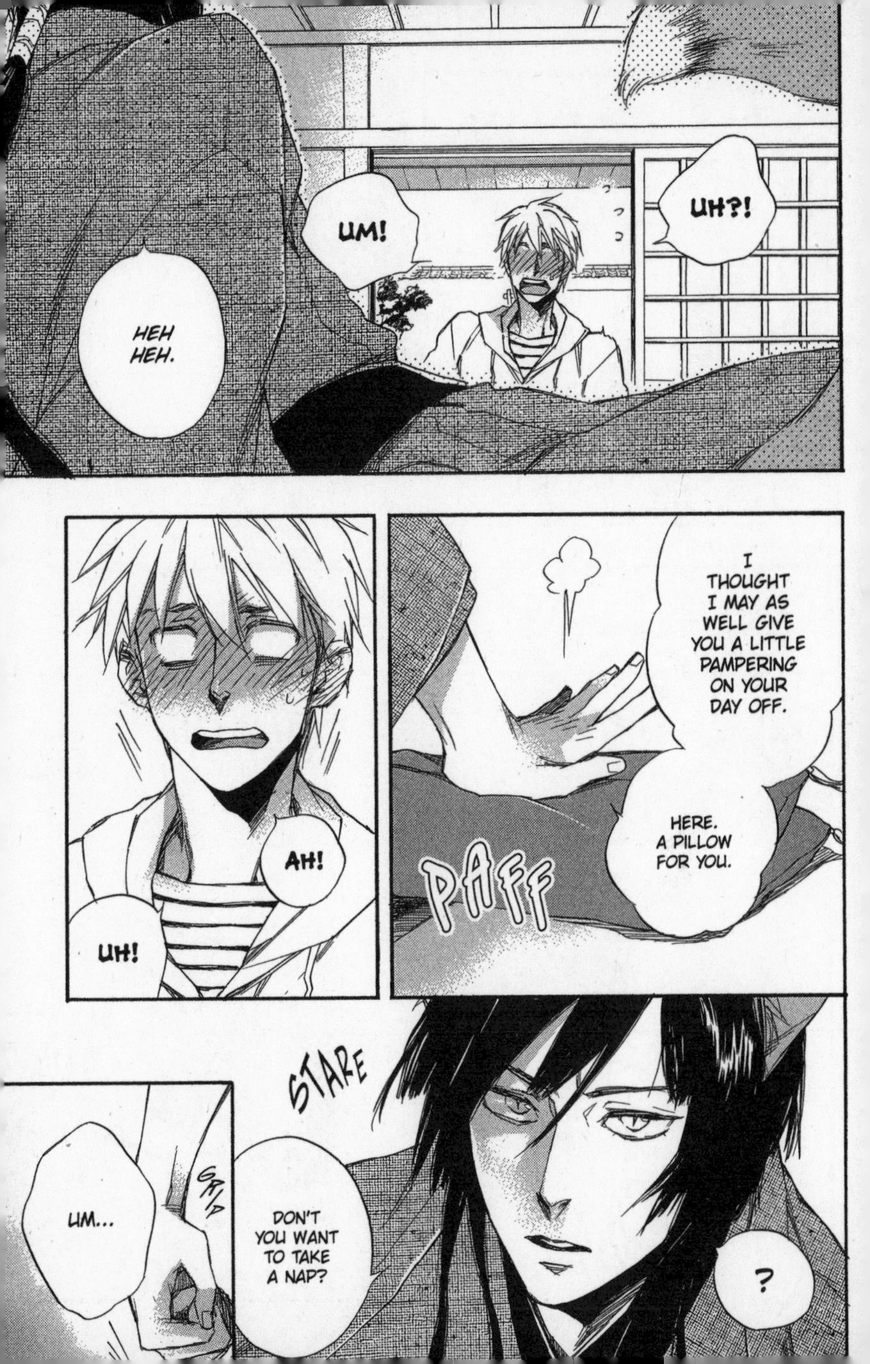
UH?!
UM!
HEH HEH.
I THOUGHT I MAY AS WELL GIVE YOU A LITTLE PAMPERING ON YOUR DAY OFF.
HERE. A PILLOW FOR YOU.
PAFF
AH!
UH!
STARE
?
DON'T YOU WANT TO TAKE A NAP?
GRIP
UM...

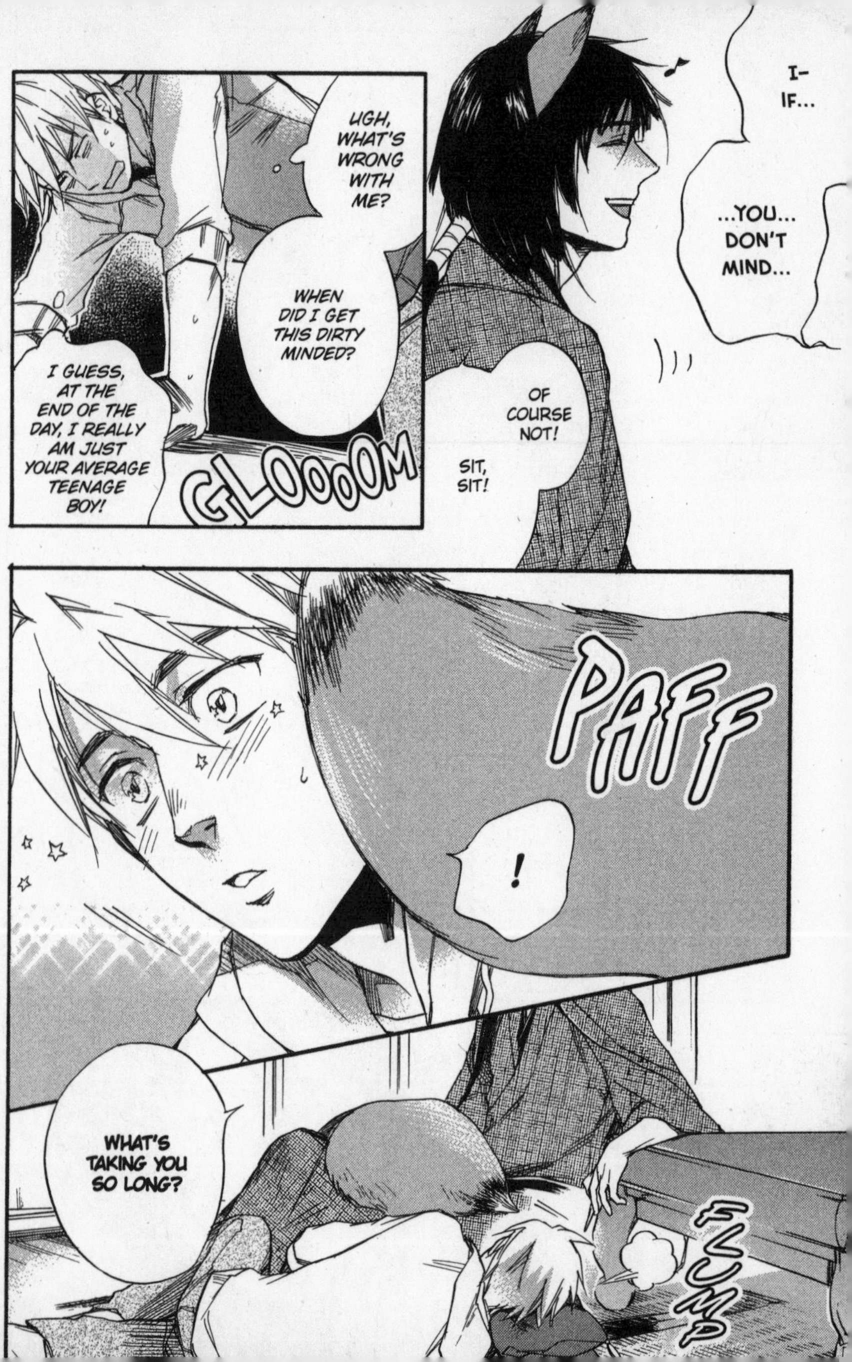
I- IF...
...YOU... DON'T MIND...
OF COURSE NOT!
SIT, SIT!
UGH, WHAT'S WRONG WITH ME?
WHEN DID I GET THIS DIRTY MINDED?
I GUESS, AT THE END OF THE DAY, I REALLY AM JUST YOUR AVERAGE TEENAGE BOY!
GLOOOOM
PAFF
!
WHAT'S TAKING YOU SO LONG?
FLUMP

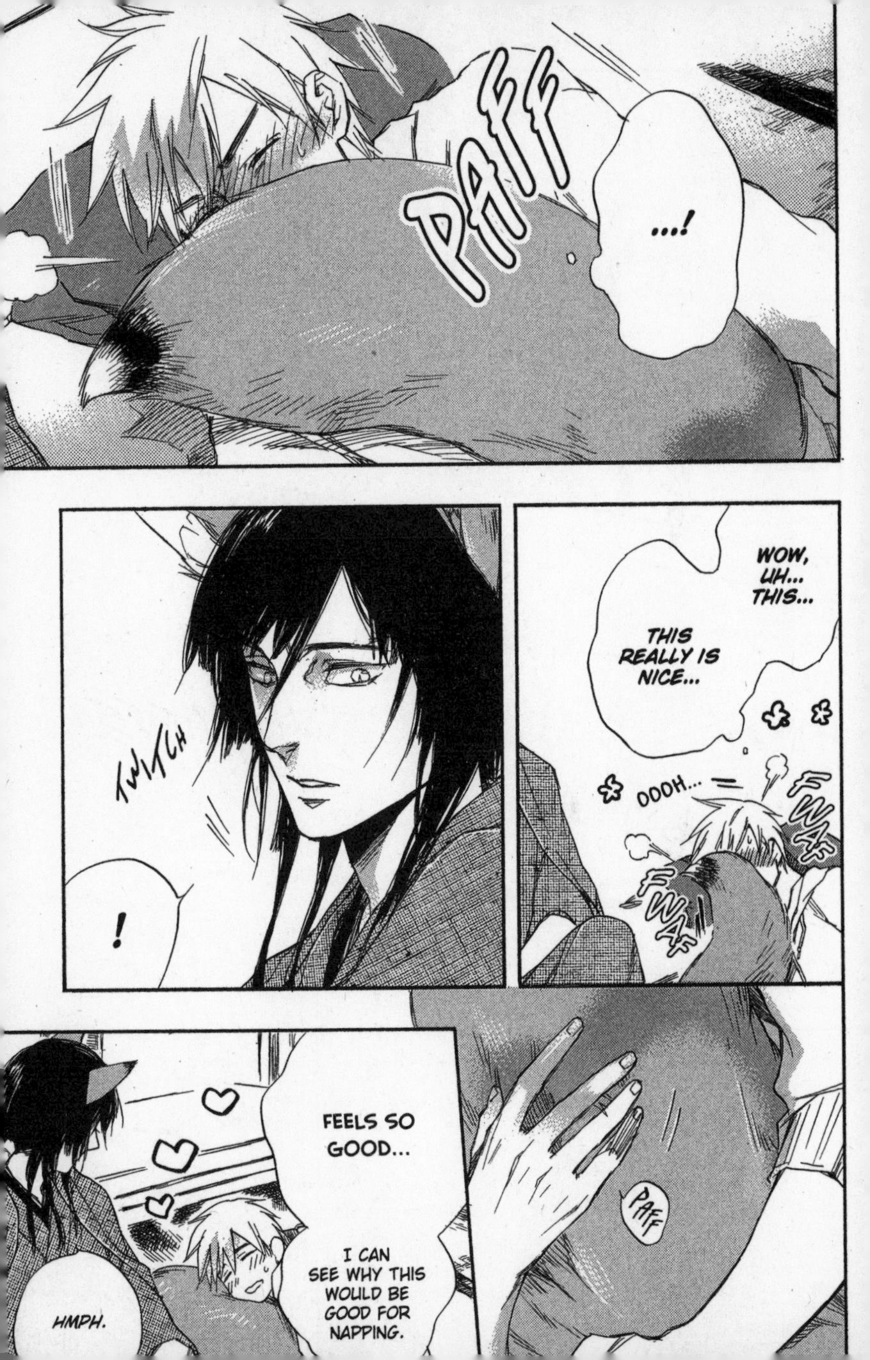
PAFF
...!
WOW, UH... THIS...
THIS REALLY IS NICE...
OOOH...
FWAF
FWAF
TWITCH
!
PAFF
FEELS SO GOOD...
I CAN SEE WHY THIS WOULD BE GOOD FOR NAPPING.
HMPH.

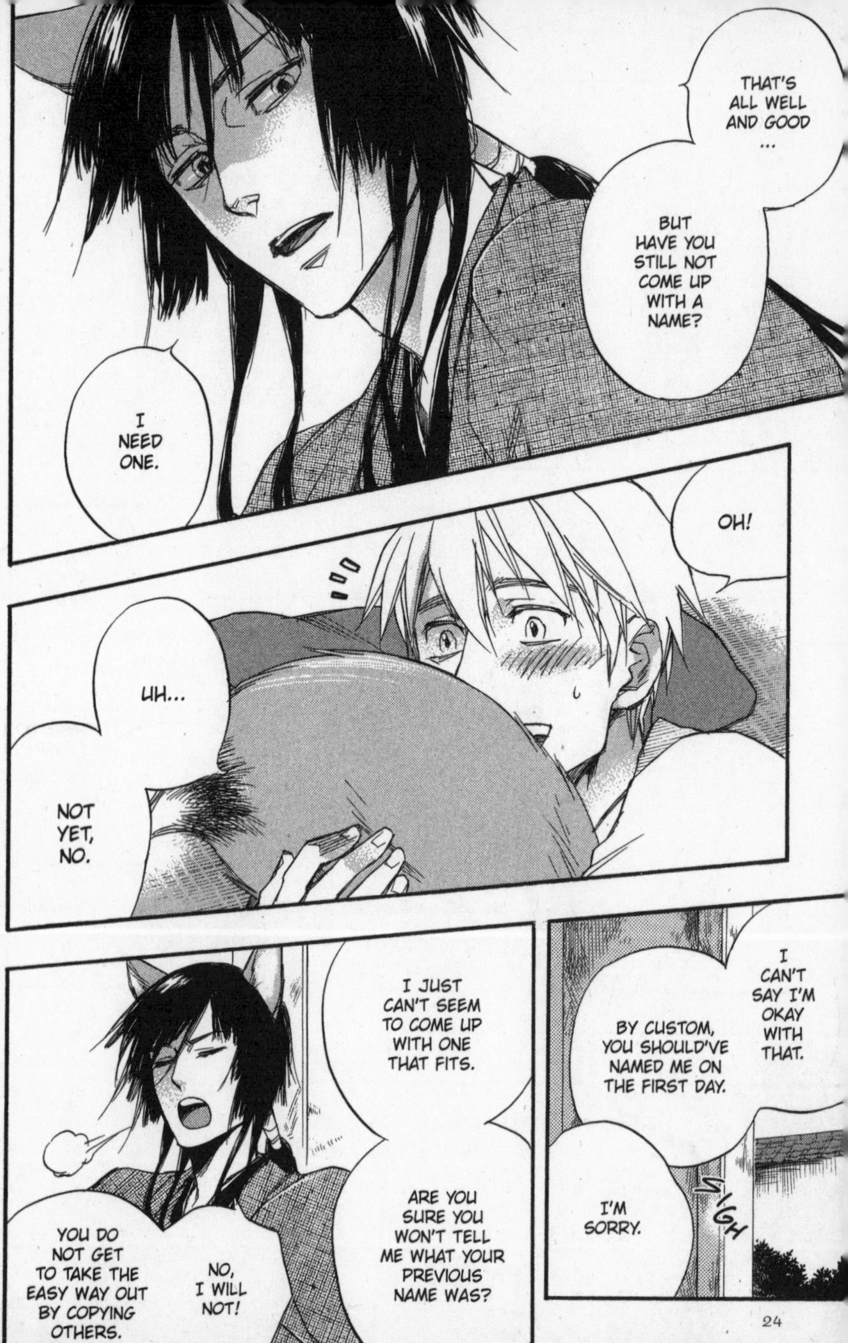
THAT'S ALL WELL AND GOOD ...
BUT HAVE YOU STILL NOT COME UP WITH A NAME?
I NEED ONE.
OH!
UH...
NOT YET, NO.
I CAN'T SAY I'M OKAY WITH THAT.
BY CUSTOM, YOU SHOULD'VE NAMED ME ON THE FIRST DAY.
I'M SORRY.
SIGH
I JUST CAN'T SEEM TO COME UP WITH ONE THAT FITS.
ARE YOU SURE YOU WON'T TELL ME WHAT YOUR PREVIOUS NAME WAS?
NO, I WILL NOT!
YOU DO NOT GET TO TAKE THE EASY WAY OUT BY COPYING OTHERS.

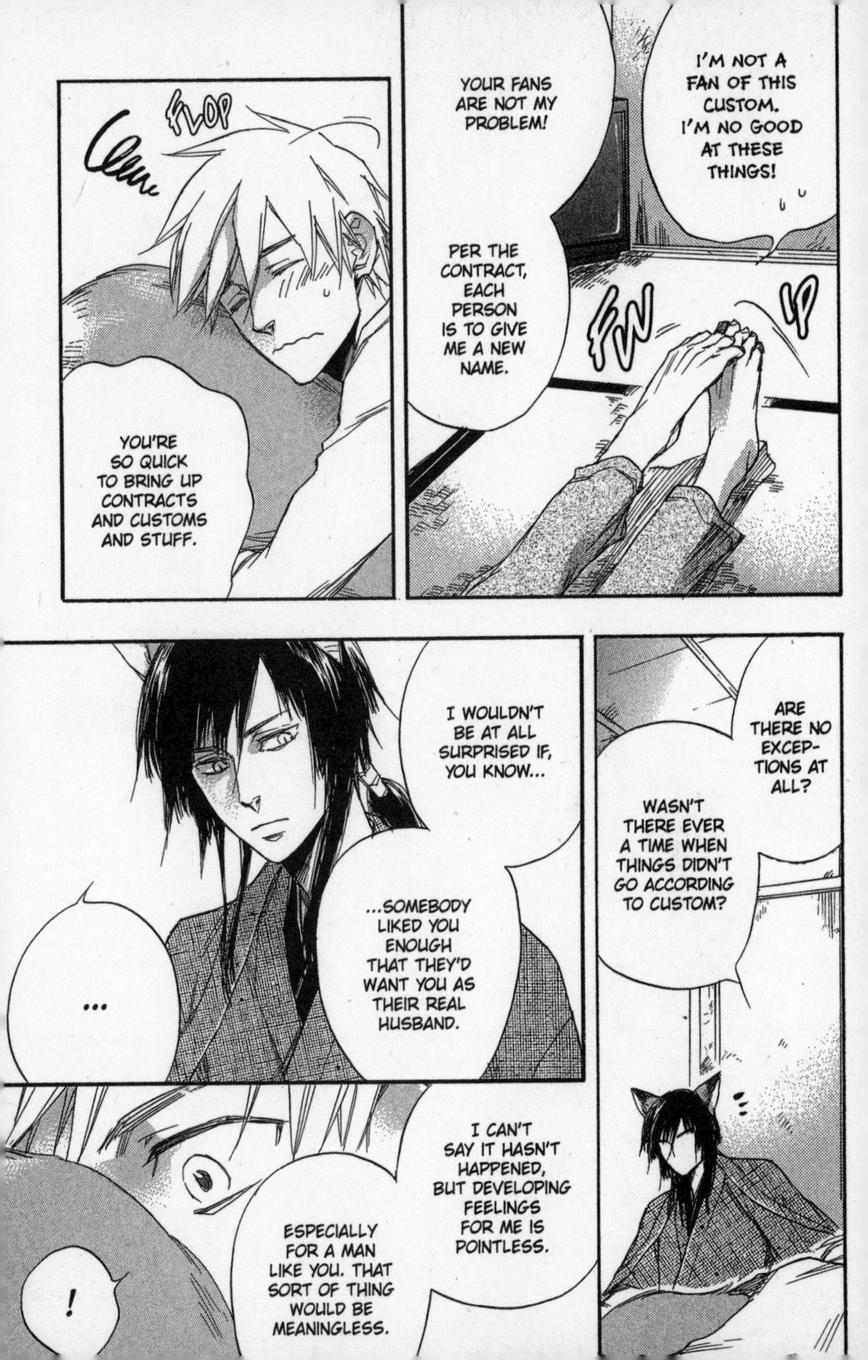
I'M NOT A FAN OF THIS CUSTOM. I'M NO GOOD AT THESE THINGS!
FWUP
YOUR FANS ARE NOT MY PROBLEM!
PER THE CONTRACT, EACH PERSON IS TO GIVE ME A NEW NAME.
FLOP
YOU'RE SO QUICK TO BRING UP CONTRACTS AND CUSTOMS AND STUFF.
ARE THERE NO EXCEP-TIONS AT ALL?
WASN'T THERE EVER A TIME WHEN THINGS DIDN'T GO ACCORDING TO CUSTOM?
I WOULDN'T BE AT ALL SURPRISED IF, YOU KNOW...
...SOMEBODY LIKED YOU ENOUGH THAT THEY'D WANT YOU AS THEIR REAL HUSBAND.
...
I CAN'T SAY IT HASN'T HAPPENED, BUT DEVELOPING FEELINGS FOR ME IS POINTLESS.
ESPECIALLY FOR A MAN LIKE YOU. THAT SORT OF THING WOULD BE MEANINGLESS.
!

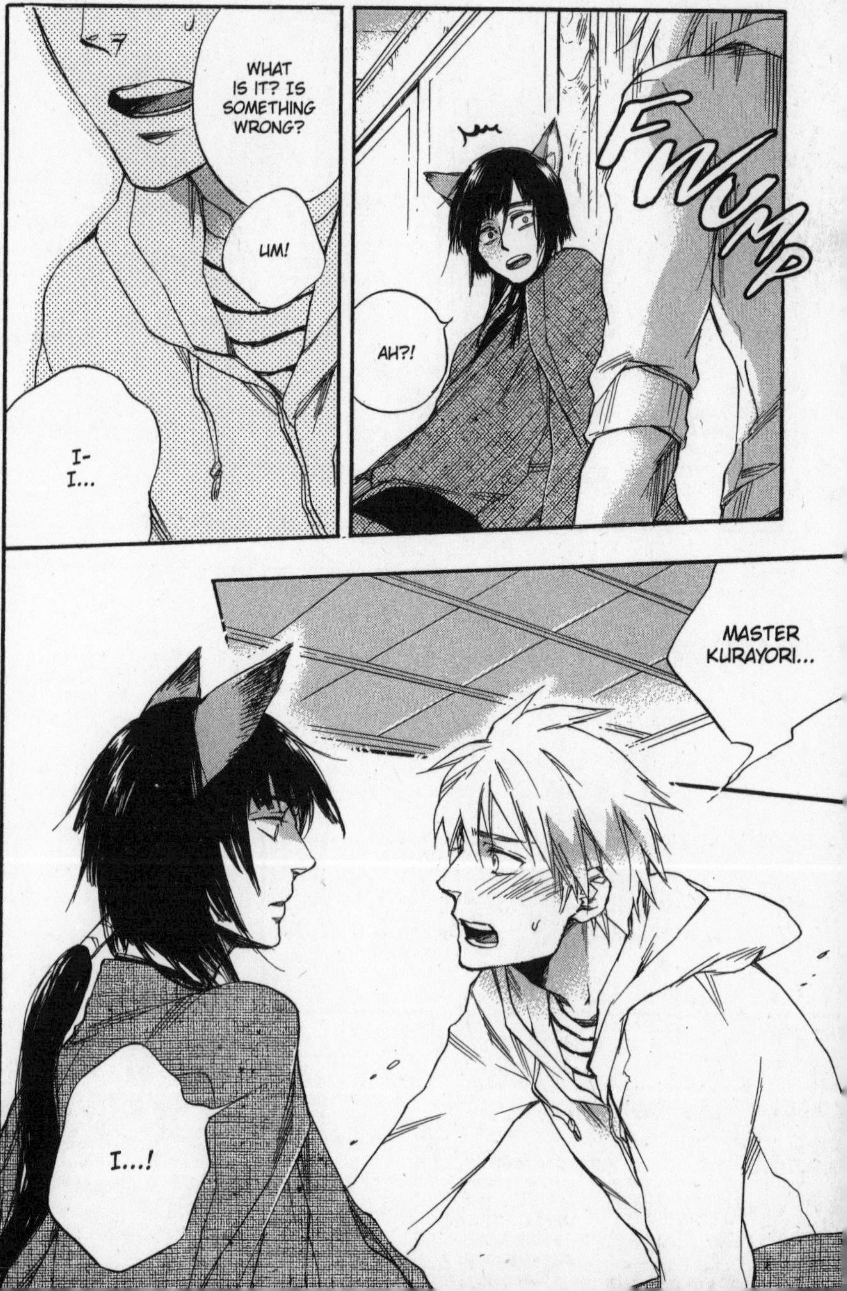
FWUMP
AH?!
WHAT IS IT? IS SOMETHING WRONG?
UM!
I- I...
MASTER KURAYORI...
I...!

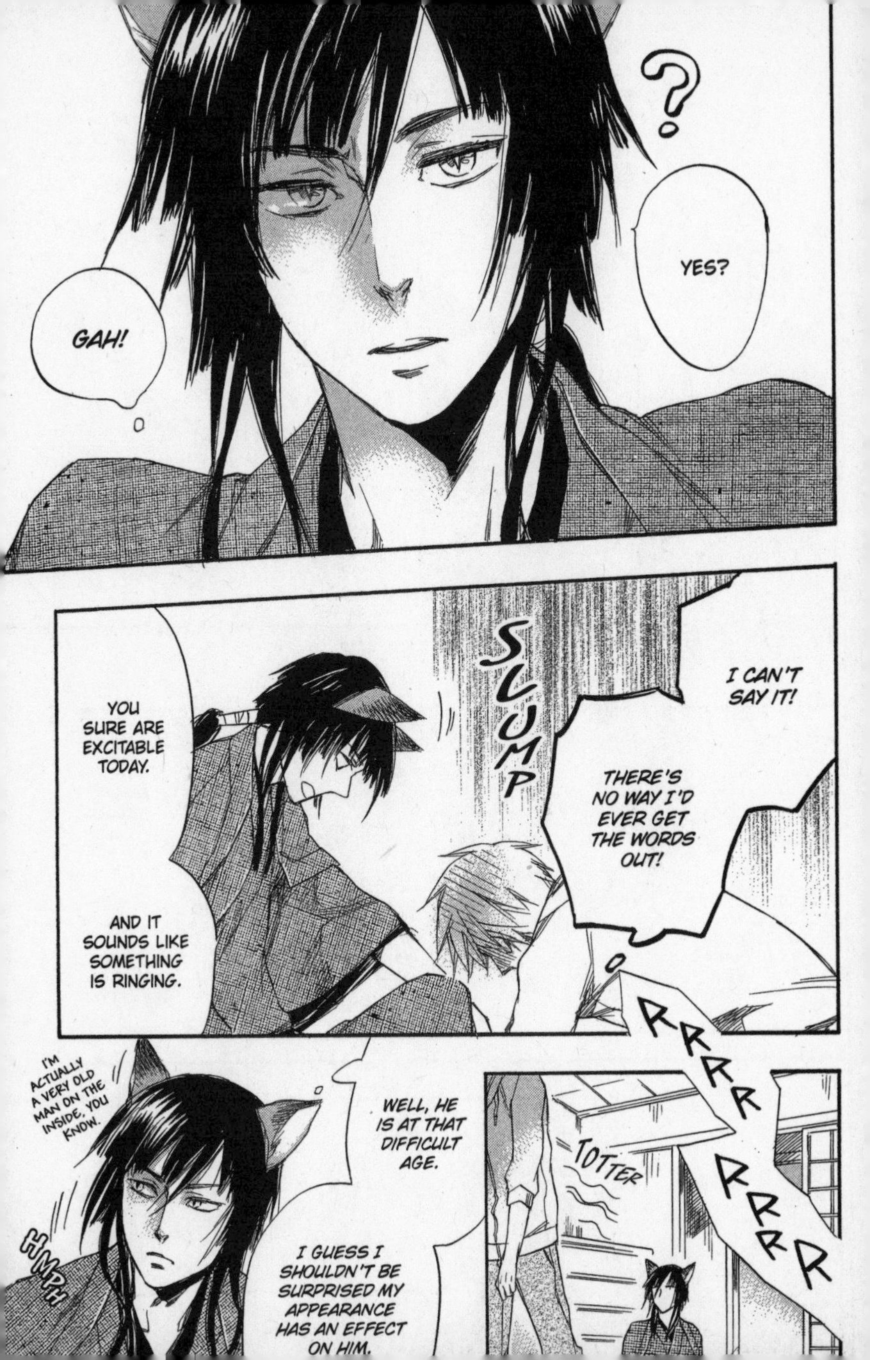
?
YES?
GAH!
I CAN'T SAY IT!
THERE'S NO WAY I'D EVER GET THE WORDS OUT!
SLUMP
YOU SURE ARE EXCITABLE TODAY.
AND IT SOUNDS LIKE SOMETHING IS RINGING.
RRRRRRRRR
TOTTER
WELL, HE IS AT THAT DIFFICULT AGE.
I GUESS I SHOULDN'T BE SURPRISED MY APPEARANCE HAS AN EFFECT ON HIM.
I'M ACTUALLY A VERY OLD MAN ON THE INSIDE, YOU KNOW.
HMPH

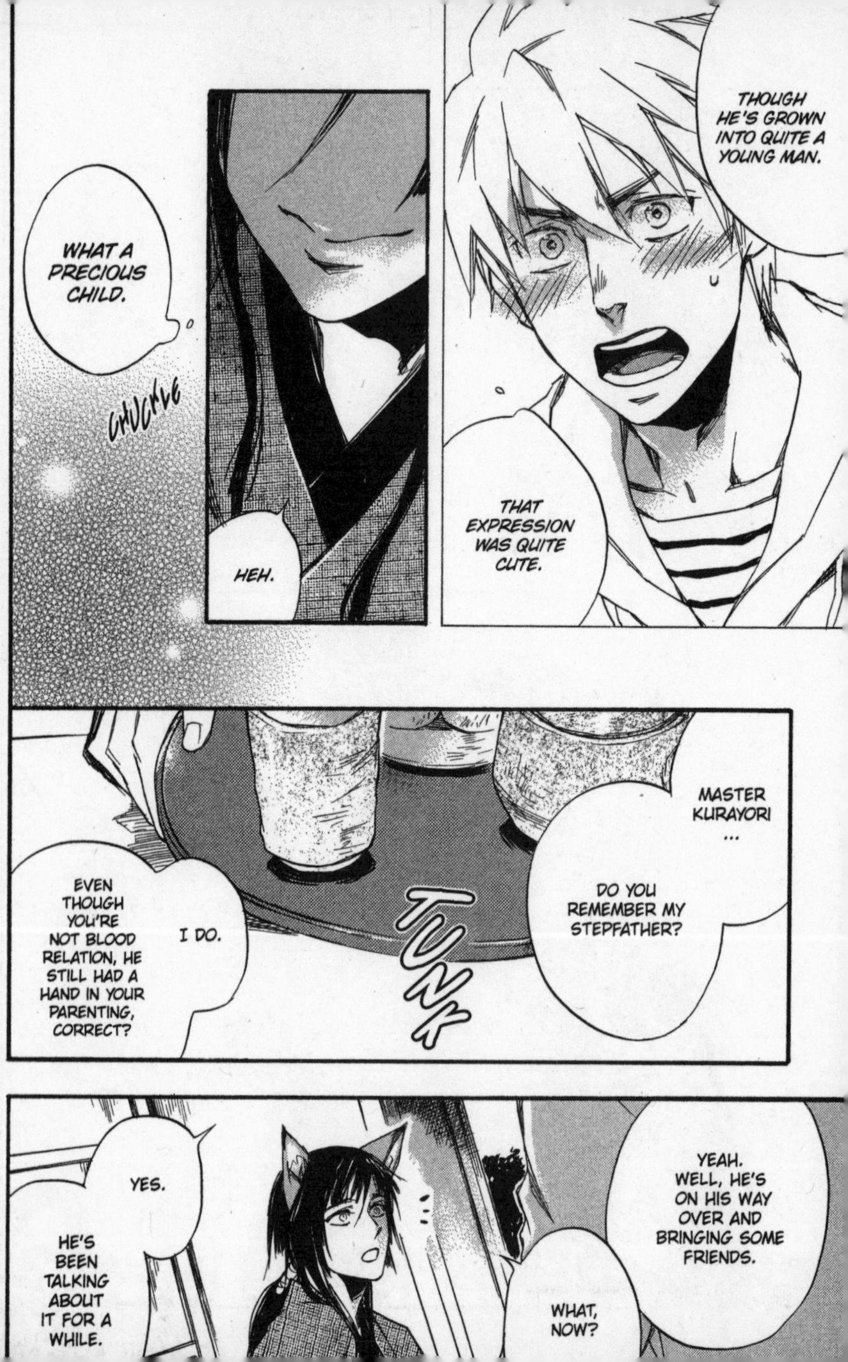
THOUGH HE'S GROWN INTO QUITE A YOUNG MAN.
THAT EXPRESSION WAS QUITE CUTE.
HEH.
WHAT A PRECIOUS CHILD.
CHUCKLE
MASTER KURAYORI ...
DO YOU REMEMBER MY STEPFATHER?
TUNK
I DO.
EVEN THOUGH YOU'RE NOT BLOOD RELATION, HE STILL HAD A HAND IN YOUR PARENTING, CORRECT?
YEAH. WELL, HE'S ON HIS WAY OVER AND BRINGING SOME FRIENDS.
WHAT, NOW?
YES.
HE'S BEEN TALKING ABOUT IT FOR A WHILE.

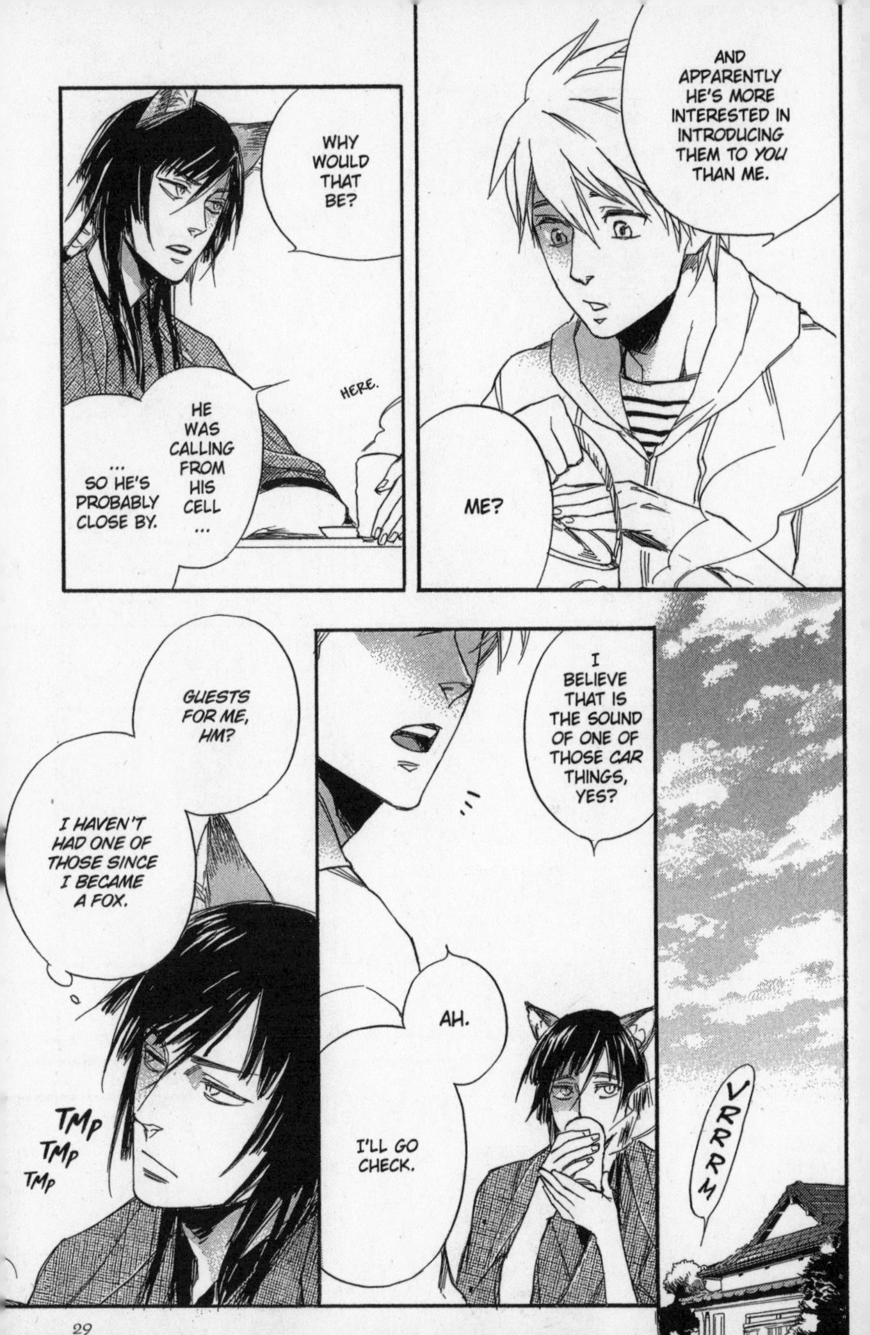
AND APPARENTLY HE'S MORE INTERESTED IN INTRODUCING THEM TO *YOU* THAN ME.
ME?
WHY WOULD THAT BE?
HERE.
HE WAS CALLING FROM HIS CELL ...
... SO HE'S PROBABLY CLOSE BY.
VRRRM
I BELIEVE THAT IS THE SOUND OF ONE OF THOSE CAR THINGS, YES?
...
AH.
I'LL GO CHECK.
GUESTS FOR ME, HM?
I HAVEN'T HAD ONE OF THOSE SINCE I BECAME A FOX.
TMP
TMP
TMP

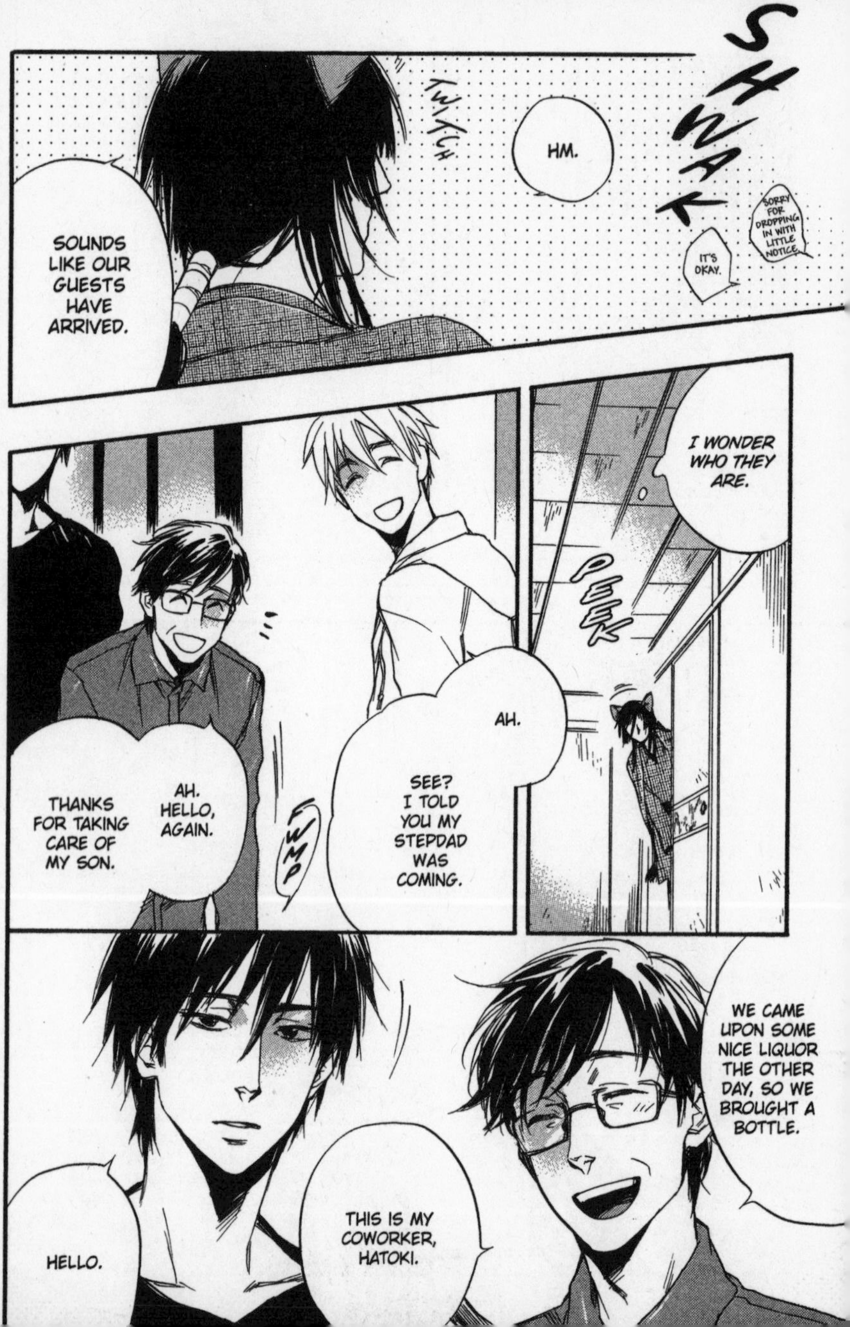
SHWAK
SORRY FOR DROPPING IN WITH LITTLE NOTICE.
IT'S OKAY.
HM.
TWITCH
SOUNDS LIKE OUR GUESTS HAVE ARRIVED.
I WONDER WHO THEY ARE.
PEEK
AH.
SEE? I TOLD YOU MY STEPDAD WAS COMING.
FWMP
AH. HELLO, AGAIN.
THANKS FOR TAKING CARE OF MY SON.
WE CAME UPON SOME NICE LIQUOR THE OTHER DAY, SO WE BROUGHT A BOTTLE.
THIS IS MY COWORKER, HATOKI.
HELLO.

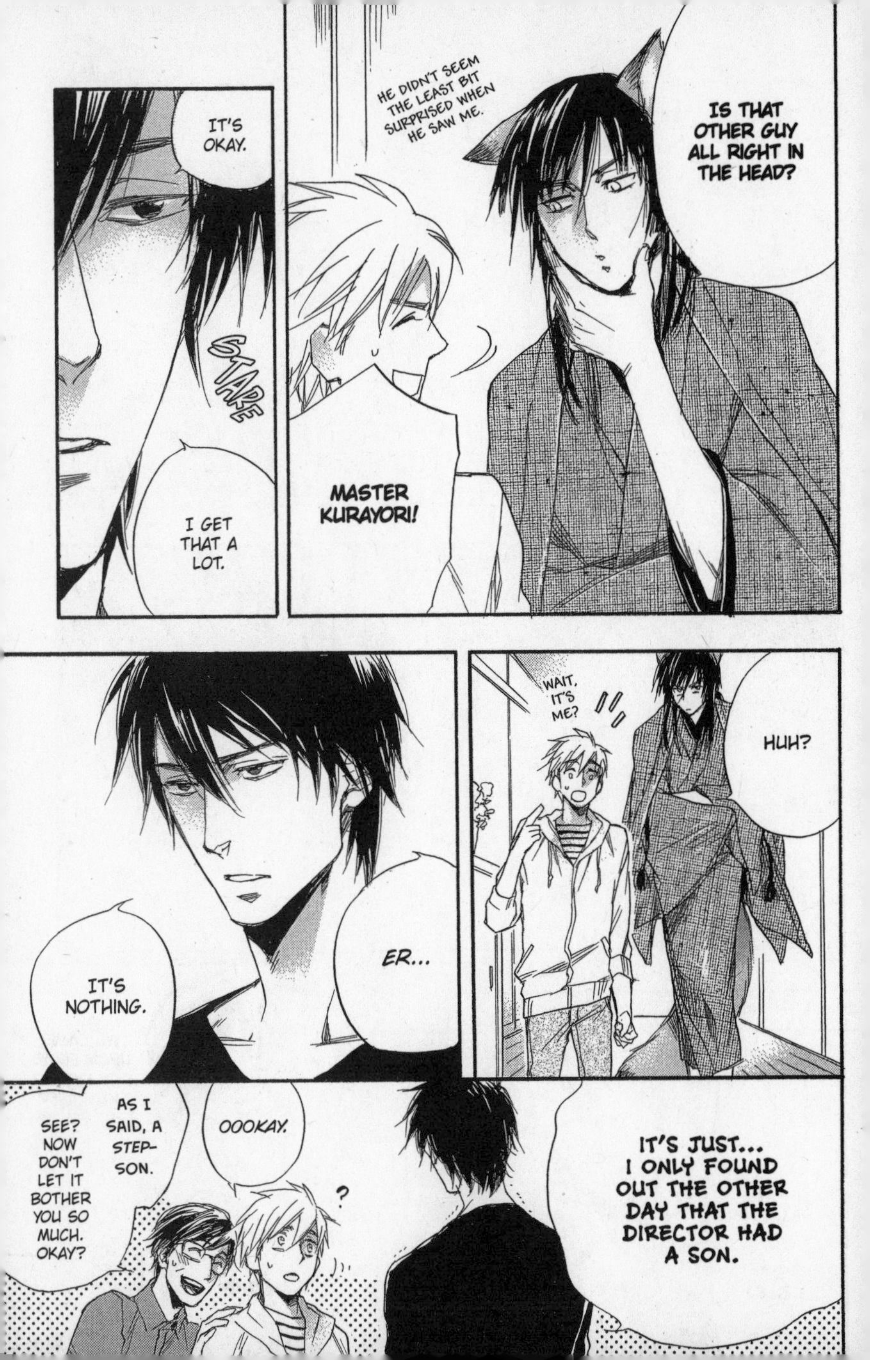
IS THAT OTHER GUY ALL RIGHT IN THE HEAD?
HE DIDN'T SEEM THE LEAST BIT SURPRISED WHEN HE SAW ME.
MASTER KURAYORI!
IT'S OKAY.
STARE
I GET THAT A LOT.
HUH?
WAIT, IT'S ME?
ER...
IT'S NOTHING.
IT'S JUST... I ONLY FOUND OUT THE OTHER DAY THAT THE DIRECTOR HAD A SON.
?
OOOKAY.
AS I SAID, A STEP-SON.
SEE? NOW DON'T LET IT BOTHER YOU SO MUCH. OKAY?

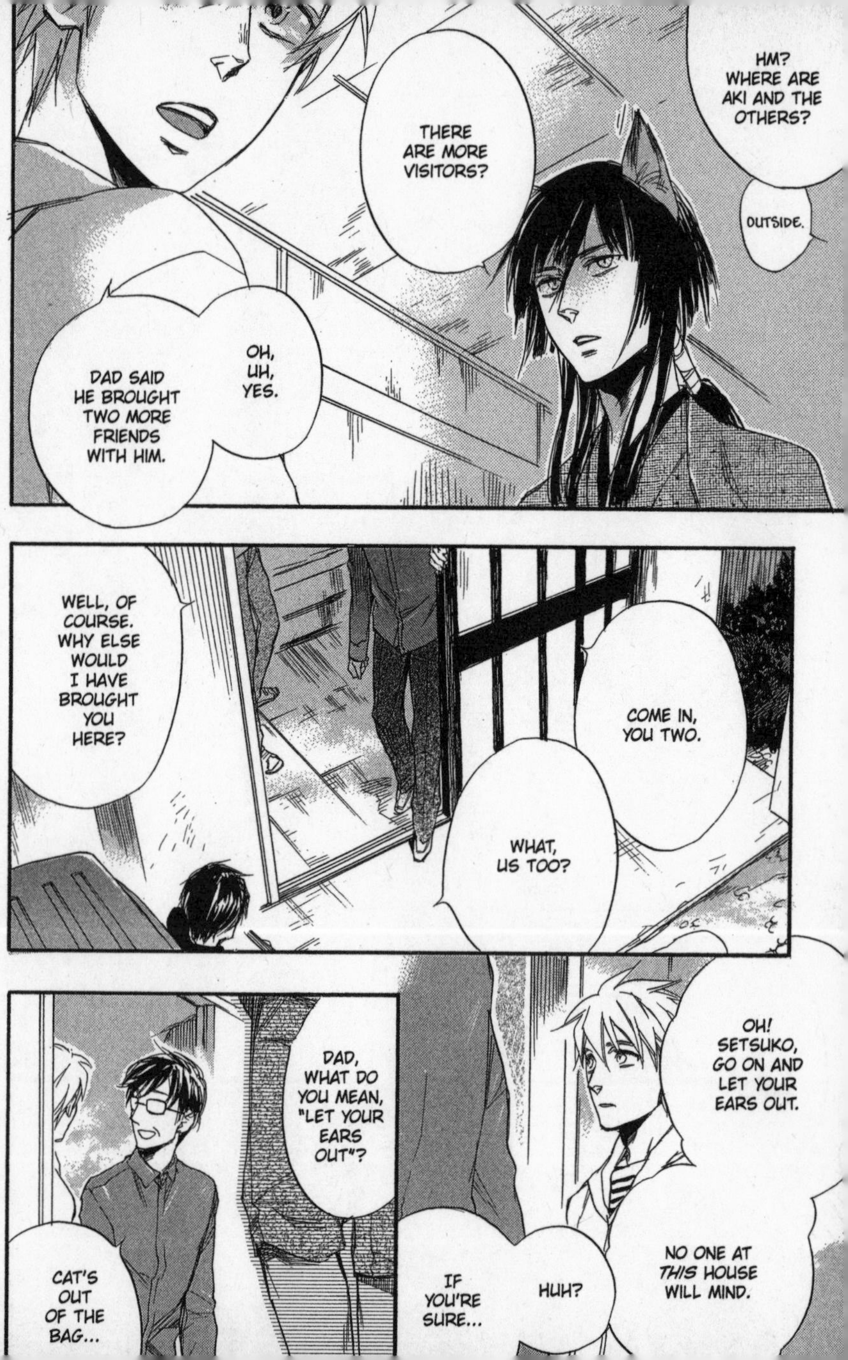
HM? WHERE ARE AKI AND THE OTHERS?
OUTSIDE.
THERE ARE MORE VISITORS?
OH, UH, YES.
DAD SAID HE BROUGHT TWO MORE FRIENDS WITH HIM.
COME IN, YOU TWO.
WHAT, US TOO?
WELL, OF COURSE. WHY ELSE WOULD I HAVE BROUGHT YOU HERE?
OH! SETSUKO, GO ON AND LET YOUR EARS OUT.
NO ONE AT *THIS* HOUSE WILL MIND.
HUH?
IF YOU'RE SURE...
DAD, WHAT DO YOU MEAN, "LET YOUR EARS OUT"?
CAT'S OUT OF THE BAG...

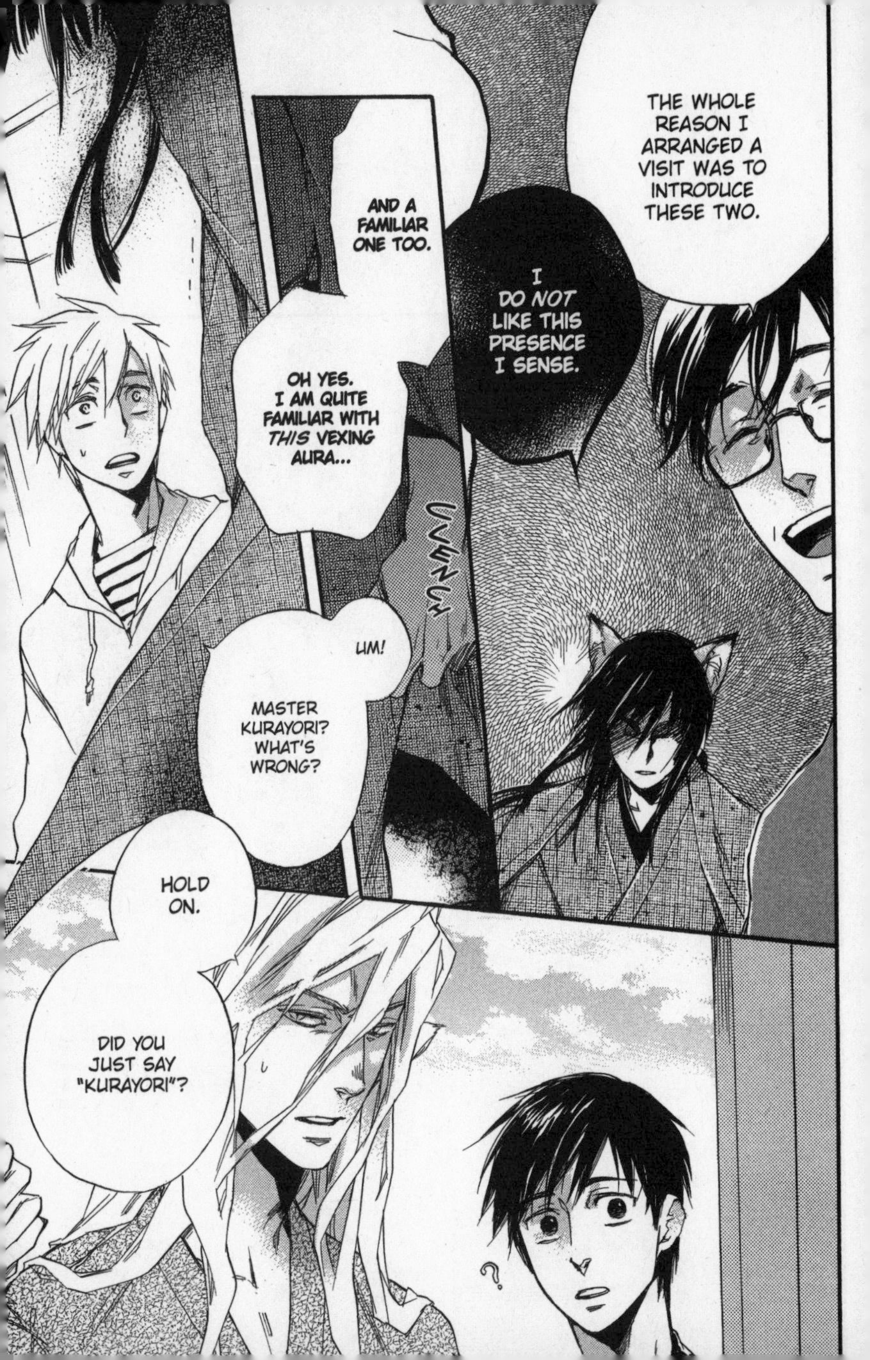
THE WHOLE REASON I ARRANGED A VISIT WAS TO INTRODUCE THESE TWO.
I DO *NOT* LIKE THIS PRESENCE I SENSE.
AND A FAMILIAR ONE TOO.
OH YES. I AM QUITE FAMILIAR WITH *THIS* VEXING AURA...
CLENCH
UM!
MASTER KURAYORI? WHAT'S WRONG?
HOLD ON.
DID YOU JUST SAY "KURAYORI"?
?

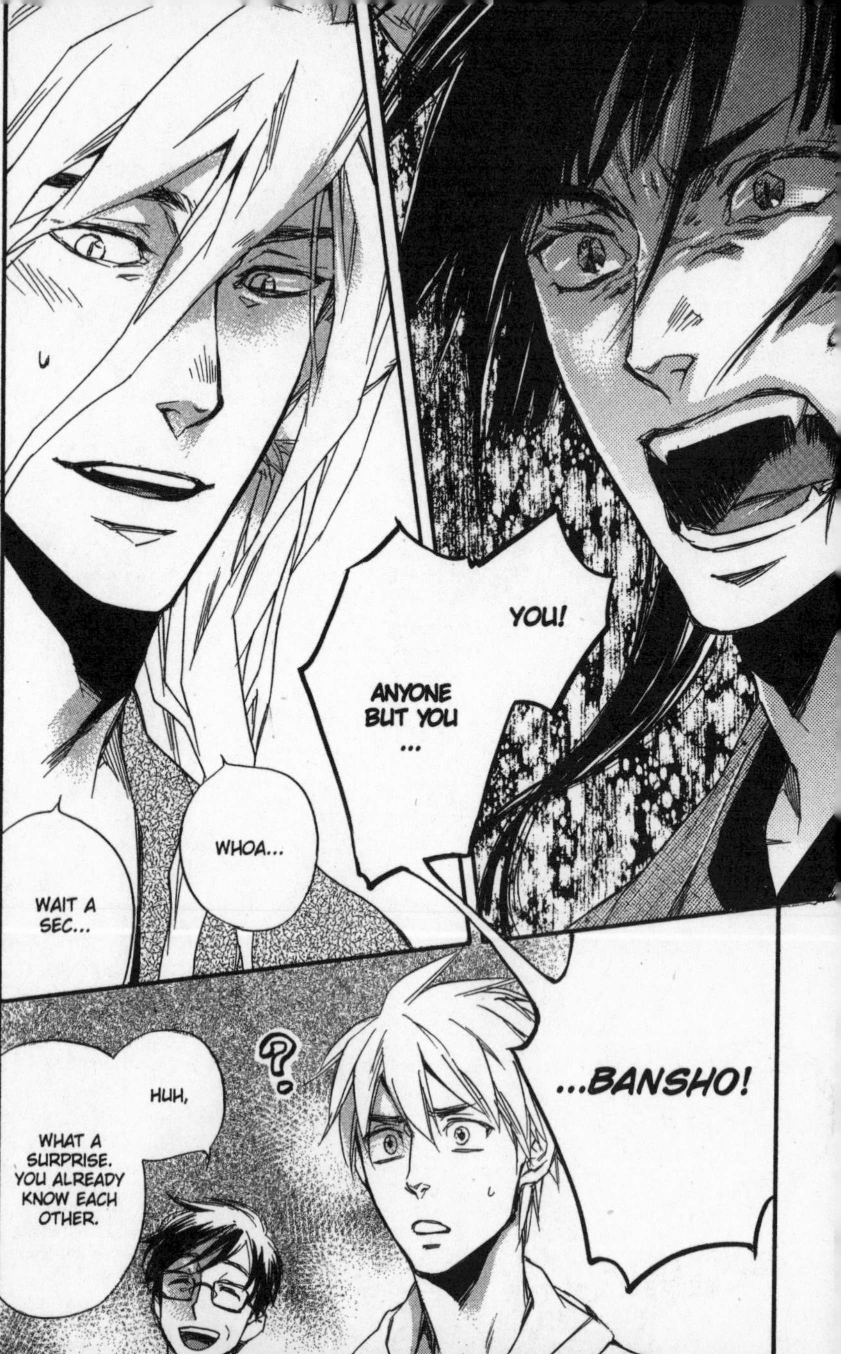
YOU!
ANYONE BUT YOU ...
WHOA...
WAIT A SEC...
...BANSHO!
?
HUH,
WHAT A SURPRISE. YOU ALREADY KNOW EACH OTHER.

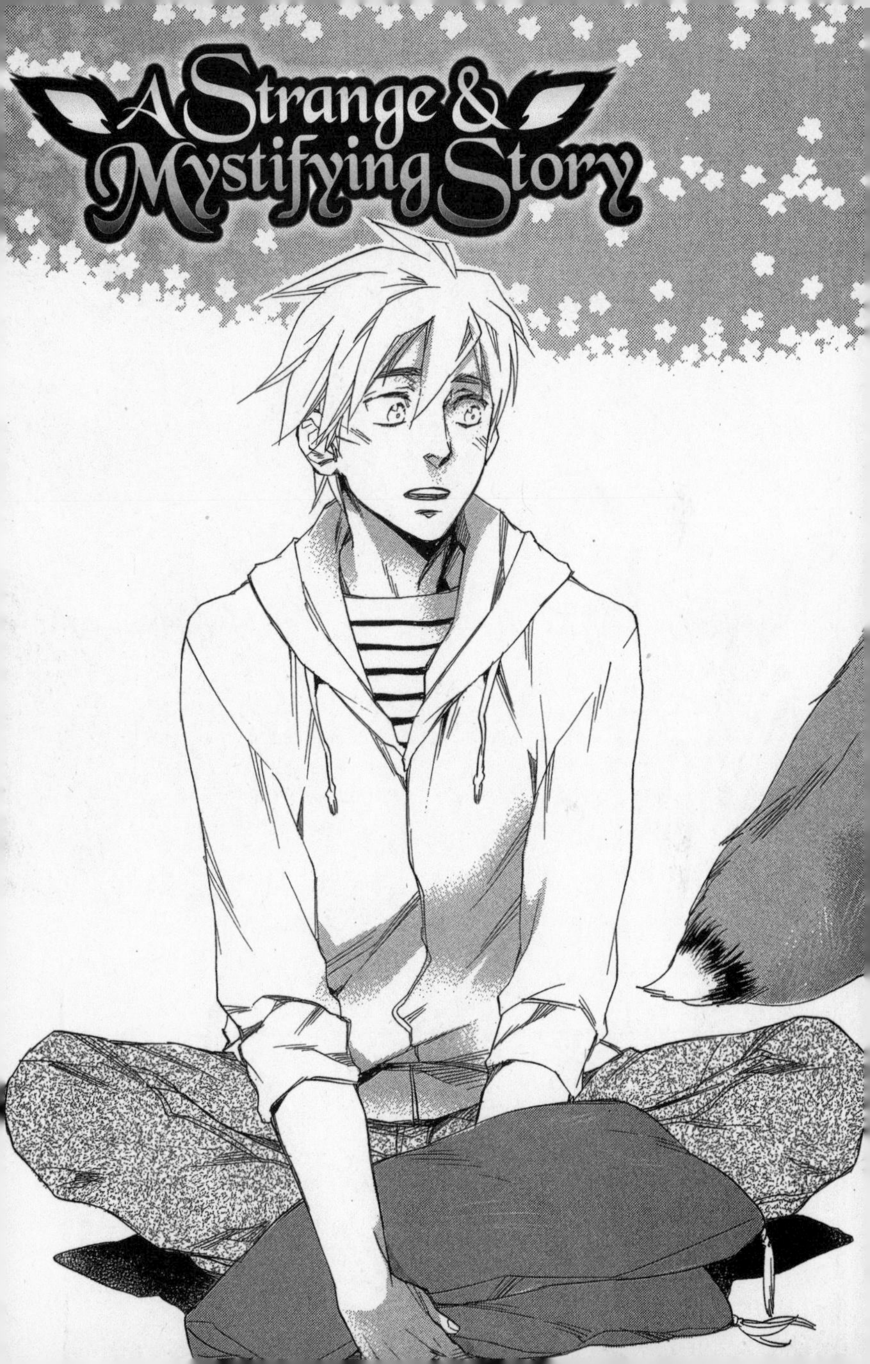
A Strange & Mystifying Story

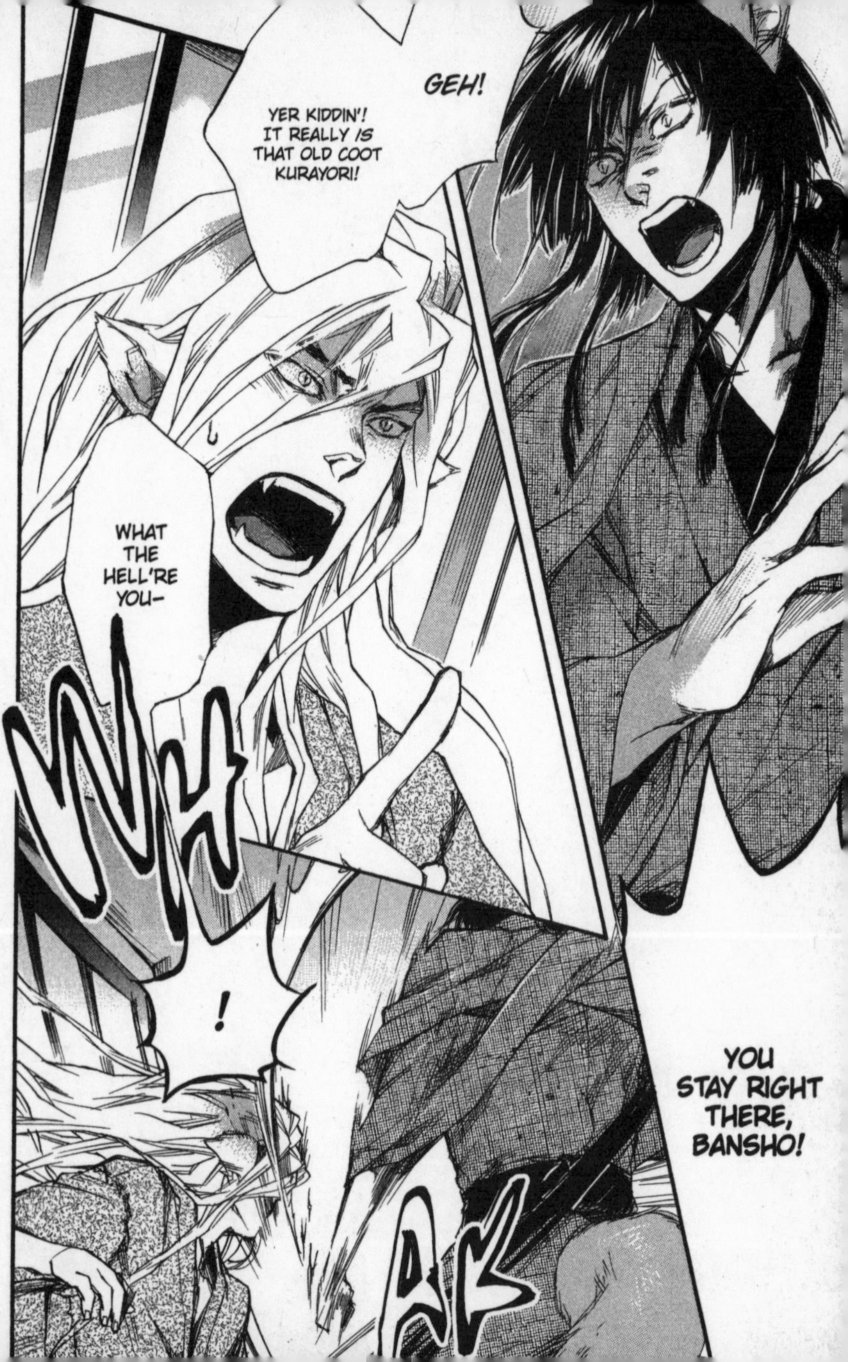
GEH!
YER KIDDIN'! IT REALLY IS THAT OLD COOT KURAYORI!
WHAT THE HELL'RE YOU-
YOU STAY RIGHT THERE, BANSHO!
WH
!
AK

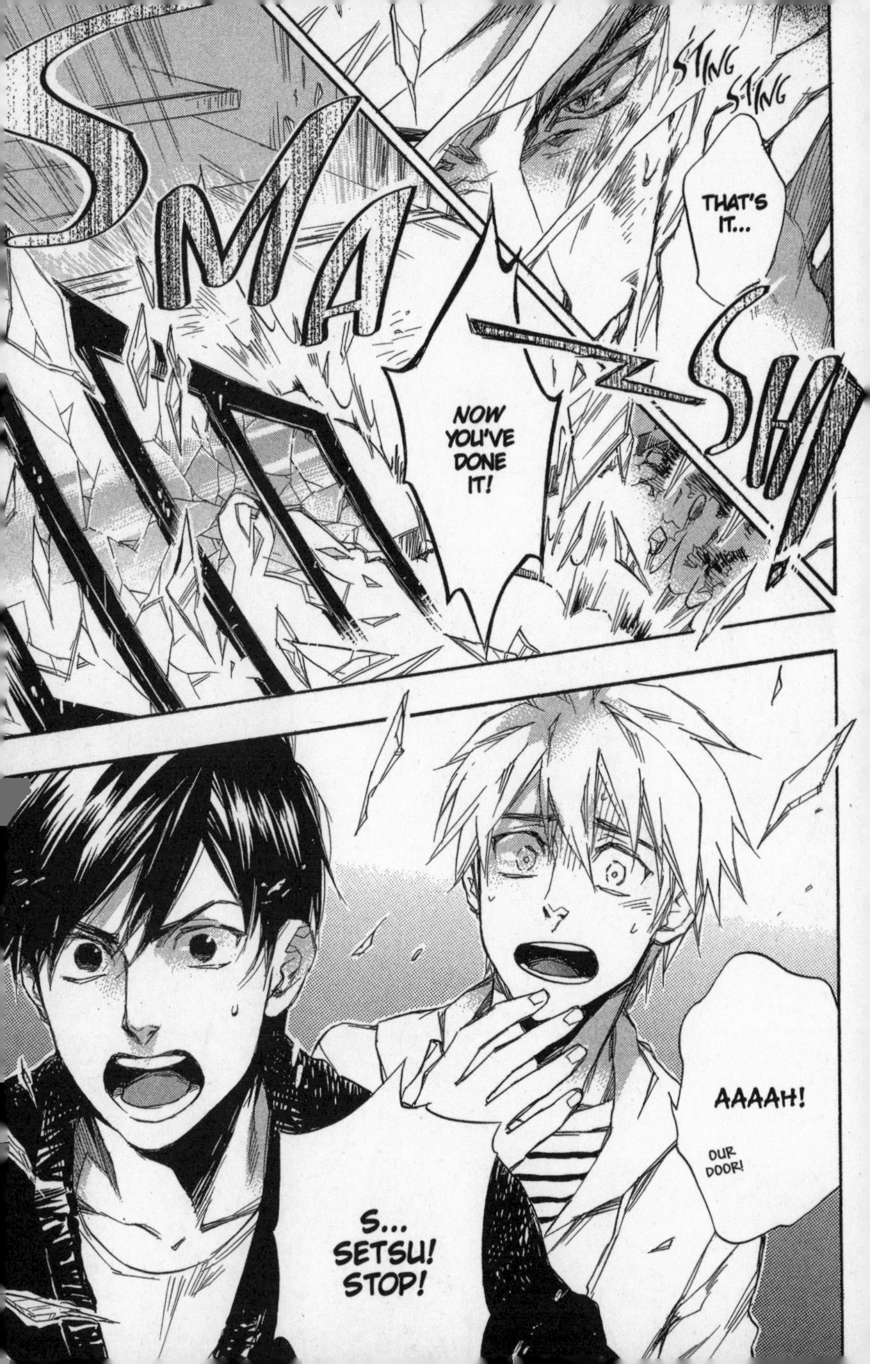
S-TING S-TING
THAT'S IT...
SMASH!
NOW YOU'VE DONE IT!
AAAAH!
OUR DOOR!
S... SETSU! STOP!

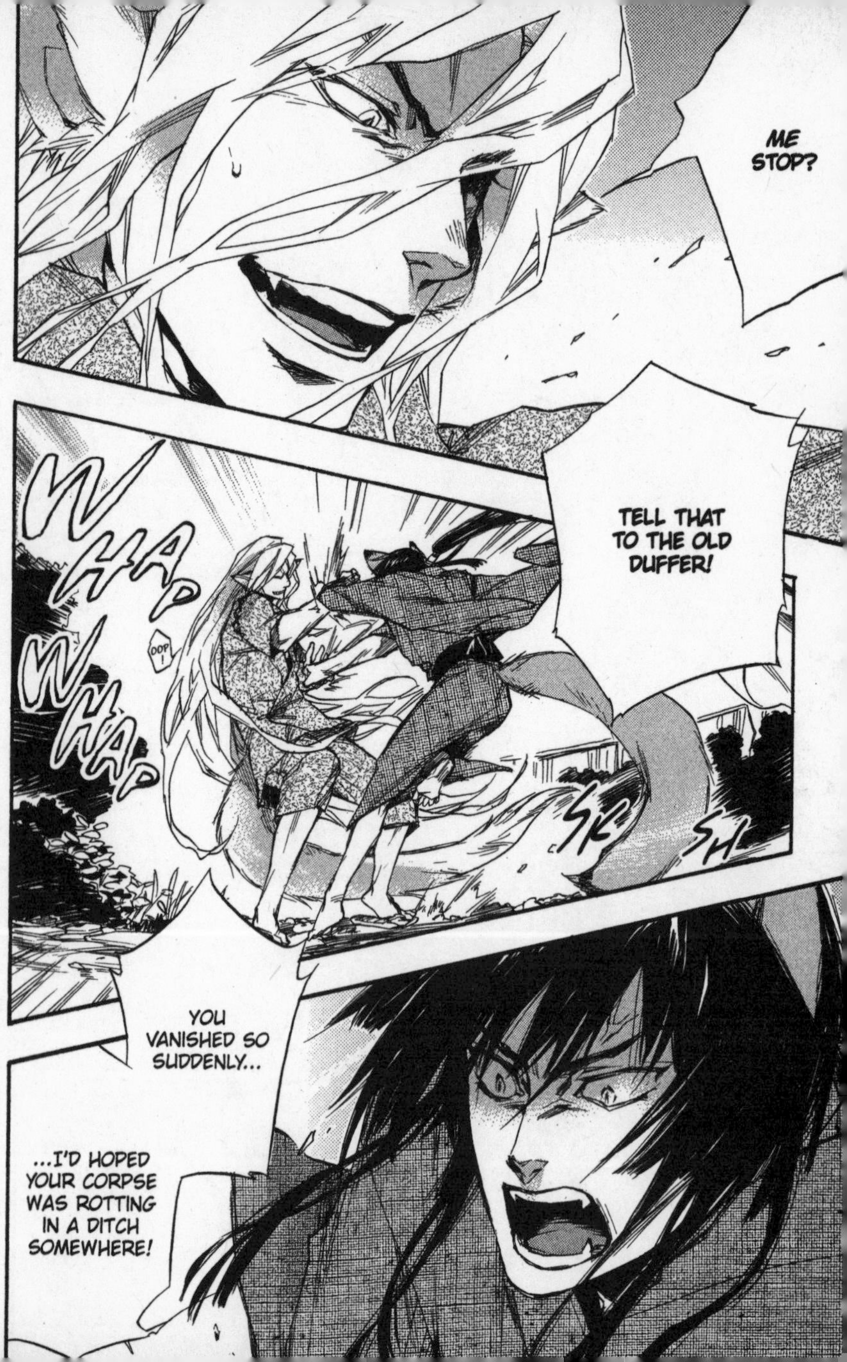
ME STOP?
TELL THAT TO THE OLD DUFFER!
WHAP
WHAP
OOP!
SKSH
YOU VANISHED SO SUDDENLY...
...I'D HOPED YOUR CORPSE WAS ROTTING IN A DITCH SOMEWHERE!

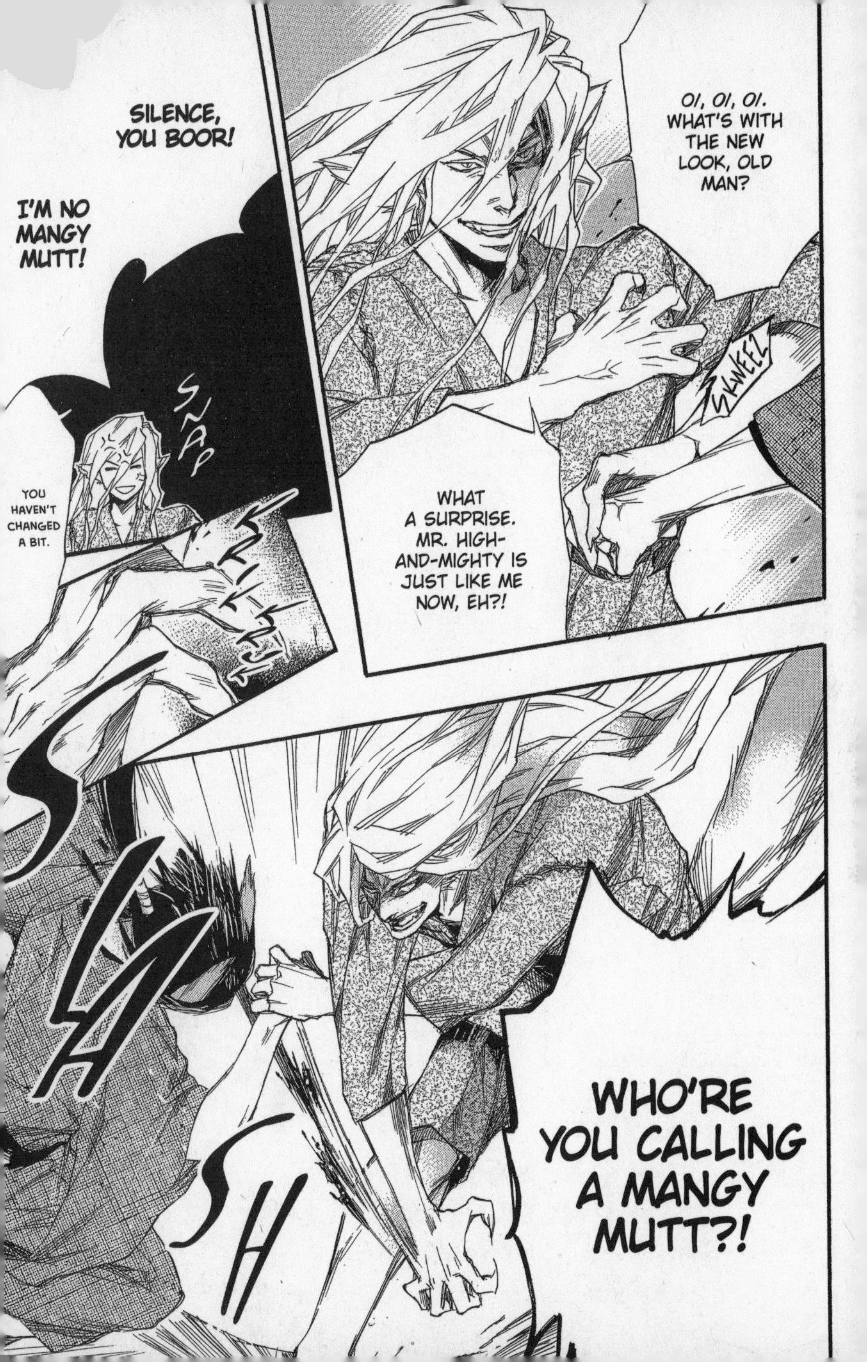
OI, OI, OI. WHAT'S WITH THE NEW LOOK, OLD MAN?
WHAT A SURPRISE. MR. HIGH-AND-MIGHTY IS JUST LIKE ME NOW, EH?!
SILENCE, YOU BOOR!
I'M NO MANGY MUTT!
SNAP
YOU HAVEN'T CHANGED A BIT.
WHO'RE YOU CALLING A MANGY MUTT?!

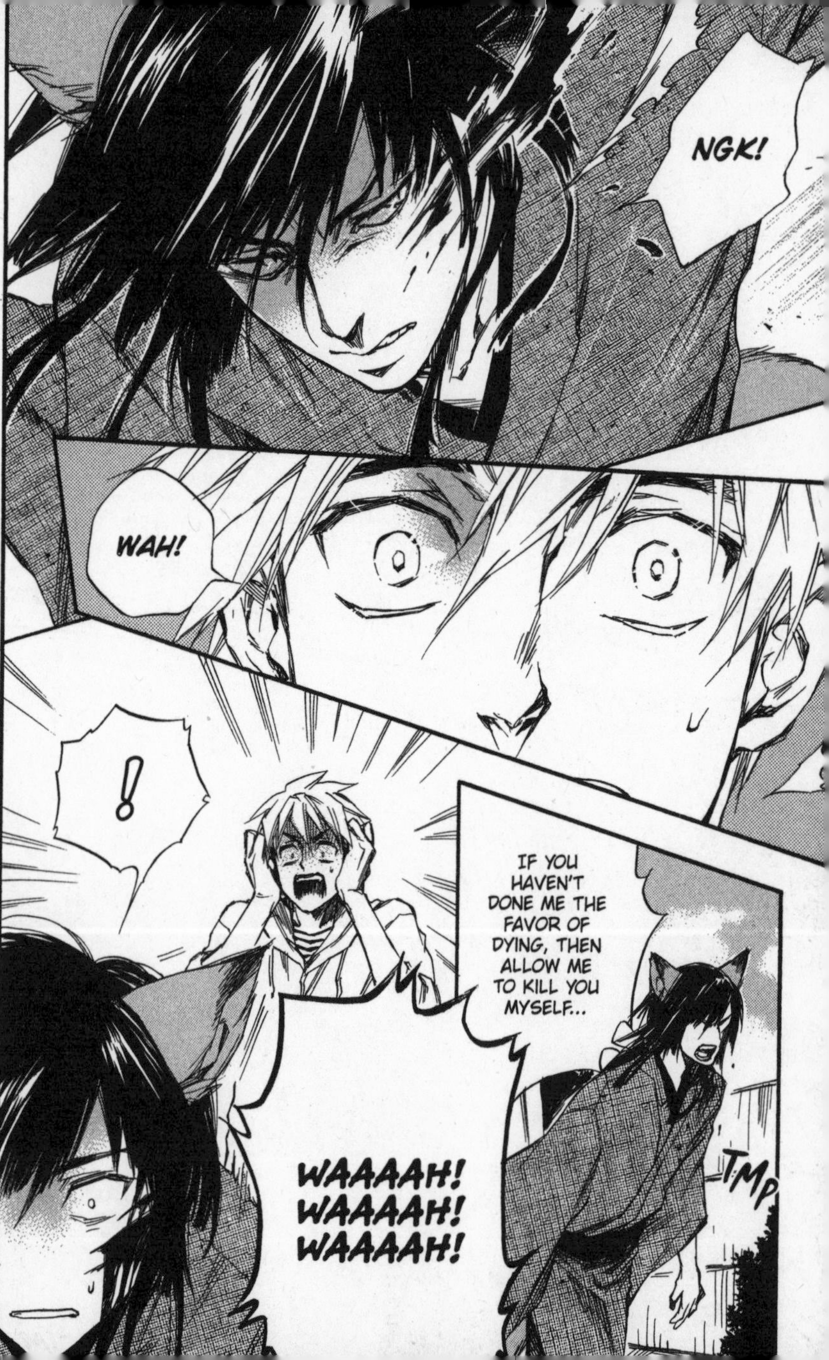
NGK!
WAH!
IF YOU HAVEN'T DONE ME THE FAVOR OF DYING, THEN ALLOW ME TO KILL YOU MYSELF...
TMP
!
WAAAAH! WAAAAH! WAAAAH!

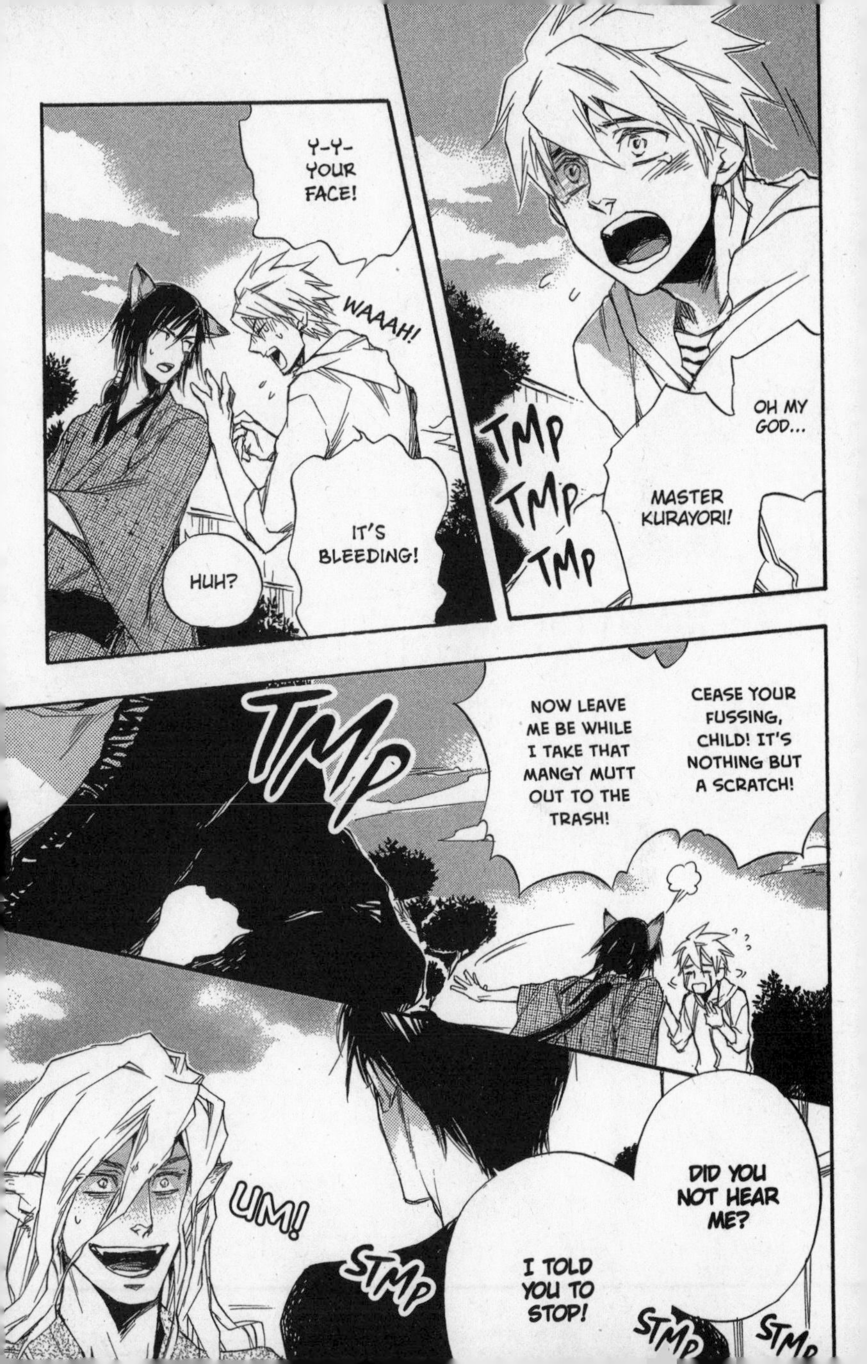
OH MY GOD...
MASTER KURAYORI!
TMP
TMP
TMP
Y-Y-YOUR FACE!
WAAAH!
IT'S BLEEDING!
HUH?
CEASE YOUR FUSSING, CHILD! IT'S NOTHING BUT A SCRATCH!
NOW LEAVE ME BE WHILE I TAKE THAT MANGY MUTT OUT TO THE TRASH!
TMP
DID YOU NOT HEAR ME?
STMP
STMP
I TOLD YOU TO STOP!
STMP
UM!

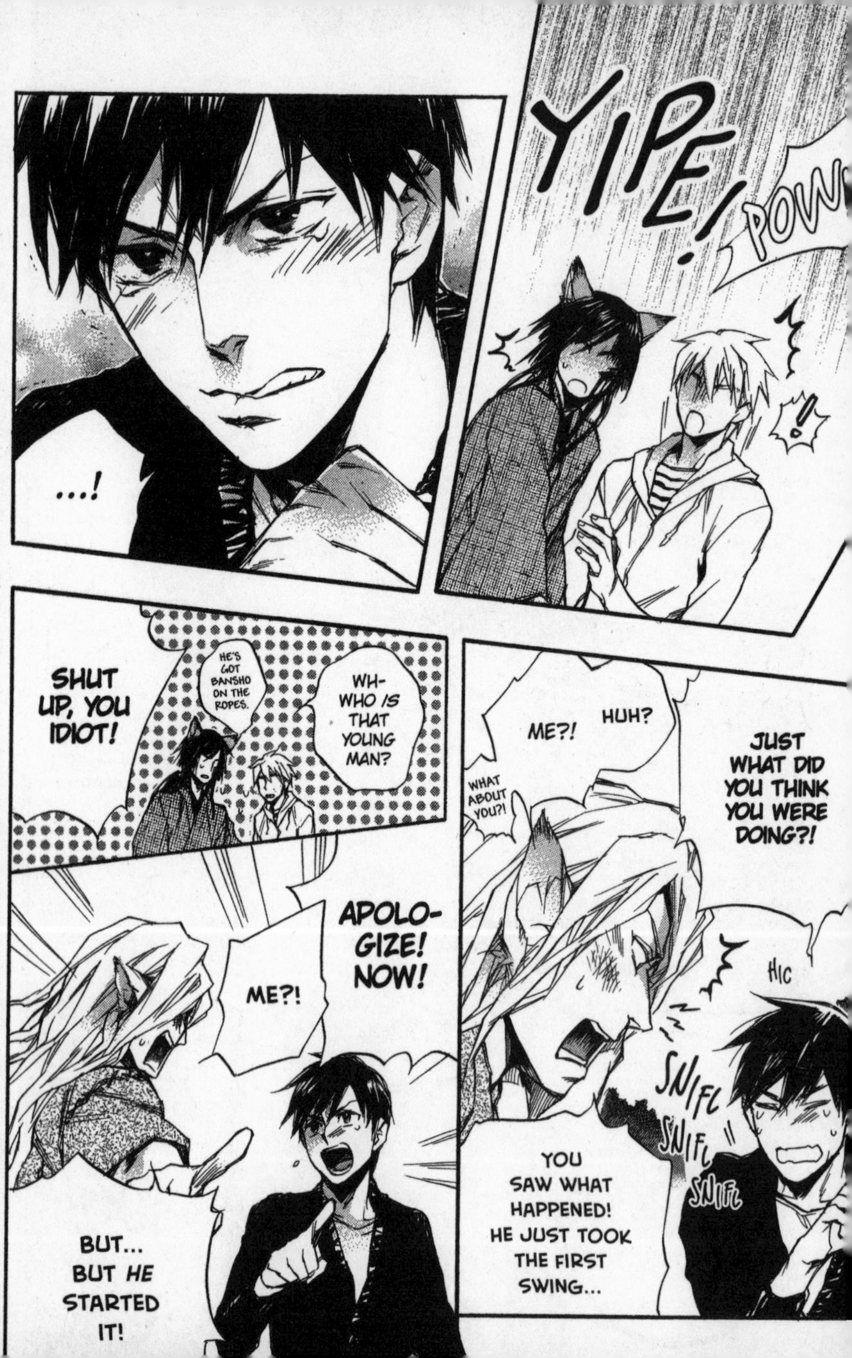
YIPE!
POW
...!
JUST WHAT DID YOU THINK YOU WERE DOING?!
HUH?
ME?!
WHAT ABOUT YOU?!
HIC
SNIFL
SNIFL
SNIFL
YOU SAW WHAT HAPPENED! HE JUST TOOK THE FIRST SWING...
WH-WHO *IS* THAT YOUNG MAN?
HE'S GOT BANSHO ON THE ROPES.
SHUT UP, YOU IDIOT!
APOLOGIZE! NOW!
ME?!
BUT... BUT *HE* STARTED IT!

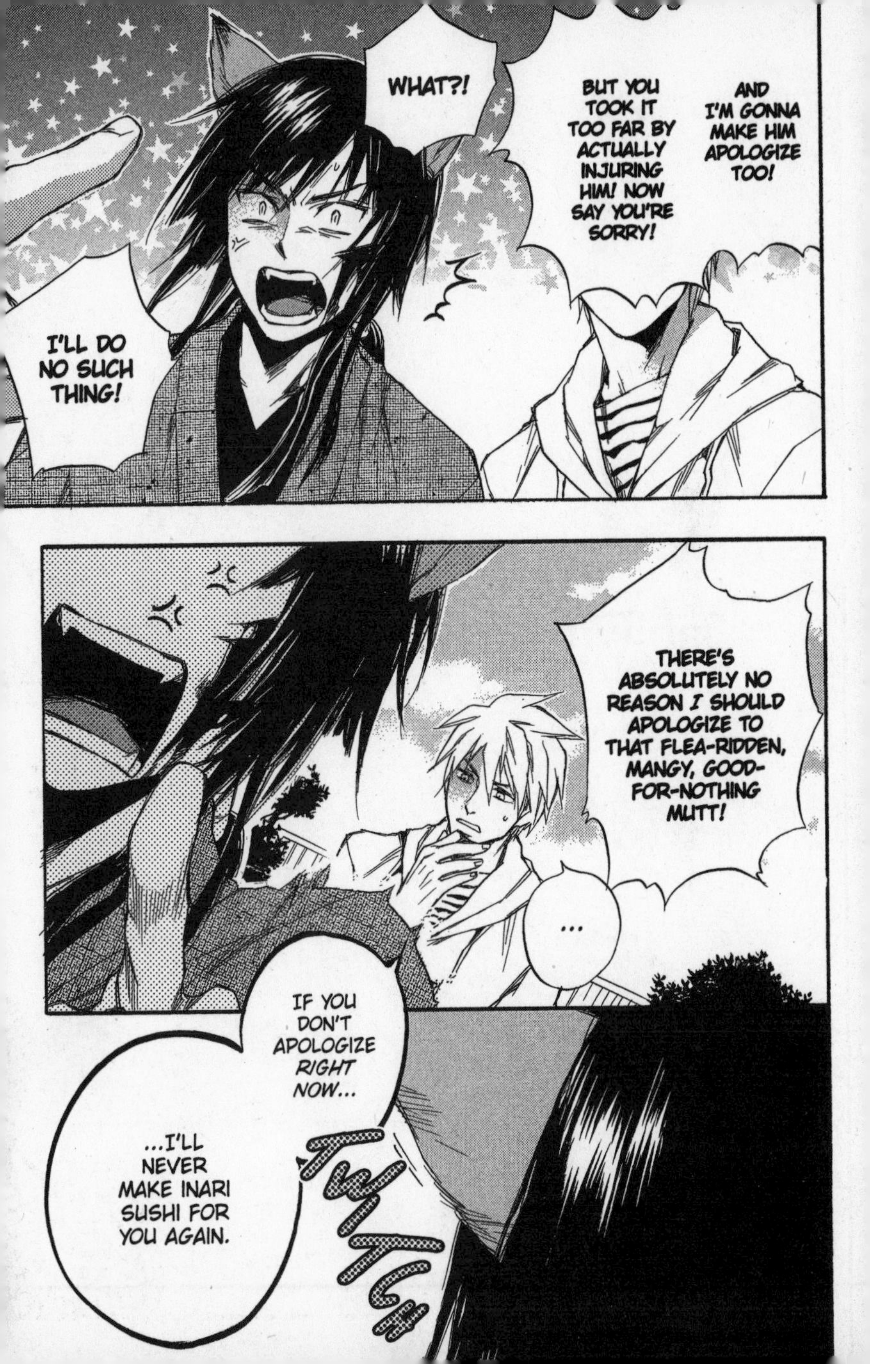
AND I'M GONNA MAKE HIM APOLOGIZE TOO!
BUT YOU TOOK IT TOO FAR BY ACTUALLY INJURING HIM! NOW SAY YOU'RE SORRY!
WHAT?!
I'LL DO NO SUCH THING!
THERE'S ABSOLUTELY NO REASON *I* SHOULD APOLOGIZE TO THAT FLEA-RIDDEN, MANGY, GOOD-FOR-NOTHING MUTT!
...
IF YOU DON'T APOLOGIZE *RIGHT* NOW...
...I'LL NEVER MAKE INARI SUSHI FOR YOU AGAIN.
TWITCH

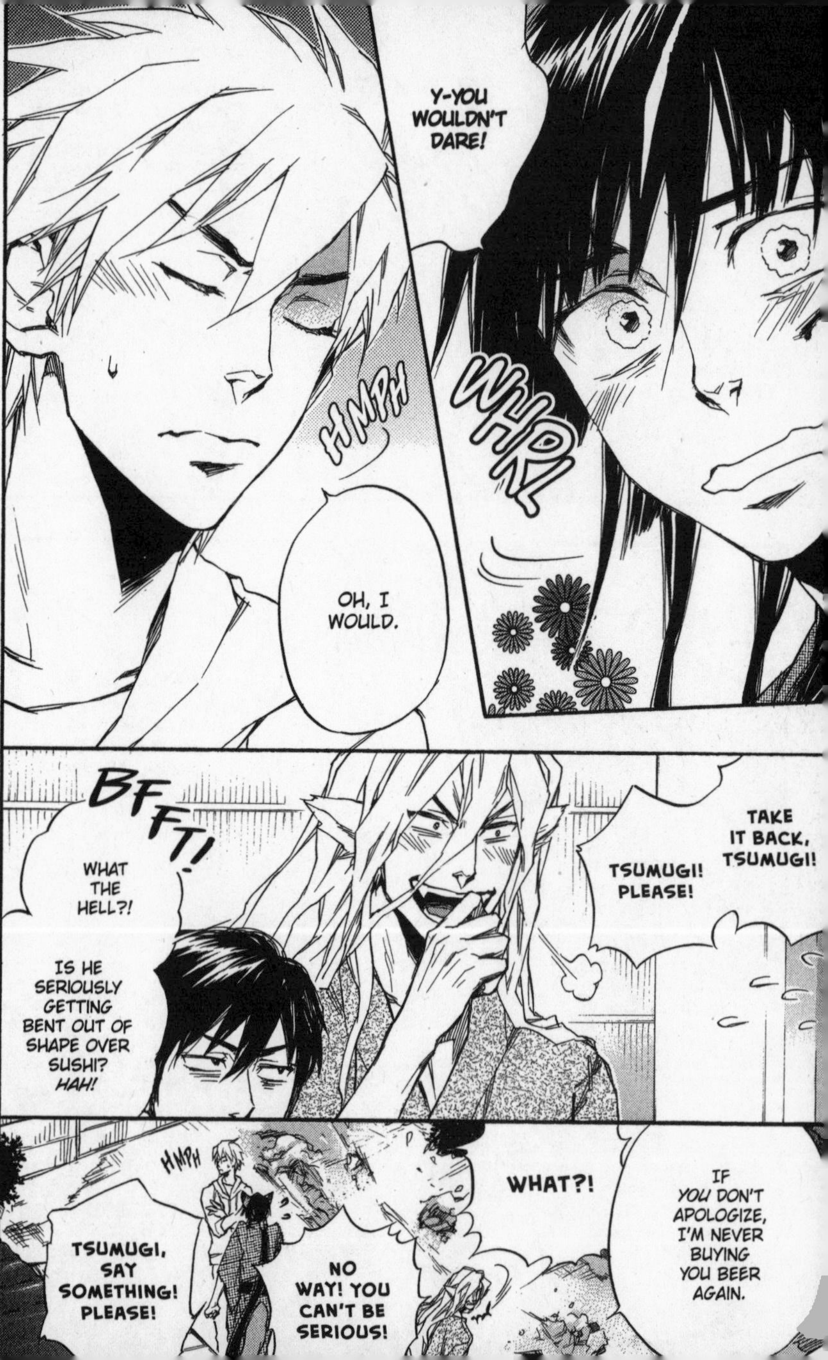
Y-YOU WOULDN'T DARE!
WHRL
HMPH
OH, I WOULD.
TAKE IT BACK, TSUMUGI!
TSUMUGI! PLEASE!
BFFT!
WHAT THE HELL?!
IS HE SERIOUSLY GETTING BENT OUT OF SHAPE OVER SUSHI? *HAH!*
IF *YOU* DON'T APOLOGIZE, I'M NEVER BUYING YOU BEER AGAIN.
WHAT?!
NO WAY! YOU CAN'T BE SERIOUS!
HMPH
TSUMUGI, SAY SOMETHING! PLEASE!

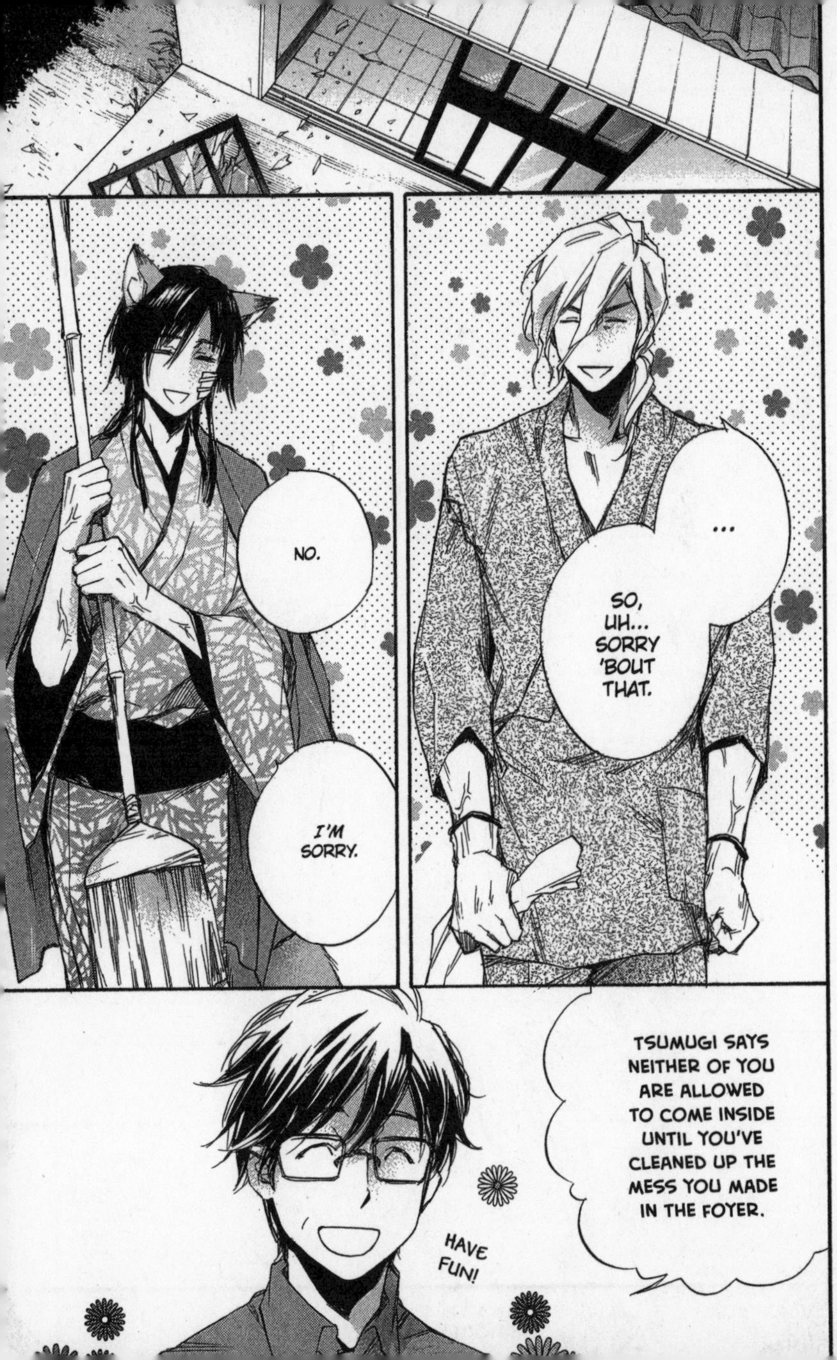
...
SO, UH... SORRY 'BOUT THAT.
NO.
I'M SORRY.
TSUMUGI SAYS NEITHER OF YOU ARE ALLOWED TO COME INSIDE UNTIL YOU'VE CLEANED UP THE MESS YOU MADE IN THE FOYER.
HAVE FUN!

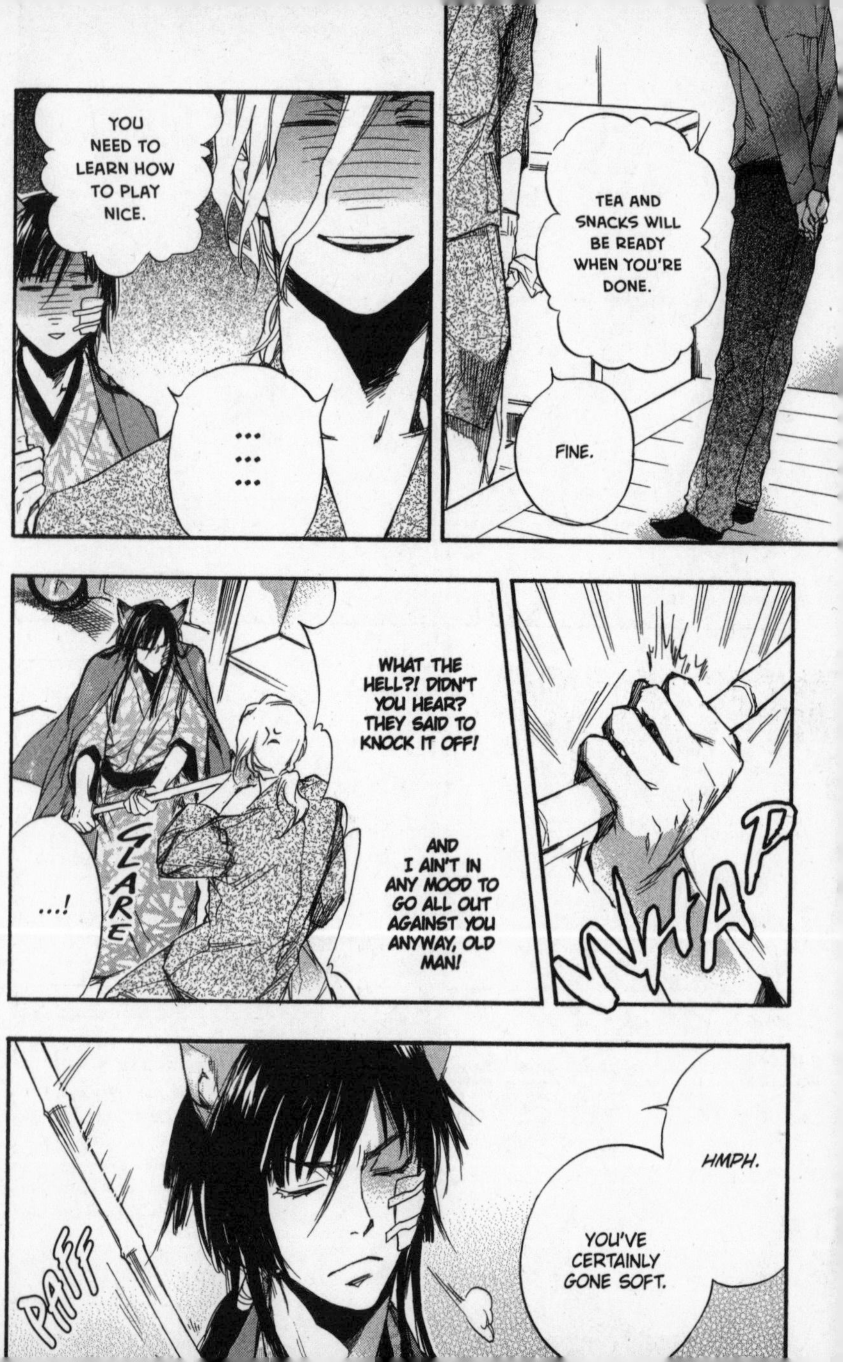
TEA AND SNACKS WILL BE READY WHEN YOU'RE DONE.
FINE.
YOU NEED TO LEARN HOW TO PLAY NICE.
... ...
WHAP
WHAT THE HELL?! DIDN'T YOU HEAR? THEY SAID TO KNOCK IT OFF!
AND I AIN'T IN ANY MOOD TO GO ALL OUT AGAINST YOU ANYWAY, OLD MAN!
GLARE
...!
HMPH.
YOU'VE CERTAINLY GONE SOFT.
PAFF

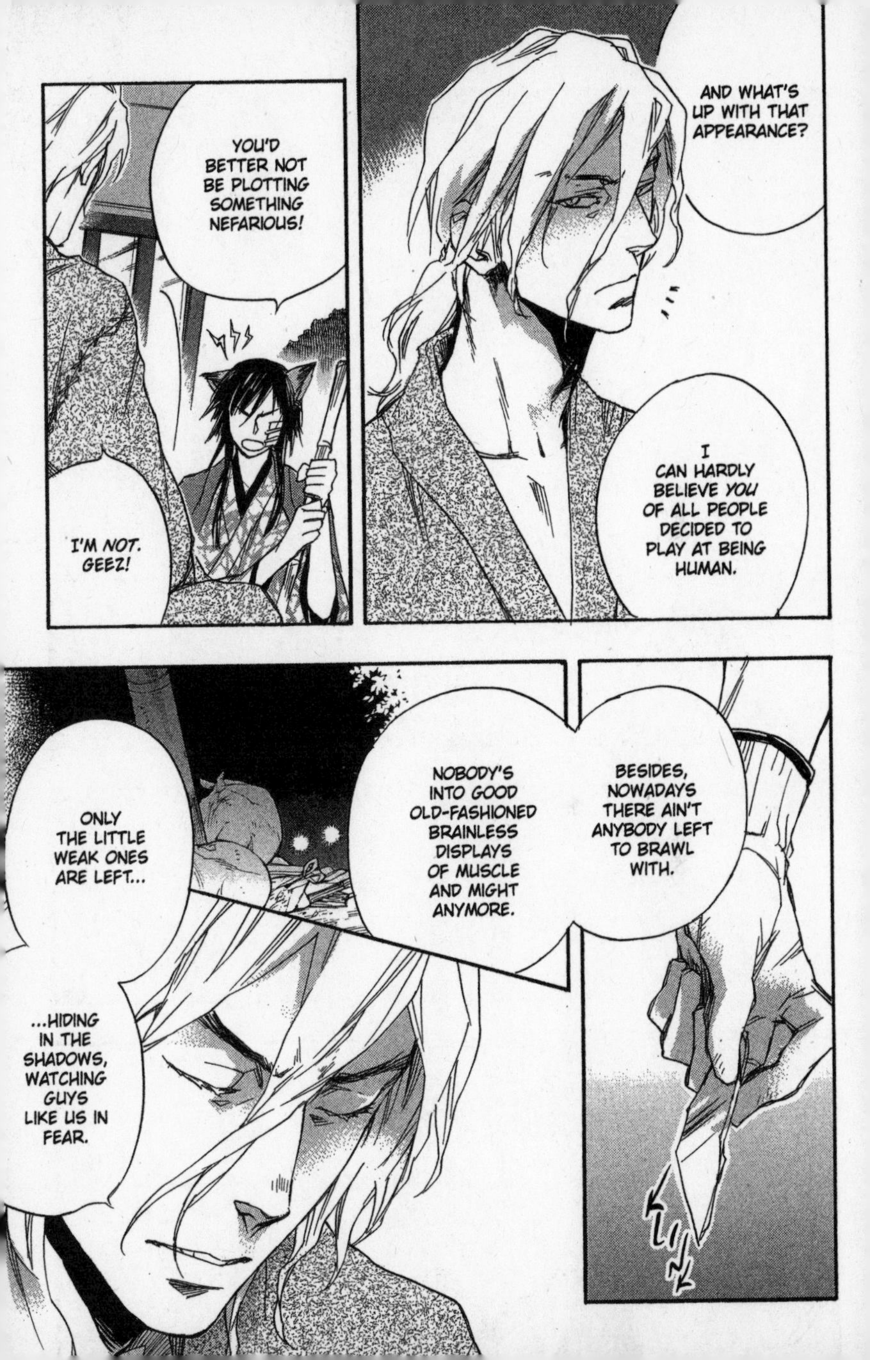
AND WHAT'S UP WITH THAT APPEARANCE?
I CAN HARDLY BELIEVE YOU OF ALL PEOPLE DECIDED TO PLAY AT BEING HUMAN.
YOU'D BETTER NOT BE PLOTTING SOMETHING NEFARIOUS!
I'M NOT. GEEZ!
BESIDES, NOWADAYS THERE AIN'T ANYBODY LEFT TO BRAWL WITH.
NOBODY'S INTO GOOD OLD-FASHIONED BRAINLESS DISPLAYS OF MUSCLE AND MIGHT ANYMORE.
KLINK
ONLY THE LITTLE WEAK ONES ARE LEFT...
...HIDING IN THE SHADOWS, WATCHING GUYS LIKE US IN FEAR.

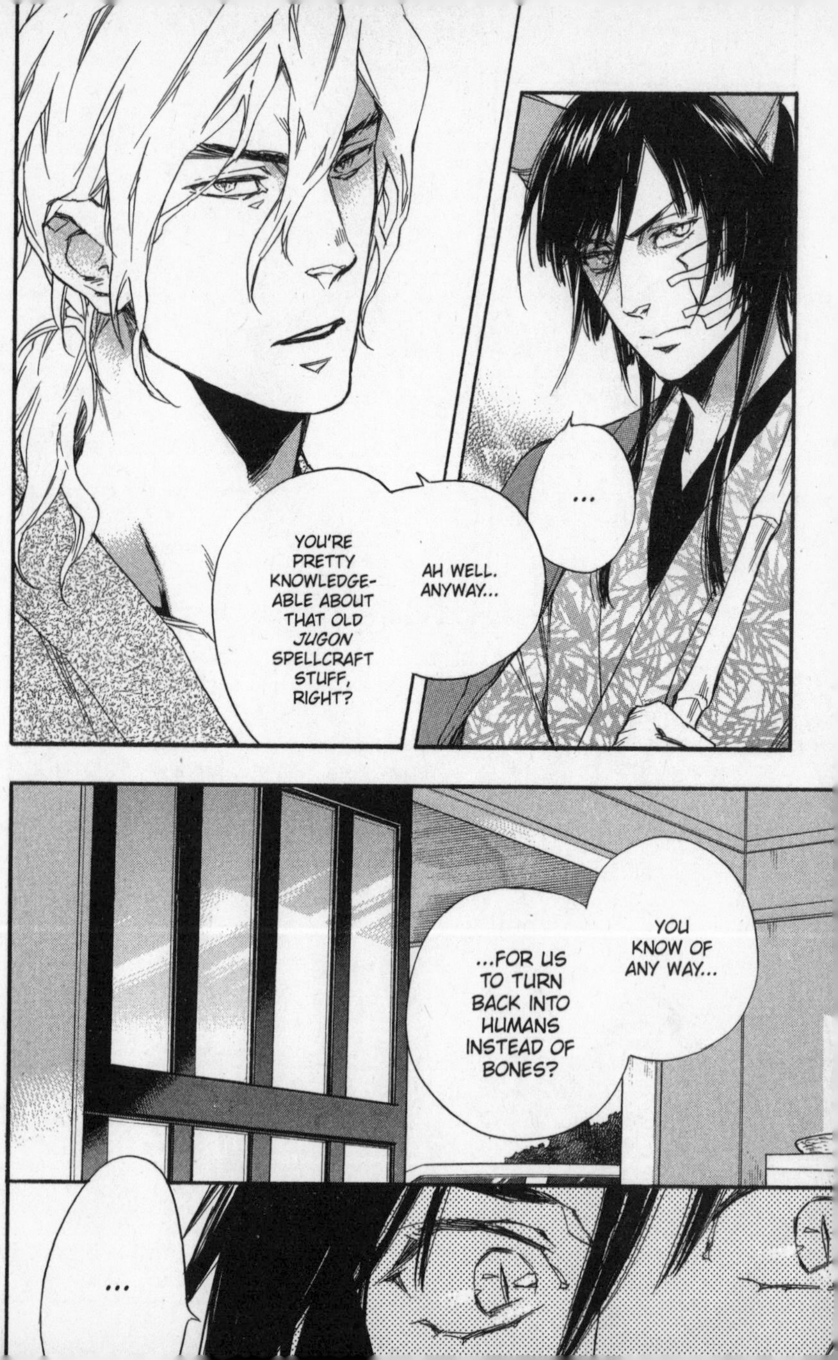
...
AH WELL. ANYWAY...
YOU'RE PRETTY KNOWLEDGE-ABLE ABOUT THAT OLD *JUGON* SPELLCRAFT STUFF, RIGHT?
YOU KNOW OF ANY WAY...
...FOR US TO TURN BACK INTO HUMANS INSTEAD OF BONES?
...

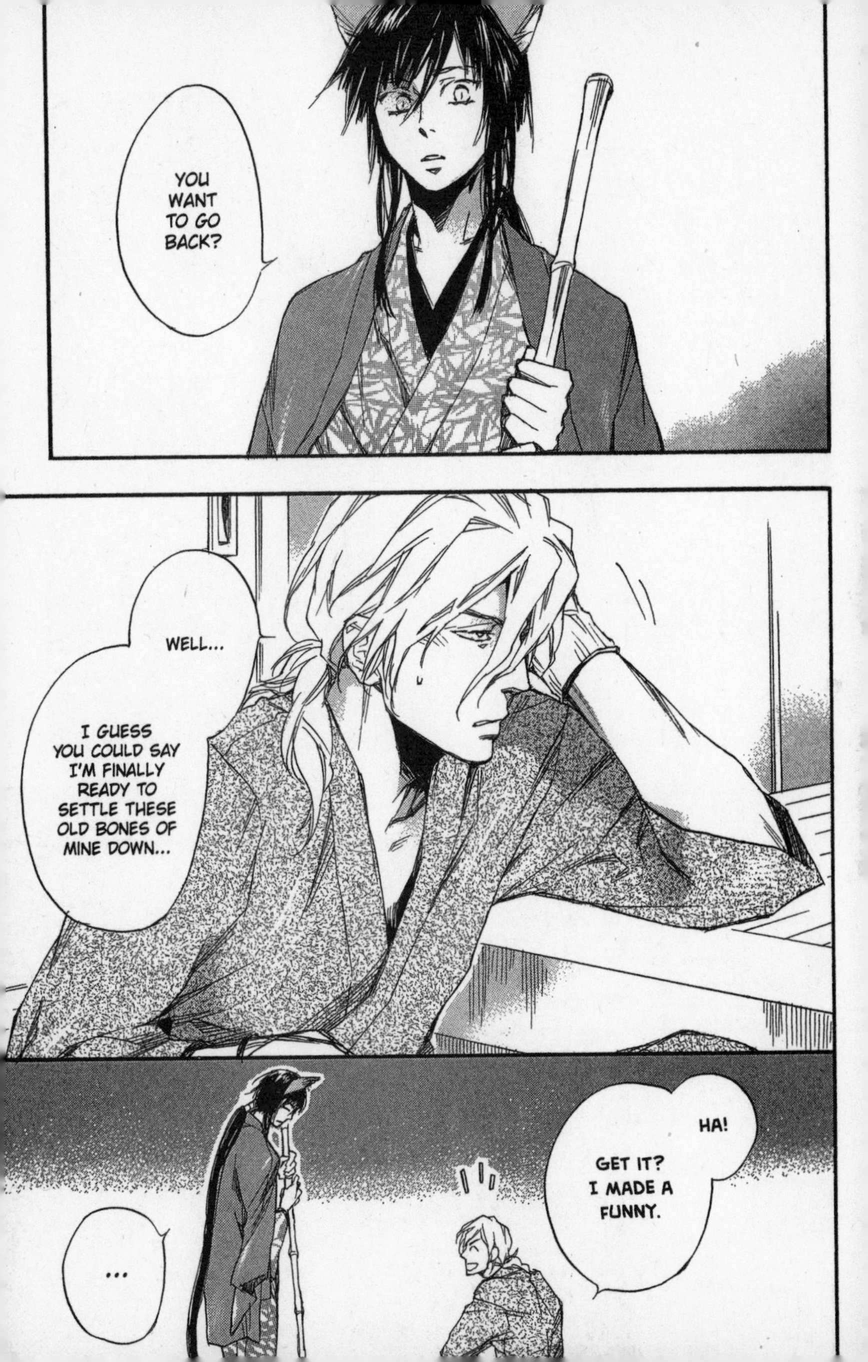
YOU WANT TO GO BACK?
WELL...
I GUESS YOU COULD SAY I'M FINALLY READY TO SETTLE THESE OLD BONES OF MINE DOWN...
HA!
GET IT? I MADE A FUNNY.
...

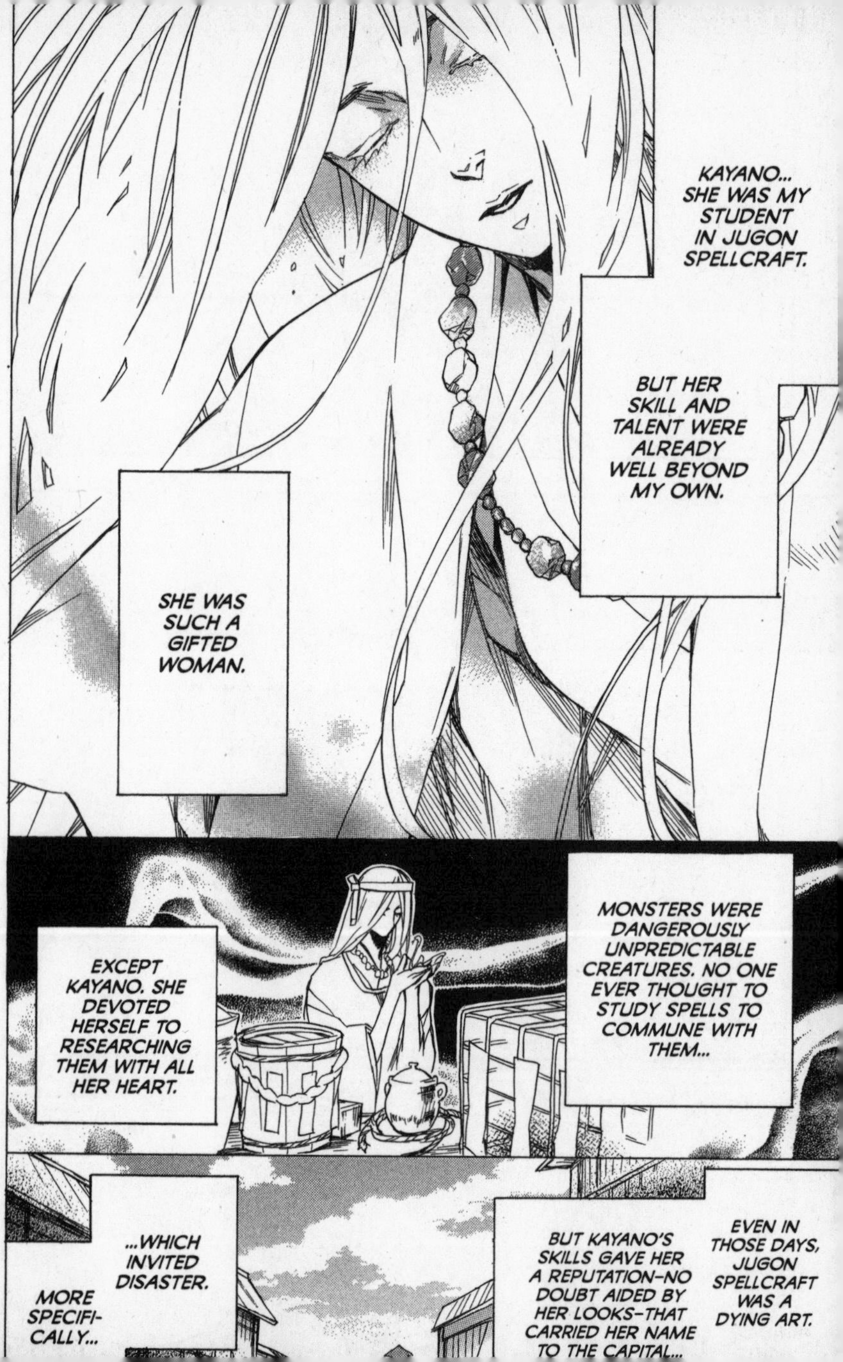
KAYANO... SHE WAS MY STUDENT IN JUGON SPELLCRAFT.
BUT HER SKILL AND TALENT WERE ALREADY WELL BEYOND MY OWN.
SHE WAS SUCH A GIFTED WOMAN.
MONSTERS WERE DANGEROUSLY UNPREDICTABLE CREATURES. NO ONE EVER THOUGHT TO STUDY SPELLS TO COMMUNE WITH THEM...
EXCEPT KAYANO. SHE DEVOTED HERSELF TO RESEARCHING THEM WITH ALL HER HEART.
EVEN IN THOSE DAYS, JUGON SPELLCRAFT WAS A DYING ART.
BUT KAYANO'S SKILLS GAVE HER A REPUTATION—NO DOUBT AIDED BY HER LOOKS—THAT CARRIED HER NAME TO THE CAPITAL...
...WHICH INVITED DISASTER.
MORE SPECIFI-CALLY...

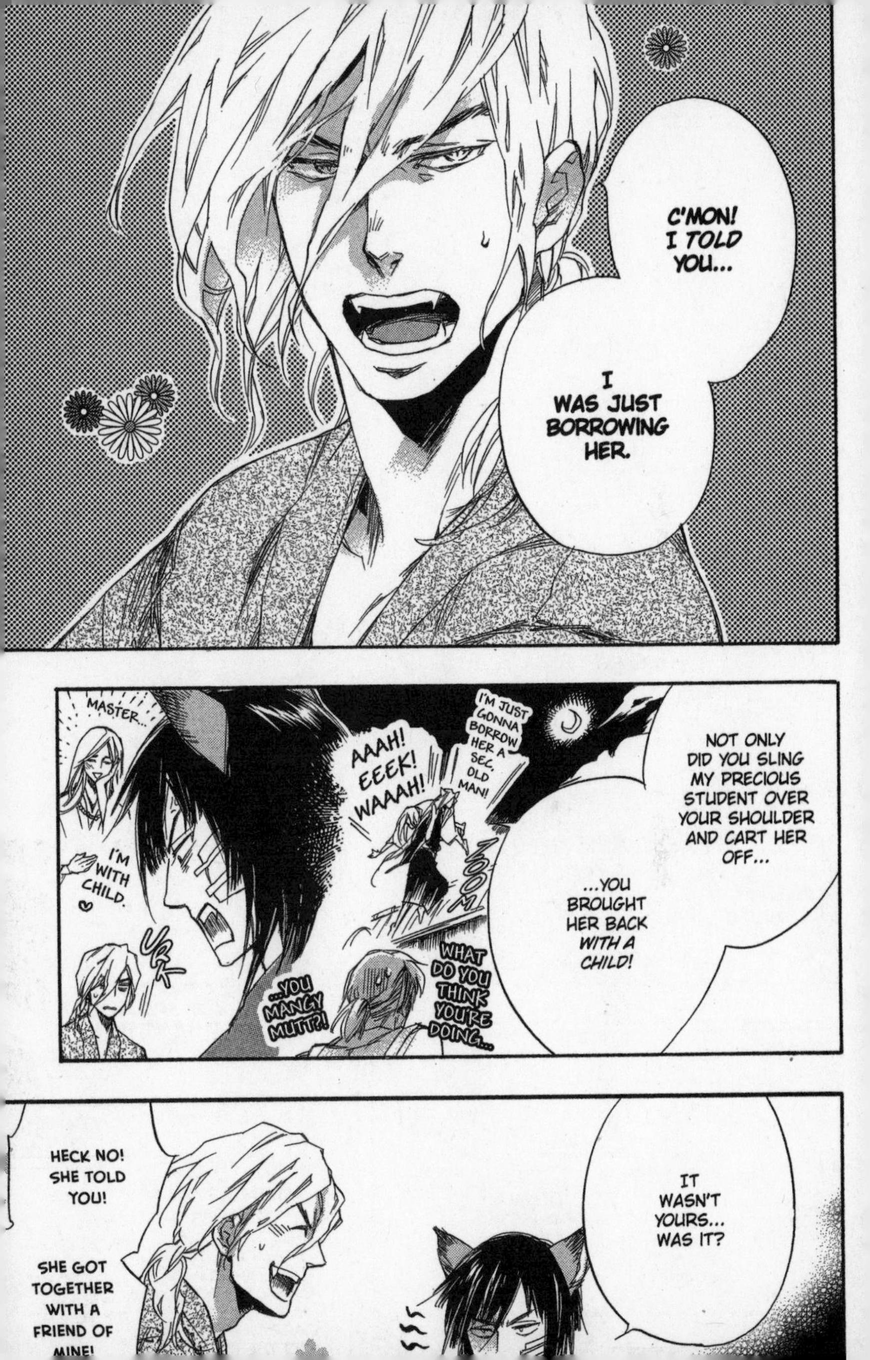
C'MON! I TOLD YOU...
I WAS JUST BORROWING HER.
NOT ONLY DID YOU SLING MY PRECIOUS STUDENT OVER YOUR SHOULDER AND CART HER OFF...
...YOU BROUGHT HER BACK WITH A CHILD!
I'M JUST GONNA BORROW HER A SEC, OLD MAN!
AAAH! EEEK! WAAAH!
VOOOM
WHAT DO YOU THINK YOU'RE DOING...
...YOU MANGY MUTT?!
MASTER...
I'M WITH CHILD.
URK
IT WASN'T YOURS... WAS IT?
HECK NO! SHE TOLD YOU!
SHE GOT TOGETHER WITH A FRIEND OF MINE!

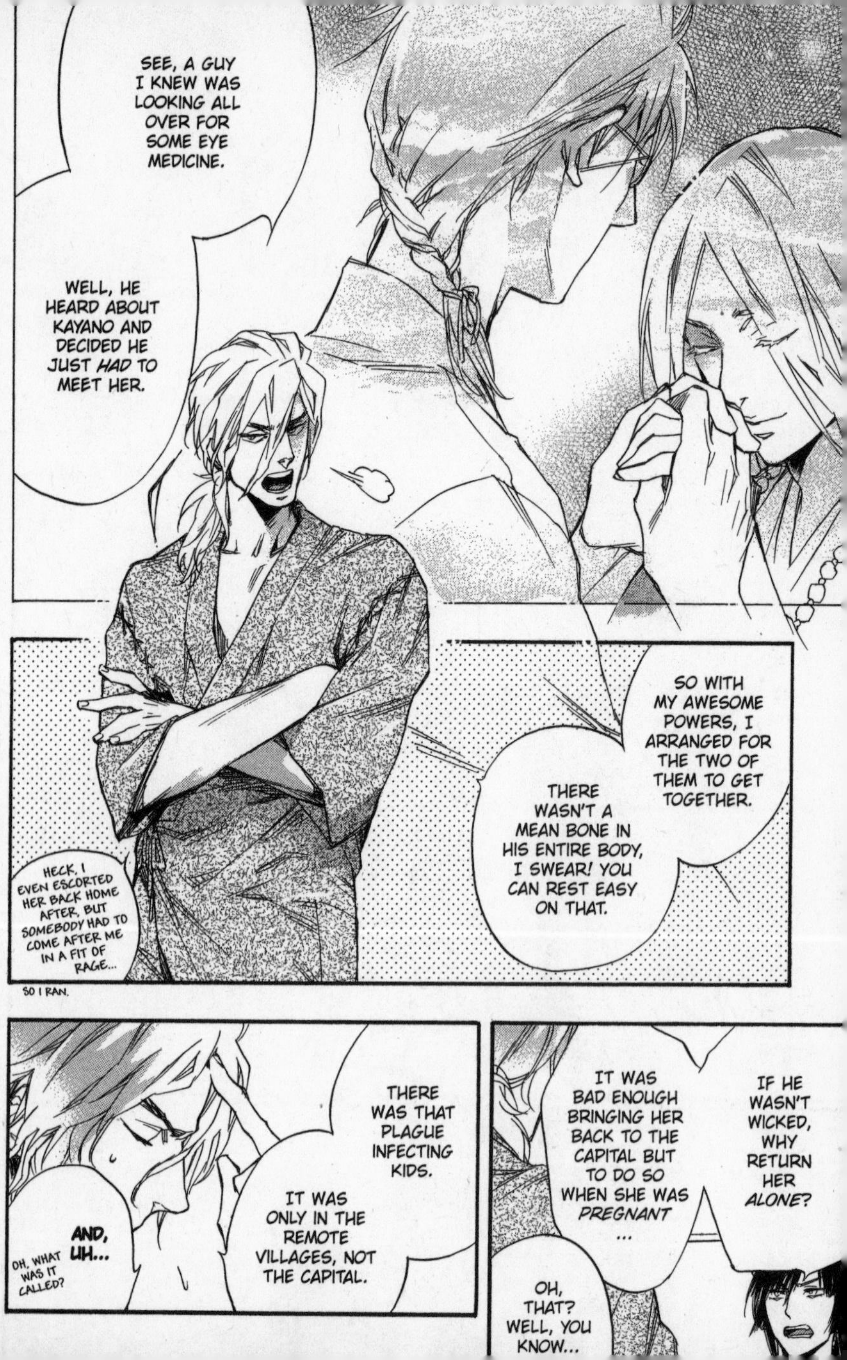

SEE, A GUY I KNEW WAS LOOKING ALL OVER FOR SOME EYE MEDICINE.
WELL, HE HEARD ABOUT KAYANO AND DECIDED HE JUST *HAD* TO MEET HER.
SO WITH MY AWESOME POWERS, I ARRANGED FOR THE TWO OF THEM TO GET TOGETHER.
THERE WASN'T A MEAN BONE IN HIS ENTIRE BODY, I SWEAR! YOU CAN REST EASY ON THAT.
HECK, I EVEN ESCORTED HER BACK HOME AFTER, BUT SOMEBODY HAD TO COME AFTER ME IN A FIT OF RAGE...
SO I RAN.
IF HE WASN'T WICKED, WHY RETURN HER *ALONE*?
IT WAS BAD ENOUGH BRINGING HER BACK TO THE CAPITAL BUT TO DO SO WHEN SHE WAS *PREGNANT*...
OH, THAT? WELL, YOU KNOW...
THERE WAS THAT PLAGUE INFECTING KIDS.
IT WAS ONLY IN THE REMOTE VILLAGES, NOT THE CAPITAL.
AND, UH...
OH, WHAT WAS IT CALLED?

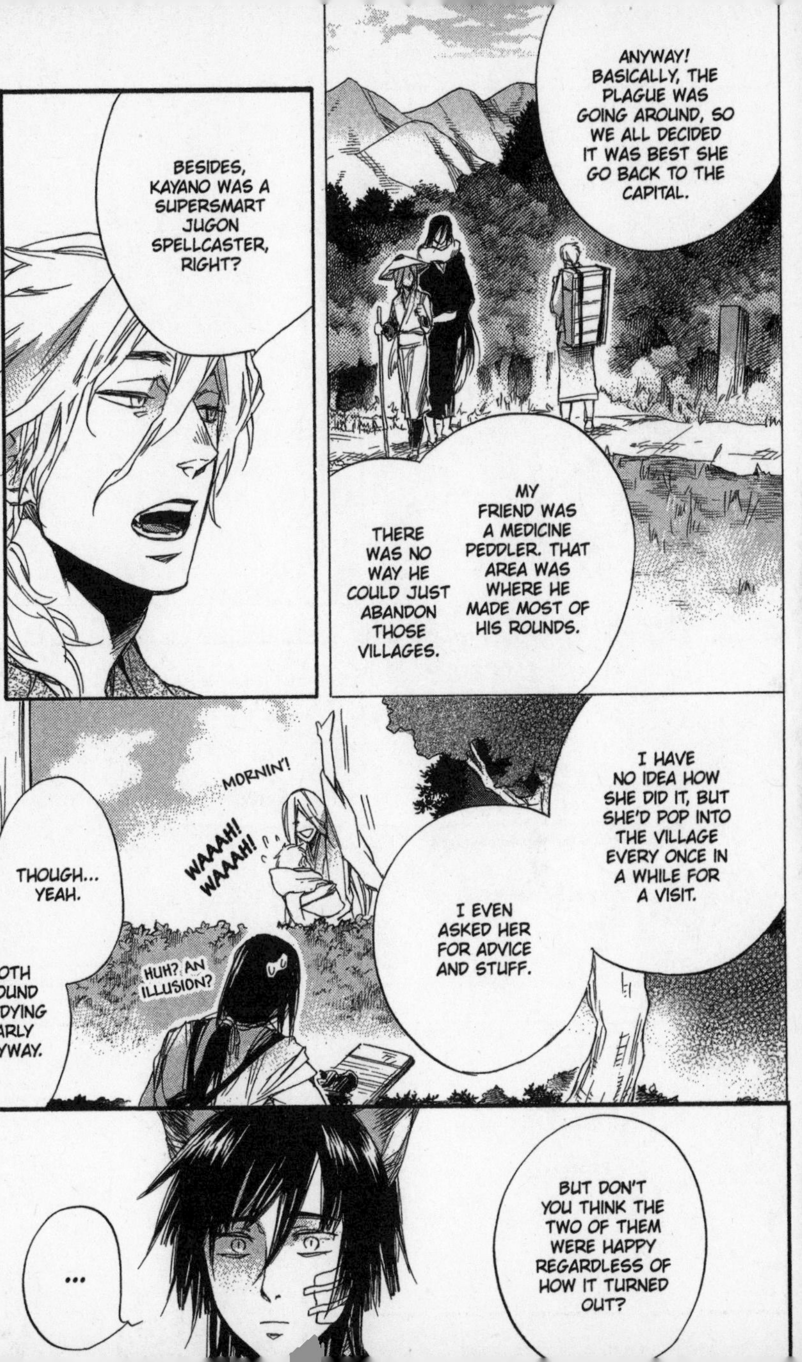
ANYWAY! BASICALLY, THE PLAGUE WAS GOING AROUND, SO WE ALL DECIDED IT WAS BEST SHE GO BACK TO THE CAPITAL.
MY FRIEND WAS A MEDICINE PEDDLER. THAT AREA WAS WHERE HE MADE MOST OF HIS ROUNDS.
THERE WAS NO WAY HE COULD JUST ABANDON THOSE VILLAGES.
BESIDES, KAYANO WAS A SUPERSMART JUGON SPELLCASTER, RIGHT?
I HAVE NO IDEA HOW SHE DID IT, BUT SHE'D POP INTO THE VILLAGE EVERY ONCE IN A WHILE FOR A VISIT.
I EVEN ASKED HER FOR ADVICE AND STUFF.
MORNIN'!
WAAAH! WAAAH!
HUH? AN ILLUSION?
THOUGH... YEAH.
BOTH WOUND UP DYING EARLY ANYWAY.
BUT DON'T YOU THINK THE TWO OF THEM WERE HAPPY REGARDLESS OF HOW IT TURNED OUT?
...

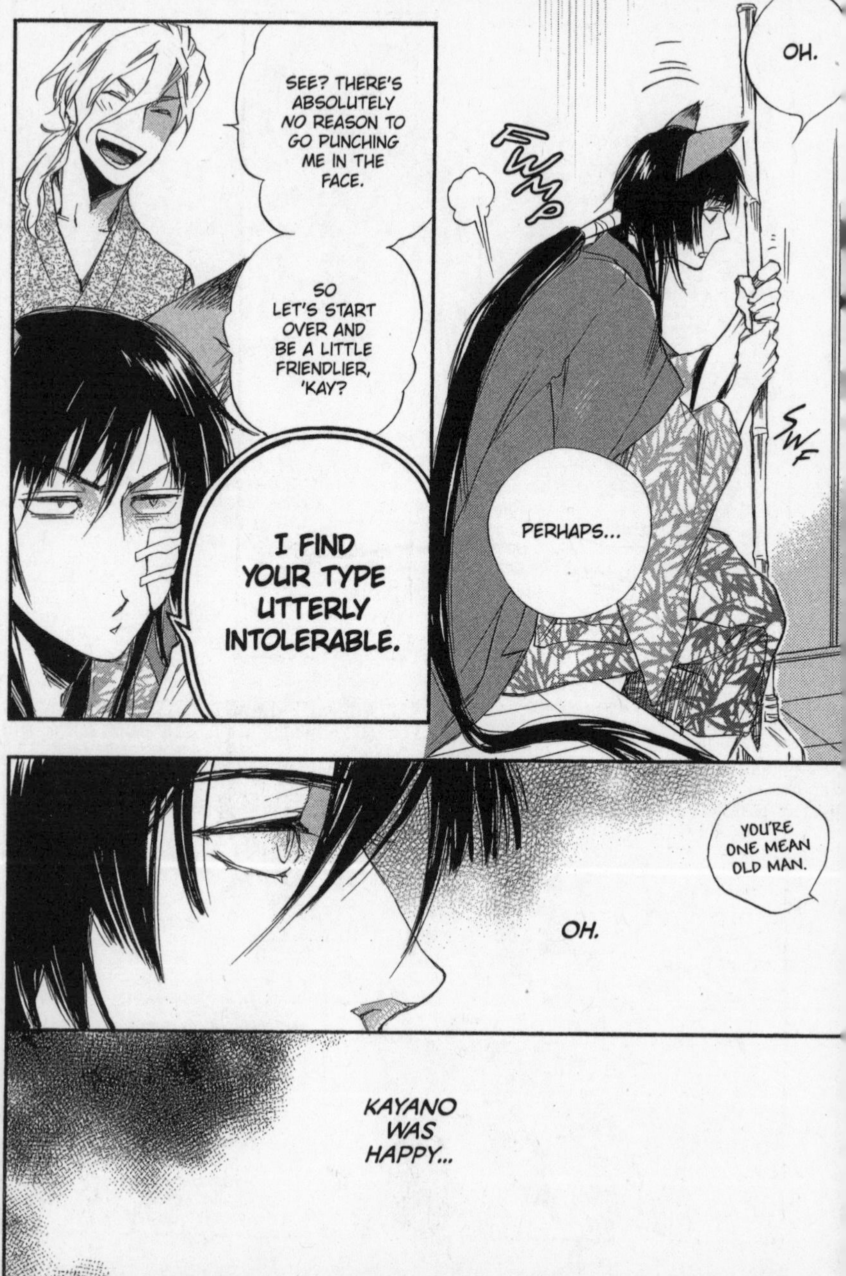
OH.
FWMP
SWF
PERHAPS...
SEE? THERE'S ABSOLUTELY NO REASON TO GO PUNCHING ME IN THE FACE.
SO LET'S START OVER AND BE A LITTLE FRIENDLIER, 'KAY?
I FIND YOUR TYPE UTTERLY INTOLERABLE.
YOU'RE ONE MEAN OLD MAN.
OH.
KAYANO WAS HAPPY...

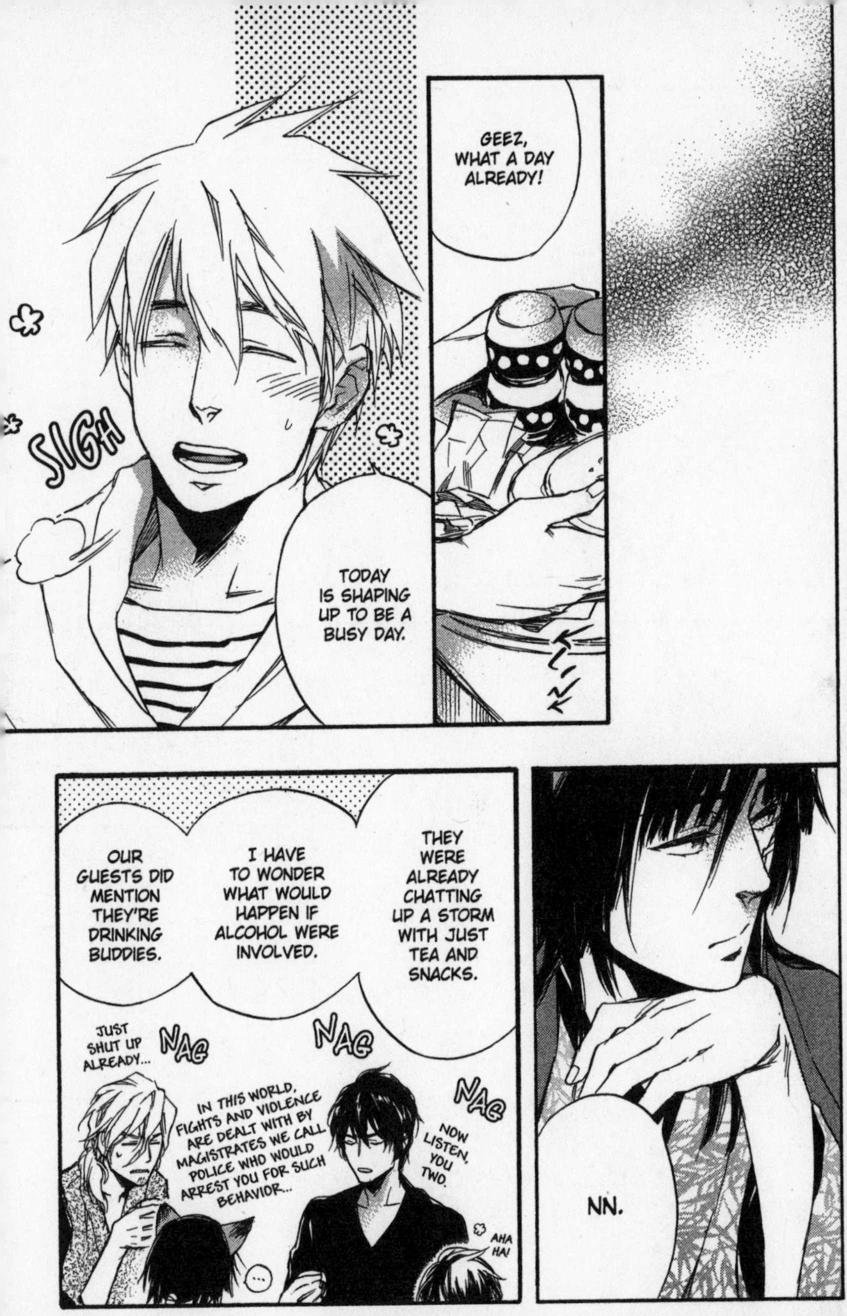

GEEZ, WHAT A DAY ALREADY!
KLINK
SIGH
TODAY IS SHAPING UP TO BE A BUSY DAY.
NN.
THEY WERE ALREADY CHATTING UP A STORM WITH JUST TEA AND SNACKS.
I HAVE TO WONDER WHAT WOULD HAPPEN IF ALCOHOL WERE INVOLVED.
OUR GUESTS DID MENTION THEY'RE DRINKING BUDDIES.
NAG
NOW LISTEN, YOU TWO.
NAG
IN THIS WORLD, FIGHTS AND VIOLENCE ARE DEALT WITH BY MAGISTRATES WE CALL POLICE WHO WOULD ARREST YOU FOR SUCH BEHAVIOR...
NAG
JUST SHUT UP ALREADY...
AHA HA!
...

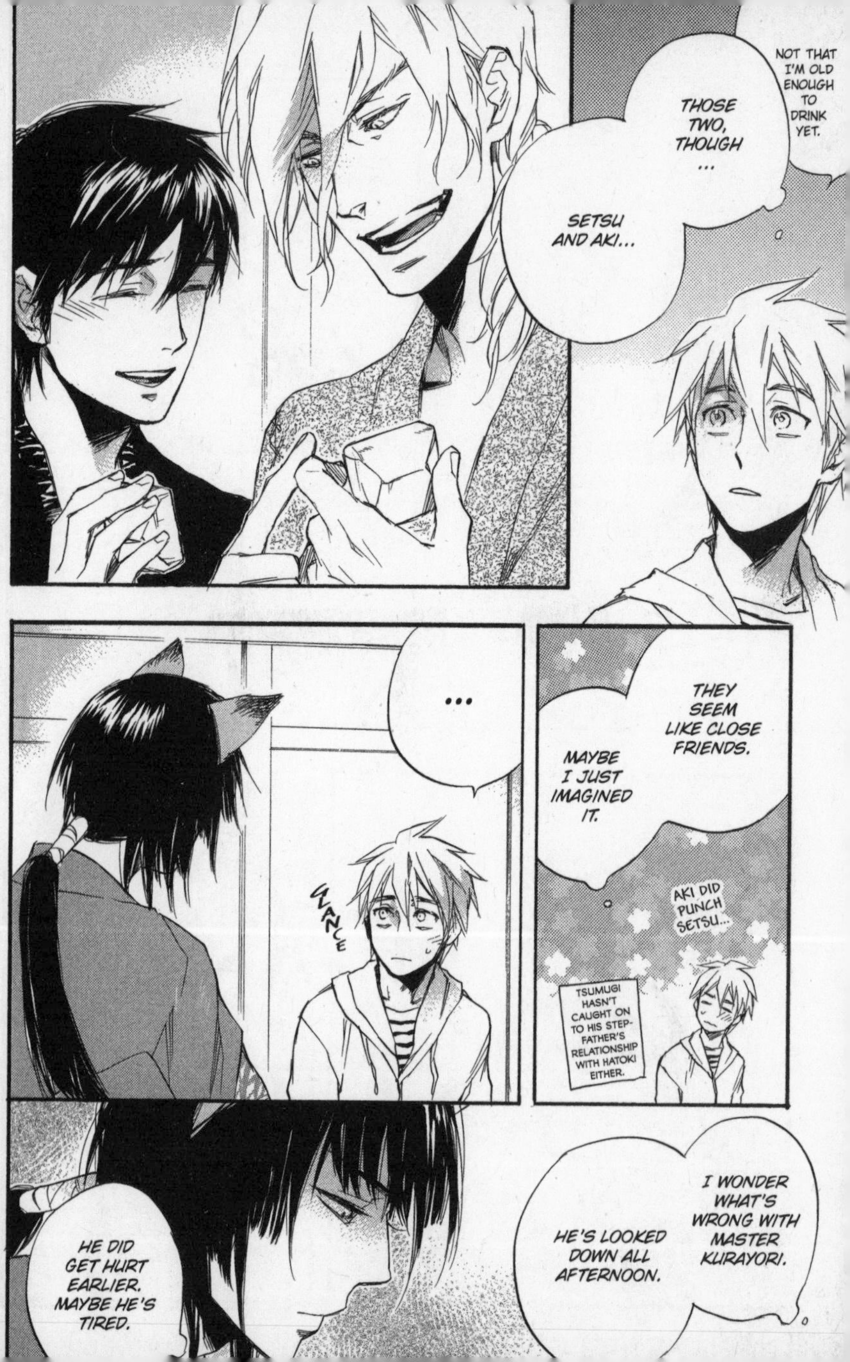
NOT THAT I'M OLD ENOUGH TO DRINK YET.
THOSE TWO, THOUGH...
SETSU AND AKI...
THEY SEEM LIKE CLOSE FRIENDS.
MAYBE I JUST IMAGINED IT.
AKI DID PUNCH SETSU...
TSUMUGI HASN'T CAUGHT ON TO HIS STEP-FATHER'S RELATIONSHIP WITH HATOKI EITHER.
...
GLANCE
I WONDER WHAT'S WRONG WITH MASTER KURAYORI.
HE'S LOOKED DOWN ALL AFTERNOON.
HE DID GET HURT EARLIER. MAYBE HE'S TIRED.

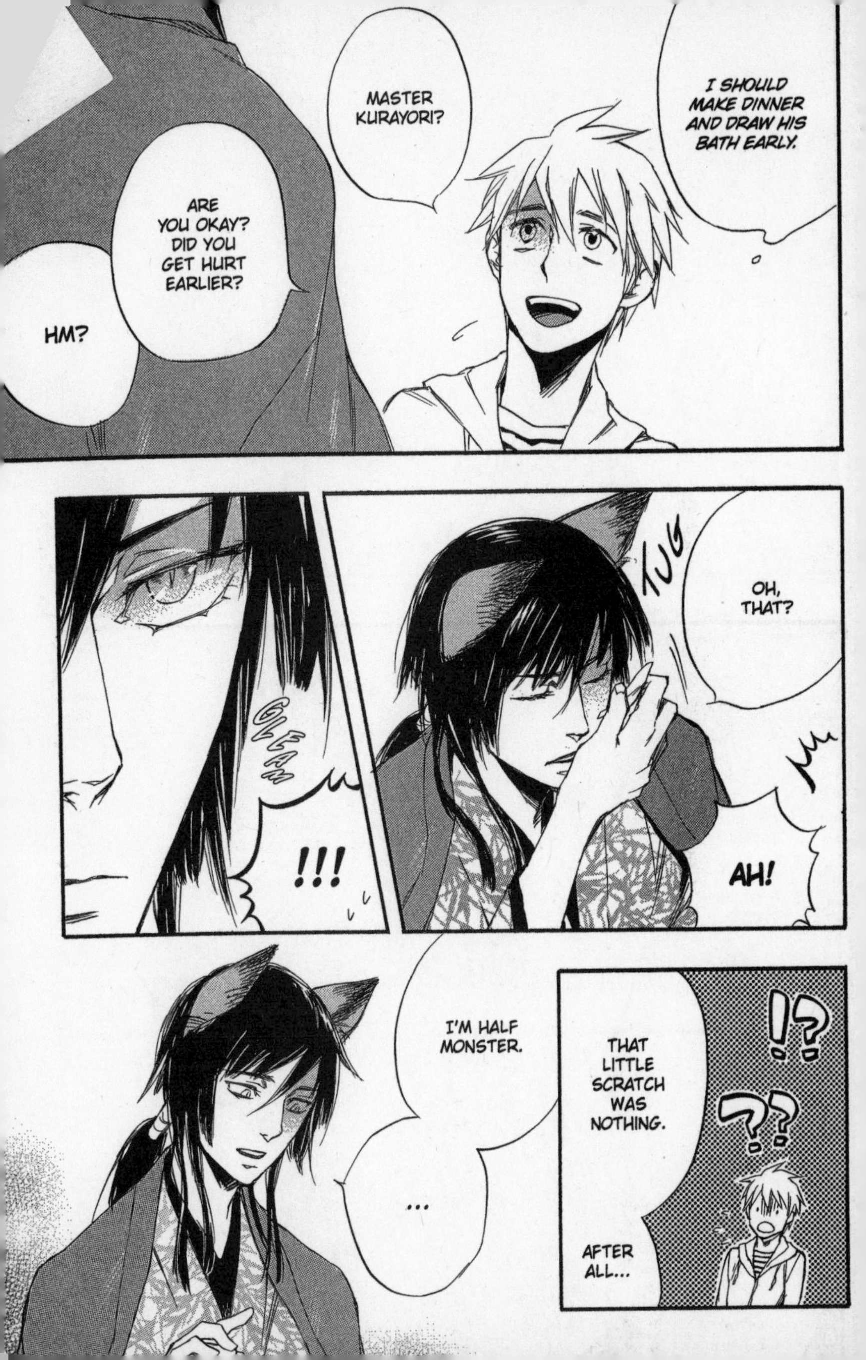
I SHOULD MAKE DINNER AND DRAW HIS BATH EARLY.
MASTER KURAYORI?
ARE YOU OKAY? DID YOU GET HURT EARLIER?
HM?
OH, THAT?
TUG
AH!
GLEAM
!!!
!?
??
THAT LITTLE SCRATCH WAS NOTHING.
AFTER ALL...
I'M HALF MONSTER.
...

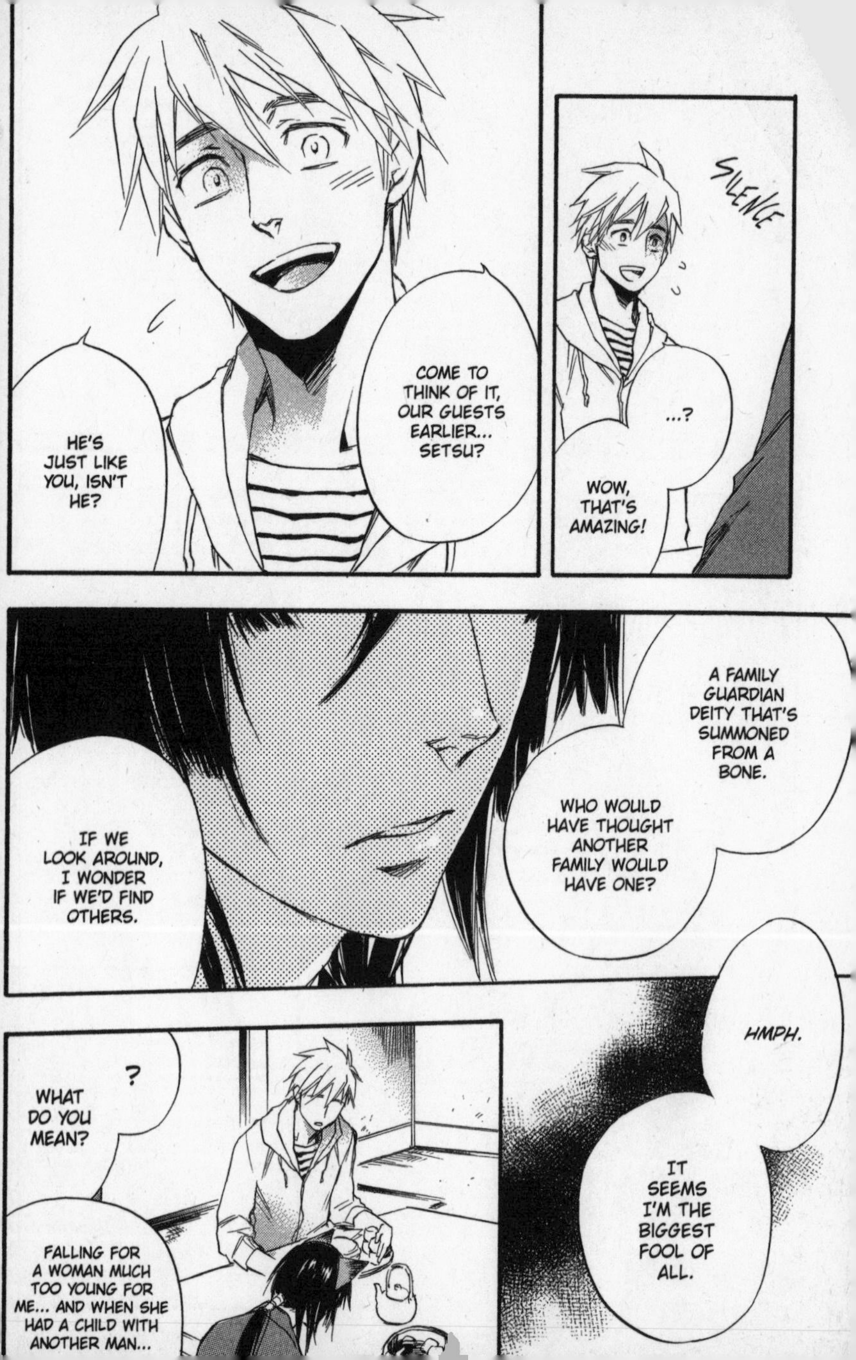
SILENCE
...?
WOW, THAT'S AMAZING!
COME TO THINK OF IT, OUR GUESTS EARLIER... SETSU?
HE'S JUST LIKE YOU, ISN'T HE?
A FAMILY GUARDIAN DEITY THAT'S SUMMONED FROM A BONE.
WHO WOULD HAVE THOUGHT ANOTHER FAMILY WOULD HAVE ONE?
IF WE LOOK AROUND, I WONDER IF WE'D FIND OTHERS.
HMPH.
IT SEEMS I'M THE BIGGEST FOOL OF ALL.
?
WHAT DO YOU MEAN?
FALLING FOR A WOMAN MUCH TOO YOUNG FOR ME... AND WHEN SHE HAD A CHILD WITH ANOTHER MAN...

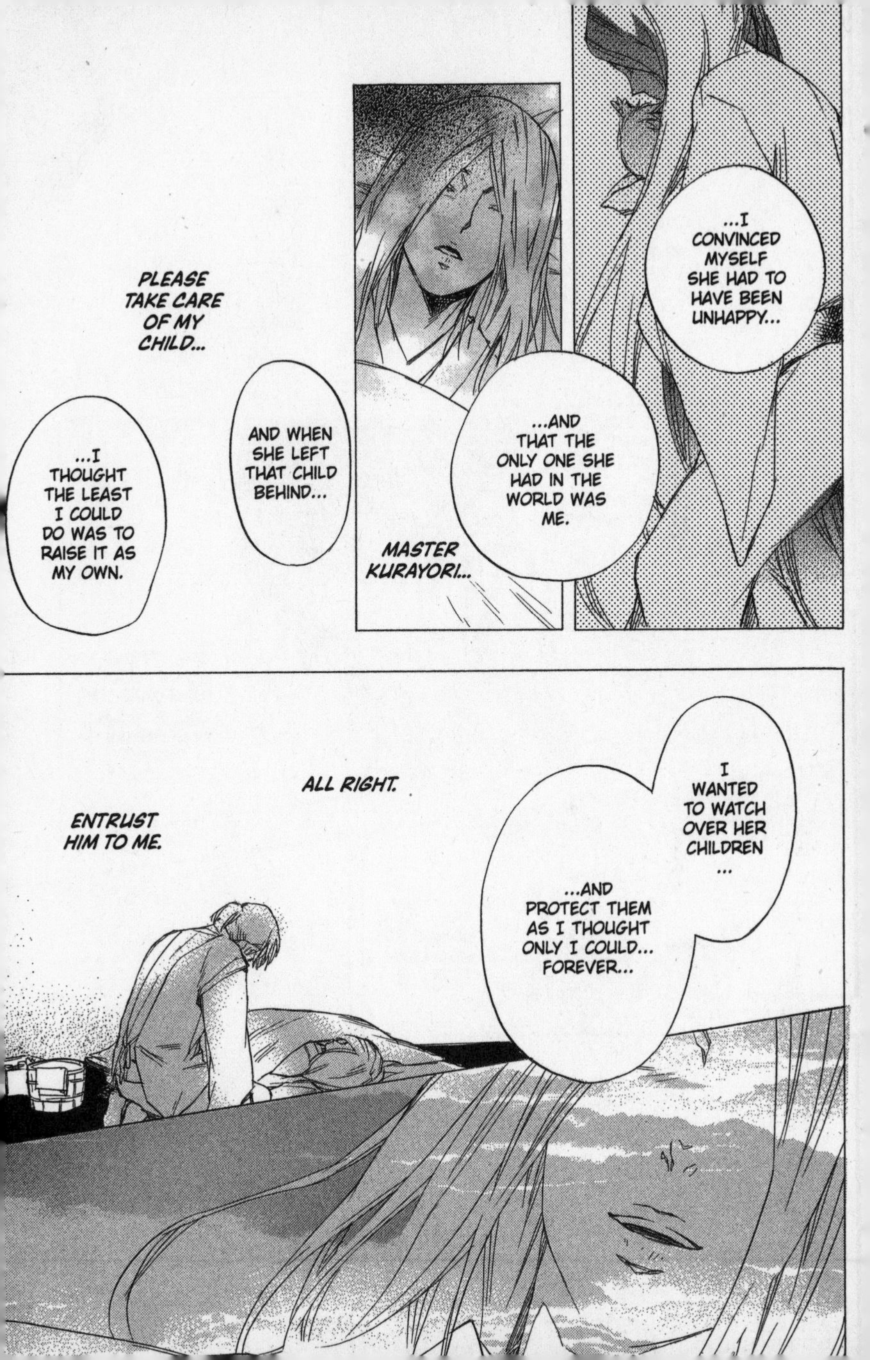
...I CONVINCED MYSELF SHE HAD TO HAVE BEEN UNHAPPY...
...AND THAT THE ONLY ONE SHE HAD IN THE WORLD WAS ME.
MASTER KURAYORI...
PLEASE TAKE CARE OF MY CHILD...
AND WHEN SHE LEFT THAT CHILD BEHIND...
...I THOUGHT THE LEAST I COULD DO WAS TO RAISE IT AS MY OWN.
I WANTED TO WATCH OVER HER CHILDREN ...
...AND PROTECT THEM AS I THOUGHT ONLY I COULD... FOREVER...
ALL RIGHT.
ENTRUST HIM TO ME.

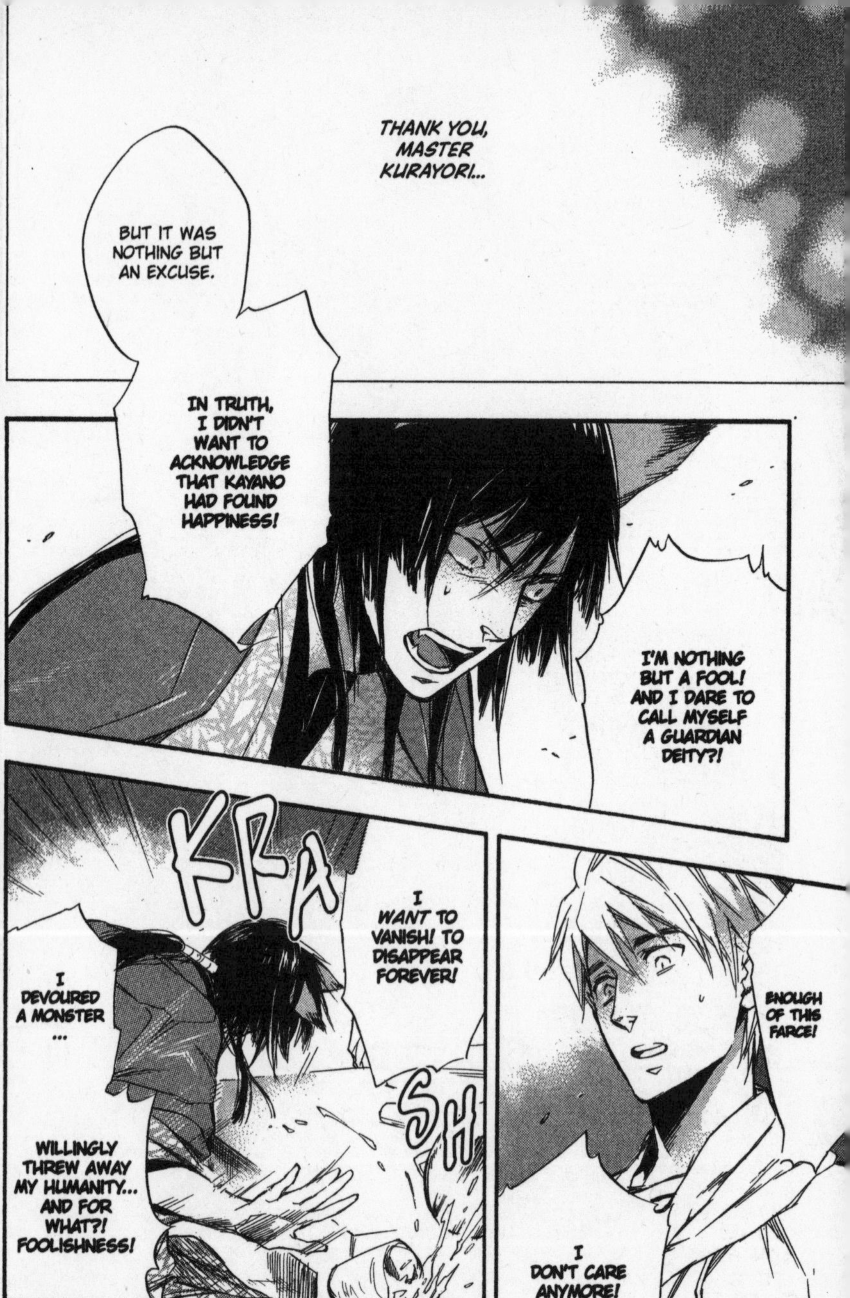
THANK YOU, MASTER KURAYORI...
BUT IT WAS NOTHING BUT AN EXCUSE.
IN TRUTH, I DIDN'T WANT TO ACKNOWLEDGE THAT KAYANO HAD FOUND HAPPINESS!
I'M NOTHING BUT A FOOL! AND I DARE TO CALL MYSELF A GUARDIAN DEITY?!
ENOUGH OF THIS FARCE!
I DON'T CARE ANYMORE!
KRA
I WANT TO VANISH! TO DISAPPEAR FOREVER!
I DEVOURED A MONSTER ...
SH
WILLINGLY THREW AWAY MY HUMANITY... AND FOR WHAT?! FOOLISHNESS!

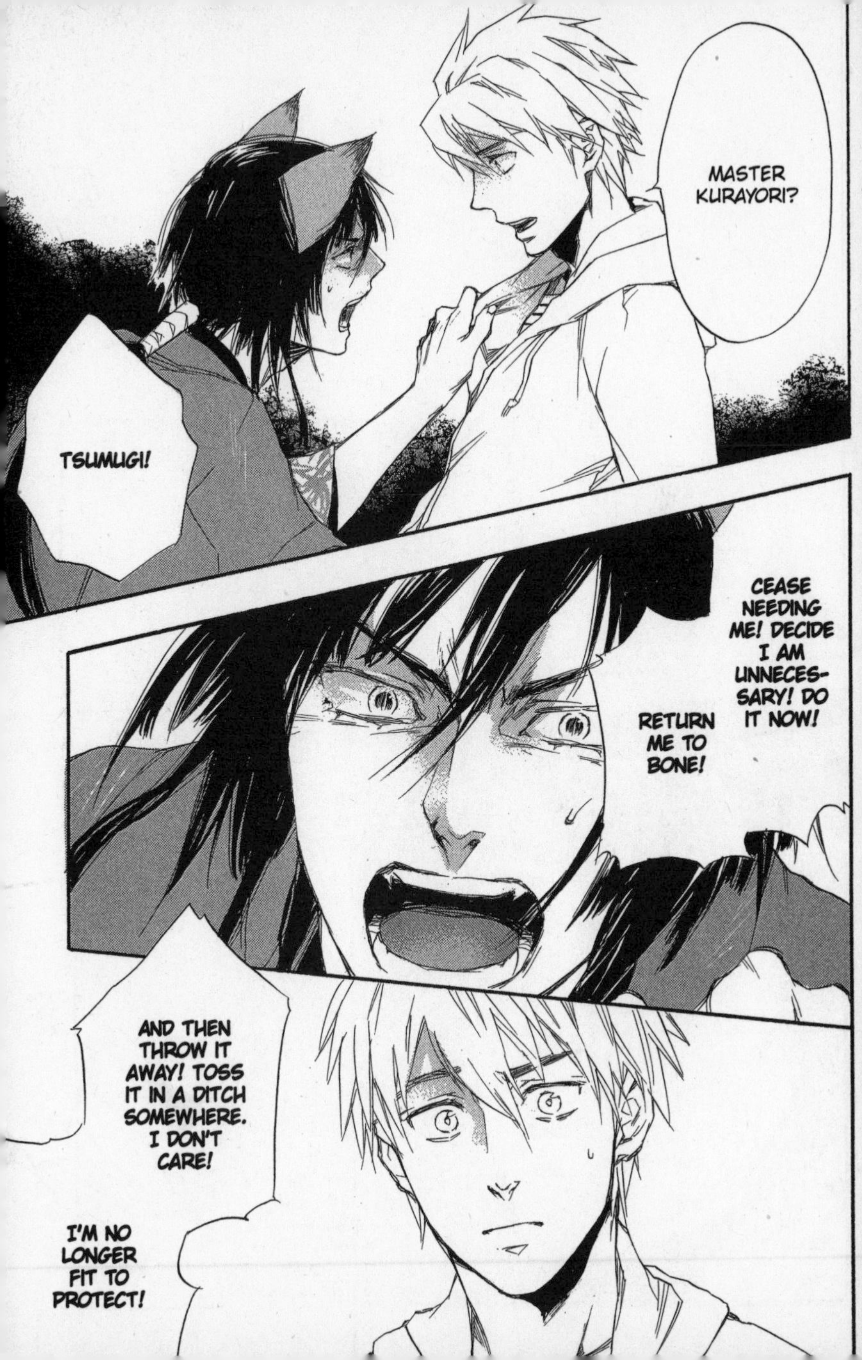
MASTER KURAYORI?
TSUMUGI!
CEASE NEEDING ME! DECIDE I AM UNNECES-SARY! DO IT NOW!
RETURN ME TO BONE!
AND THEN THROW IT AWAY! TOSS IT IN A DITCH SOMEWHERE. I DON'T CARE!
I'M NO LONGER FIT TO PROTECT!

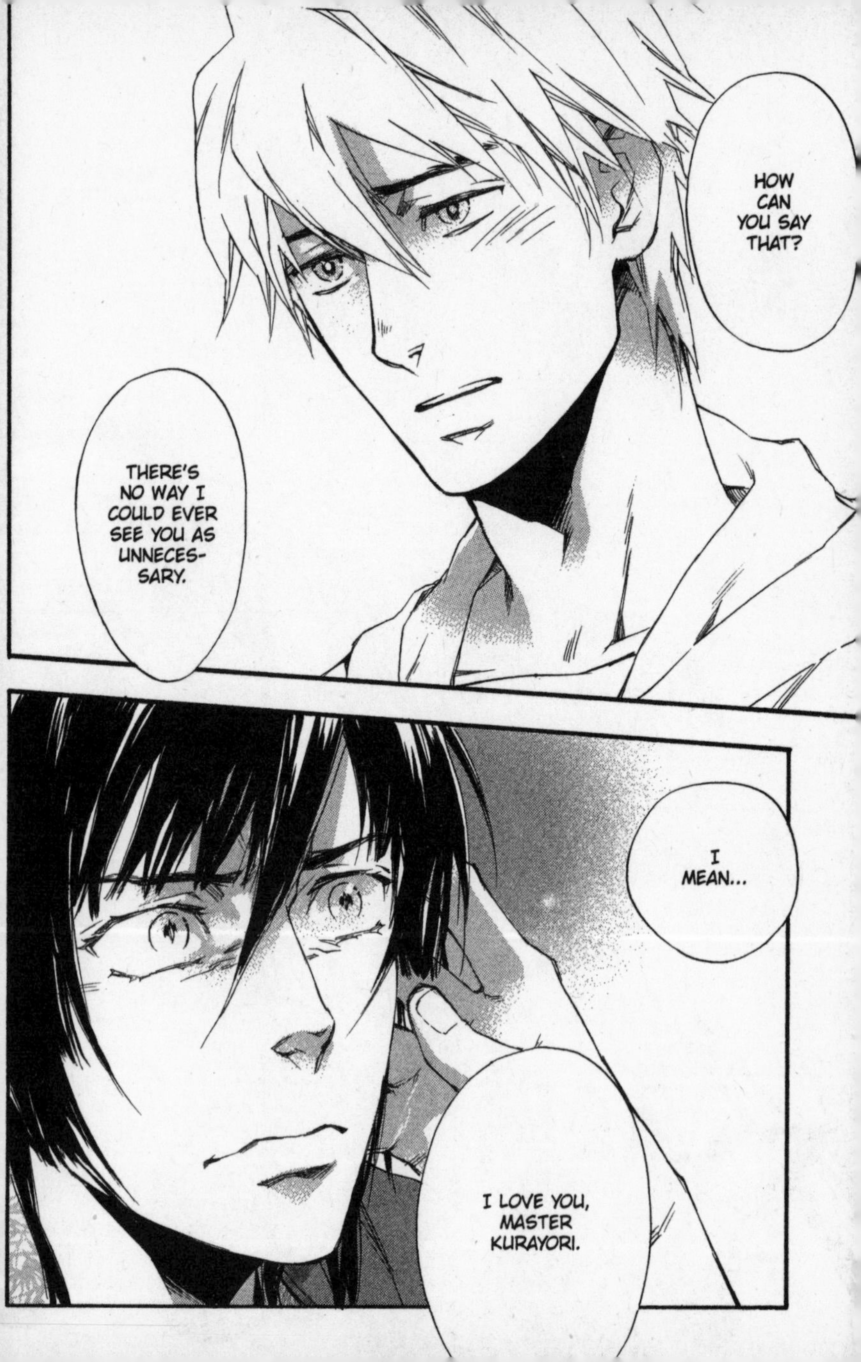
HOW CAN YOU SAY THAT?
THERE'S NO WAY I COULD EVER SEE YOU AS UNNECES-SARY.
I MEAN...
I LOVE YOU, MASTER KURAYORI.

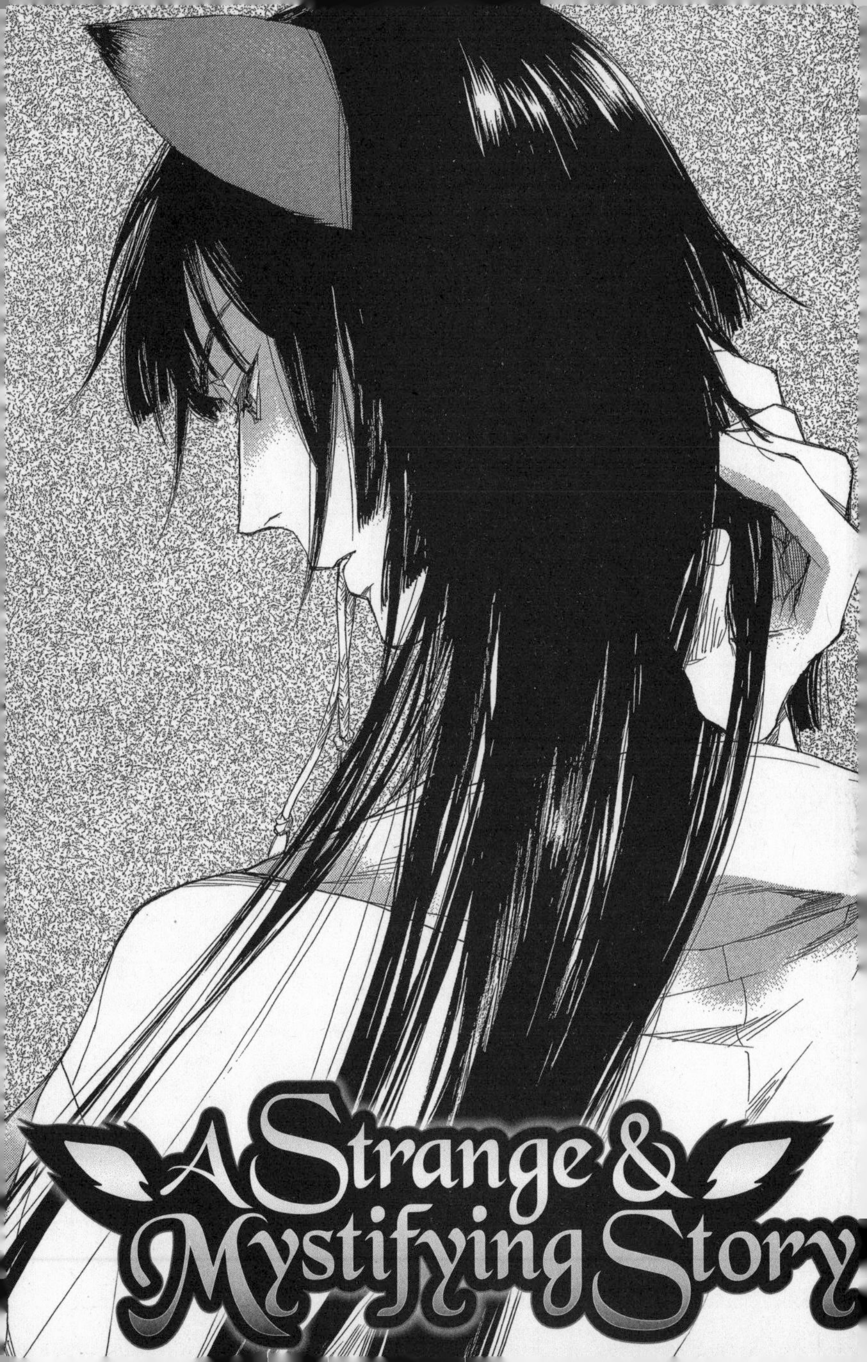
A Strange & Mystifying Story

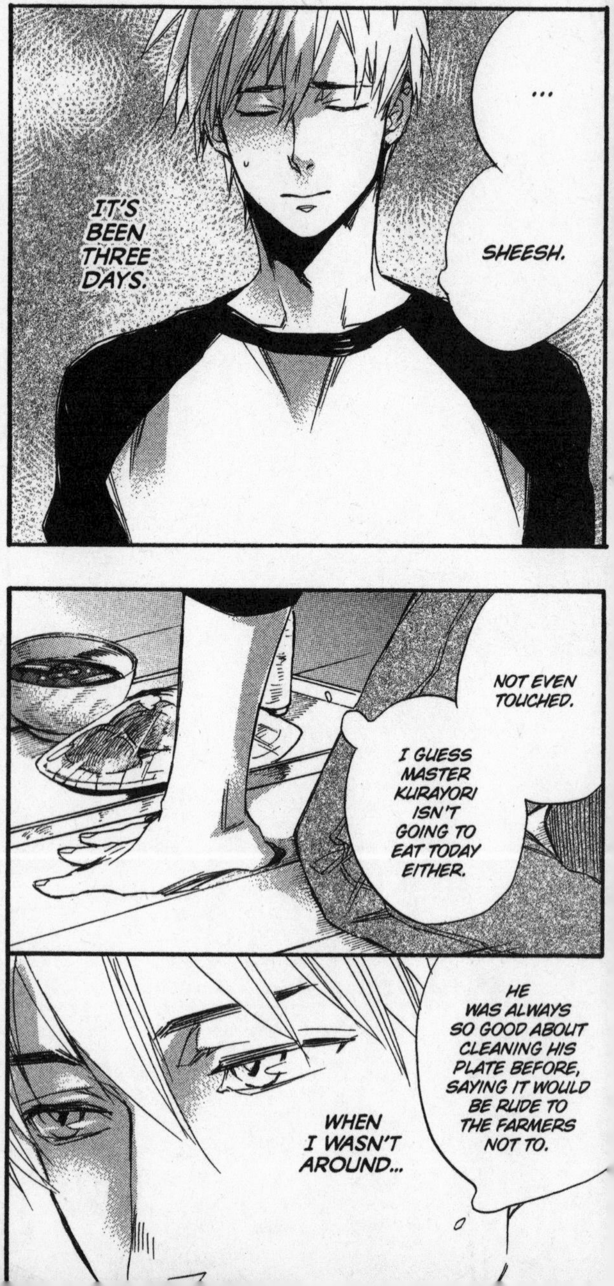
...
SHEESH.
IT'S BEEN THREE DAYS.
NOT EVEN TOUCHED.
I GUESS MASTER KURAYORI ISN'T GOING TO EAT TODAY EITHER.
HE WAS ALWAYS SO GOOD ABOUT CLEANING HIS PLATE BEFORE, SAYING IT WOULD BE RUDE TO THE FARMERS NOT TO.
WHEN I WASN'T AROUND...

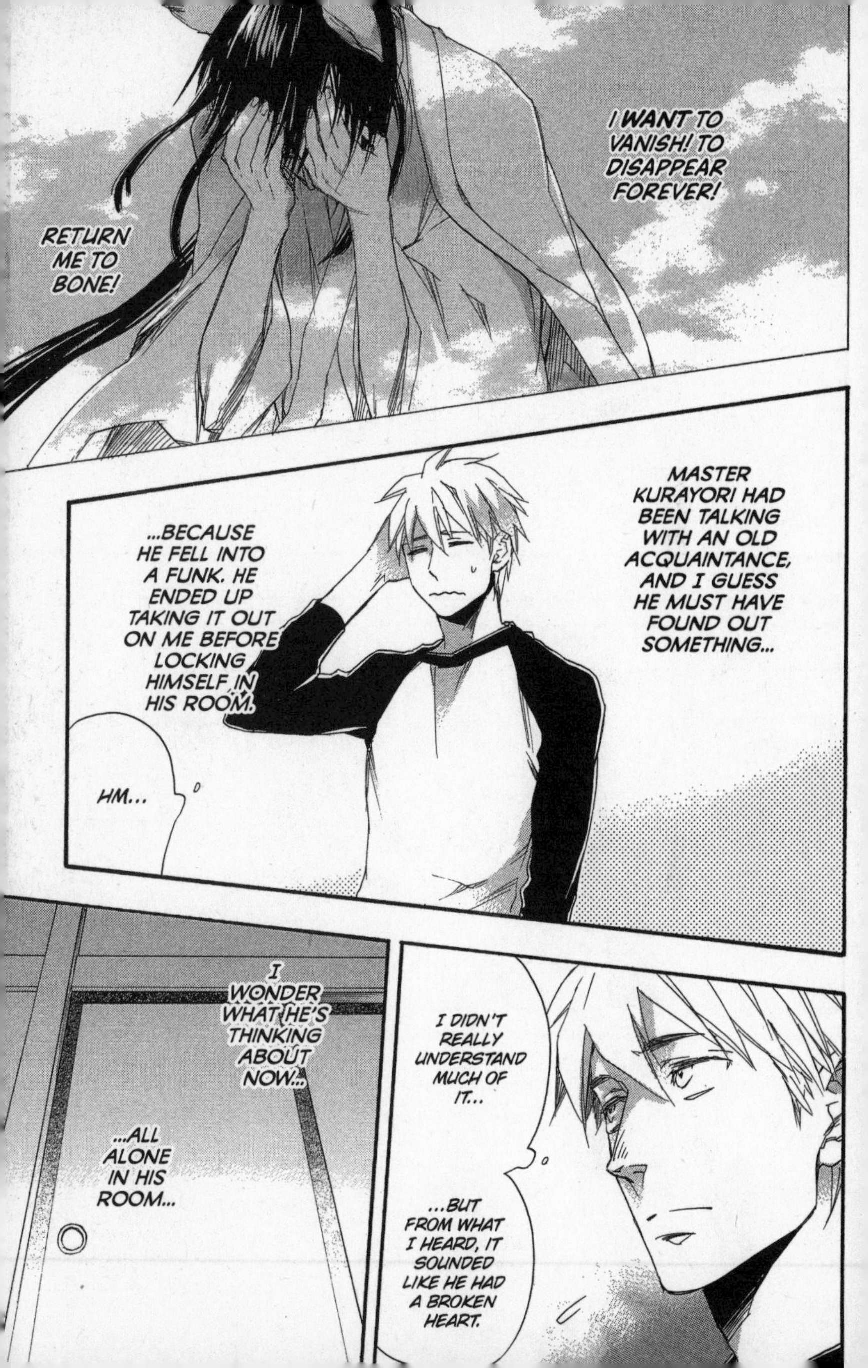
I WANT TO VANISH! TO DISAPPEAR FOREVER!
RETURN ME TO BONE!
MASTER KURAYORI HAD BEEN TALKING WITH AN OLD ACQUAINTANCE, AND I GUESS HE MUST HAVE FOUND OUT SOMETHING...
...BECAUSE HE FELL INTO A FUNK. HE ENDED UP TAKING IT OUT ON ME BEFORE LOCKING HIMSELF IN HIS ROOM.
HM...
I DIDN'T REALLY UNDERSTAND MUCH OF IT...
...BUT FROM WHAT I HEARD, IT SOUNDED LIKE HE HAD A BROKEN HEART.
I WONDER WHAT HE'S THINKING ABOUT NOW...
...ALL ALONE IN HIS ROOM...

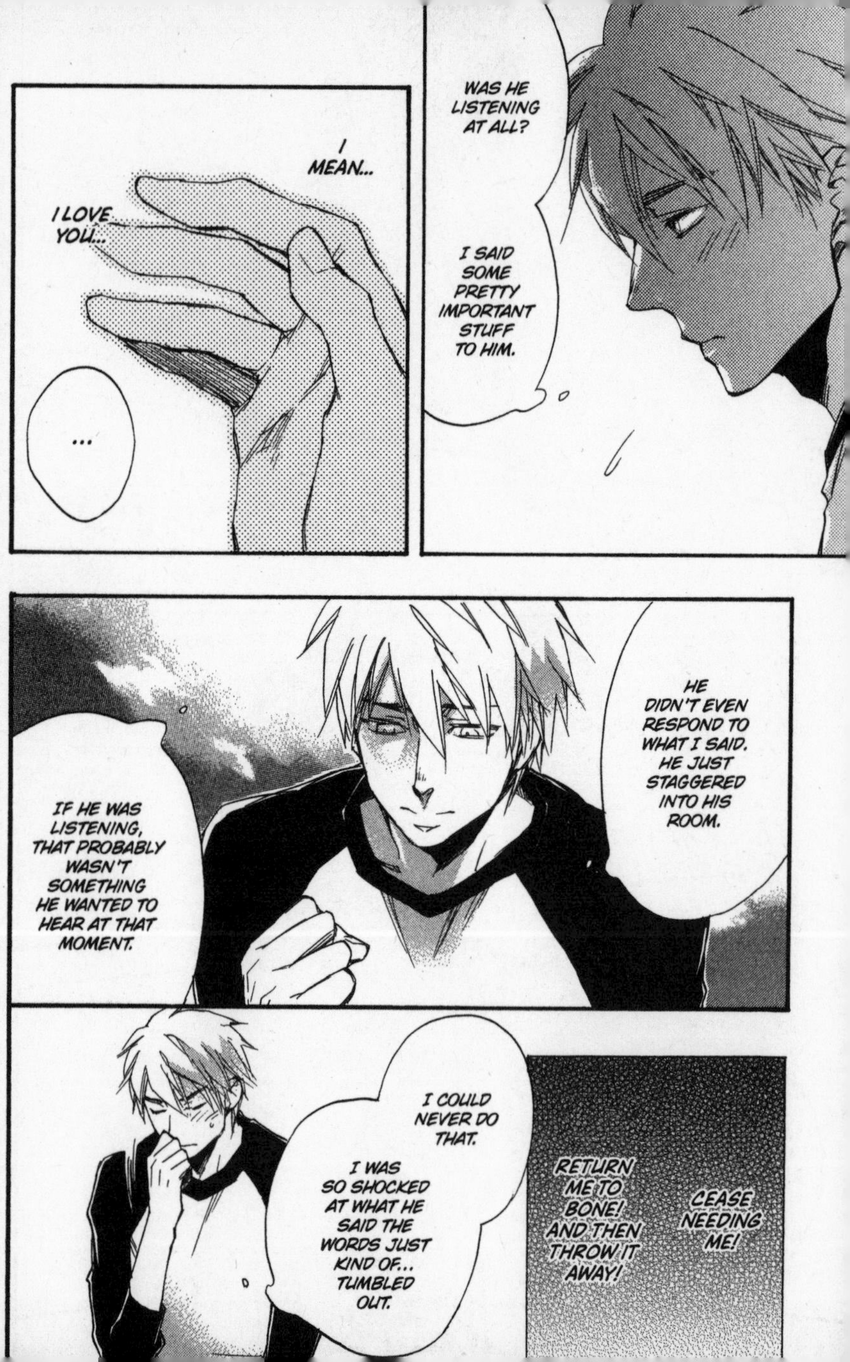

WAS HE LISTENING AT ALL?
I SAID SOME PRETTY IMPORTANT STUFF TO HIM.
I MEAN...
I LOVE YOU...
...
HE DIDN'T EVEN RESPOND TO WHAT I SAID. HE JUST STAGGERED INTO HIS ROOM.
IF HE WAS LISTENING, THAT PROBABLY WASN'T SOMETHING HE WANTED TO HEAR AT THAT MOMENT.
CEASE NEEDING ME!
RETURN ME TO BONE! AND THEN THROW IT AWAY!
I COULD NEVER DO THAT.
I WAS SO SHOCKED AT WHAT HE SAID THE WORDS JUST KIND OF... TUMBLED OUT.

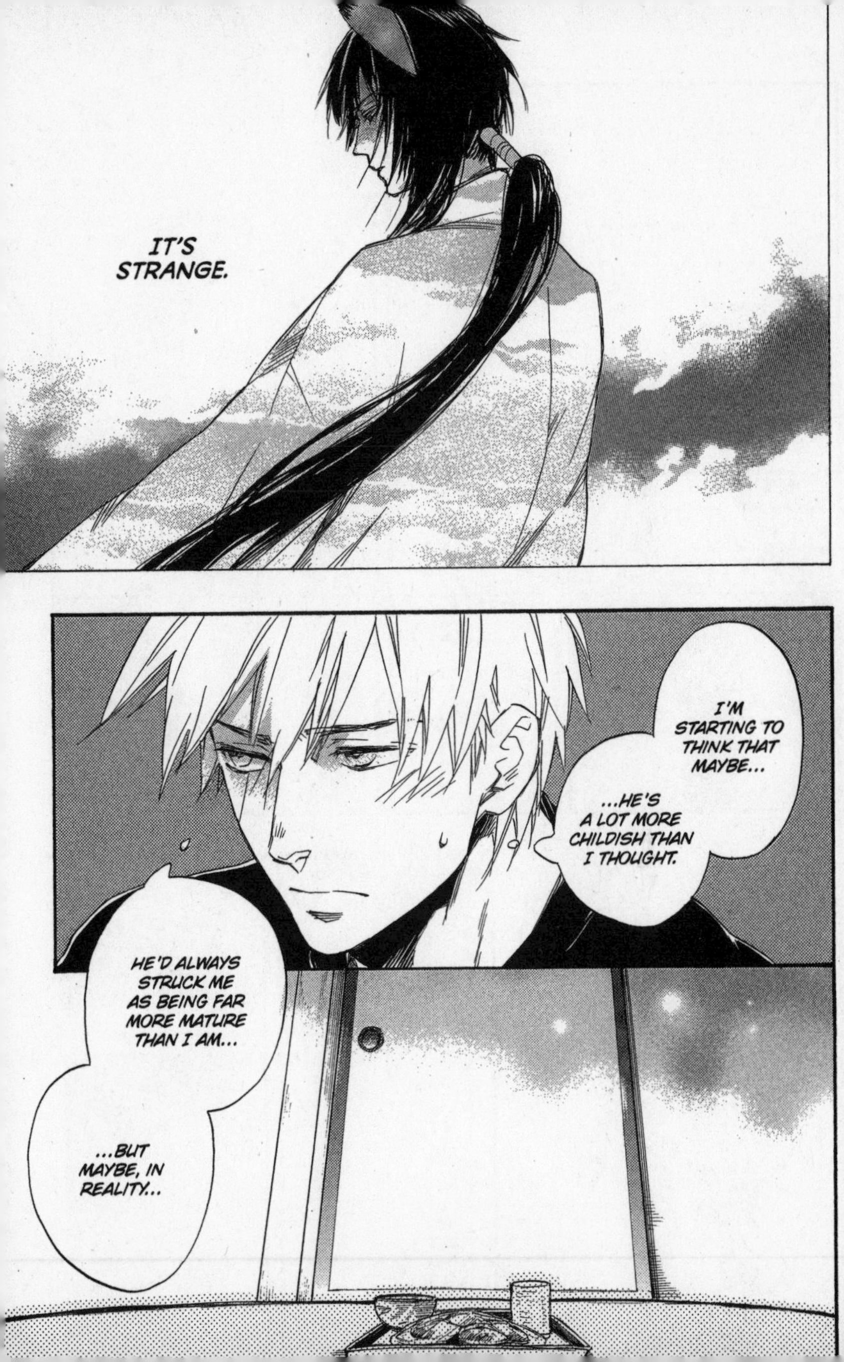
IT'S STRANGE.
I'M STARTING TO THINK THAT MAYBE...
...HE'S A LOT MORE CHILDISH THAN I THOUGHT.
HE'D ALWAYS STRUCK ME AS BEING FAR MORE MATURE THAN I AM...
...BUT MAYBE, IN REALITY...

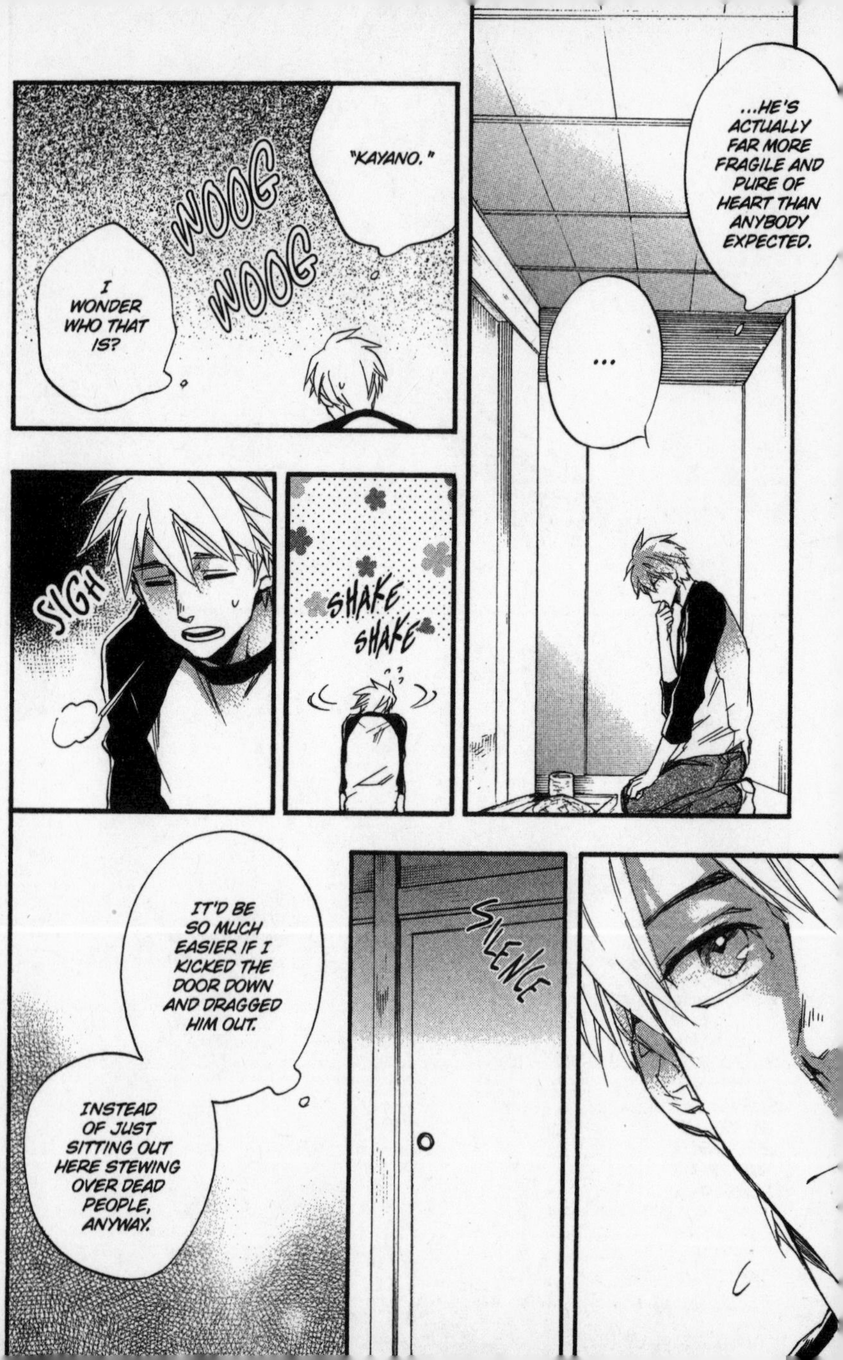
...HE'S ACTUALLY FAR MORE FRAGILE AND PURE OF HEART THAN ANYBODY EXPECTED.
...
"KAYANO."
WOOG WOOG
I WONDER WHO THAT IS?
SHAKE SHAKE
SIGH
SILENCE
IT'D BE SO MUCH EASIER IF I KICKED THE DOOR DOWN AND DRAGGED HIM OUT.
INSTEAD OF JUST SITTING OUT HERE STEWING OVER DEAD PEOPLE, ANYWAY.

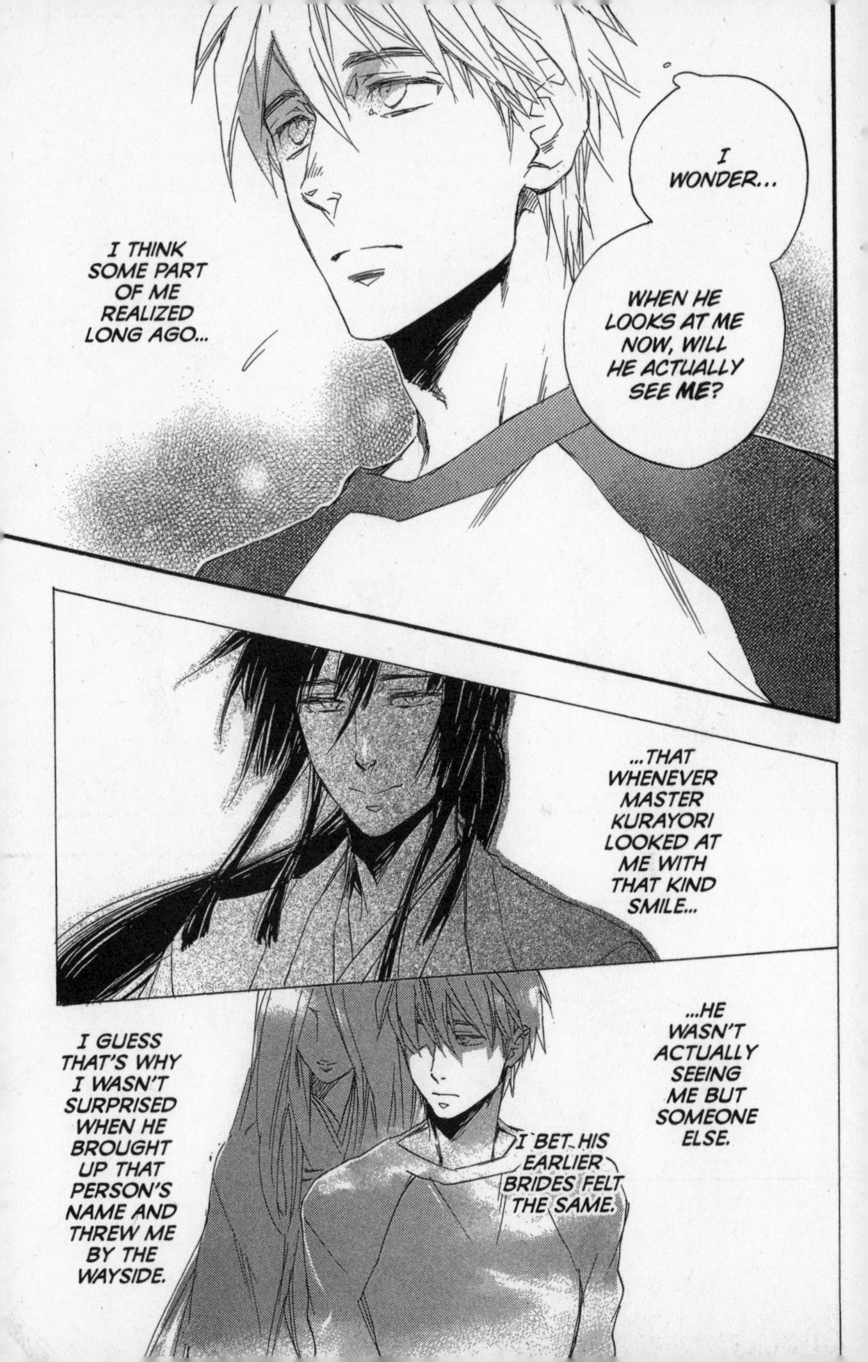
I WONDER...
WHEN HE LOOKS AT ME NOW, WILL HE ACTUALLY SEE ME?
I THINK SOME PART OF ME REALIZED LONG AGO...
...THAT WHENEVER MASTER KURAYORI LOOKED AT ME WITH THAT KIND SMILE...
...HE WASN'T ACTUALLY SEEING ME BUT SOMEONE ELSE.
I BET HIS EARLIER BRIDES FELT THE SAME.
I GUESS THAT'S WHY I WASN'T SURPRISED WHEN HE BROUGHT UP THAT PERSON'S NAME AND THREW ME BY THE WAYSIDE.

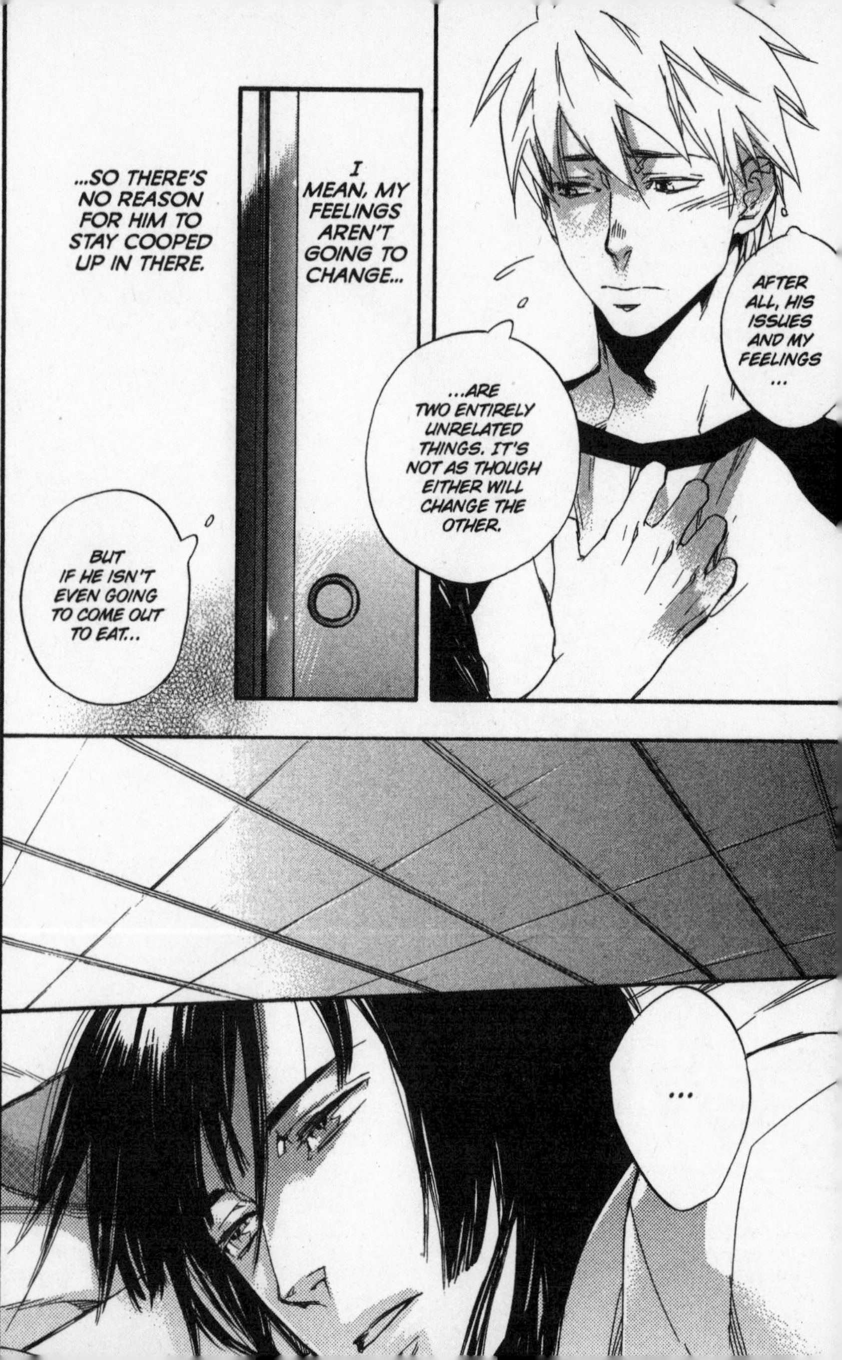
AFTER ALL, HIS ISSUES AND MY FEELINGS...
...ARE TWO ENTIRELY UNRELATED THINGS. IT'S NOT AS THOUGH EITHER WILL CHANGE THE OTHER.
I MEAN, MY FEELINGS AREN'T GOING TO CHANGE...
...SO THERE'S NO REASON FOR HIM TO STAY COOPED UP IN THERE.
BUT IF HE ISN'T EVEN GOING TO COME OUT TO EAT...
...

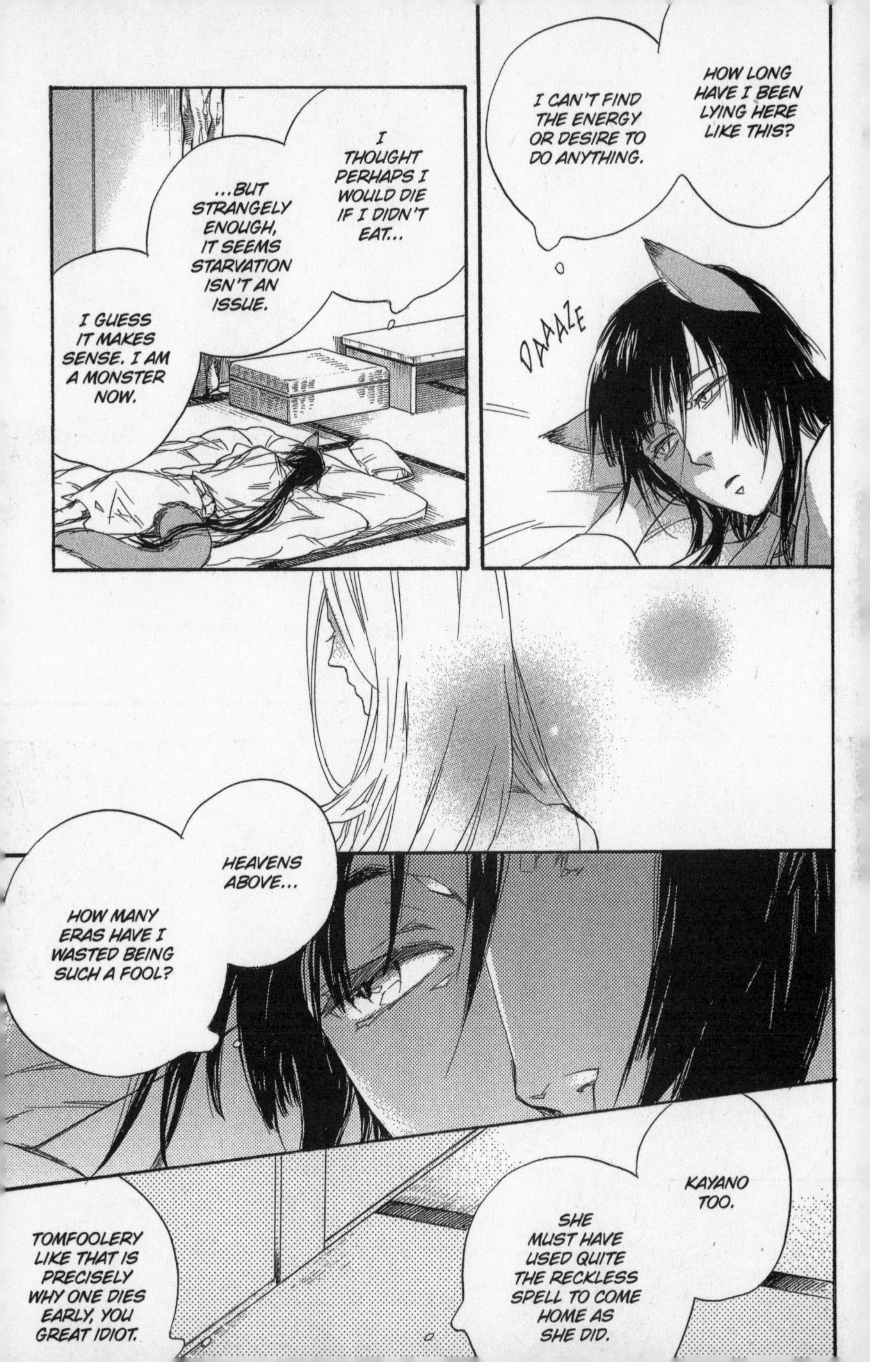
HOW LONG HAVE I BEEN LYING HERE LIKE THIS?
I CAN'T FIND THE ENERGY OR DESIRE TO DO ANYTHING.
DAAAZE
I THOUGHT PERHAPS I WOULD DIE IF I DIDN'T EAT...
...BUT STRANGELY ENOUGH, IT SEEMS STARVATION ISN'T AN ISSUE.
I GUESS IT MAKES SENSE. I AM A MONSTER NOW.
HEAVENS ABOVE...
HOW MANY ERAS HAVE I WASTED BEING SUCH A FOOL?
KAYANO TOO.
SHE MUST HAVE USED QUITE THE RECKLESS SPELL TO COME HOME AS SHE DID.
TOMFOOLERY LIKE THAT IS PRECISELY WHY ONE DIES EARLY, YOU GREAT IDIOT.

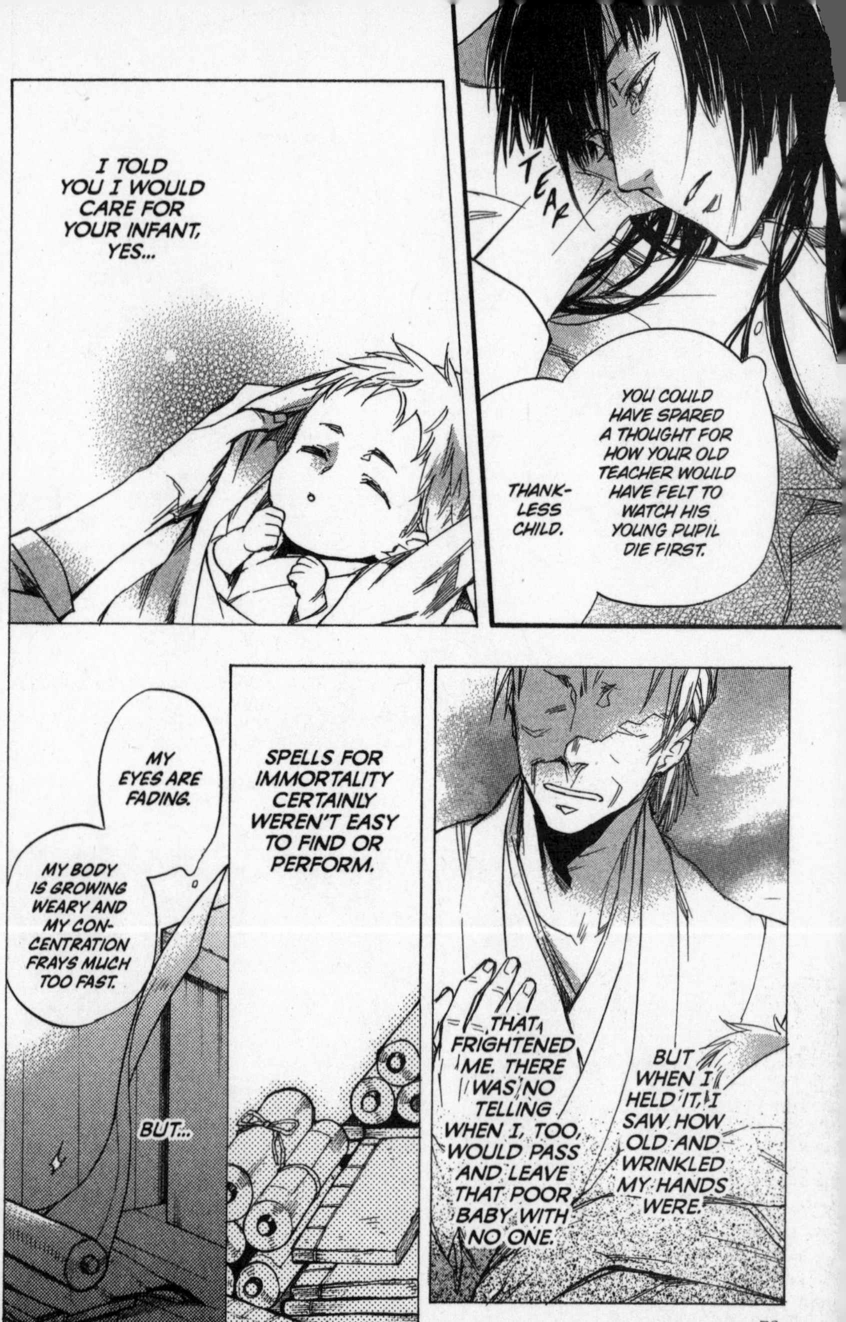
TEAR
YOU COULD HAVE SPARED A THOUGHT FOR HOW YOUR OLD TEACHER WOULD HAVE FELT TO WATCH HIS YOUNG PUPIL DIE FIRST.
THANK-LESS CHILD.
I TOLD YOU I WOULD CARE FOR YOUR INFANT, YES...
BUT WHEN I HELD IT, I SAW HOW OLD AND WRINKLED MY HANDS WERE.
THAT FRIGHTENED ME. THERE WAS NO TELLING WHEN I, TOO, WOULD PASS AND LEAVE THAT POOR BABY WITH NO ONE.
SPELLS FOR IMMORTALITY CERTAINLY WEREN'T EASY TO FIND OR PERFORM.
MY EYES ARE FADING.
MY BODY IS GROWING WEARY AND MY CON-CENTRATION FRAYS MUCH TOO FAST.
BUT...

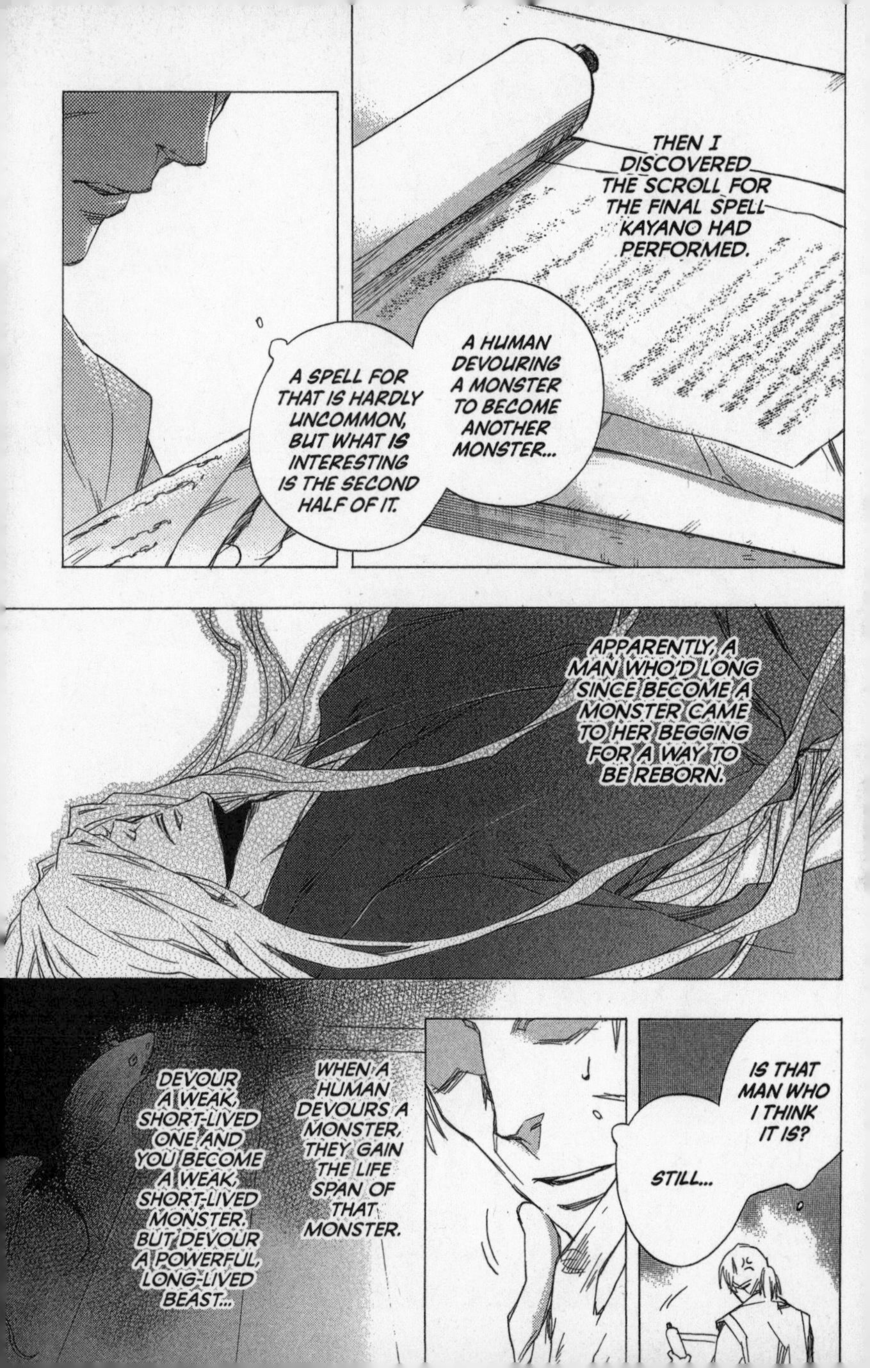
THEN I DISCOVERED THE SCROLL FOR THE FINAL SPELL KAYANO HAD PERFORMED.
A HUMAN DEVOURING A MONSTER TO BECOME ANOTHER MONSTER...
A SPELL FOR THAT IS HARDLY UNCOMMON, BUT WHAT IS INTERESTING IS THE SECOND HALF OF IT.
APPARENTLY, A MAN WHO'D LONG SINCE BECOME A MONSTER CAME TO HER BEGGING FOR A WAY TO BE REBORN.
IS THAT MAN WHO I THINK IT IS?
STILL...
WHEN A HUMAN DEVOURS A MONSTER, THEY GAIN THE LIFE SPAN OF THAT MONSTER.
DEVOUR A WEAK, SHORT-LIVED ONE AND YOU BECOME A WEAK, SHORT-LIVED MONSTER. BUT DEVOUR A POWERFUL, LONG-LIVED BEAST...

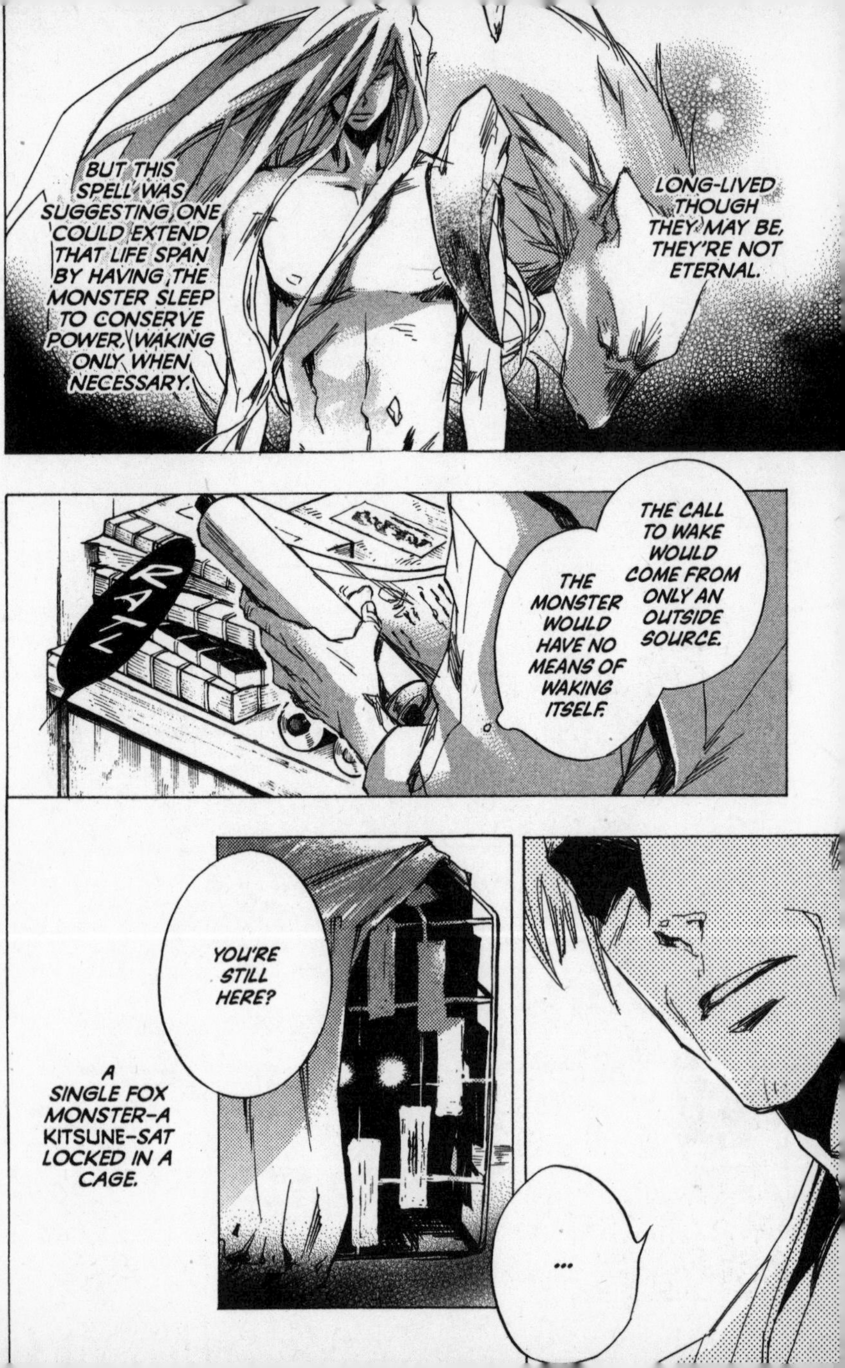
LONG-LIVED THOUGH THEY MAY BE, THEY'RE NOT ETERNAL.
BUT THIS SPELL WAS SUGGESTING ONE COULD EXTEND THAT LIFE SPAN BY HAVING THE MONSTER SLEEP TO CONSERVE POWER, WAKING ONLY WHEN NECESSARY.
THE CALL TO WAKE WOULD COME FROM ONLY AN OUTSIDE SOURCE.
THE MONSTER WOULD HAVE NO MEANS OF WAKING ITSELF.
RATL
...
YOU'RE STILL HERE?
A SINGLE FOX MONSTER—A KITSUNE—SAT LOCKED IN A CAGE.

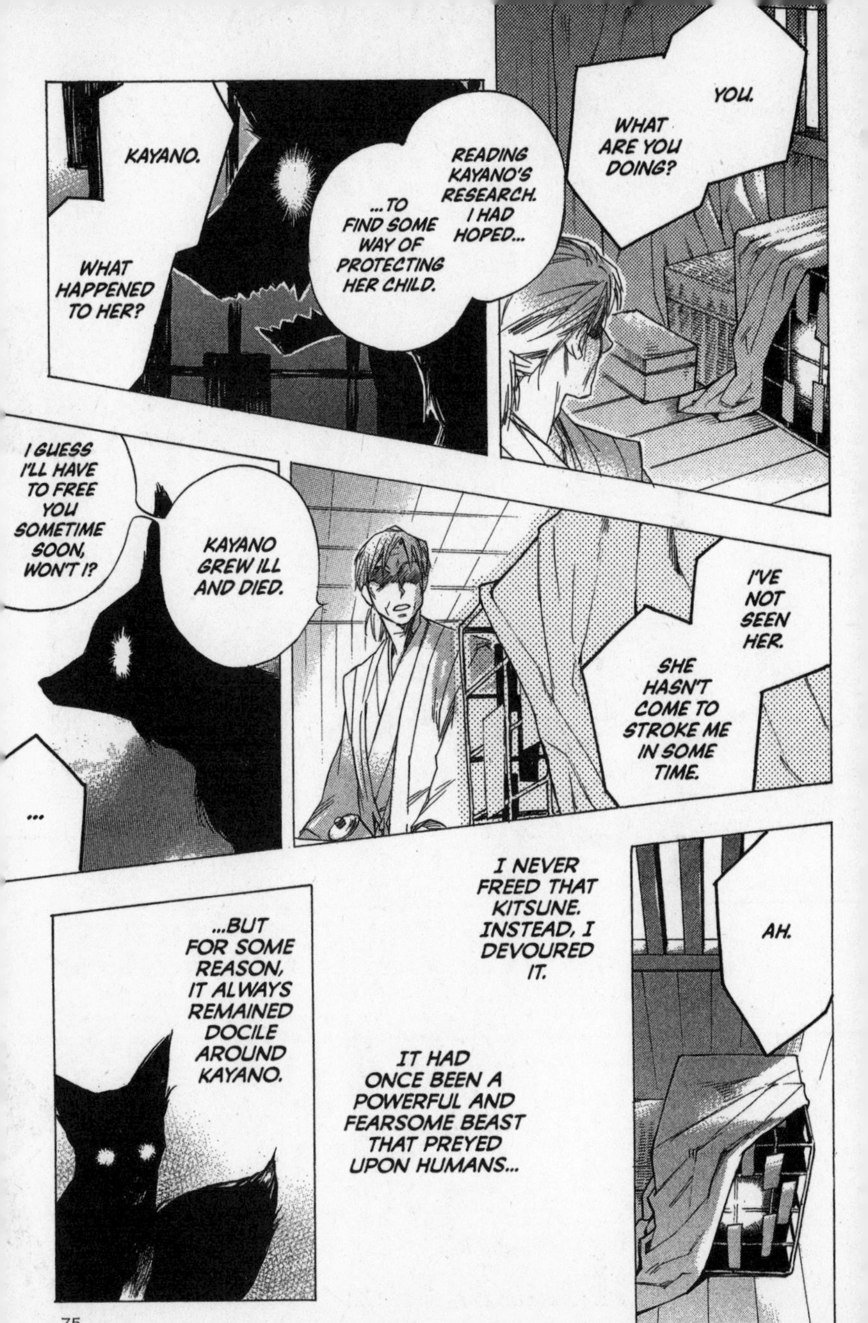
YOU.
WHAT ARE YOU DOING?
READING KAYANO'S RESEARCH. I HAD HOPED...
...TO FIND SOME WAY OF PROTECTING HER CHILD.
KAYANO.
WHAT HAPPENED TO HER?
I'VE NOT SEEN HER.
SHE HASN'T COME TO STROKE ME IN SOME TIME.
KAYANO GREW ILL AND DIED.
I GUESS I'LL HAVE TO FREE YOU SOMETIME SOON, WON'T I?
...
AH.
I NEVER FREED THAT KITSUNE. INSTEAD, I DEVOURED IT.
IT HAD ONCE BEEN A POWERFUL AND FEARSOME BEAST THAT PREYED UPON HUMANS...
...BUT FOR SOME REASON, IT ALWAYS REMAINED DOCILE AROUND KAYANO.

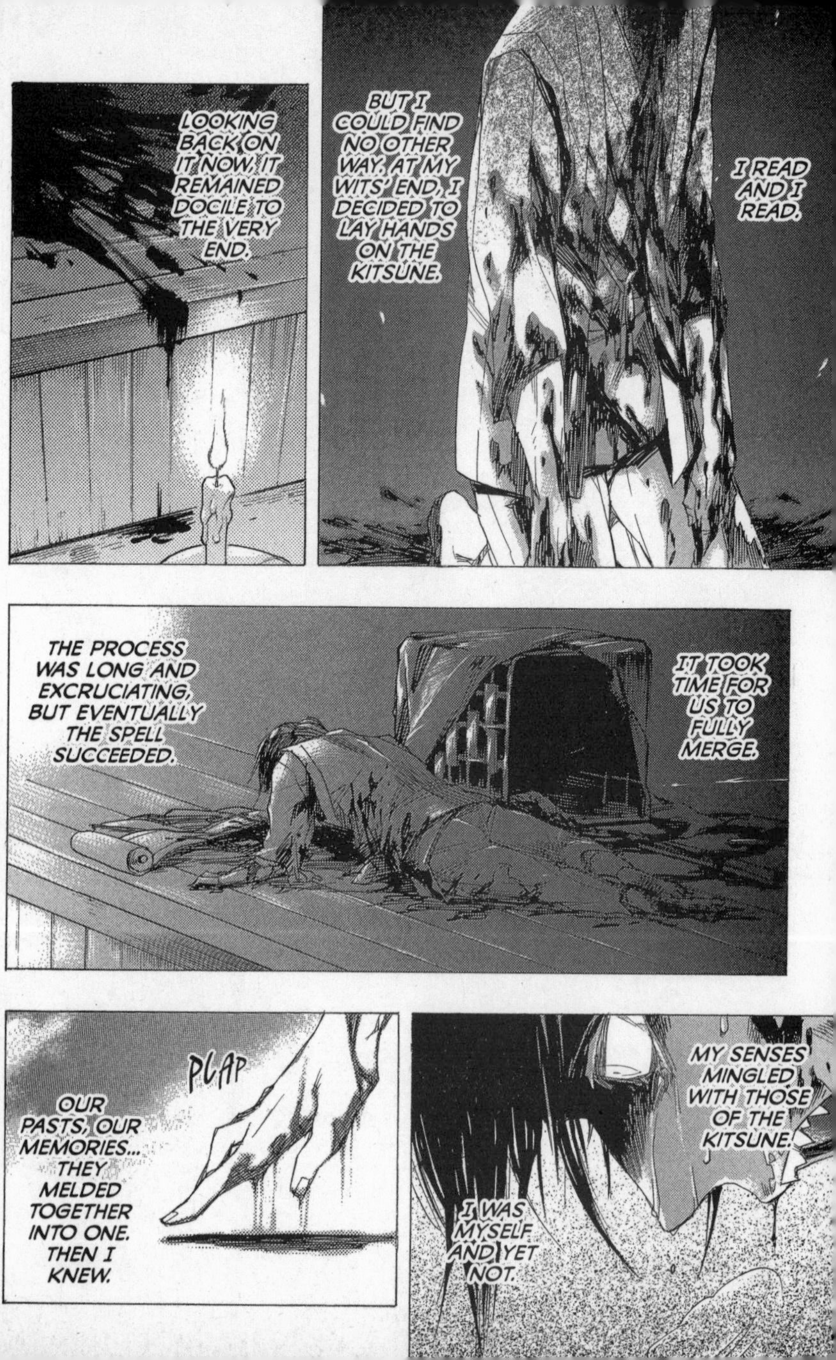
I READ AND I READ.
BUT I COULD FIND NO OTHER WAY. AT MY WITS' END, I DECIDED TO LAY HANDS ON THE KITSUNE.
LOOKING BACK ON IT NOW, IT REMAINED DOCILE TO THE VERY END.
IT TOOK TIME FOR US TO FULLY MERGE.
THE PROCESS WAS LONG AND EXCRUCIATING, BUT EVENTUALLY THE SPELL SUCCEEDED.
MY SENSES MINGLED WITH THOSE OF THE KITSUNE.
I WAS MYSELF AND YET NOT.
PLAP
OUR PASTS, OUR MEMORIES... THEY MELDED TOGETHER INTO ONE. THEN I KNEW.

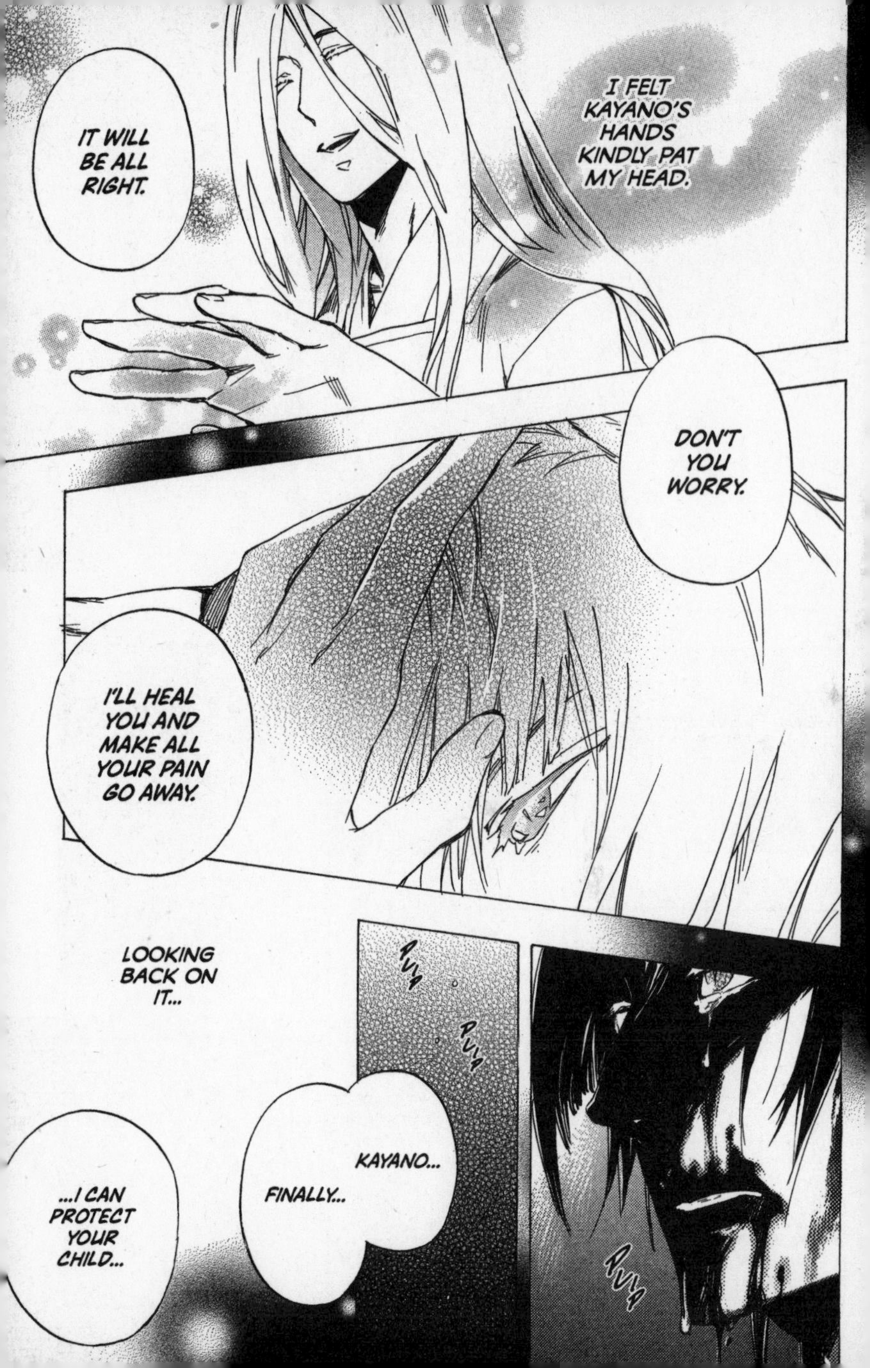
I FELT KAYANO'S HANDS KINDLY PAT MY HEAD.
IT WILL BE ALL RIGHT.
DON'T YOU WORRY.
I'LL HEAL YOU AND MAKE ALL YOUR PAIN GO AWAY.
KAYANO... FINALLY...
LOOKING BACK ON IT...
...I CAN PROTECT YOUR CHILD...

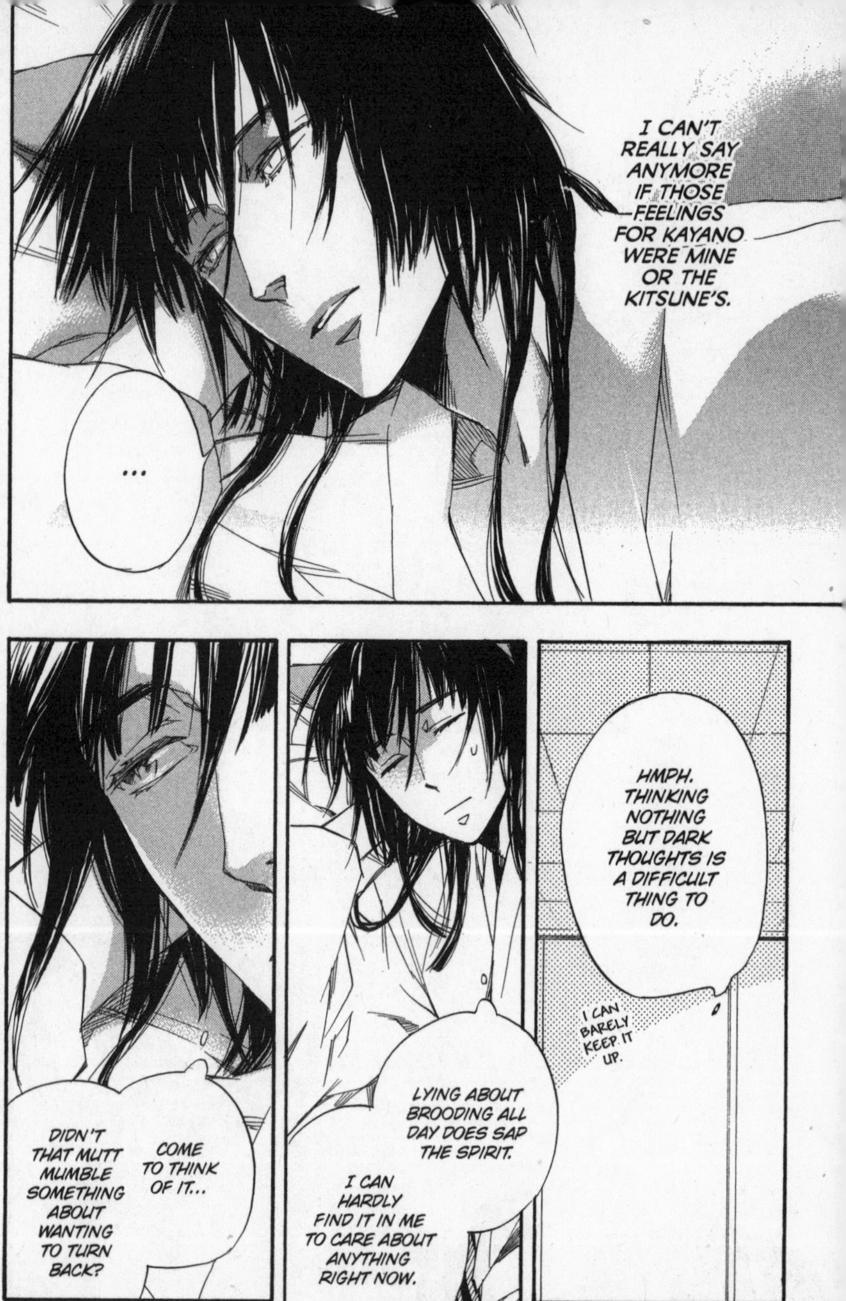
I CAN'T REALLY SAY ANYMORE IF THOSE FEELINGS FOR KAYANO WERE MINE OR THE KITSUNE'S.
...
HMPH. THINKING NOTHING BUT DARK THOUGHTS IS A DIFFICULT THING TO DO.
I CAN BARELY KEEP IT UP.
LYING ABOUT BROODING ALL DAY DOES SAP THE SPIRIT.
I CAN HARDLY FIND IT IN ME TO CARE ABOUT ANYTHING RIGHT NOW.
COME TO THINK OF IT...
DIDN'T THAT MUTT MUMBLE SOMETHING ABOUT WANTING TO TURN BACK?

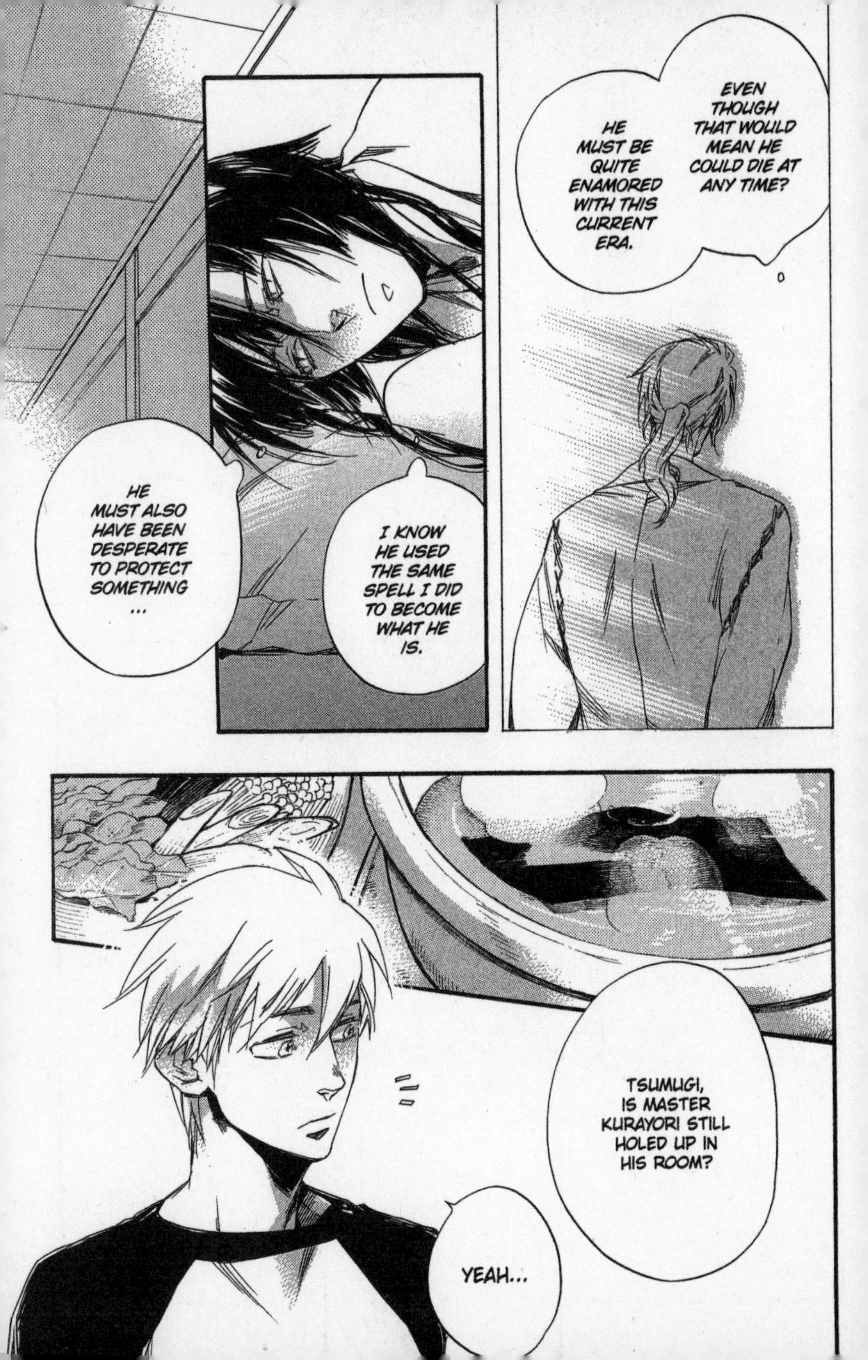
HE MUST BE QUITE ENAMORED WITH THIS CURRENT ERA. EVEN THOUGH THAT WOULD MEAN HE COULD DIE AT ANY TIME?
I KNOW HE USED THE SAME SPELL I DID TO BECOME WHAT HE IS.
HE MUST ALSO HAVE BEEN DESPERATE TO PROTECT SOMETHING...
TSUMUGI, IS MASTER KURAYORI STILL HOLED UP IN HIS ROOM?
YEAH...

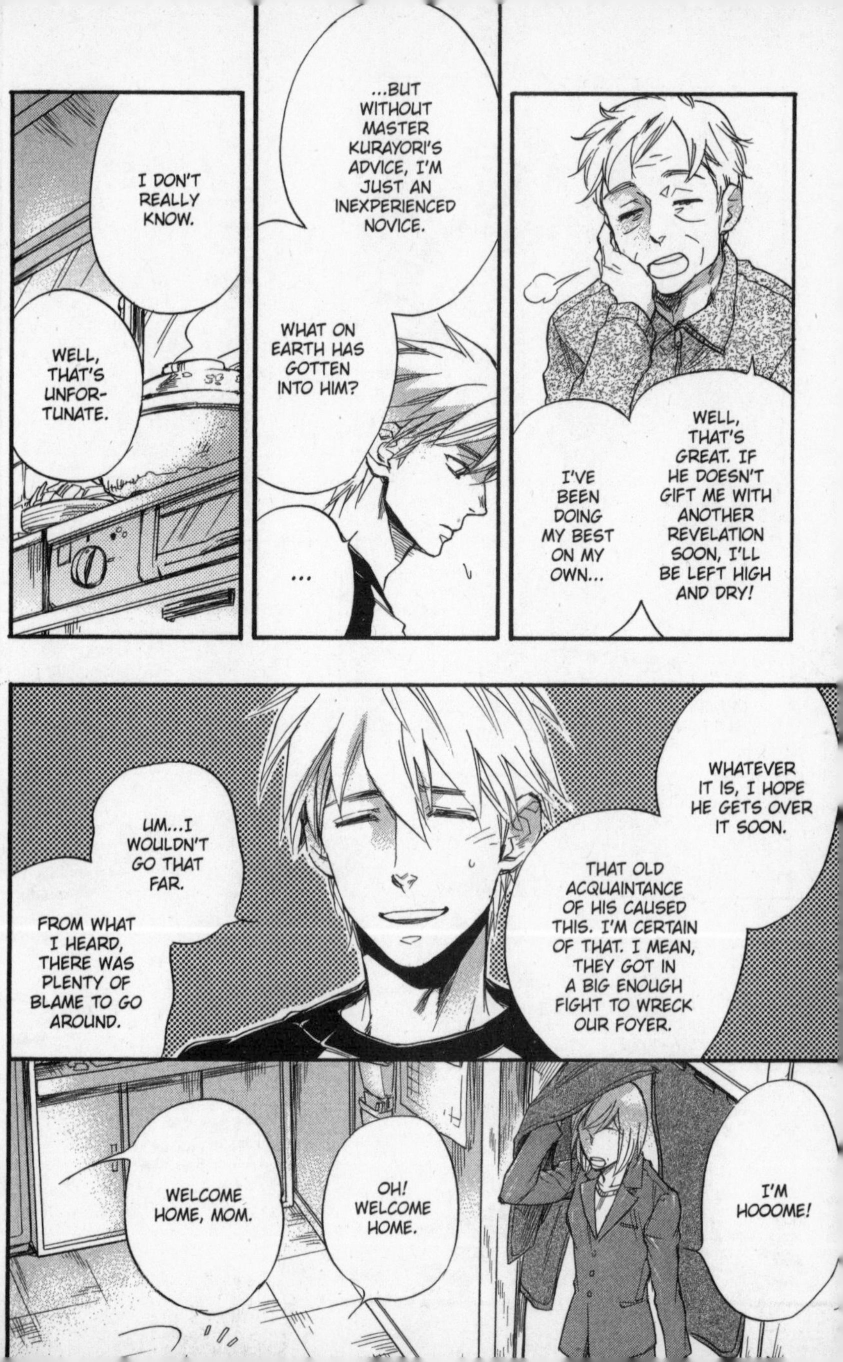
WELL, THAT'S GREAT. IF HE DOESN'T GIFT ME WITH ANOTHER REVELATION SOON, I'LL BE LEFT HIGH AND DRY!
I'VE BEEN DOING MY BEST ON MY OWN...
...BUT WITHOUT MASTER KURAYORI'S ADVICE, I'M JUST AN INEXPERIENCED NOVICE.
WHAT ON EARTH HAS GOTTEN INTO HIM?
...
I DON'T REALLY KNOW.
WELL, THAT'S UNFORTUNATE.
WHATEVER IT IS, I HOPE HE GETS OVER IT SOON.
THAT OLD ACQUAINTANCE OF HIS CAUSED THIS. I'M CERTAIN OF THAT. I MEAN, THEY GOT IN A BIG ENOUGH FIGHT TO WRECK OUR FOYER.
UM...I WOULDN'T GO THAT FAR.
FROM WHAT I HEARD, THERE WAS PLENTY OF BLAME TO GO AROUND.
I'M HOOOME!
OH! WELCOME HOME.
WELCOME HOME, MOM.

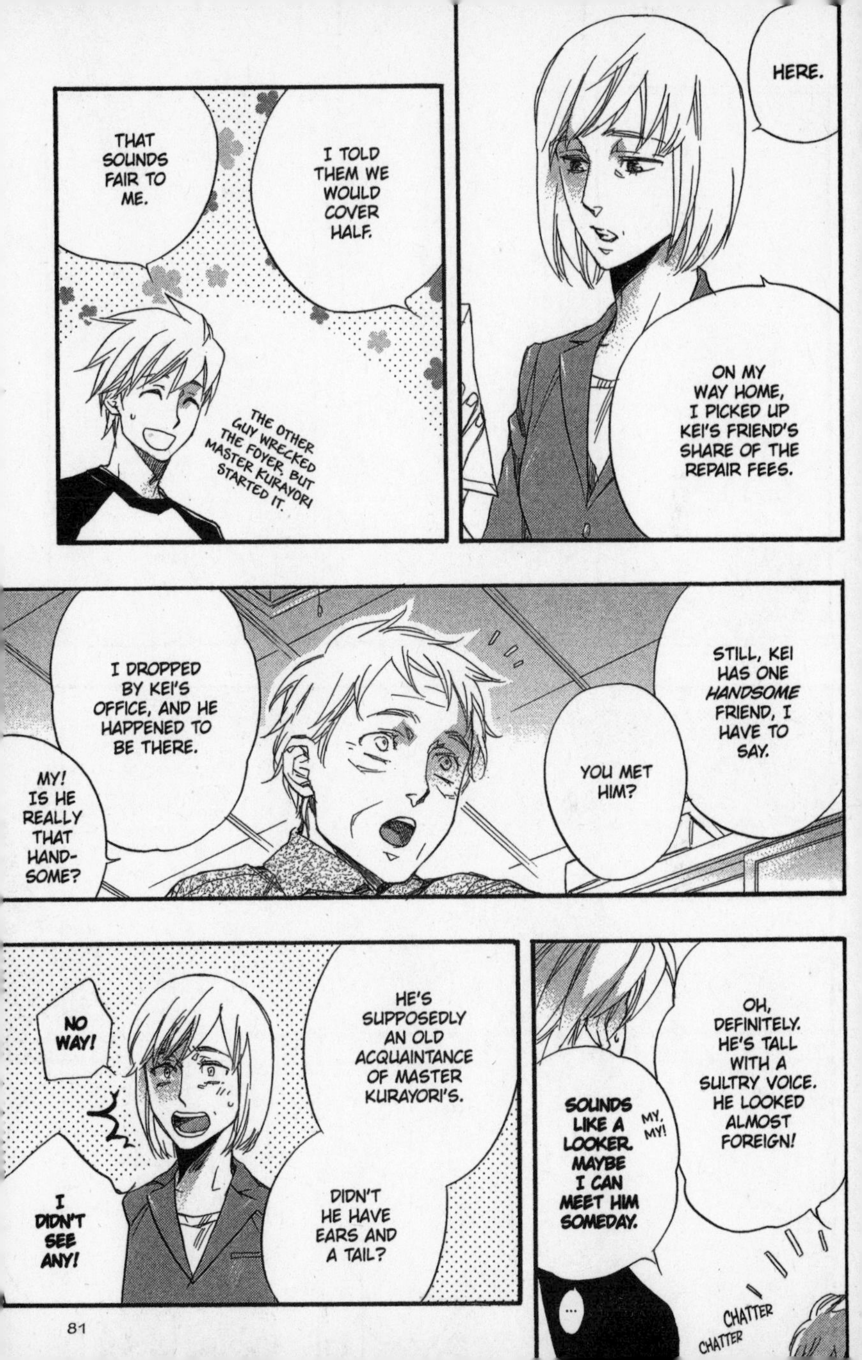
HERE.
ON MY WAY HOME, I PICKED UP KEI'S FRIEND'S SHARE OF THE REPAIR FEES.
I TOLD THEM WE WOULD COVER HALF.
THAT SOUNDS FAIR TO ME.
THE OTHER GUY WRECKED THE FOYER, BUT MASTER KURAYORI STARTED IT.
STILL, KEI HAS ONE *HANDSOME* FRIEND, I HAVE TO SAY.
YOU MET HIM?
I DROPPED BY KEI'S OFFICE, AND HE HAPPENED TO BE THERE.
MY! IS HE REALLY THAT HANDSOME?
OH, DEFINITELY. HE'S TALL WITH A SULTRY VOICE. HE LOOKED ALMOST FOREIGN!
MY, MY!
SOUNDS LIKE A LOOKER. MAYBE I CAN MEET HIM SOMEDAY.
...
CHATTER
CHATTER
HE'S SUPPOSEDLY AN OLD ACQUAINTANCE OF MASTER KURAYORI'S.
NO WAY!
DIDN'T HE HAVE EARS AND A TAIL?
I DIDN'T SEE ANY!

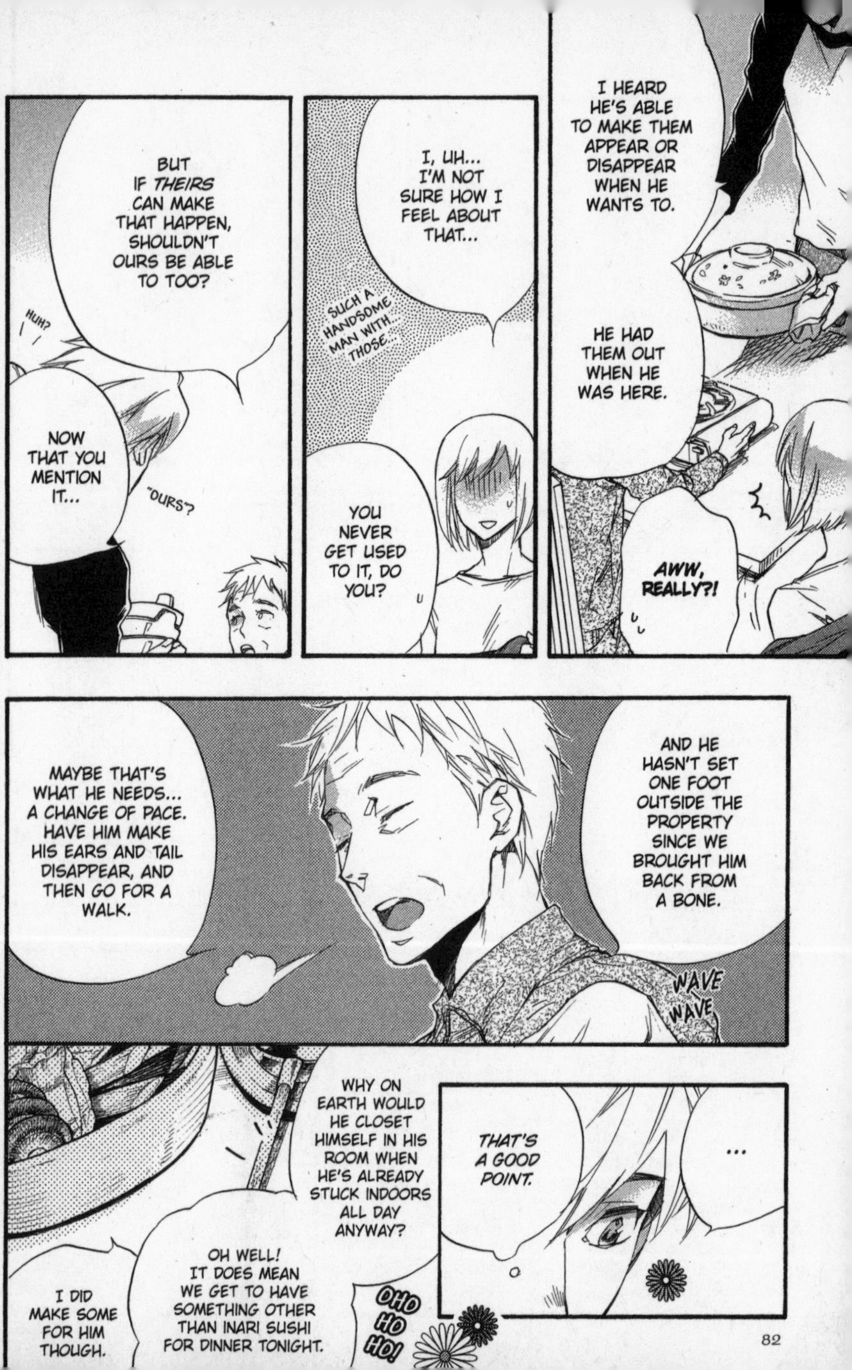
I HEARD HE'S ABLE TO MAKE THEM APPEAR OR DISAPPEAR WHEN HE WANTS TO.
HE HAD THEM OUT WHEN HE WAS HERE.
AWW, REALLY?!
I, UH... I'M NOT SURE HOW I FEEL ABOUT THAT...
SUCH A HANDSOME MAN WITH THOSE...
YOU NEVER GET USED TO IT, DO YOU?
BUT IF *THEIRS* CAN MAKE THAT HAPPEN, SHOULDN'T OURS BE ABLE TO TOO?
HUH?
NOW THAT YOU MENTION IT...
"OURS"?
AND HE HASN'T SET ONE FOOT OUTSIDE THE PROPERTY SINCE WE BROUGHT HIM BACK FROM A BONE.
WAVE WAVE
MAYBE THAT'S WHAT HE NEEDS... A CHANGE OF PACE. HAVE HIM MAKE HIS EARS AND TAIL DISAPPEAR, AND THEN GO FOR A WALK.
...
THAT'S A GOOD POINT.
WHY ON EARTH WOULD HE CLOSET HIMSELF IN HIS ROOM WHEN HE'S ALREADY STUCK INDOORS ALL DAY ANYWAY?
OH WELL! IT DOES MEAN WE GET TO HAVE SOMETHING OTHER THAN INARI SUSHI FOR DINNER TONIGHT.
OHO HO HO!
I DID MAKE SOME FOR HIM THOUGH.

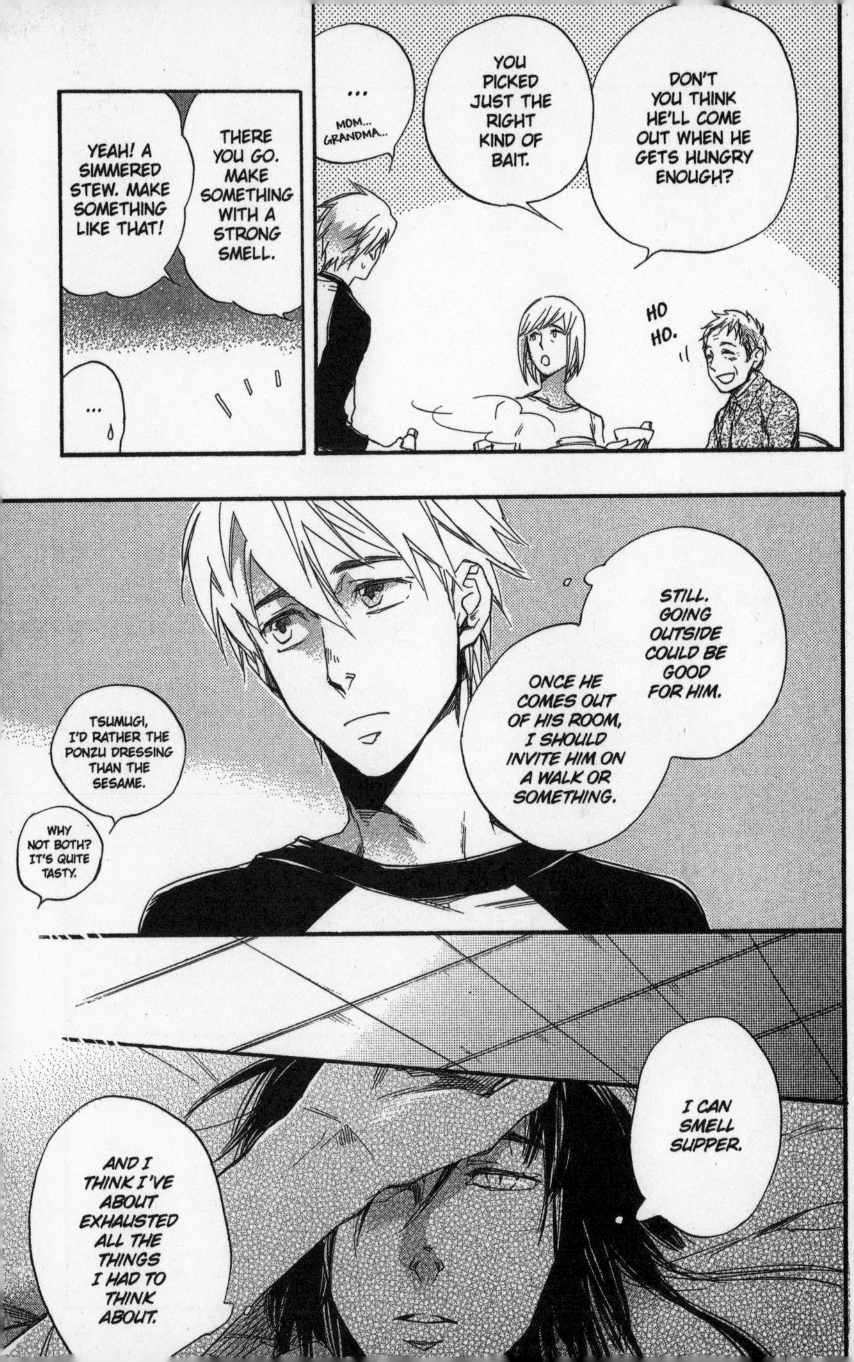
DON'T YOU THINK HE'LL COME OUT WHEN HE GETS HUNGRY ENOUGH?
YOU PICKED JUST THE RIGHT KIND OF BAIT.
...
MOM... GRANDMA...
HO HO.
THERE YOU GO. MAKE SOMETHING WITH A STRONG SMELL.
YEAH! A SIMMERED STEW. MAKE SOMETHING LIKE THAT!
...
STILL. GOING OUTSIDE COULD BE GOOD FOR HIM.
ONCE HE COMES OUT OF HIS ROOM, I SHOULD INVITE HIM ON A WALK OR SOMETHING.
TSUMUGI, I'D RATHER THE PONZU DRESSING THAN THE SESAME.
WHY NOT BOTH? IT'S QUITE TASTY.
I CAN SMELL SUPPER.
AND I THINK I'VE ABOUT EXHAUSTED ALL THE THINGS I HAD TO THINK ABOUT.

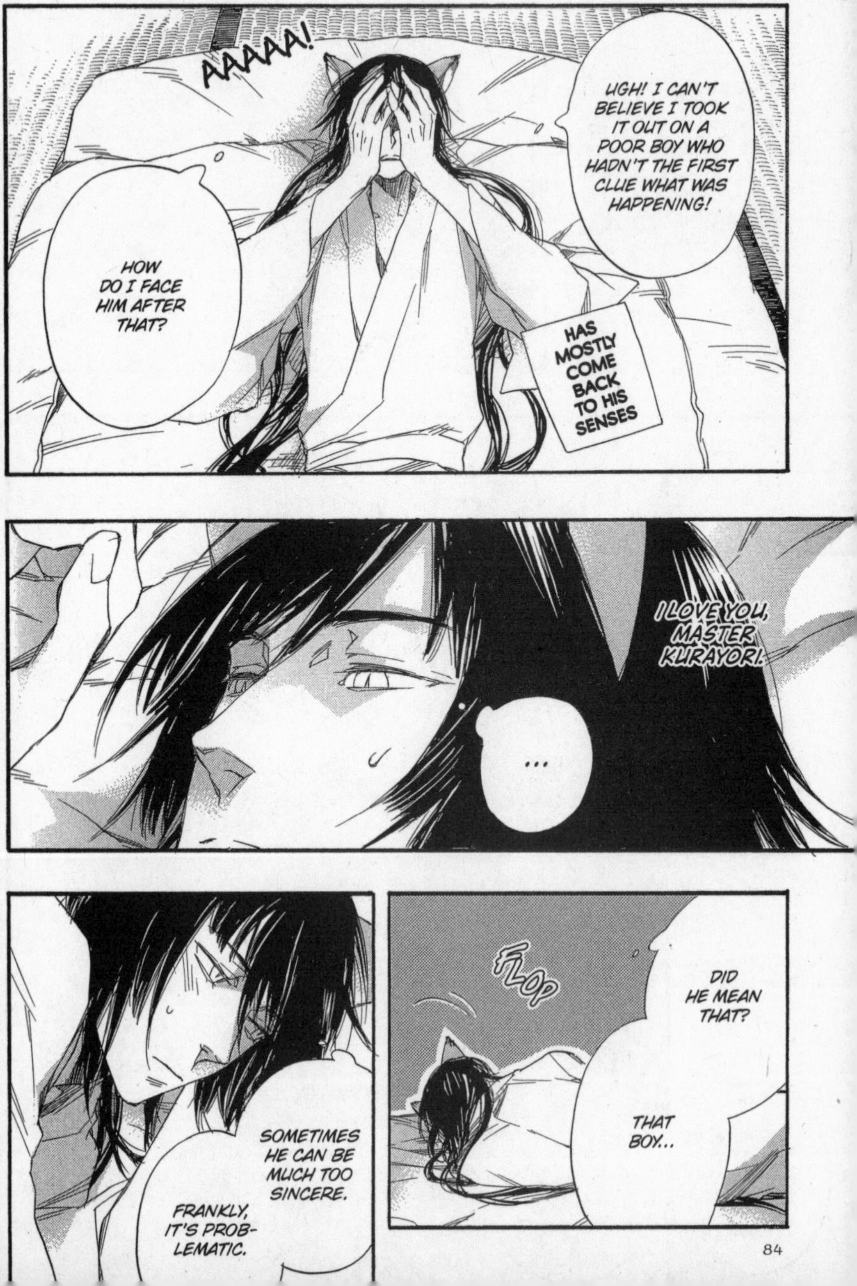
AAAAA!
UGH! I CAN'T BELIEVE I TOOK IT OUT ON A POOR BOY WHO HADN'T THE FIRST CLUE WHAT WAS HAPPENING!
HAS MOSTLY COME BACK TO HIS SENSES
HOW DO I FACE HIM AFTER THAT?
I LOVE YOU, MASTER KURAYORI.
...
FLOP
DID HE MEAN THAT?
THAT BOY...
SOMETIMES HE CAN BE MUCH TOO SINCERE.
FRANKLY, IT'S PROB-LEMATIC.

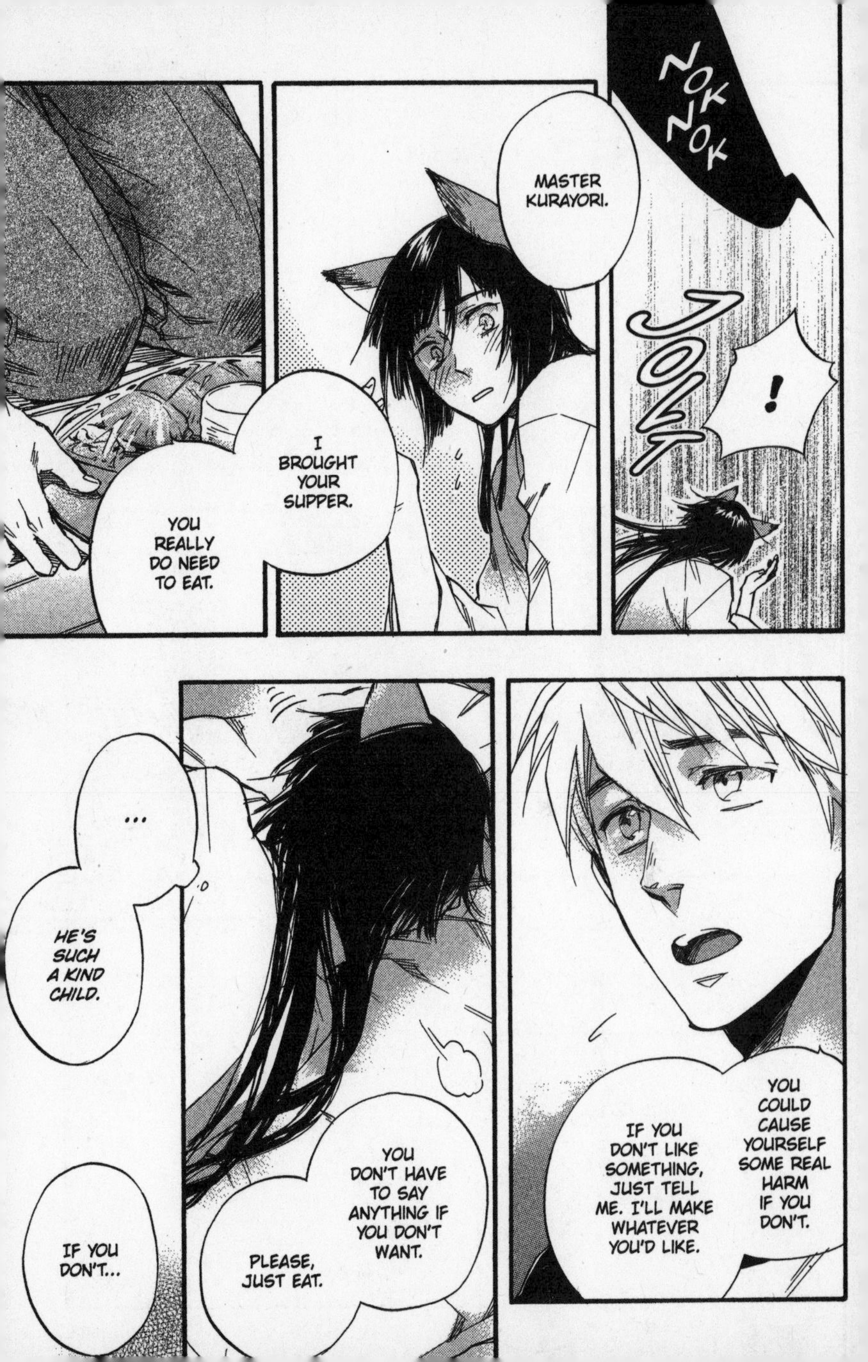
NOK NOK
JOLT
!
MASTER KURAYORI.
I BROUGHT YOUR SUPPER.
YOU REALLY DO NEED TO EAT.
YOU COULD CAUSE YOURSELF SOME REAL HARM IF YOU DON'T.
IF YOU DON'T LIKE SOMETHING, JUST TELL ME. I'LL MAKE WHATEVER YOU'D LIKE.
...
HE'S SUCH A KIND CHILD.
YOU DON'T HAVE TO SAY ANYTHING IF YOU DON'T WANT.
PLEASE, JUST EAT.
IF YOU DON'T...

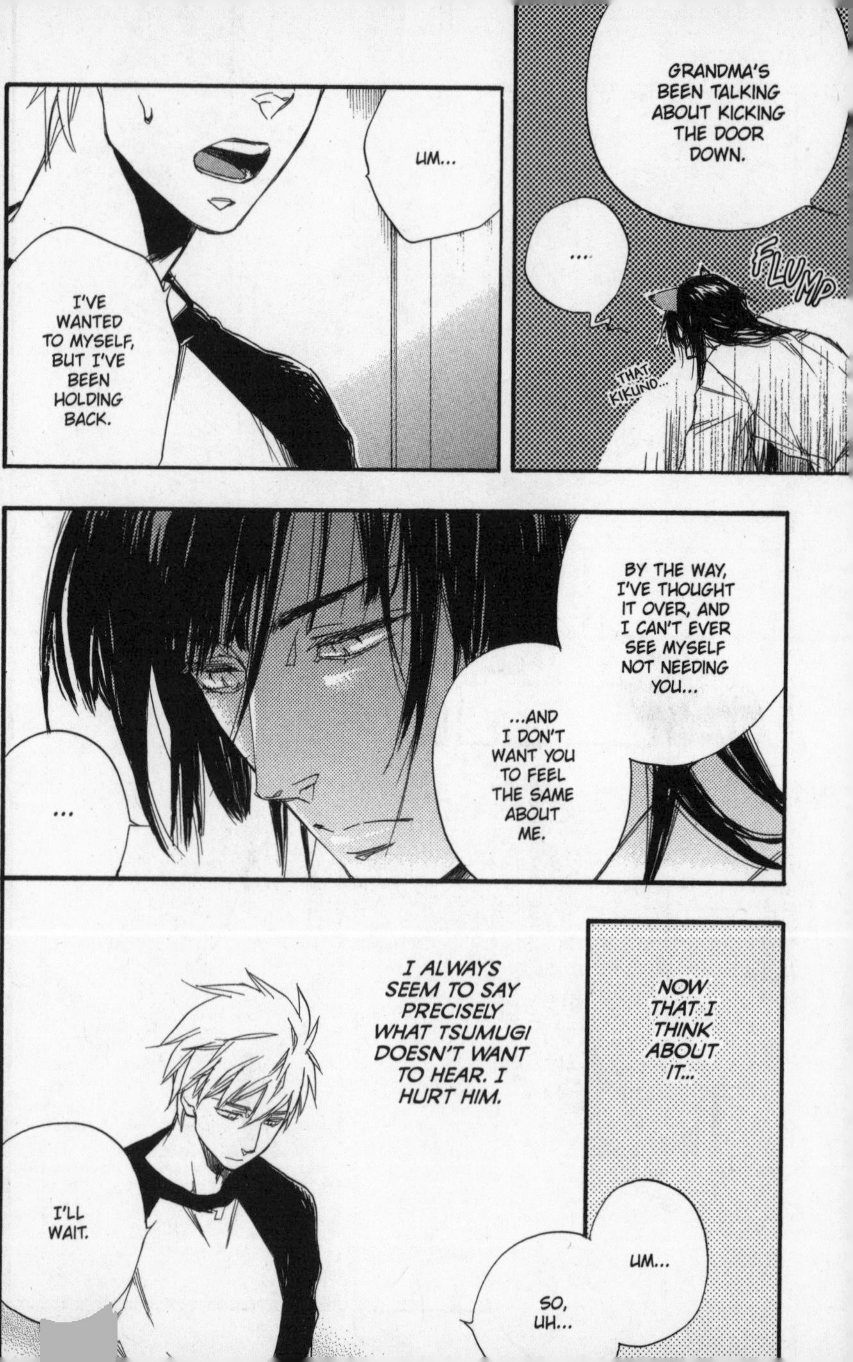
GRANDMA'S BEEN TALKING ABOUT KICKING THE DOOR DOWN.
...
FLUMP
THAT KIKUNO...
UM...
I'VE WANTED TO MYSELF, BUT I'VE BEEN HOLDING BACK.
BY THE WAY, I'VE THOUGHT IT OVER, AND I CAN'T EVER SEE MYSELF NOT NEEDING YOU...
...AND I DON'T WANT YOU TO FEEL THE SAME ABOUT ME.
...
NOW THAT I THINK ABOUT IT...
I ALWAYS SEEM TO SAY PRECISELY WHAT TSUMUGI DOESN'T WANT TO HEAR. I HURT HIM.
UM...
SO, UH...
I'LL WAIT.

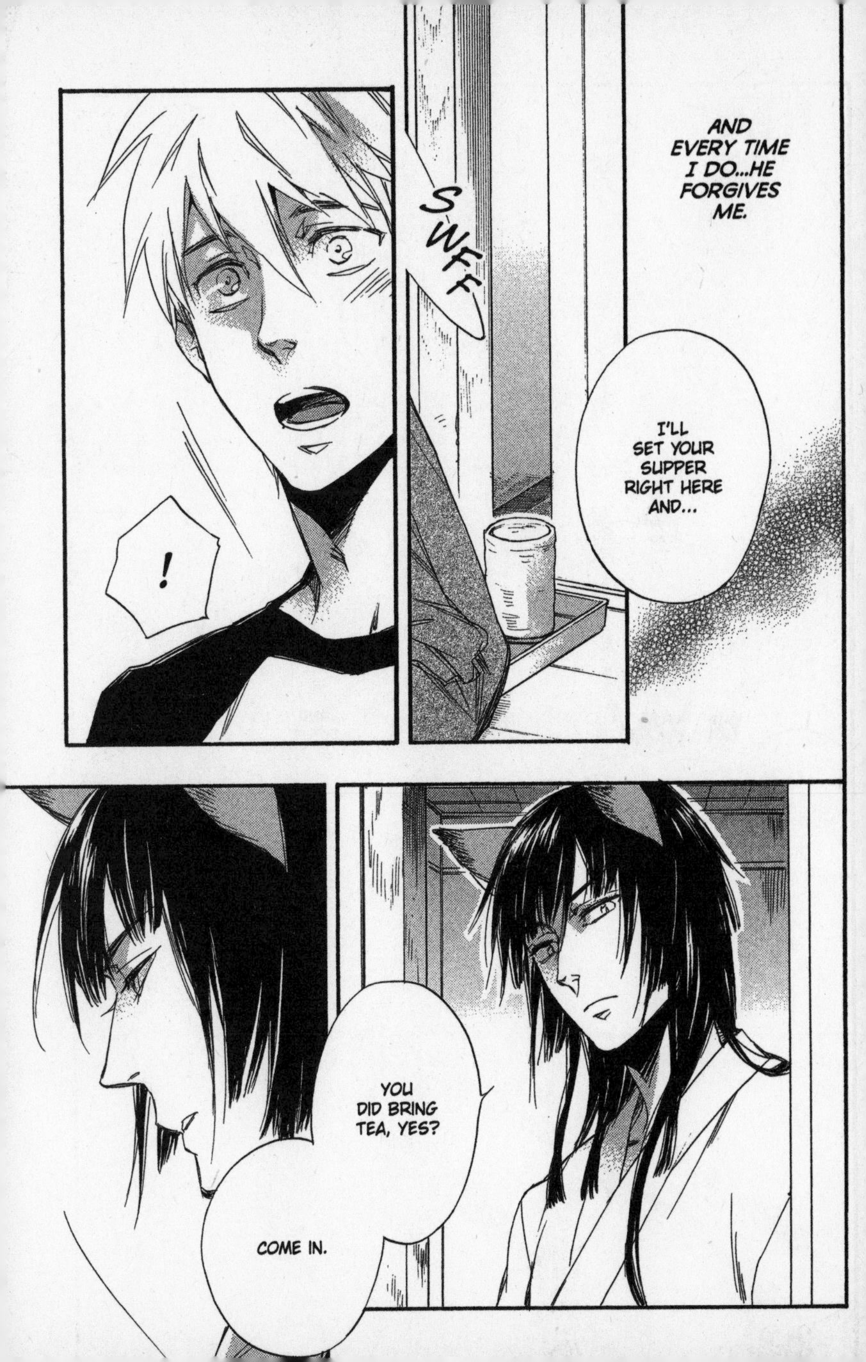
AND EVERY TIME I DO...HE FORGIVES ME.
I'LL SET YOUR SUPPER RIGHT HERE AND...
SWFF
!
YOU DID BRING TEA, YES?
COME IN.

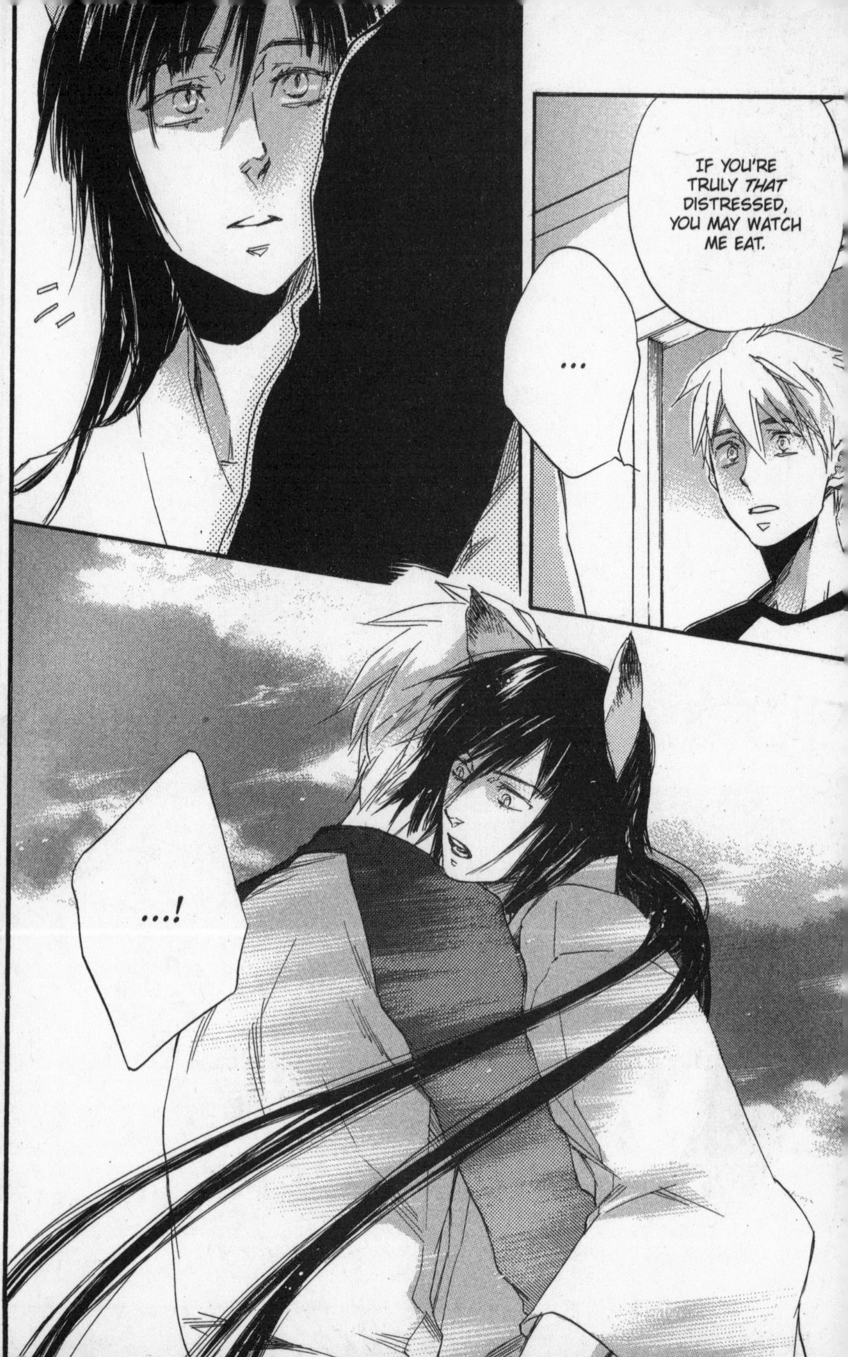
IF YOU'RE TRULY *THAT* DISTRESSED, YOU MAY WATCH ME EAT.
...
...!

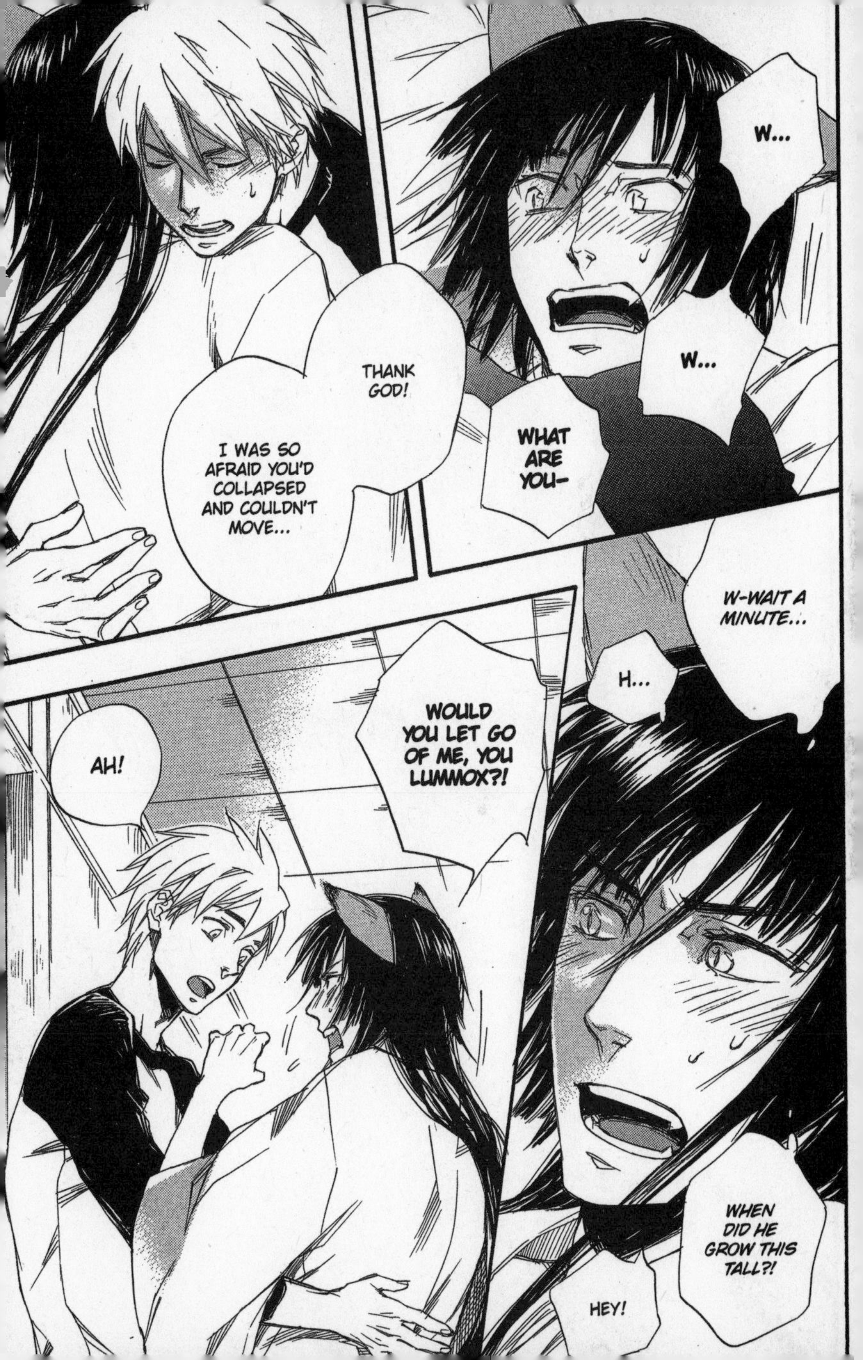
W...
W...
WHAT ARE YOU-
THANK GOD!
I WAS SO AFRAID YOU'D COLLAPSED AND COULDN'T MOVE...
W-WAIT A MINUTE...
H...
WHEN DID HE GROW THIS TALL?!
HEY!
WOULD YOU LET GO OF ME, YOU LUMMOX?!
AH!

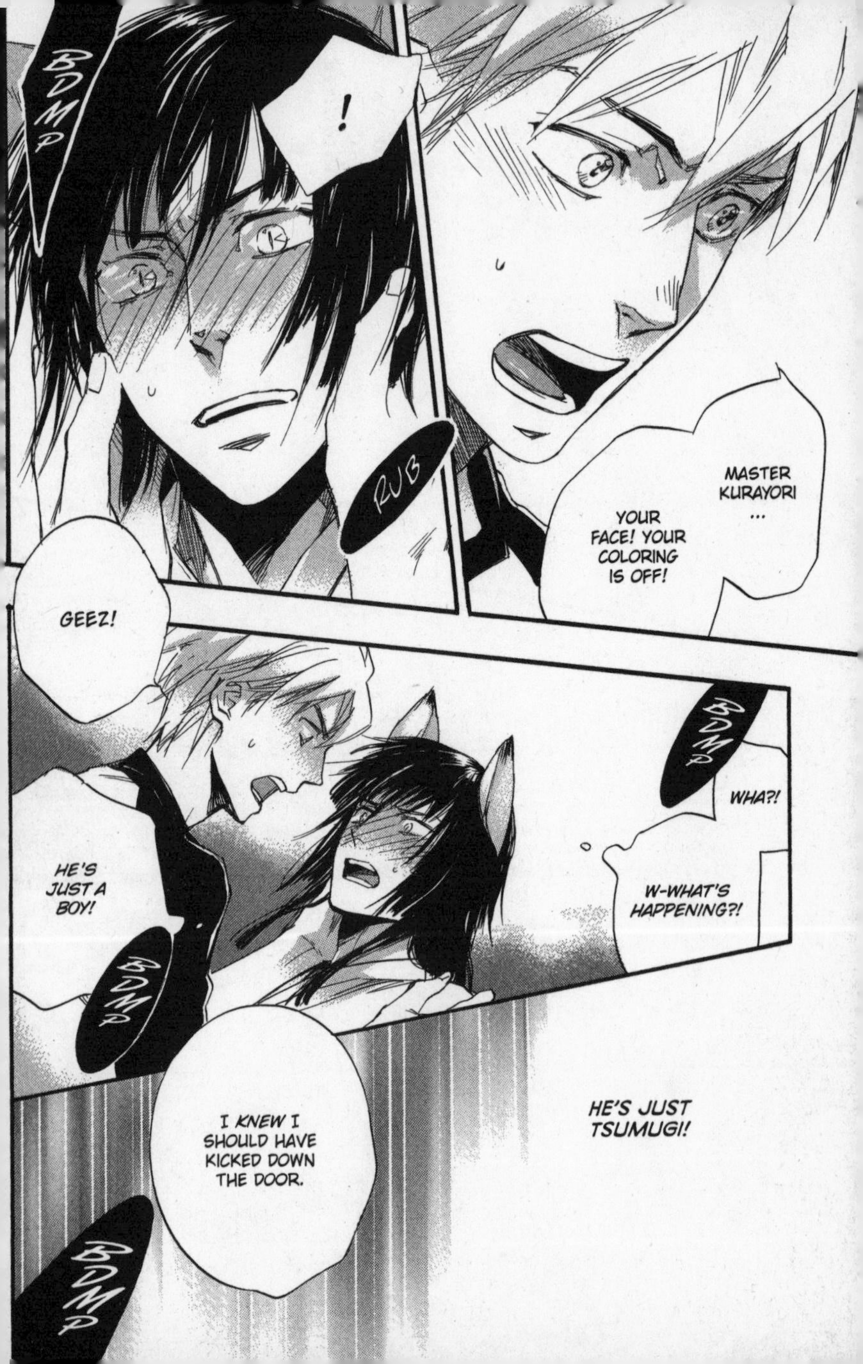
MASTER KURAYORI ...
YOUR FACE! YOUR COLORING IS OFF!
RUB
!
BDMP
BDMP
WHA?!
W-WHAT'S HAPPENING?!
GEEZ!
HE'S JUST A BOY!
BDMP
HE'S JUST TSUMUGI!
I KNEW I SHOULD HAVE KICKED DOWN THE DOOR.
BDMP

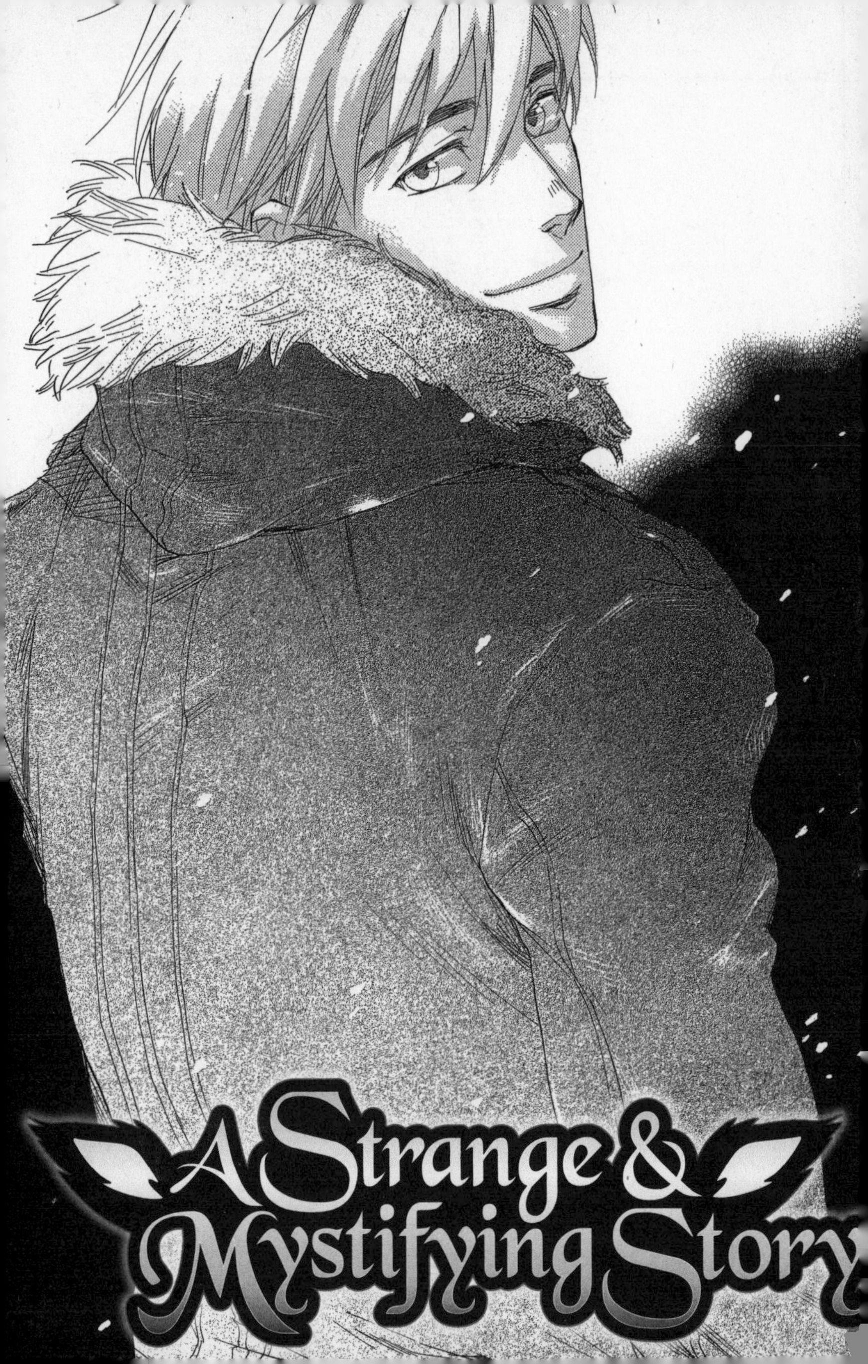
A Strange & Mystifying Story

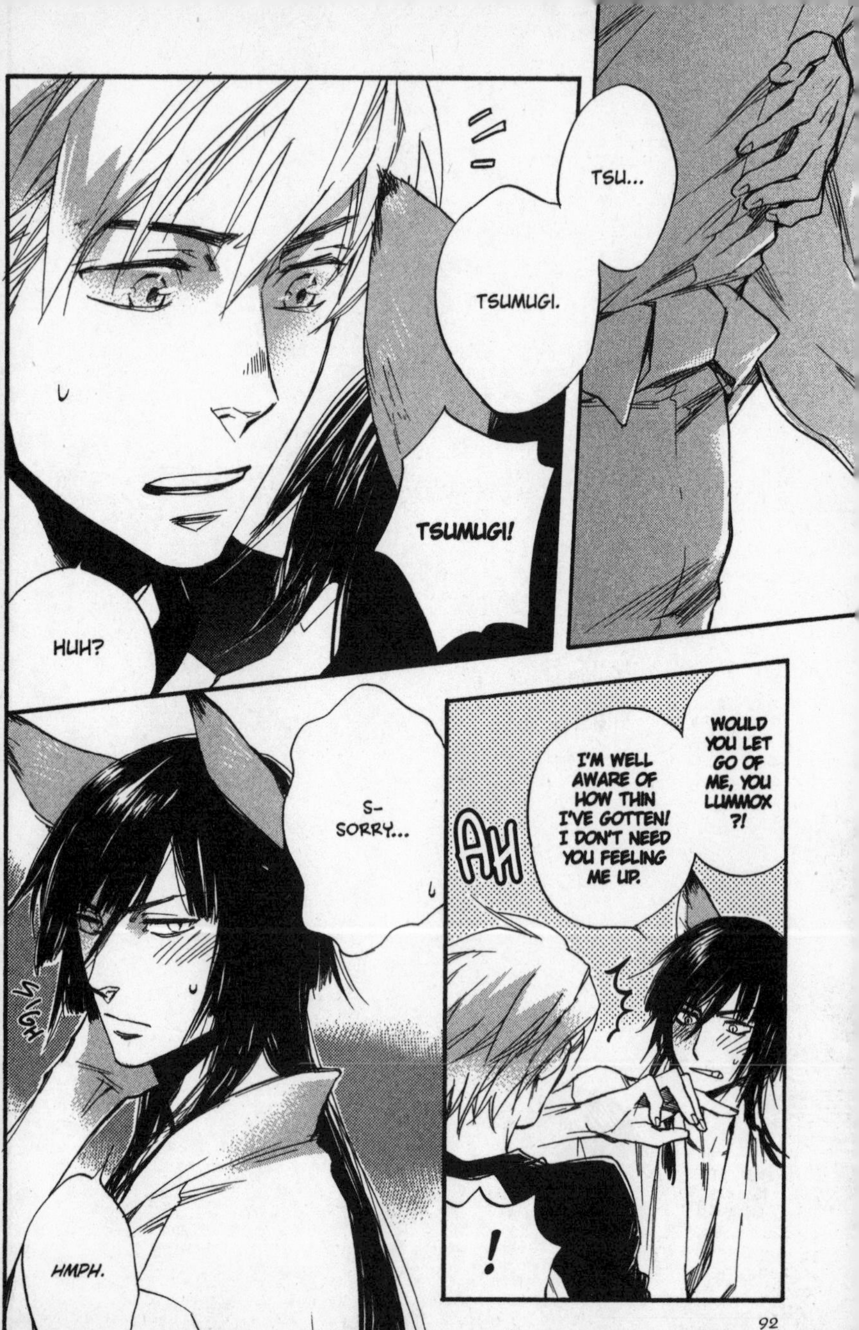
TSU...
TSUMUGI.
TSUMUGI!
HUH?
WOULD YOU LET GO OF ME, YOU LUMMOX?!
I'M WELL AWARE OF HOW THIN I'VE GOTTEN! I DON'T NEED YOU FEELING ME UP.
AH
!
S-SORRY...
SIGH
HMPH.

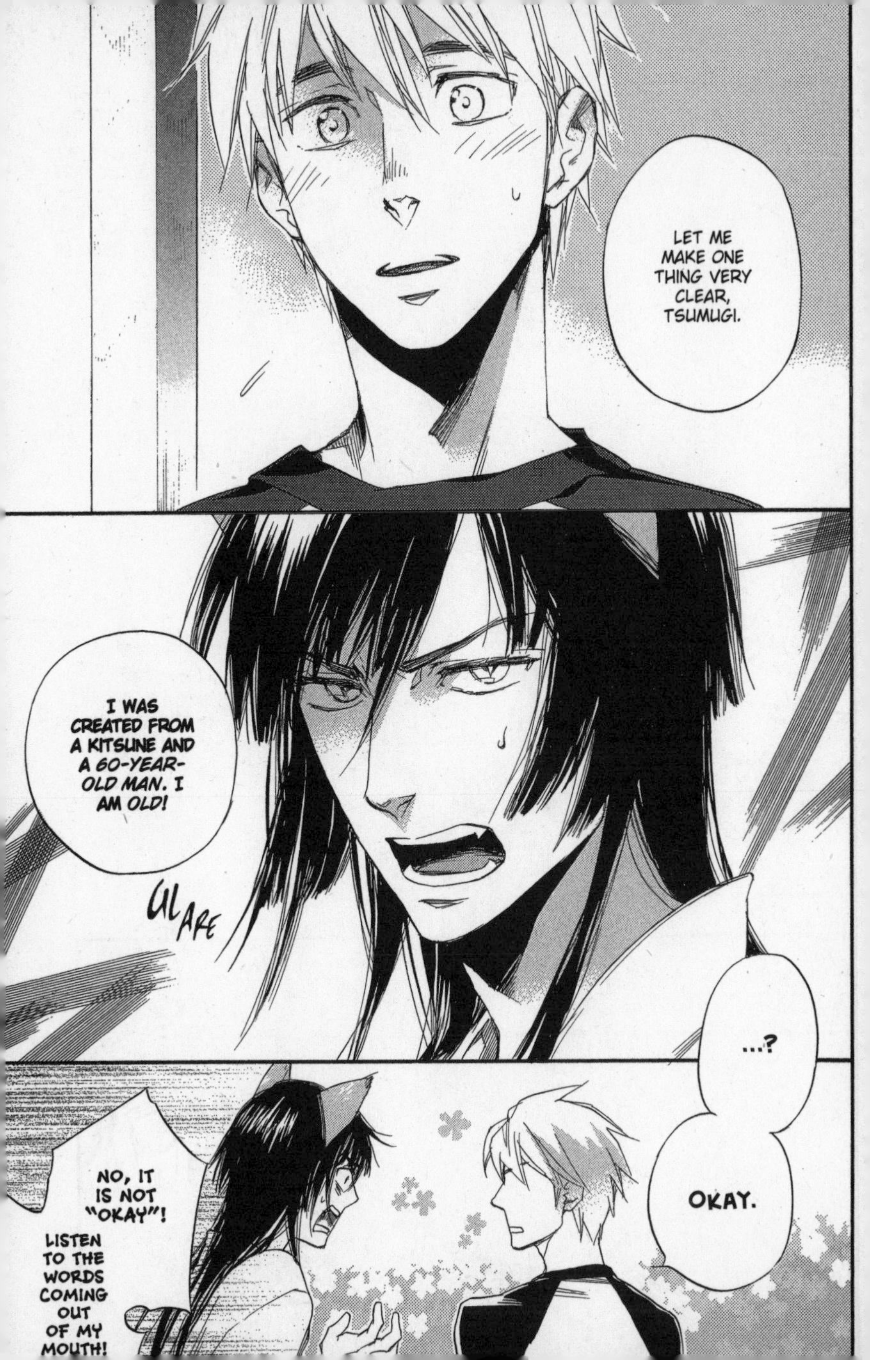
LET ME MAKE ONE THING VERY CLEAR, TSUMUGI.
I WAS CREATED FROM A KITSUNE AND A 60-YEAR-OLD MAN. I AM OLD!
GLARE
...?
OKAY.
NO, IT IS NOT "OKAY"!
LISTEN TO THE WORDS COMING OUT OF MY MOUTH!

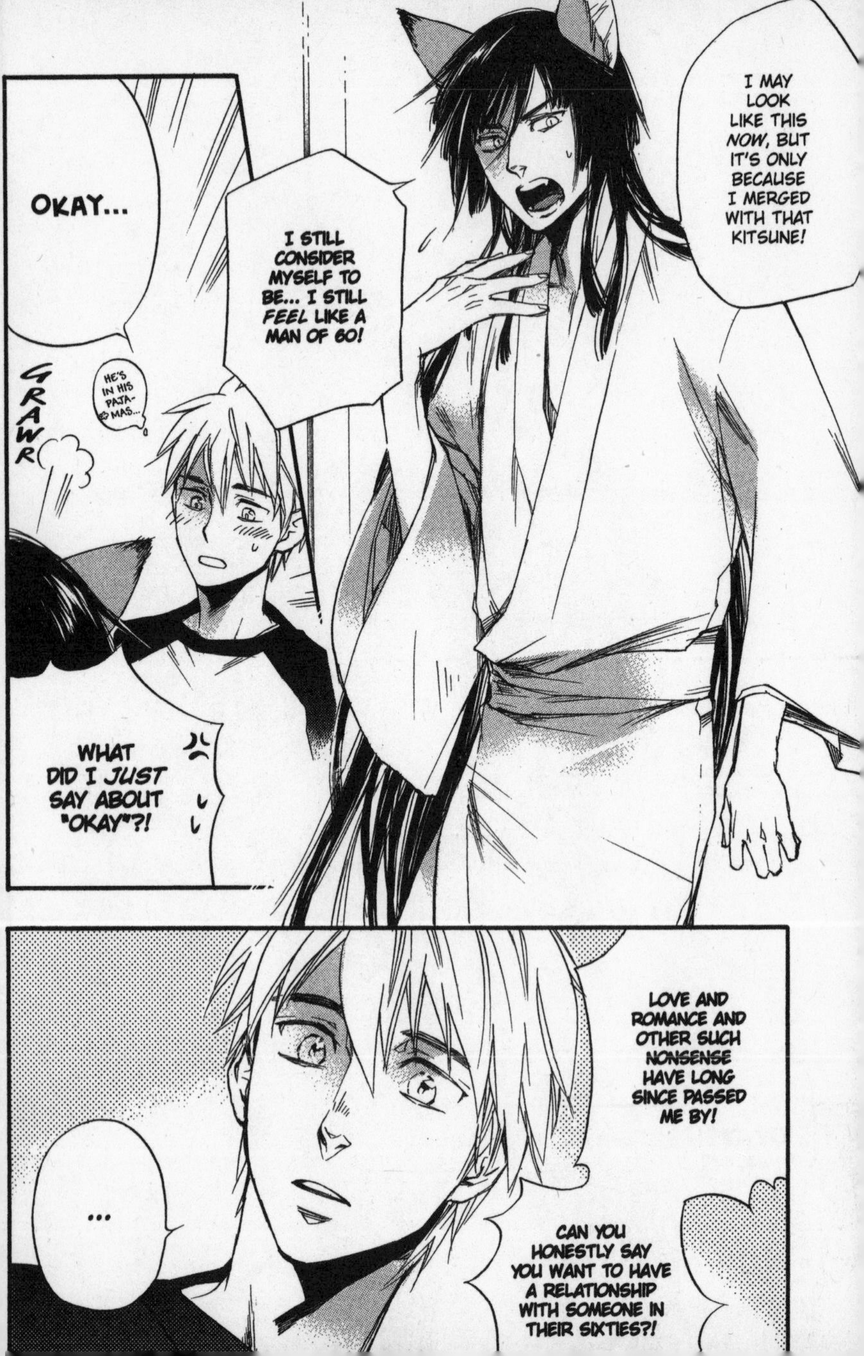
I MAY LOOK LIKE THIS *NOW*, BUT IT'S ONLY BECAUSE I MERGED WITH THAT KITSUNE!
I STILL CONSIDER MYSELF TO BE... I STILL *FEEL* LIKE A MAN OF 60!
OKAY...
HE'S IN HIS PAJAMAS...
GRAWR
WHAT DID I *JUST* SAY ABOUT "OKAY"?!
LOVE AND ROMANCE AND OTHER SUCH NONSENSE HAVE LONG SINCE PASSED ME BY!
CAN YOU HONESTLY SAY YOU WANT TO HAVE A RELATIONSHIP WITH SOMEONE IN THEIR SIXTIES?!
...

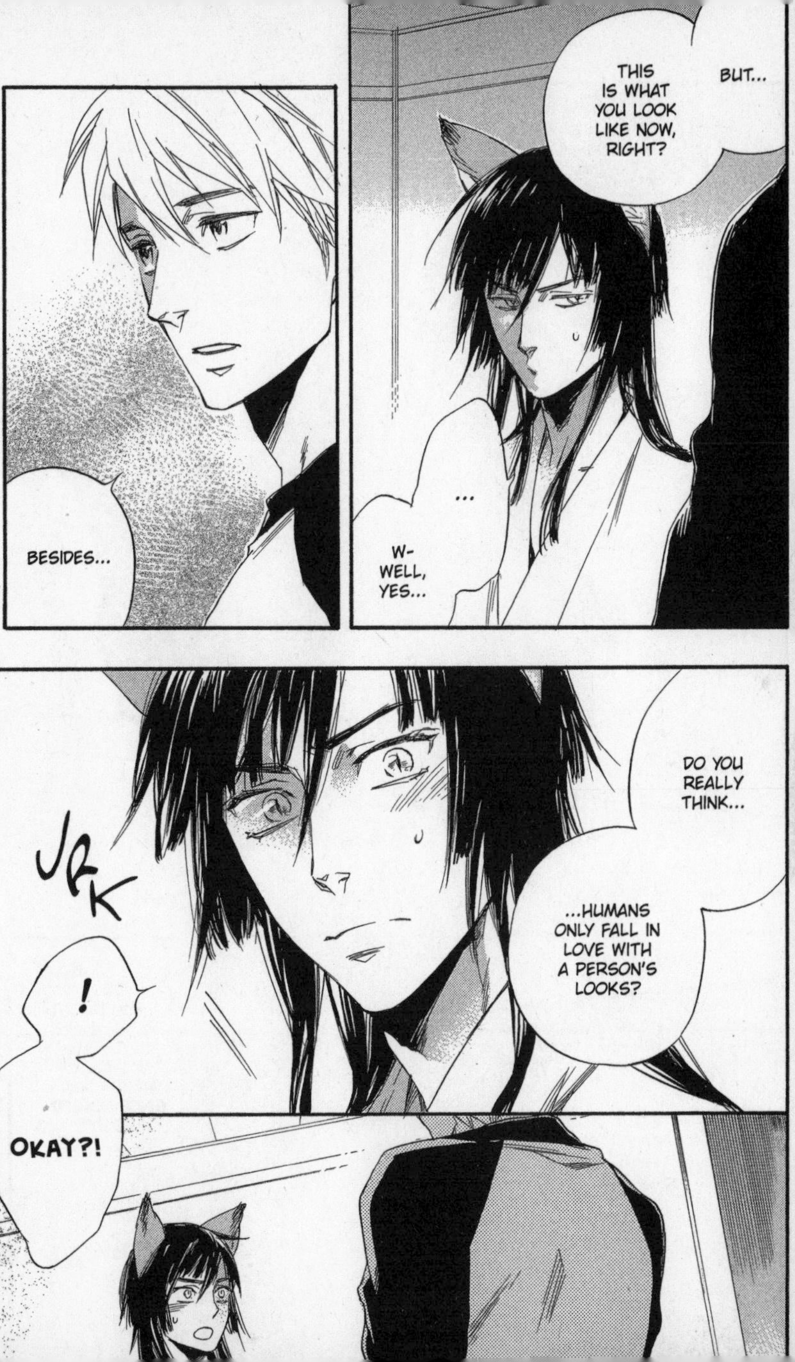
BUT...
THIS IS WHAT YOU LOOK LIKE NOW, RIGHT?
...
W-WELL, YES...
BESIDES...
DO YOU REALLY THINK...
...HUMANS ONLY FALL IN LOVE WITH A PERSON'S LOOKS?
JRK
!
OKAY?!

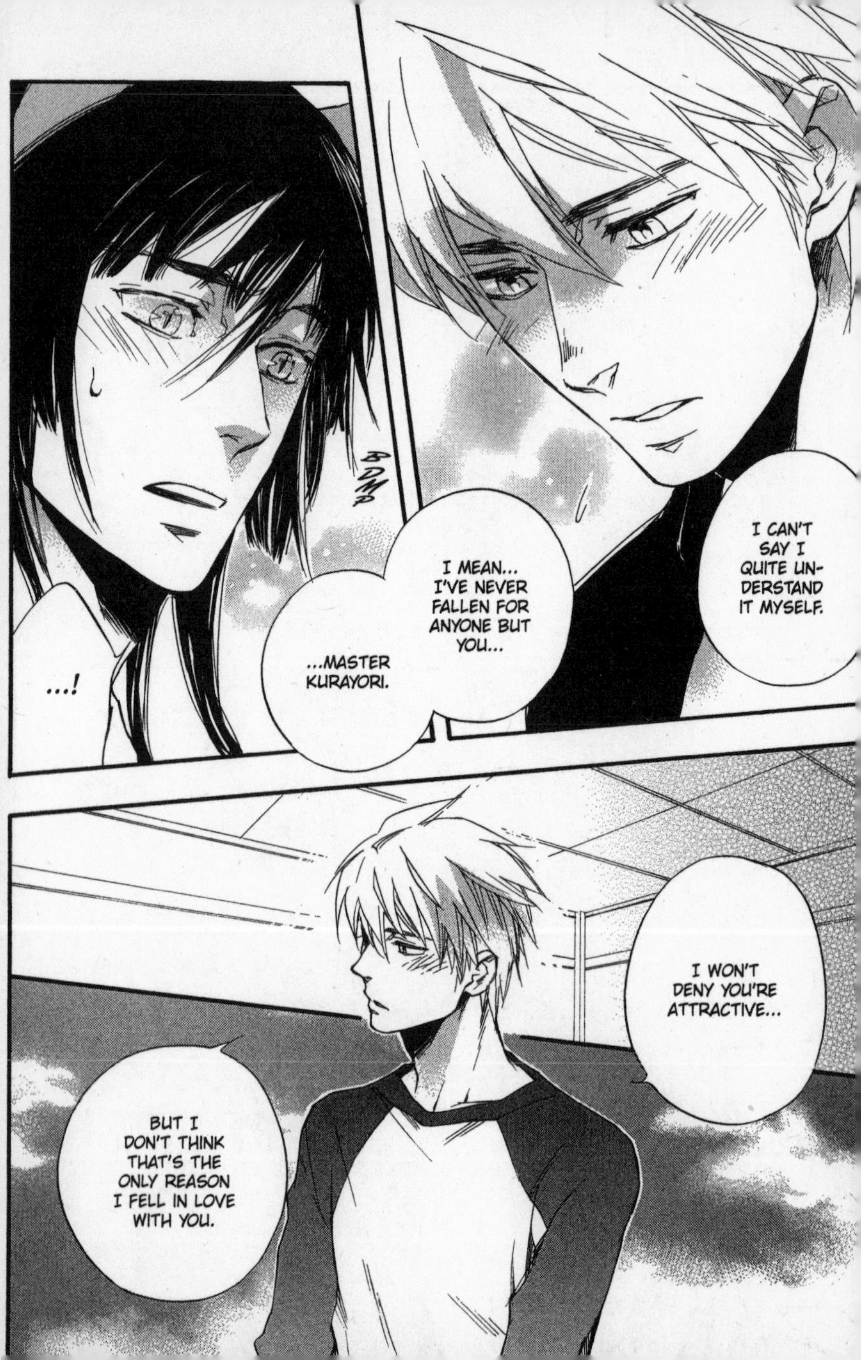
I CAN'T SAY I QUITE UN-DERSTAND IT MYSELF.
I MEAN... I'VE NEVER FALLEN FOR ANYONE BUT YOU...
...MASTER KURAYORI.
BDMP
...!
I WON'T DENY YOU'RE ATTRACTIVE...
BUT I DON'T THINK THAT'S THE ONLY REASON I FELL IN LOVE WITH YOU.

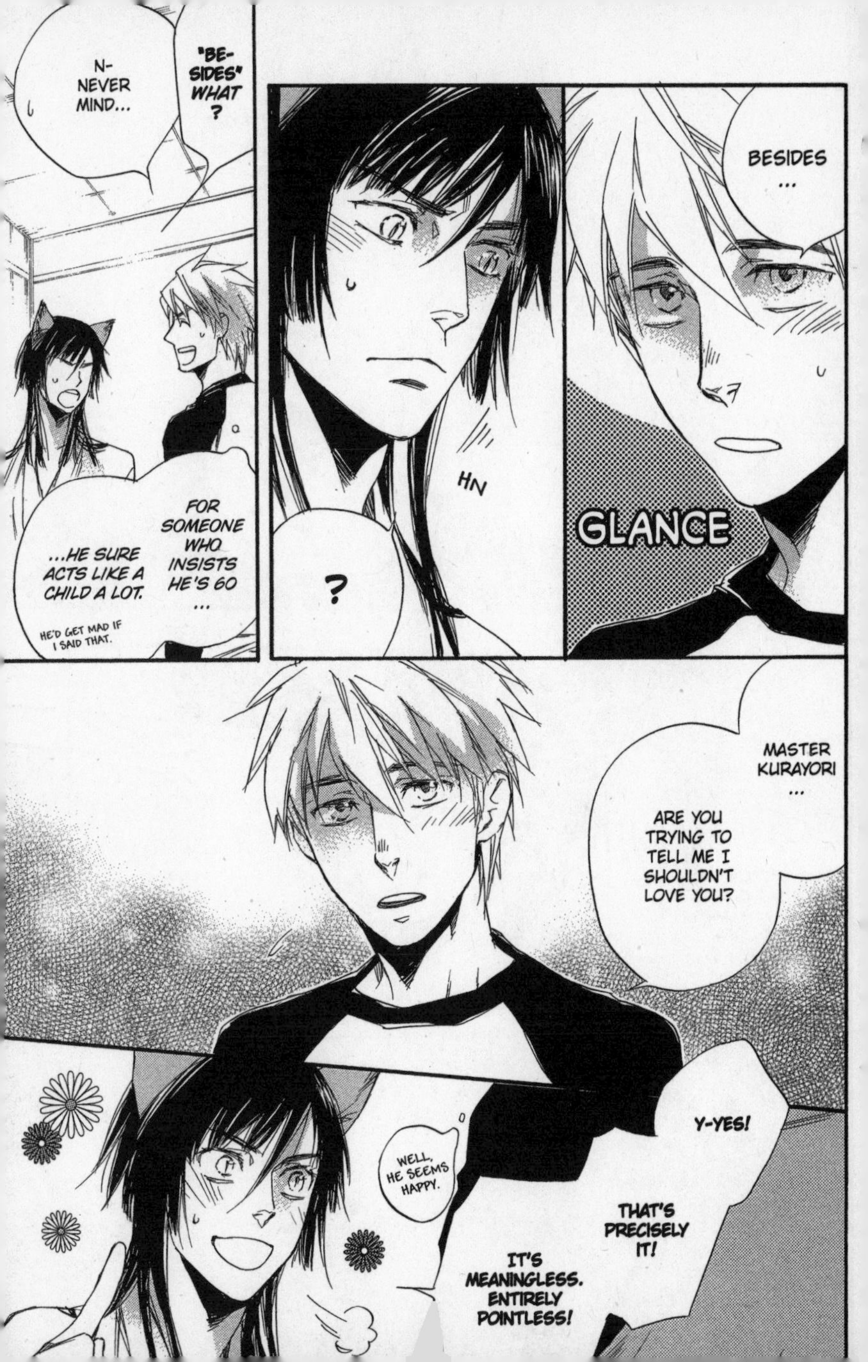
BESIDES ...
GLANCE
HN
?
"BE-SIDES" WHAT?
N-NEVER MIND...
FOR SOMEONE WHO INSISTS HE'S 60 ...
...HE SURE ACTS LIKE A CHILD A LOT.
HE'D GET MAD IF I SAID THAT.
MASTER KURAYORI ...
ARE YOU TRYING TO TELL ME I SHOULDN'T LOVE YOU?
Y-YES!
THAT'S PRECISELY IT!
IT'S MEANINGLESS. ENTIRELY POINTLESS!
WELL, HE SEEMS HAPPY.

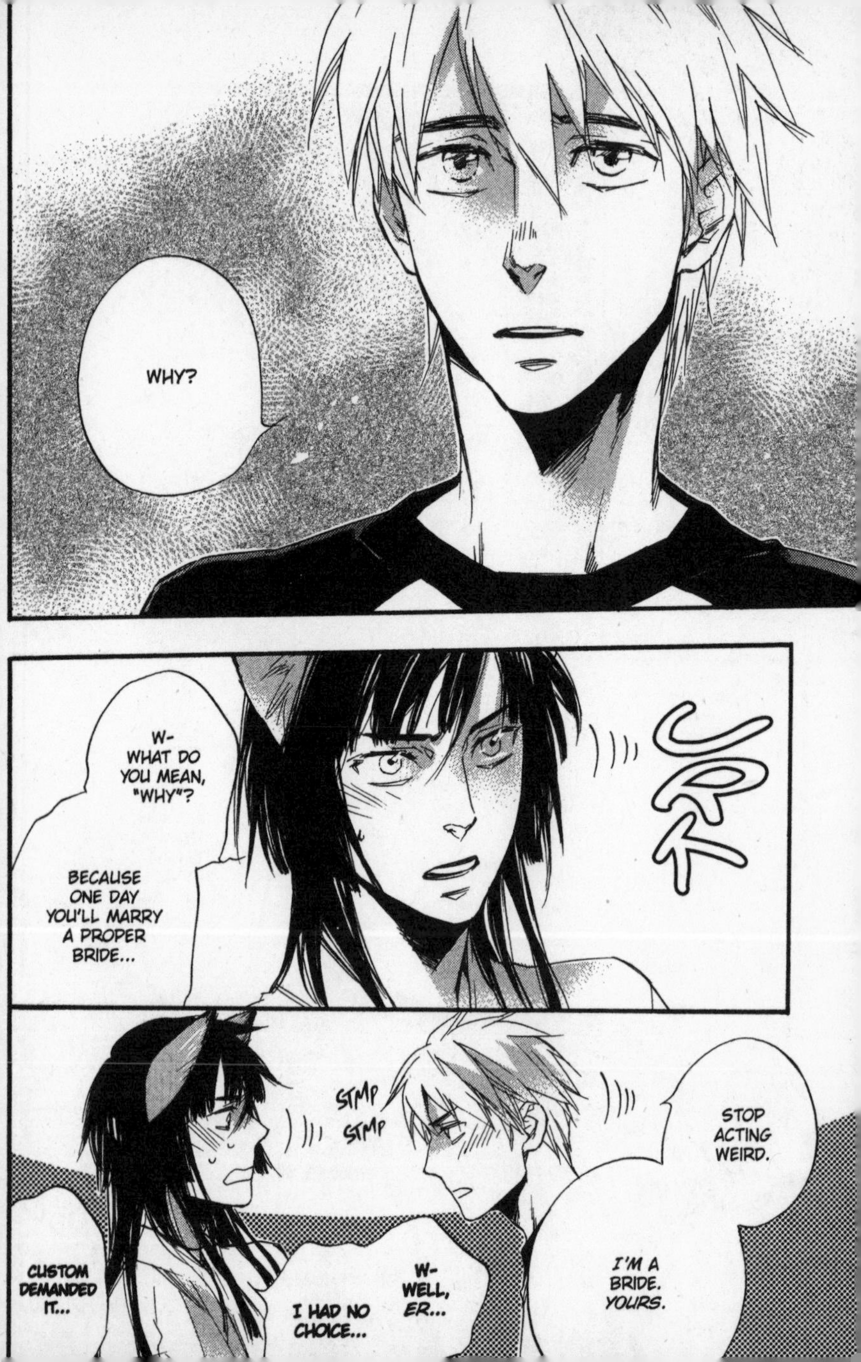
WHY?
URK
W- WHAT DO YOU MEAN, "WHY"?
BECAUSE ONE DAY YOU'LL MARRY A PROPER BRIDE...
STOP ACTING WEIRD.
I'M A BRIDE. YOURS.
STMP STMP
W- WELL, ER...
I HAD NO CHOICE...
CUSTOM DEMANDED IT...

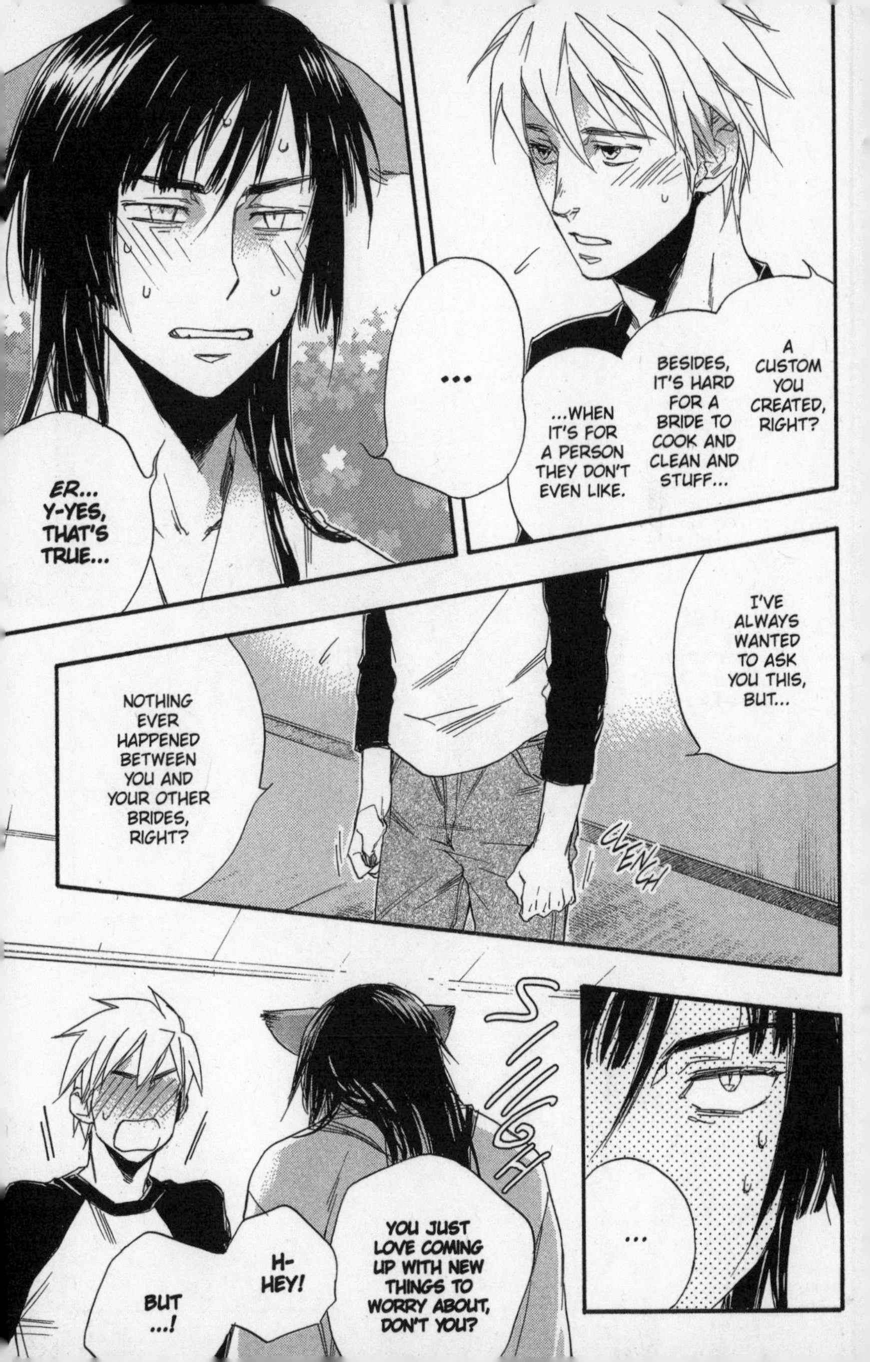
A CUSTOM YOU CREATED, RIGHT?
BESIDES, IT'S HARD FOR A BRIDE TO COOK AND CLEAN AND STUFF...
...WHEN IT'S FOR A PERSON THEY DON'T EVEN LIKE.
...
ER... Y-YES, THAT'S TRUE...
I'VE ALWAYS WANTED TO ASK YOU THIS, BUT...
NOTHING EVER HAPPENED BETWEEN YOU AND YOUR OTHER BRIDES, RIGHT?
CLENCH
...
SIIGH
YOU JUST LOVE COMING UP WITH NEW THINGS TO WORRY ABOUT, DON'T YOU?
H-HEY!
BUT ...!

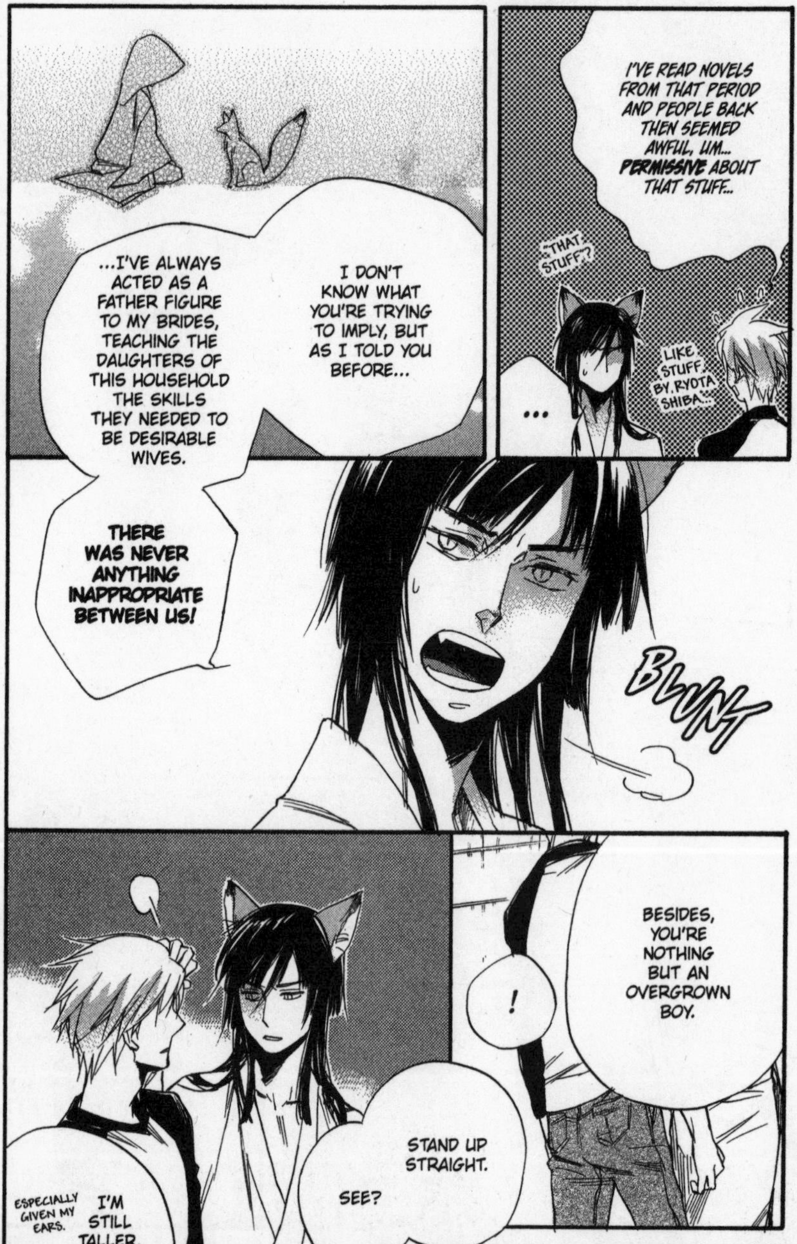
I'VE READ NOVELS FROM THAT PERIOD AND PEOPLE BACK THEN SEEMED AWFUL, UM... PERMISSIVE ABOUT THAT STUFF...
"THAT STUFF"?
LIKE STUFF BY RYOTA SHIBA...
...
I DON'T KNOW WHAT YOU'RE TRYING TO IMPLY, BUT AS I TOLD YOU BEFORE...
...I'VE ALWAYS ACTED AS A FATHER FIGURE TO MY BRIDES, TEACHING THE DAUGHTERS OF THIS HOUSEHOLD THE SKILLS THEY NEEDED TO BE DESIRABLE WIVES.
THERE WAS NEVER ANYTHING INAPPROPRIATE BETWEEN US!
BLUNT
BESIDES, YOU'RE NOTHING BUT AN OVERGROWN BOY.
!
STAND UP STRAIGHT.
SEE?
I'M STILL TALLER.
ESPECIALLY GIVEN MY EARS.

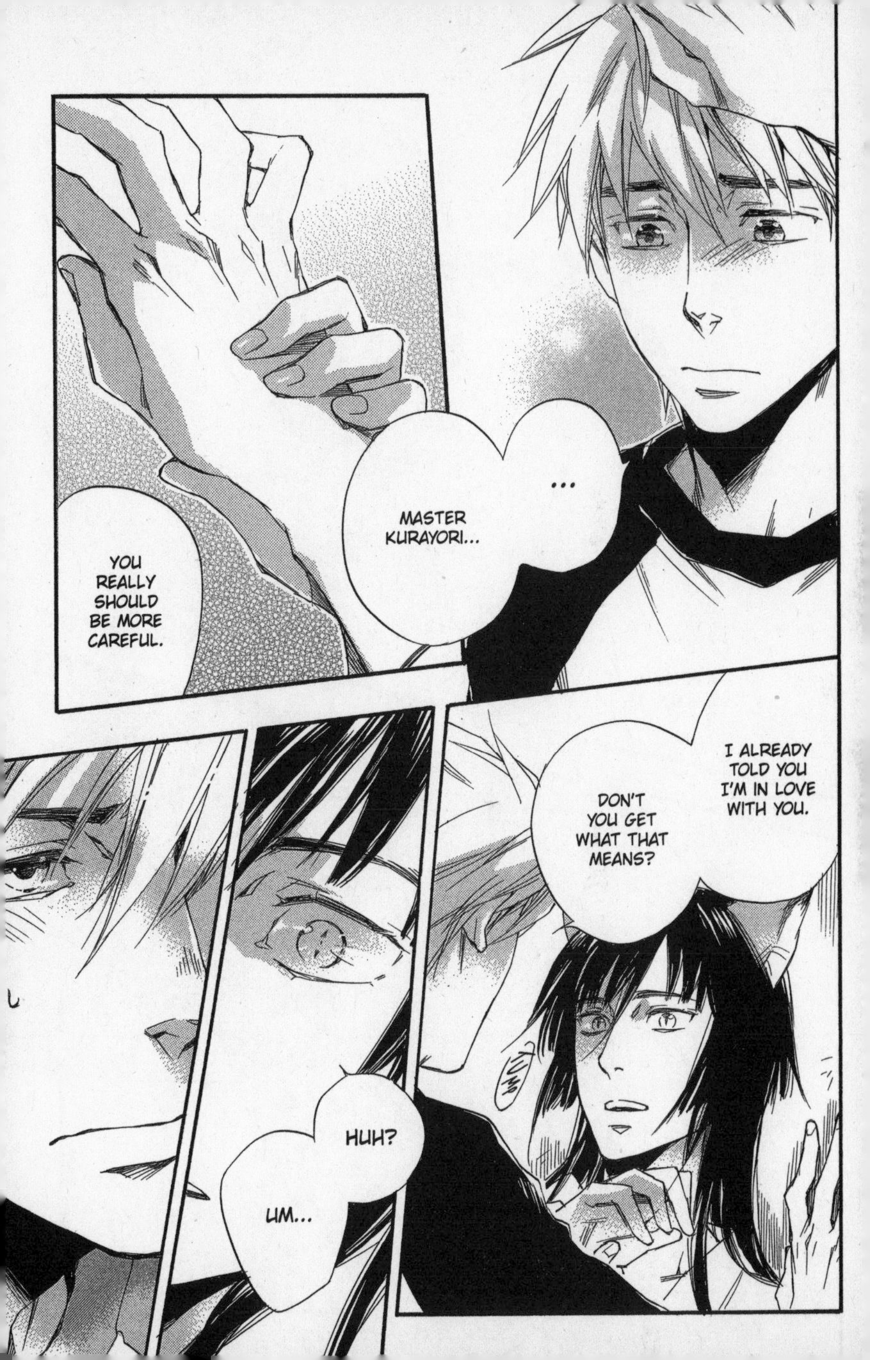
...
MASTER KURAYORI...
YOU REALLY SHOULD BE MORE CAREFUL.
I ALREADY TOLD YOU I'M IN LOVE WITH YOU.
DON'T YOU GET WHAT THAT MEANS?
HUH?
UM...

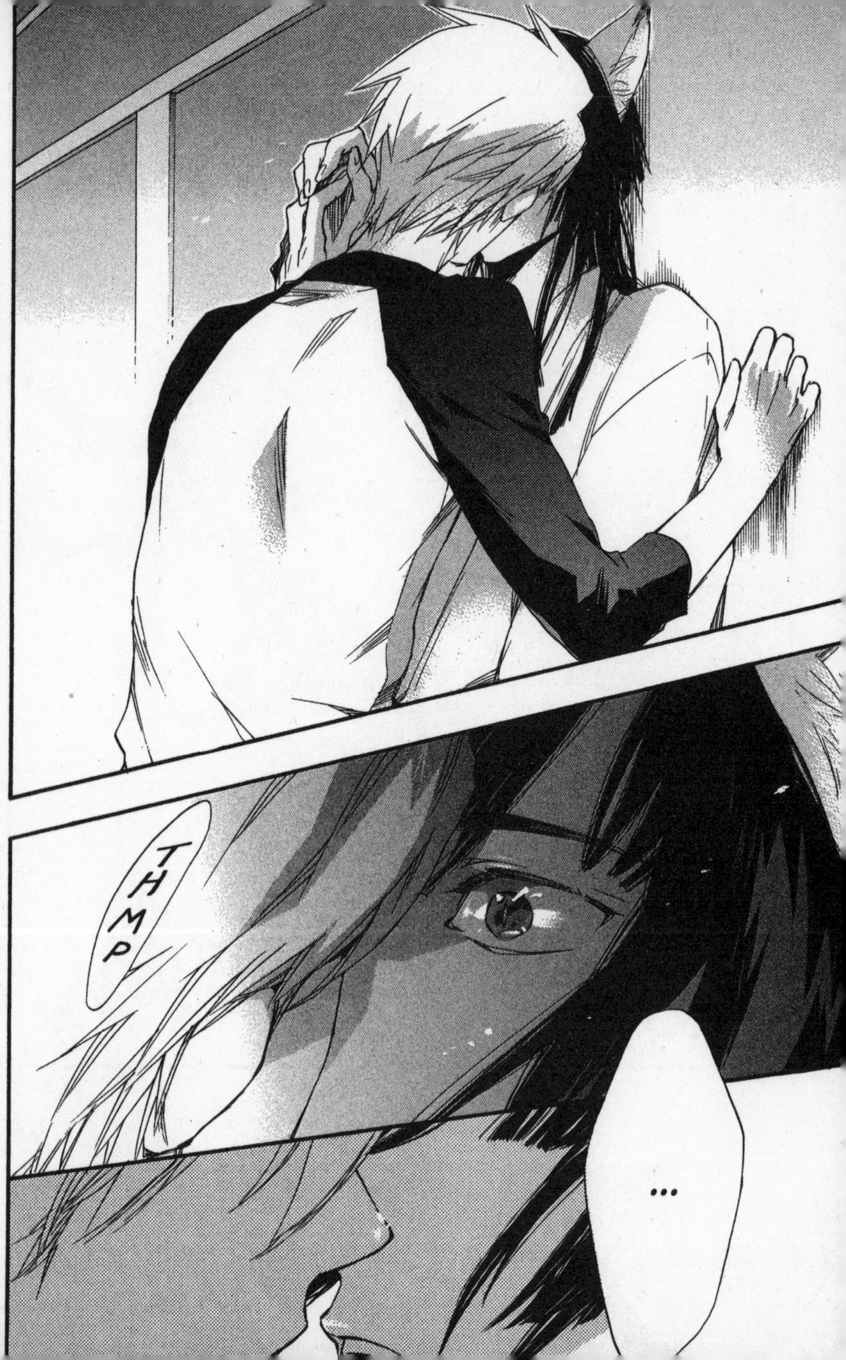
THMP
...

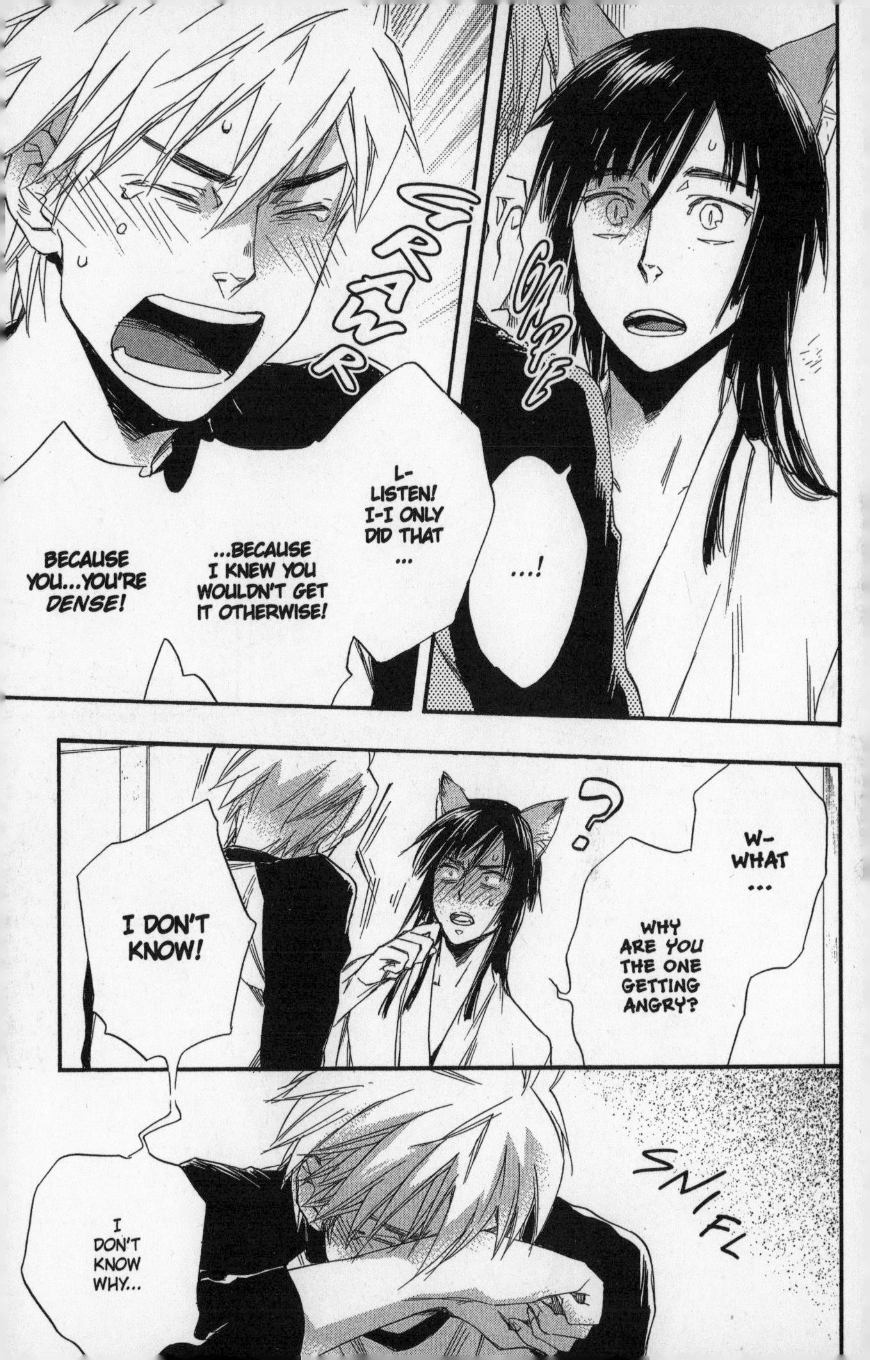
...!
RAWR
L- LISTEN! I-I ONLY DID THAT ...
...BECAUSE I KNEW YOU WOULDN'T GET IT OTHERWISE!
BECAUSE YOU...YOU'RE *DENSE!*
W- WHAT ...
WHY ARE YOU THE ONE GETTING ANGRY?
I DON'T KNOW!
SNIFL
I DON'T KNOW WHY...

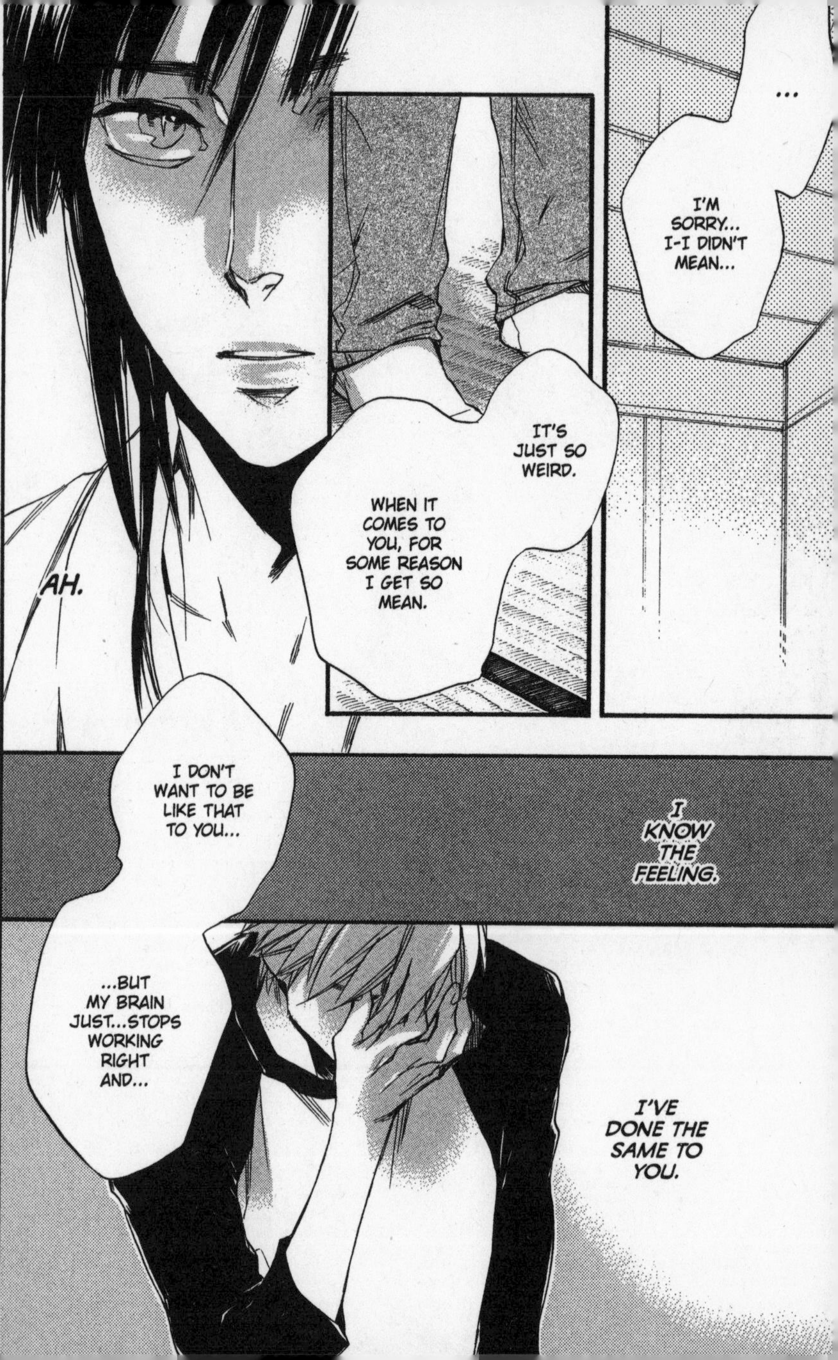
...
I'M SORRY... I-I DIDN'T MEAN...
IT'S JUST SO WEIRD.
WHEN IT COMES TO YOU, FOR SOME REASON I GET SO MEAN.
AH.
I KNOW THE FEELING.
I DON'T WANT TO BE LIKE THAT TO YOU...
...BUT MY BRAIN JUST...STOPS WORKING RIGHT AND...
I'VE DONE THE SAME TO YOU.

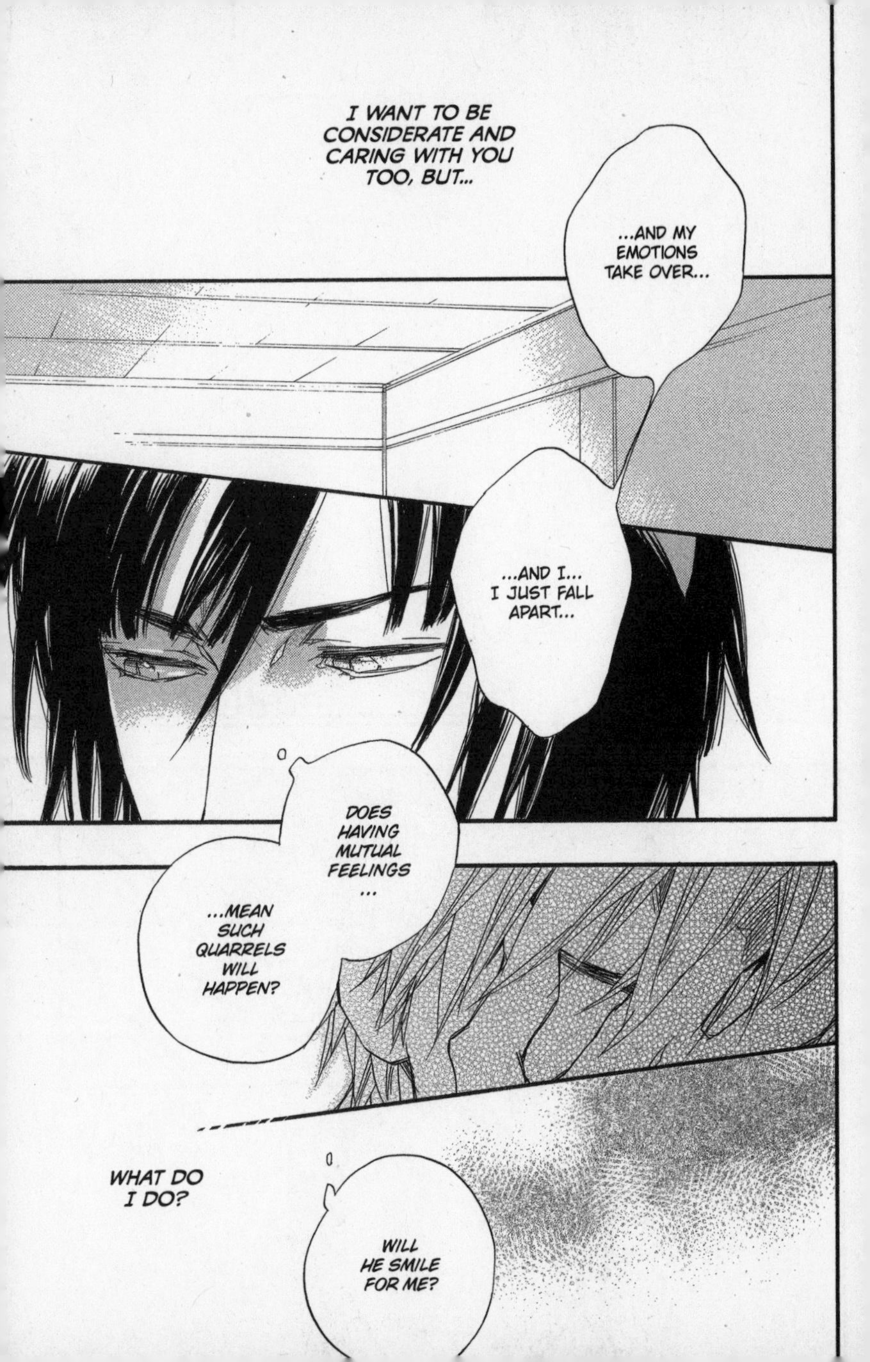
I WANT TO BE CONSIDERATE AND CARING WITH YOU TOO, BUT...
...AND MY EMOTIONS TAKE OVER...
...AND I... I JUST FALL APART...
DOES HAVING MUTUAL FEELINGS...
...MEAN SUCH QUARRELS WILL HAPPEN?
WHAT DO I DO?
WILL HE SMILE FOR ME?

WHAT CAN I DO FOR YOU?

TSUMU—

GURRRGL

...?

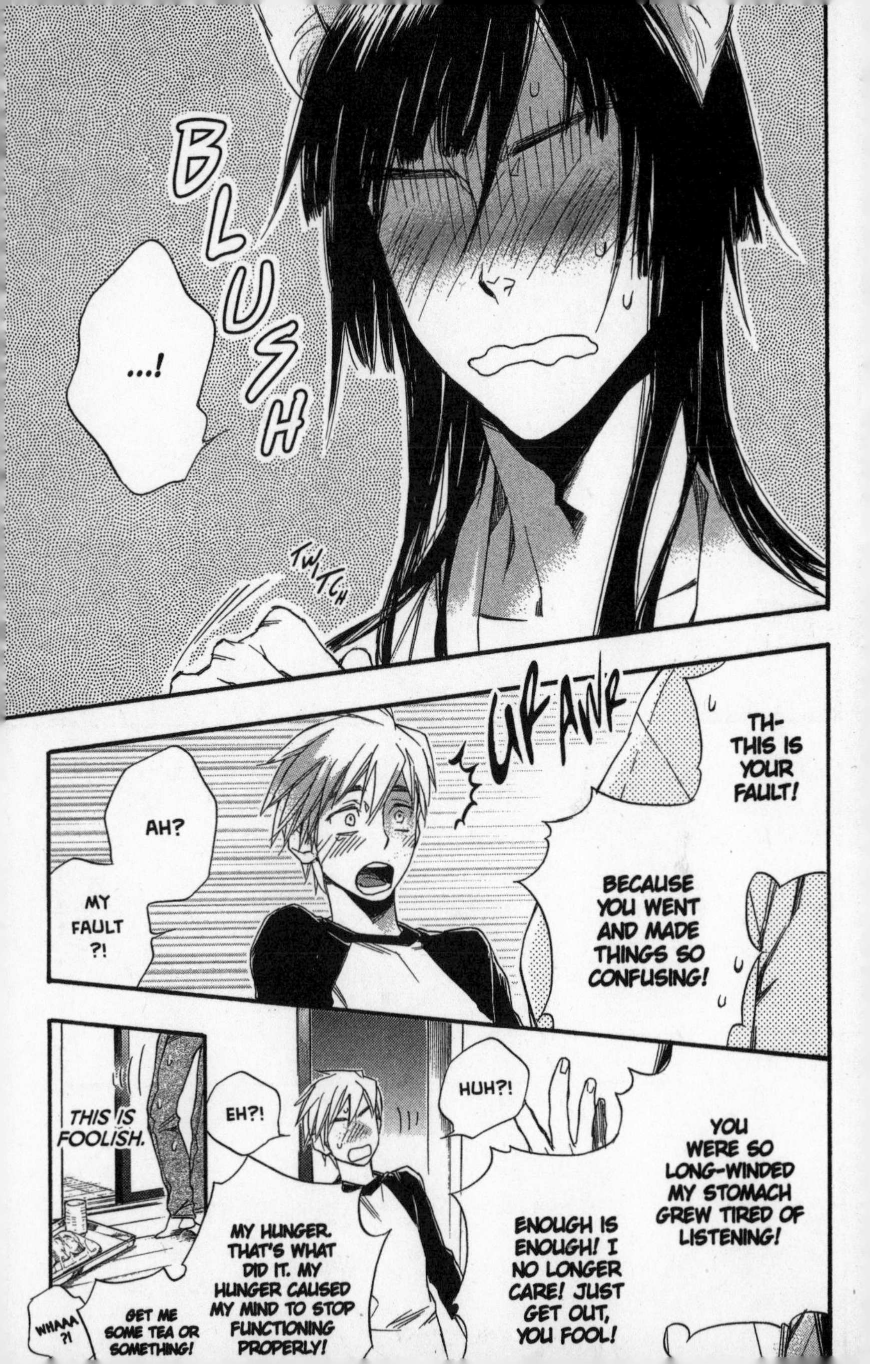
BLUSH
...!
TWITCH
TH- THIS IS YOUR FAULT!
BECAUSE YOU WENT AND MADE THINGS SO CONFUSING!
AH?
MY FAULT ?!
YOU WERE SO LONG-WINDED MY STOMACH GREW TIRED OF LISTENING!
HUH?!
ENOUGH IS ENOUGH! I NO LONGER CARE! JUST GET OUT, YOU FOOL!
EH?!
MY HUNGER. THAT'S WHAT DID IT. MY HUNGER CAUSED MY MIND TO STOP FUNCTIONING PROPERLY!
THIS IS FOOLISH.
GET ME SOME TEA OR SOMETHING!
WHAAA ?!

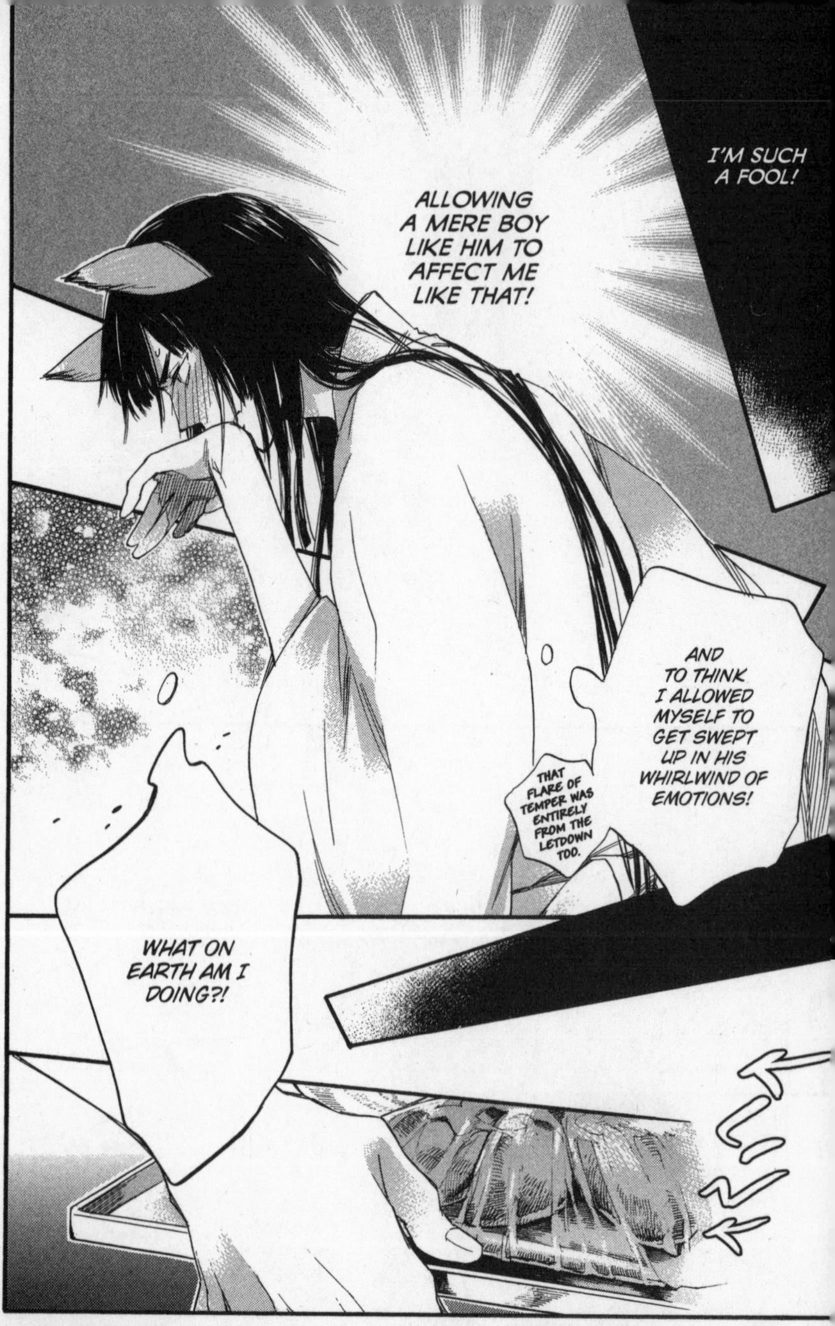
I'M SUCH A FOOL!
ALLOWING A MERE BOY LIKE HIM TO AFFECT ME LIKE THAT!
AND TO THINK I ALLOWED MYSELF TO GET SWEPT UP IN HIS WHIRLWIND OF EMOTIONS!
THAT FLARE OF TEMPER WAS ENTIRELY FROM THE LETDOWN TOO.
WHAT ON EARTH AM I DOING?!

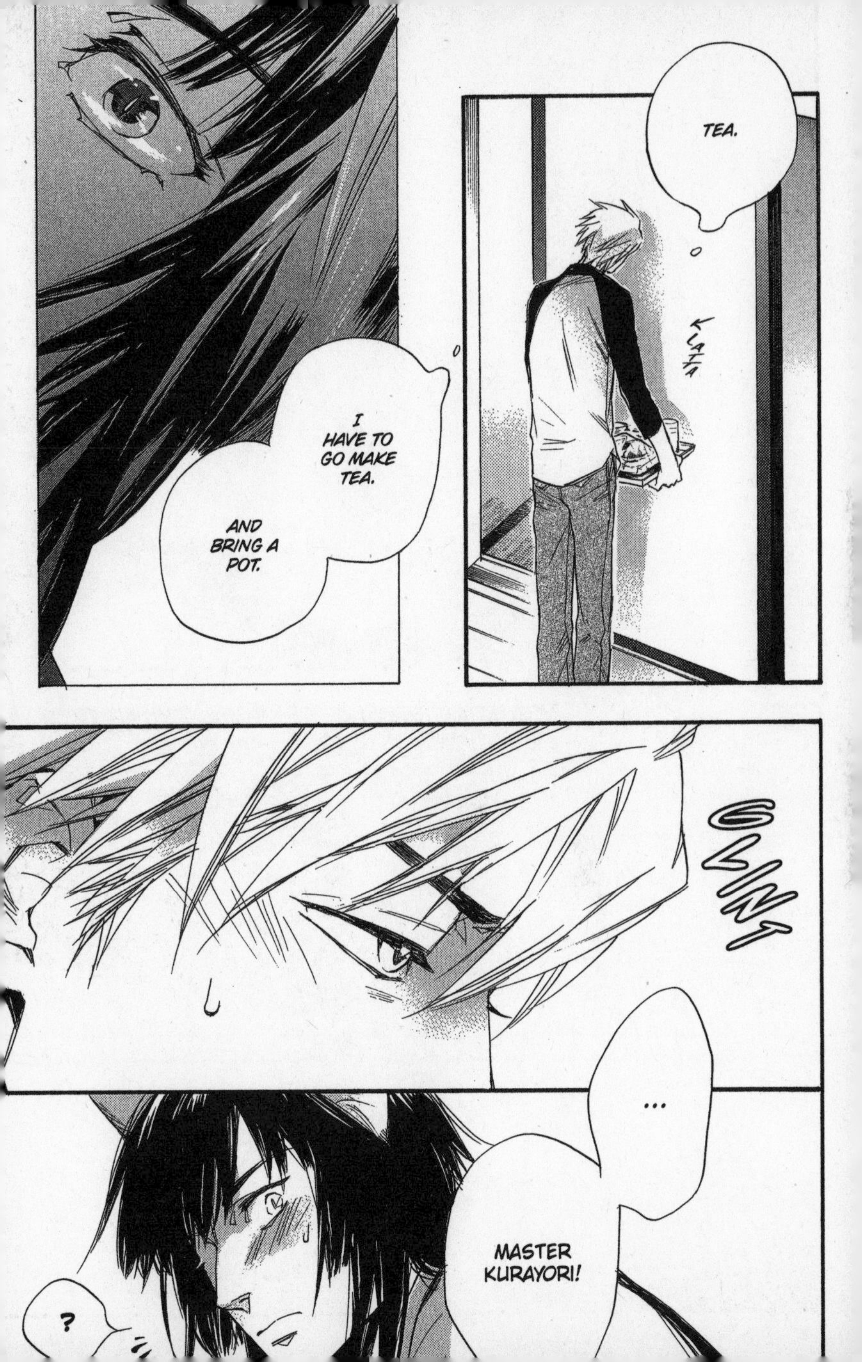
TEA.
KLAKA
I HAVE TO GO MAKE TEA.
AND BRING A POT.
GLINT
...
MASTER KURAYORI!
?

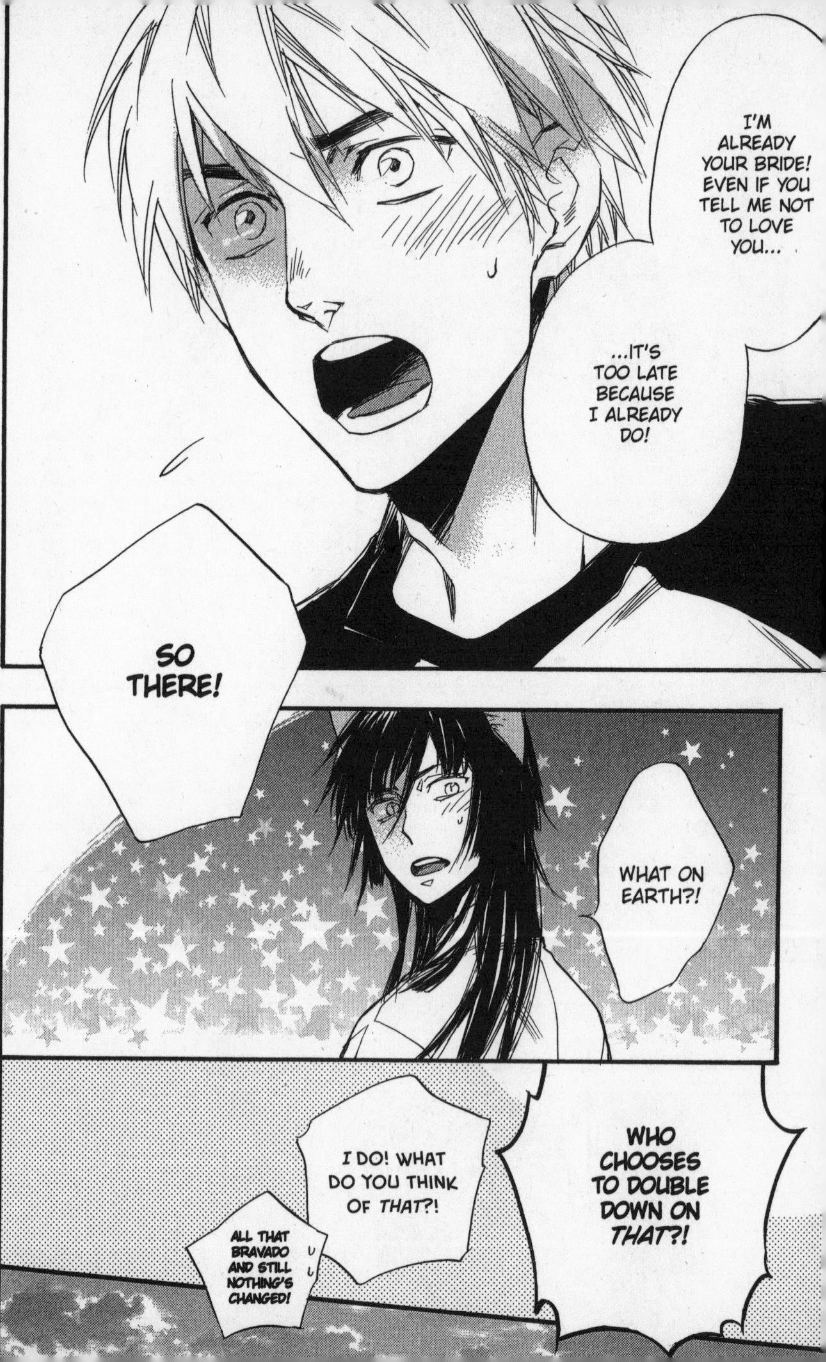
I'M ALREADY YOUR BRIDE! EVEN IF YOU TELL ME NOT TO LOVE YOU...
...IT'S TOO LATE BECAUSE I ALREADY DO!
SO THERE!
WHAT ON EARTH?!
WHO CHOOSES TO DOUBLE DOWN ON *THAT*?!
I DO! WHAT DO YOU THINK OF *THAT*?!
ALL THAT BRAVADO AND STILL NOTHING'S CHANGED!

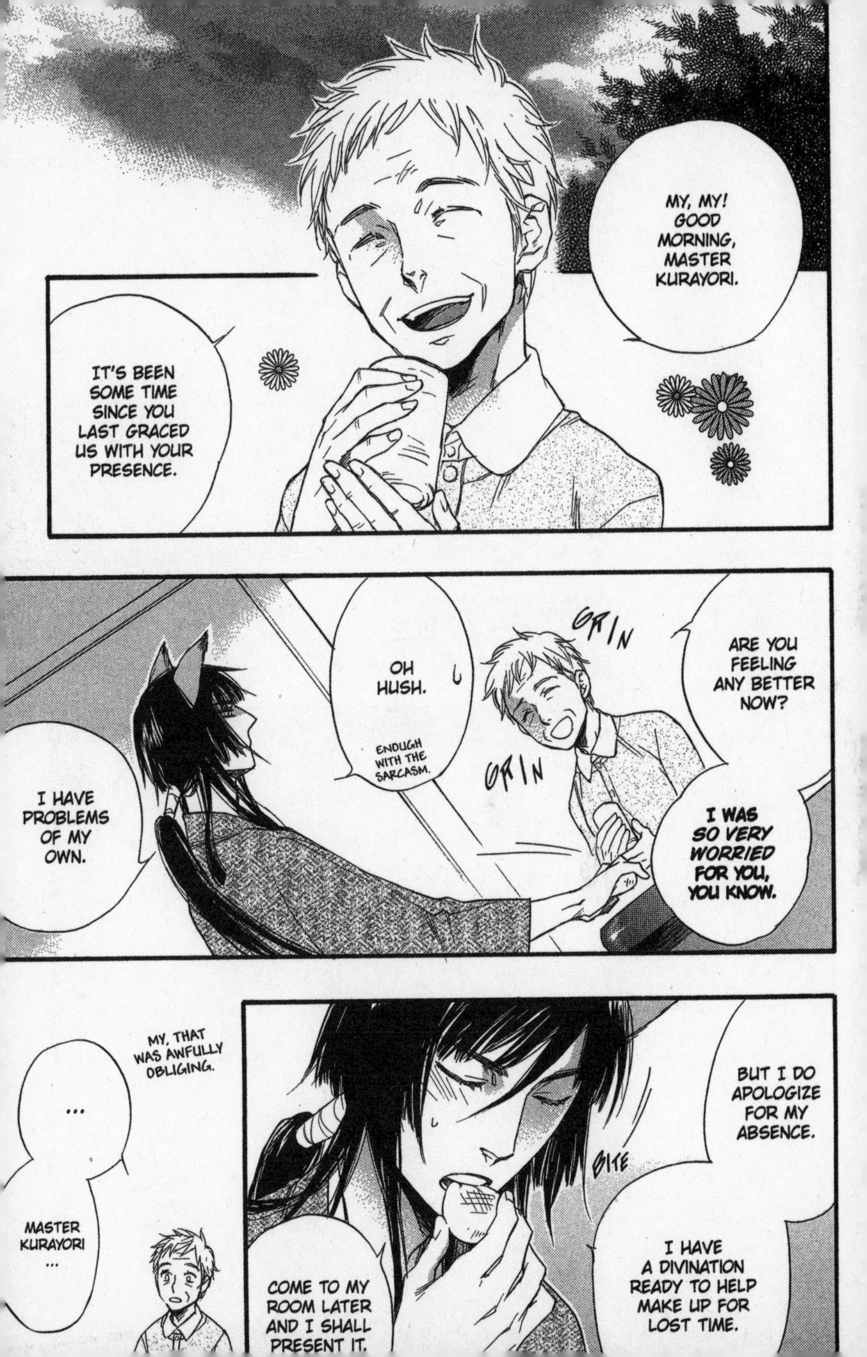
MY, MY! GOOD MORNING, MASTER KURAYORI.
IT'S BEEN SOME TIME SINCE YOU LAST GRACED US WITH YOUR PRESENCE.
GRIN
ARE YOU FEELING ANY BETTER NOW?
GRIN
I WAS *SO VERY WORRIED* FOR YOU, YOU KNOW.
OH HUSH.
ENOUGH WITH THE SARCASM.
I HAVE PROBLEMS OF MY OWN.
BUT I DO APOLOGIZE FOR MY ABSENCE.
BITE
I HAVE A DIVINATION READY TO HELP MAKE UP FOR LOST TIME.
COME TO MY ROOM LATER AND I SHALL PRESENT IT.
MY, THAT WAS AWFULLY OBLIGING.
...
MASTER KURAYORI ...

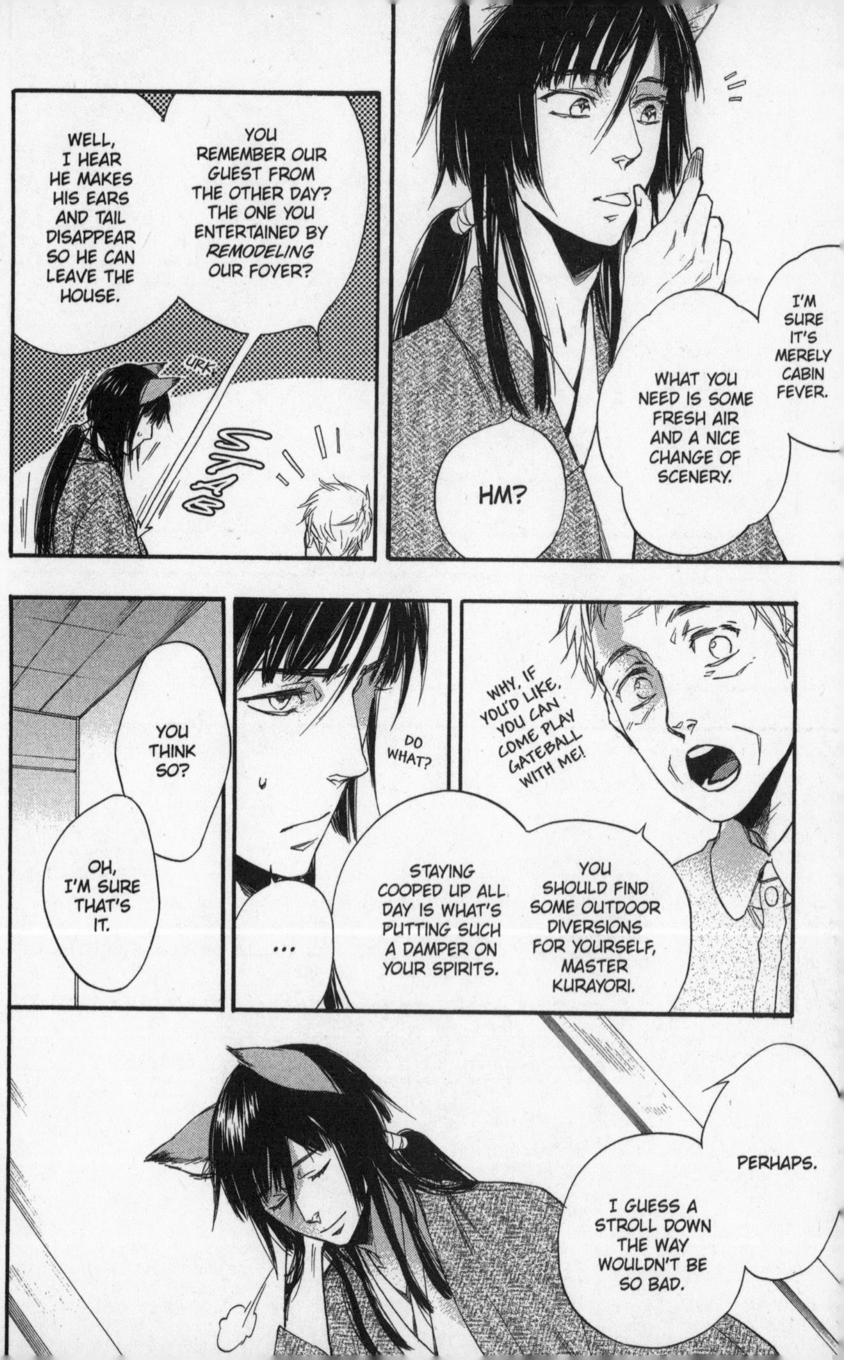
I'M SURE IT'S MERELY CABIN FEVER.
WHAT YOU NEED IS SOME FRESH AIR AND A NICE CHANGE OF SCENERY.
HM?
YOU REMEMBER OUR GUEST FROM THE OTHER DAY? THE ONE YOU ENTERTAINED BY *REMODELING* OUR FOYER?
WELL, I HEAR HE MAKES HIS EARS AND TAIL DISAPPEAR SO HE CAN LEAVE THE HOUSE.
URK
WHY, IF YOU'D LIKE, YOU CAN COME PLAY GATEBALL WITH ME!
DO WHAT?
YOU SHOULD FIND SOME OUTDOOR DIVERSIONS FOR YOURSELF, MASTER KURAYORI.
STAYING COOPED UP ALL DAY IS WHAT'S PUTTING SUCH A DAMPER ON YOUR SPIRITS.
...
YOU THINK SO?
OH, I'M SURE THAT'S IT.
PERHAPS.
I GUESS A STROLL DOWN THE WAY WOULDN'T BE SO BAD.

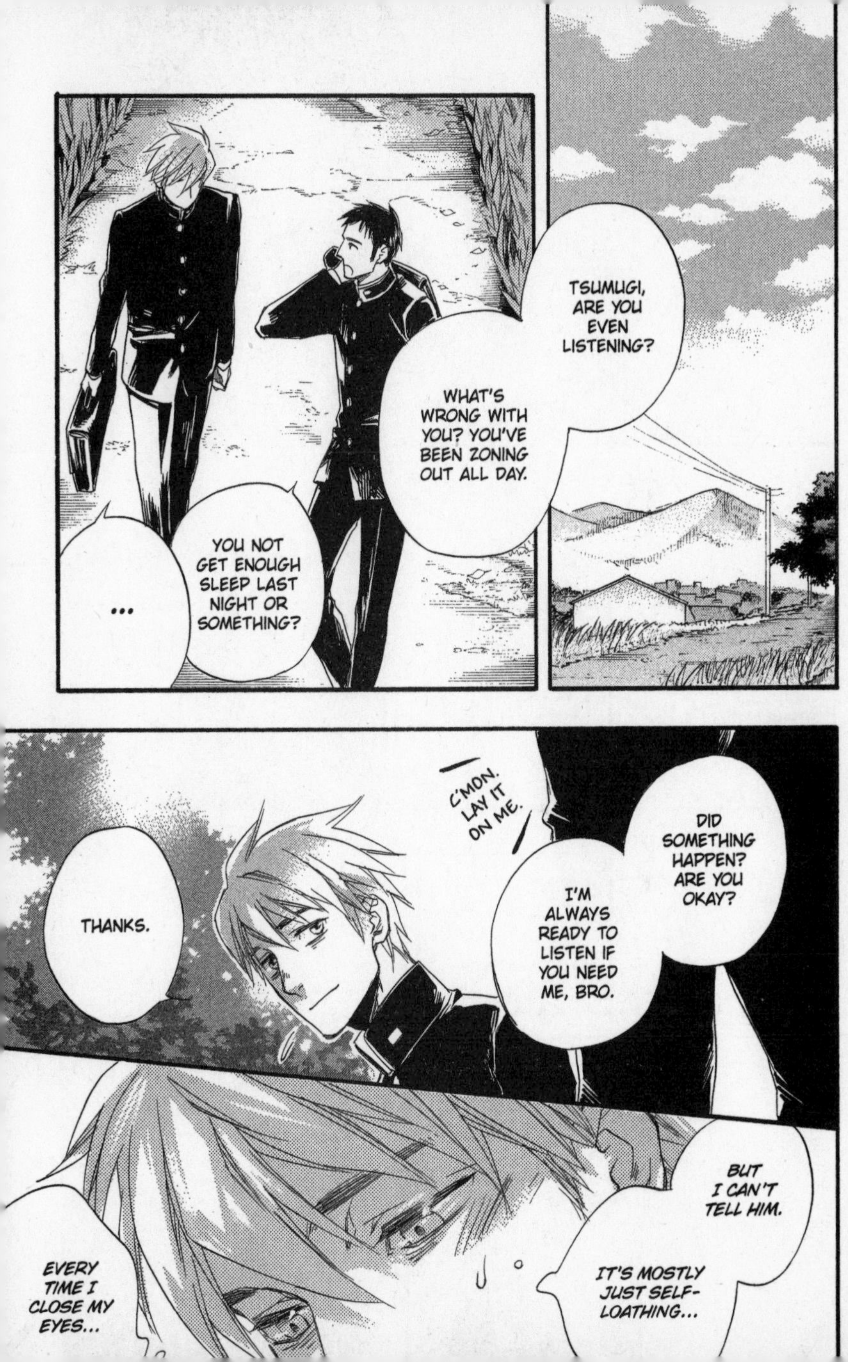
TSUMUGI, ARE YOU EVEN LISTENING?
WHAT'S WRONG WITH YOU? YOU'VE BEEN ZONING OUT ALL DAY.
YOU NOT GET ENOUGH SLEEP LAST NIGHT OR SOMETHING?
...
DID SOMETHING HAPPEN? ARE YOU OKAY?
C'MON. LAY IT ON ME.
I'M ALWAYS READY TO LISTEN IF YOU NEED ME, BRO.
THANKS.
BUT I CAN'T TELL HIM.
IT'S MOSTLY JUST SELF-LOATHING...
EVERY TIME I CLOSE MY EYES...

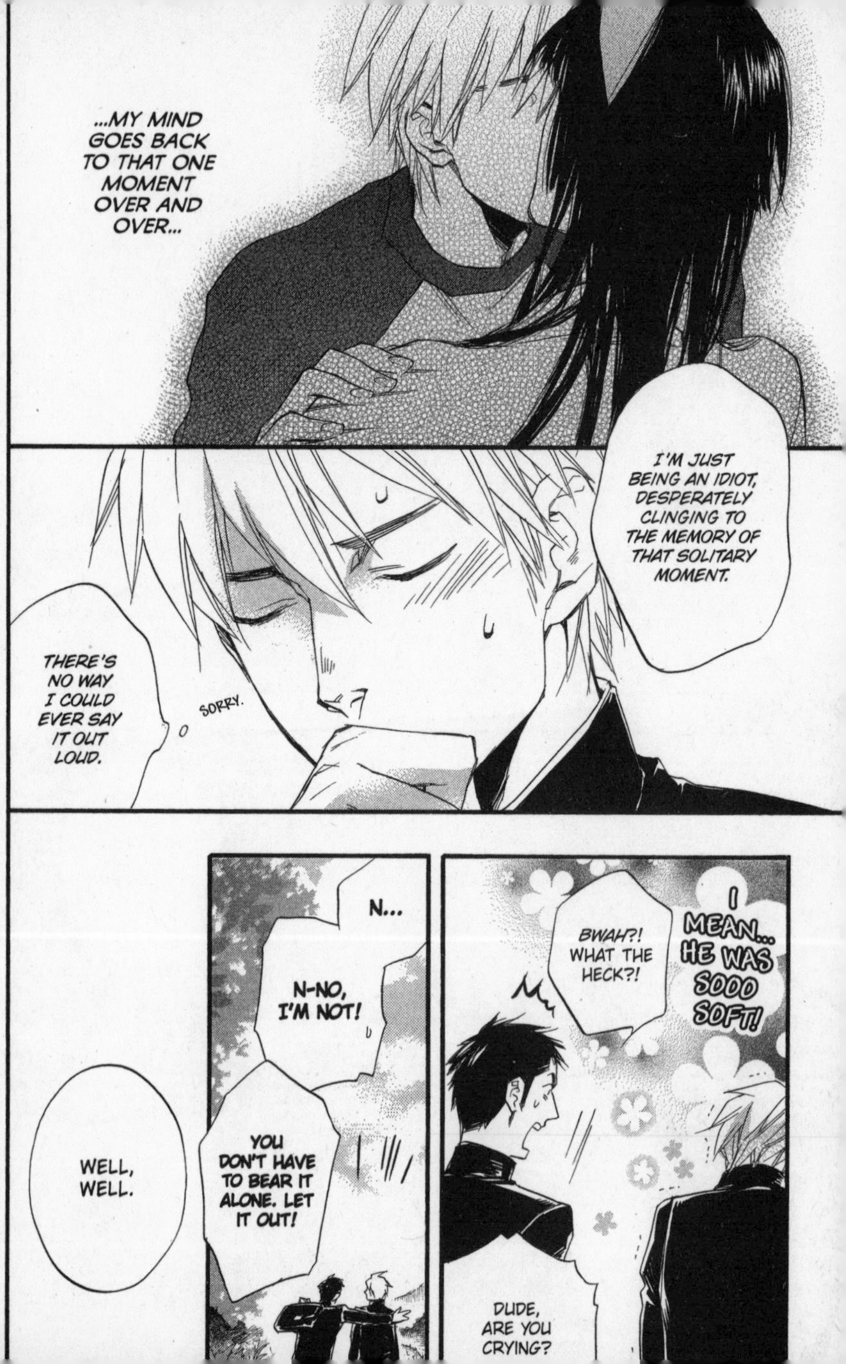
...MY MIND GOES BACK TO THAT ONE MOMENT OVER AND OVER...
I'M JUST BEING AN IDIOT, DESPERATELY CLINGING TO THE MEMORY OF THAT SOLITARY MOMENT.
SORRY.
THERE'S NO WAY I COULD EVER SAY IT OUT LOUD.
I MEAN... HE WAS SOOO SOFT!
BWAH?! WHAT THE HECK?!
DUDE, ARE YOU CRYING?
N...
N-NO, I'M NOT!
YOU DON'T HAVE TO BEAR IT ALONE. LET IT OUT!
WELL, WELL.

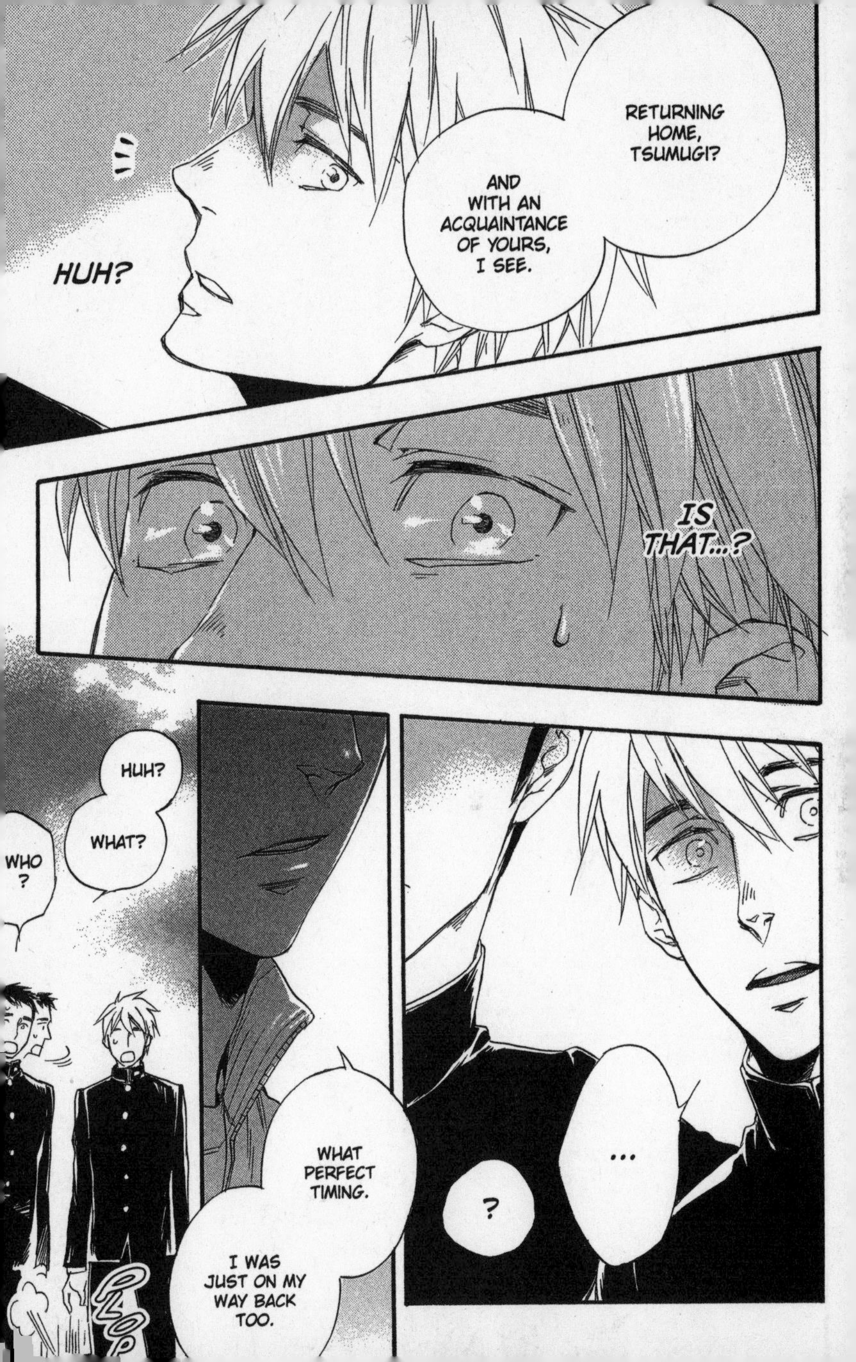
RETURNING HOME, TSUMUGI?
AND WITH AN ACQUAINTANCE OF YOURS, I SEE.
HUH?
IS THAT...?
...
?
WHAT PERFECT TIMING.
I WAS JUST ON MY WAY BACK TOO.
HUH?
WHAT?
WHO?
PLOP

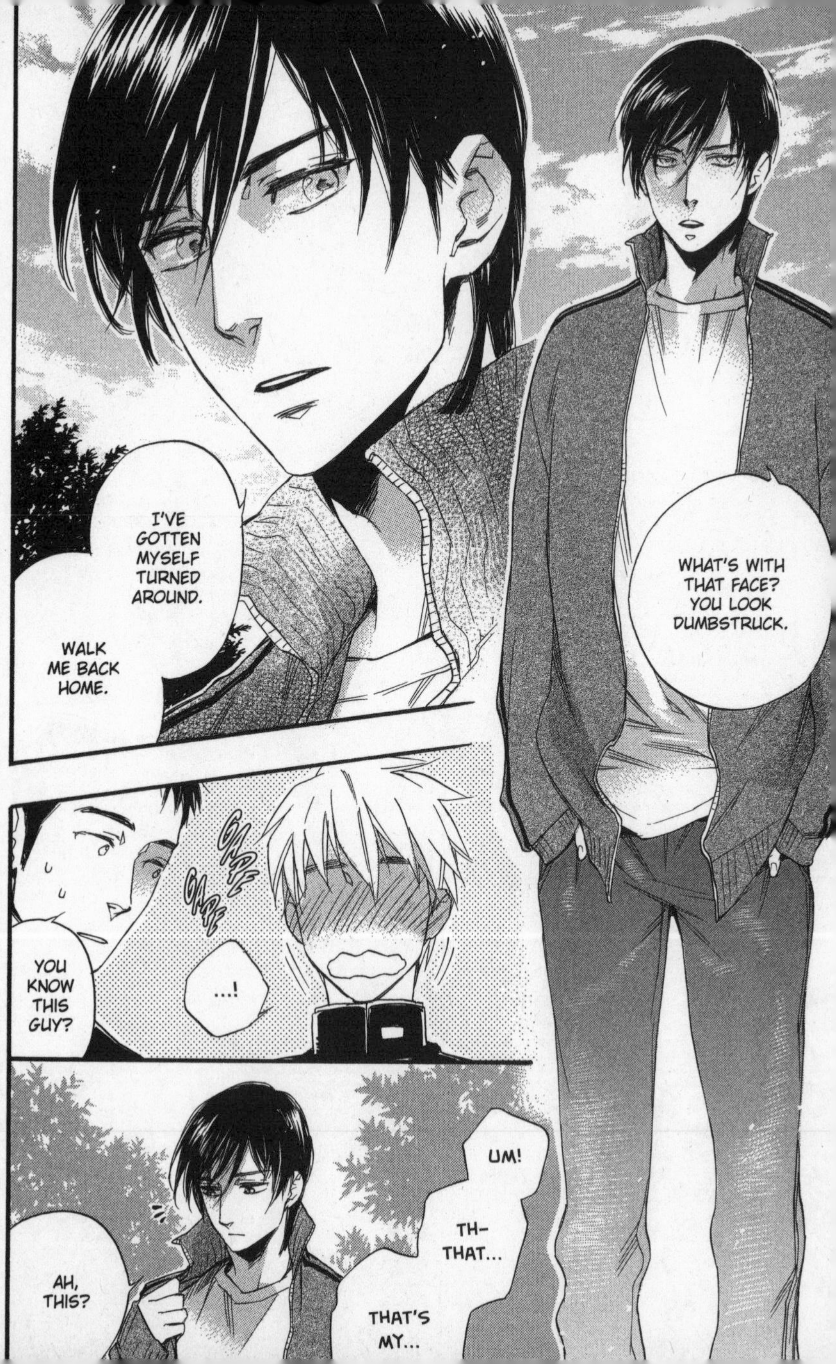
WHAT'S WITH THAT FACE? YOU LOOK DUMBSTRUCK.
I'VE GOTTEN MYSELF TURNED AROUND.
WALK ME BACK HOME.
GAPE
GAPE
...!
YOU KNOW THIS GUY?
UM!
TH- THAT...
THAT'S MY...
AH, THIS?

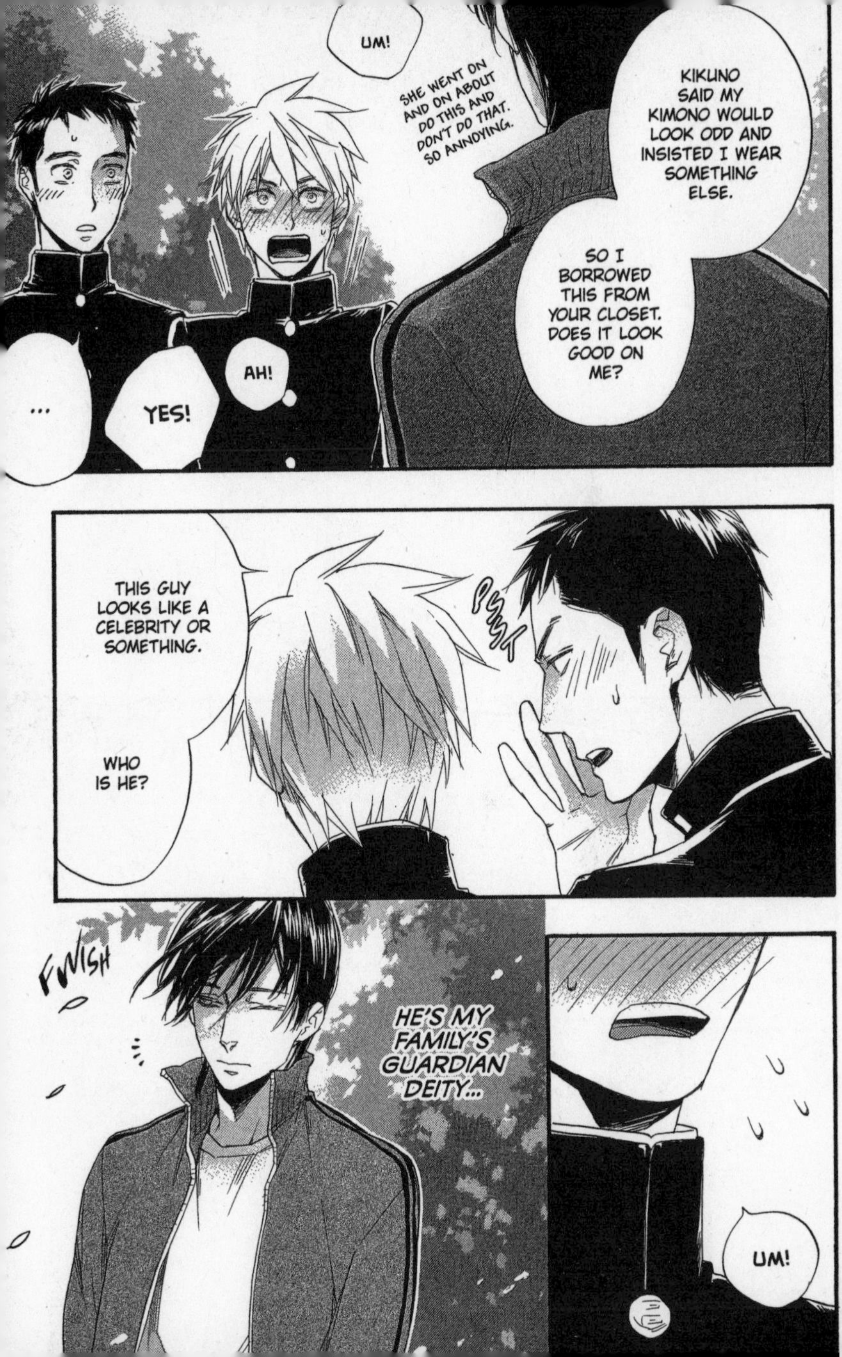
KIKUNO SAID MY KIMONO WOULD LOOK ODD AND INSISTED I WEAR SOMETHING ELSE.
SHE WENT ON AND ON ABOUT DO THIS AND DON'T DO THAT. SO ANNOYING.
SO I BORROWED THIS FROM YOUR CLOSET. DOES IT LOOK GOOD ON ME?
UM!
AH!
YES!
...
PSST
THIS GUY LOOKS LIKE A CELEBRITY OR SOMETHING.
WHO IS HE?
UM!
HE'S MY FAMILY'S GUARDIAN DEITY...
FWISH

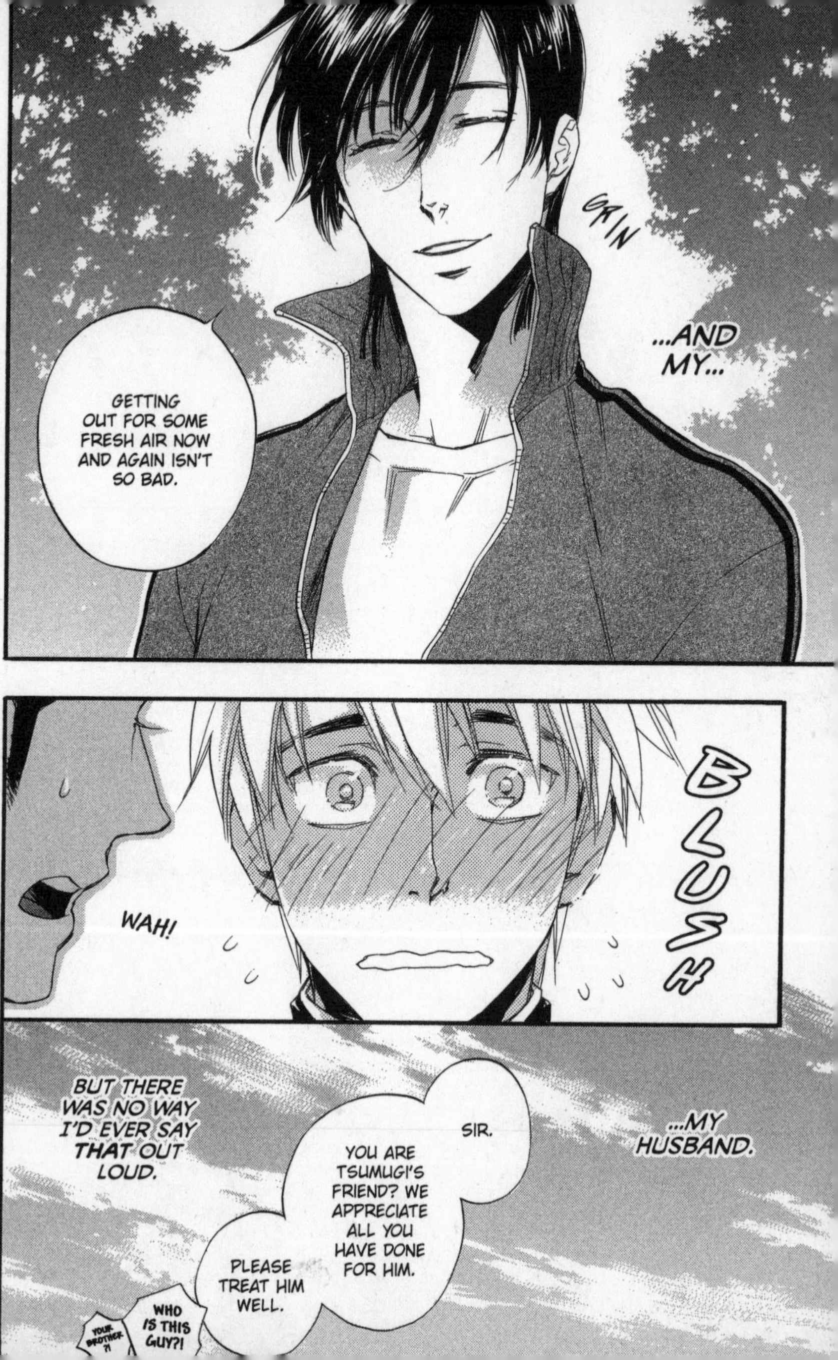
GRIN
...AND MY...
GETTING OUT FOR SOME FRESH AIR NOW AND AGAIN ISN'T SO BAD.
BLUSH
WAH!
...MY HUSBAND.
SIR.
YOU ARE TSUMUGI'S FRIEND? WE APPRECIATE ALL YOU HAVE DONE FOR HIM.
BUT THERE WAS NO WAY I'D EVER SAY THAT OUT LOUD.
PLEASE TREAT HIM WELL.
WHO IS THIS GUY?!
YOUR BROTHER ?!

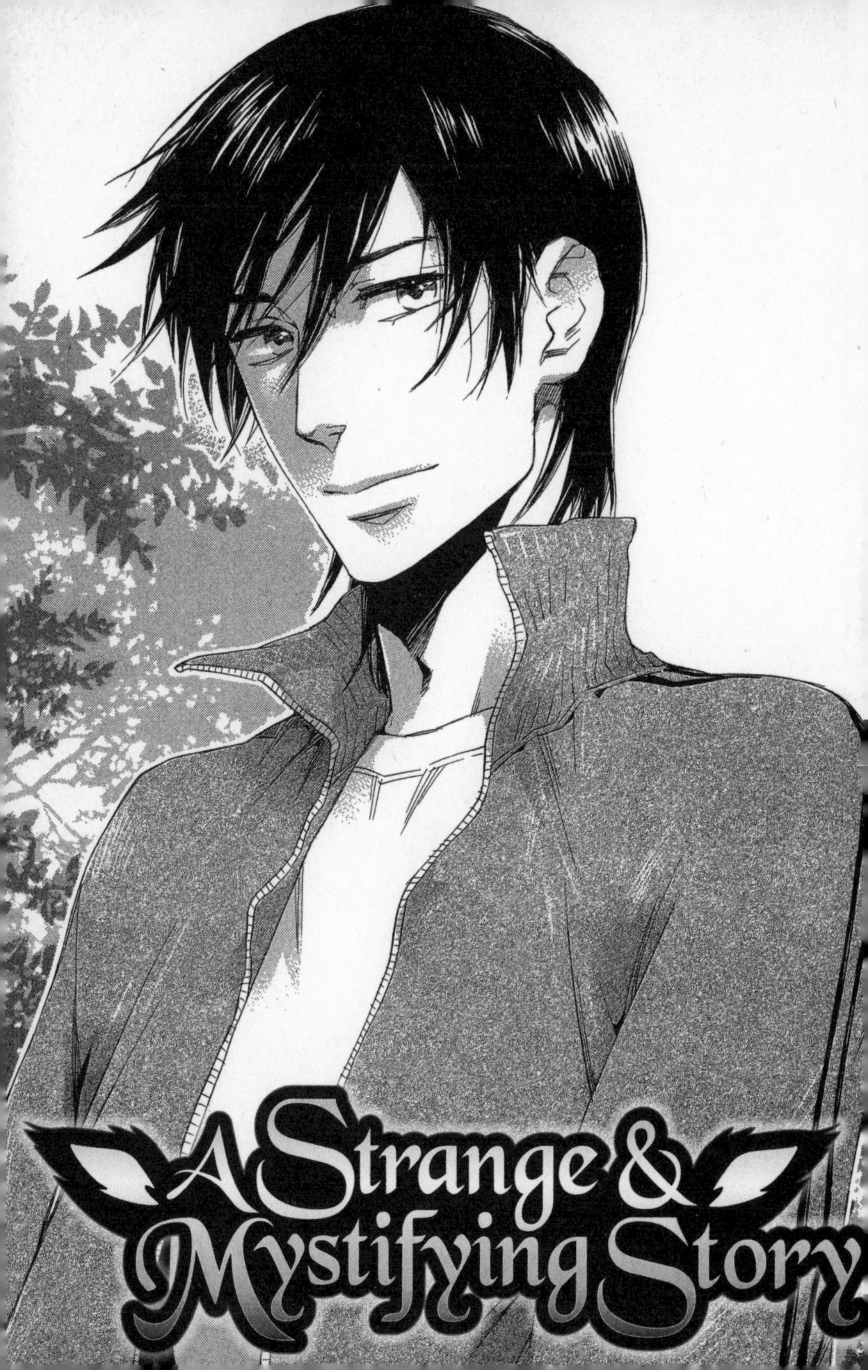
A Strange &
Mystifying Story

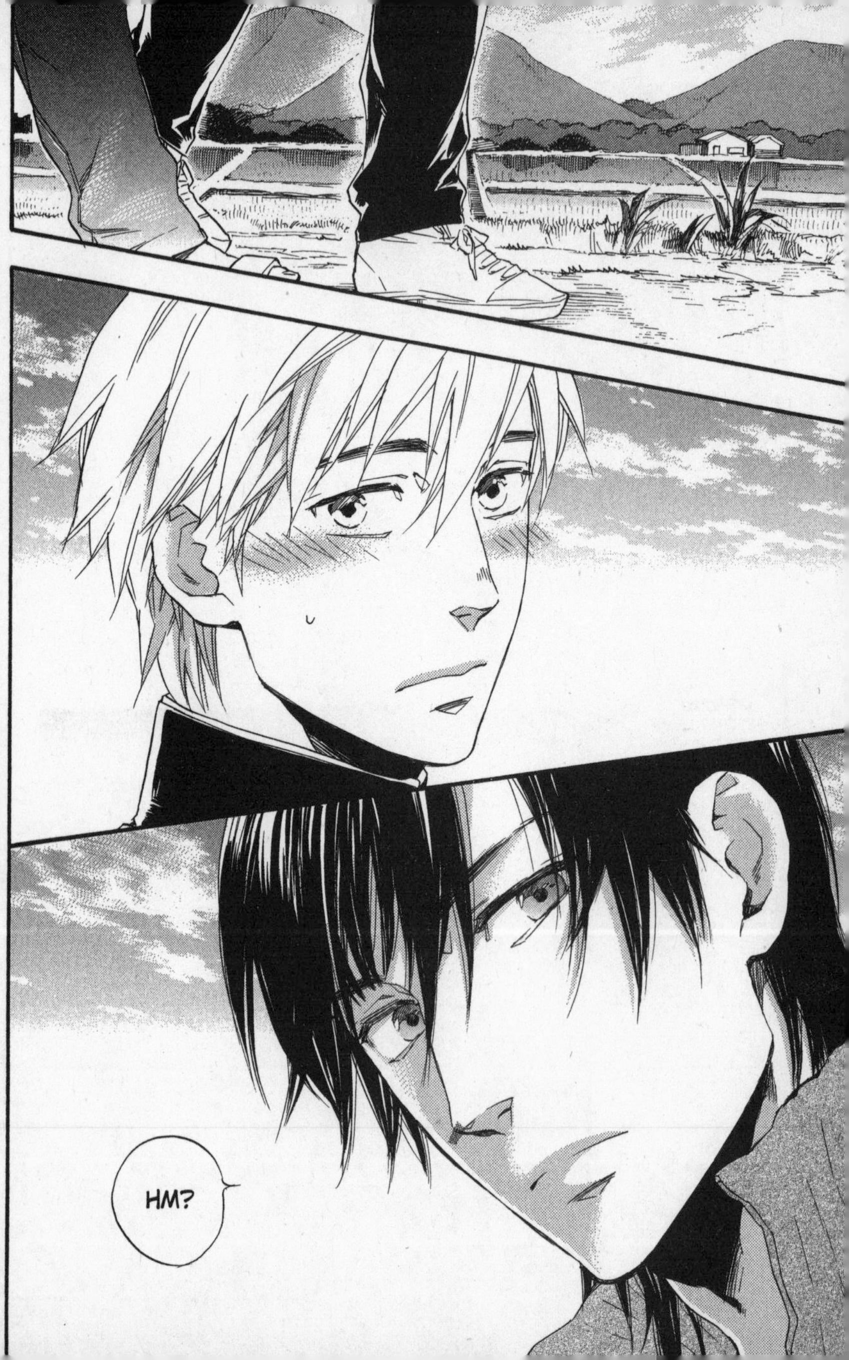
HM?

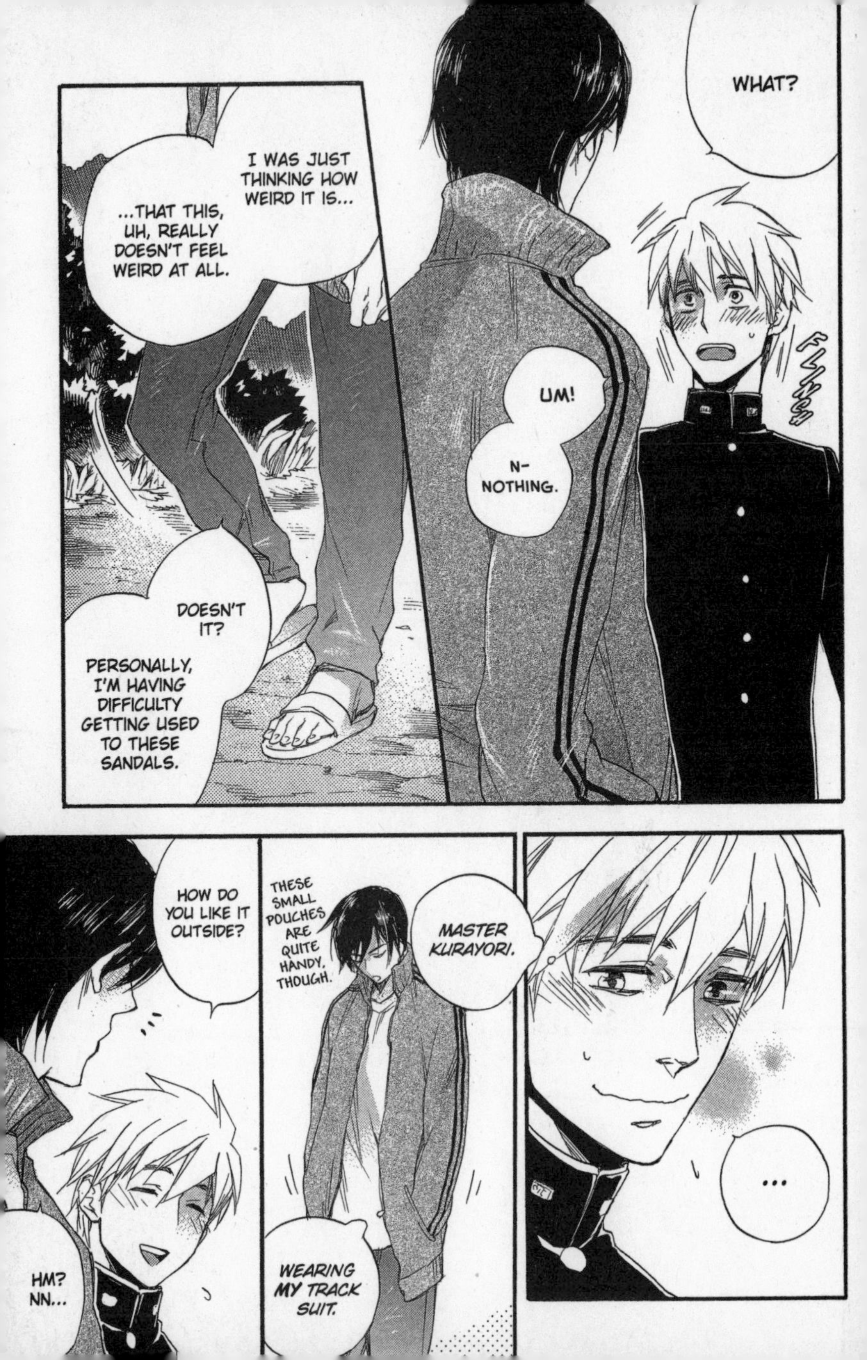
WHAT?
I WAS JUST THINKING HOW WEIRD IT IS...
...THAT THIS, UH, REALLY DOESN'T FEEL WEIRD AT ALL.
UM!
N-NOTHING.
FLINCH
DOESN'T IT?
PERSONALLY, I'M HAVING DIFFICULTY GETTING USED TO THESE SANDALS.
MASTER KURAYORI.
...
THESE SMALL POUCHES ARE QUITE HANDY, THOUGH.
WEARING MY TRACK SUIT.
HOW DO YOU LIKE IT OUTSIDE?
HM? NN...

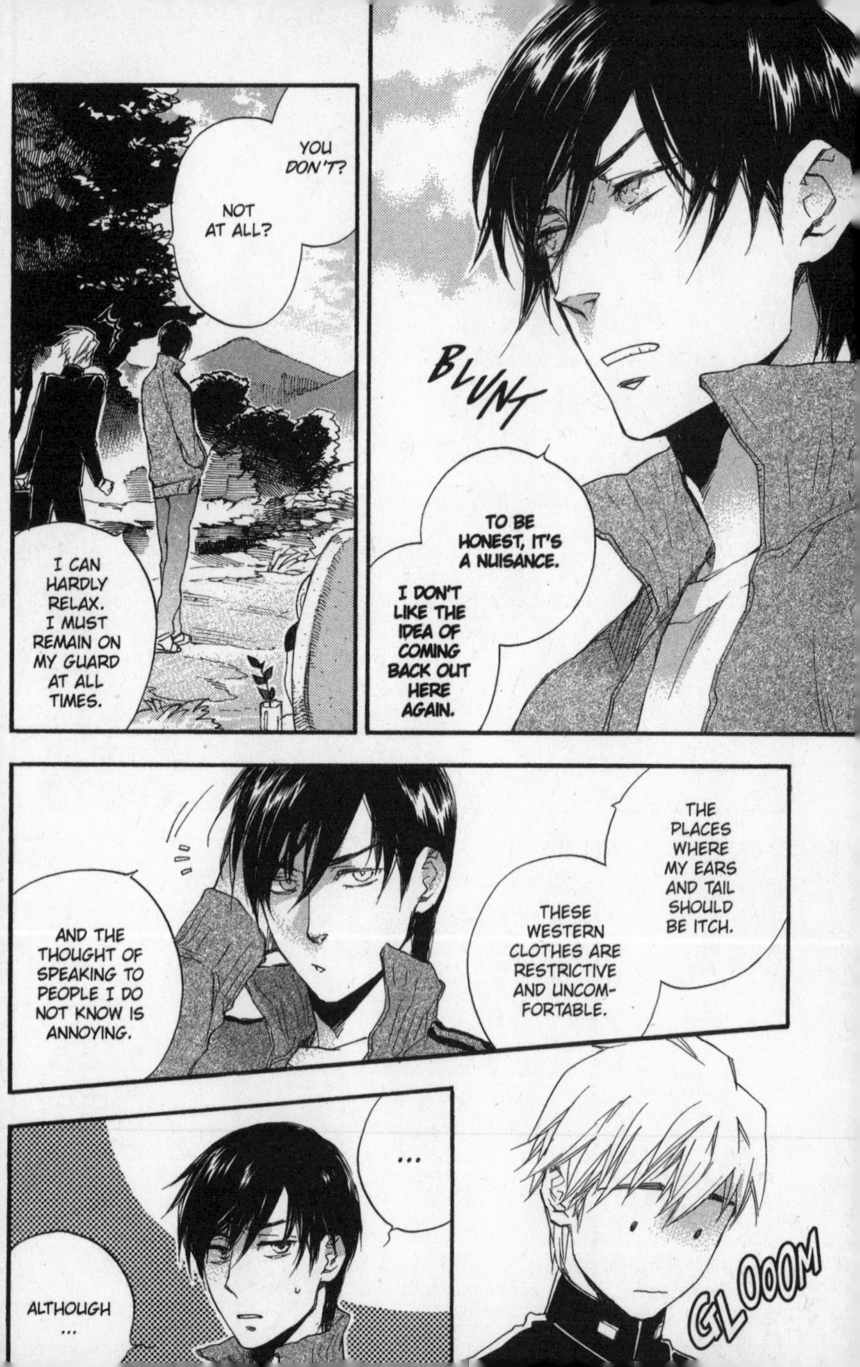
BLUNT
TO BE HONEST, IT'S A NUISANCE.
I DON'T LIKE THE IDEA OF COMING BACK OUT HERE AGAIN.
YOU DON'T?
NOT AT ALL?
I CAN HARDLY RELAX. I MUST REMAIN ON MY GUARD AT ALL TIMES.
THE PLACES WHERE MY EARS AND TAIL SHOULD BE ITCH.
THESE WESTERN CLOTHES ARE RESTRICTIVE AND UNCOM-FORTABLE.
AND THE THOUGHT OF SPEAKING TO PEOPLE I DO NOT KNOW IS ANNOYING.
GLOOOM
...
ALTHOUGH ...

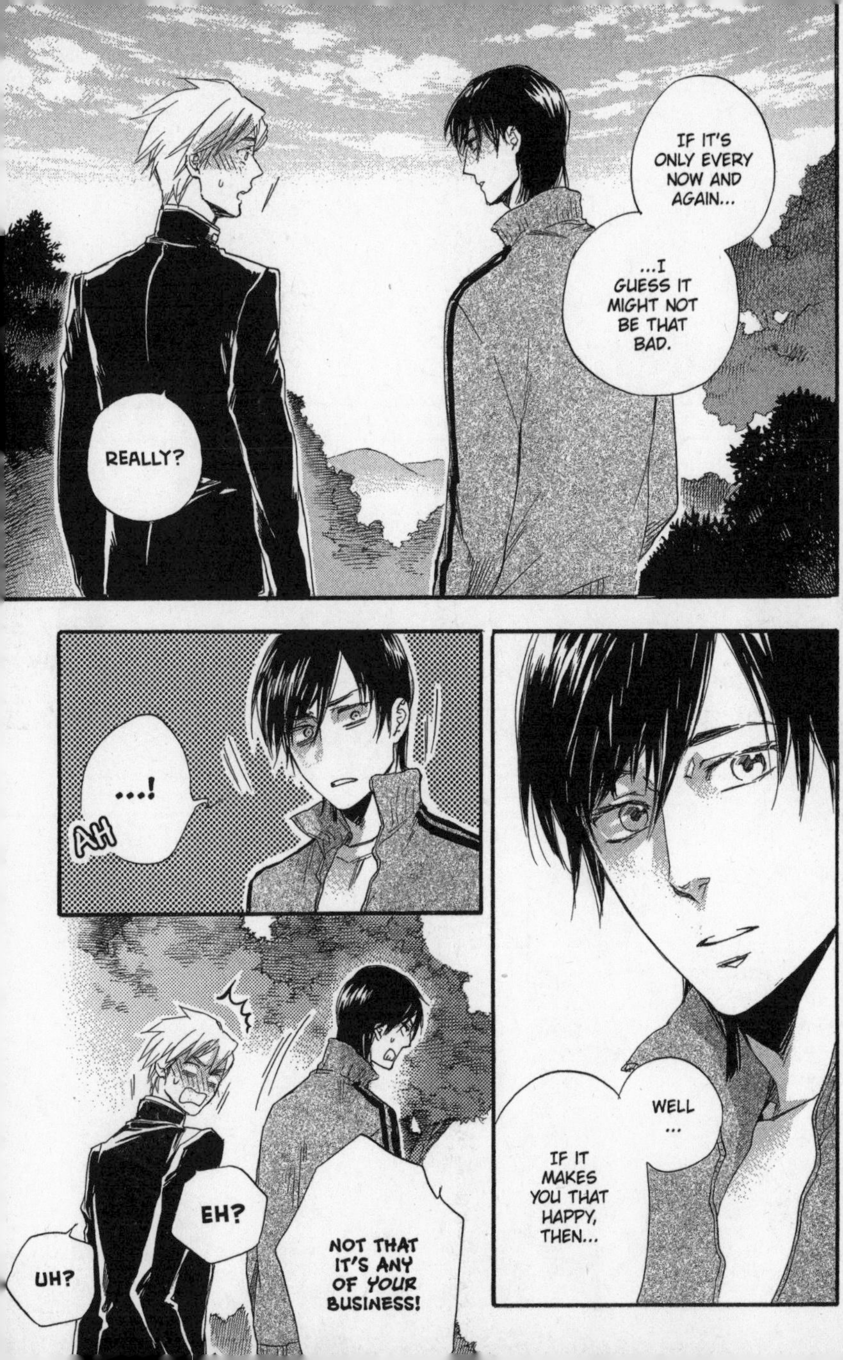
IF IT'S ONLY EVERY NOW AND AGAIN...
...I GUESS IT MIGHT NOT BE THAT BAD.
REALLY?
WELL ...
IF IT MAKES YOU THAT HAPPY, THEN...
...!
AH
NOT THAT IT'S ANY OF YOUR BUSINESS!
EH?
UH?

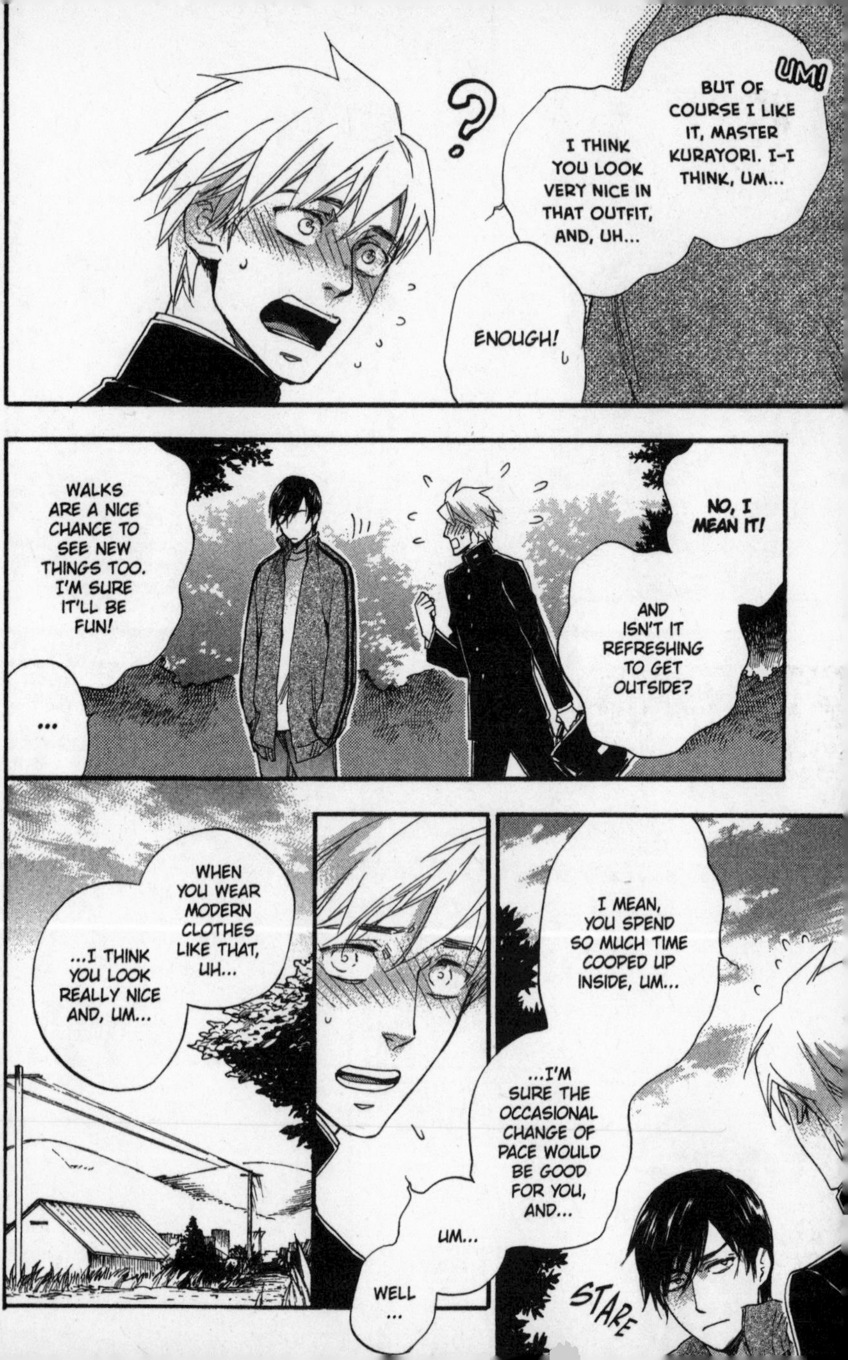
UM!
BUT OF COURSE I LIKE IT, MASTER KURAYORI. I-I THINK, UM...
I THINK YOU LOOK VERY NICE IN THAT OUTFIT, AND, UH...
ENOUGH!
NO, I MEAN IT!
AND ISN'T IT REFRESHING TO GET OUTSIDE?
WALKS ARE A NICE CHANCE TO SEE NEW THINGS TOO. I'M SURE IT'LL BE FUN!
...
I MEAN, YOU SPEND SO MUCH TIME COOPED UP INSIDE, UM...
...I'M SURE THE OCCASIONAL CHANGE OF PACE WOULD BE GOOD FOR YOU, AND...
STARE
UM...
WELL ...
WHEN YOU WEAR MODERN CLOTHES LIKE THAT, UH...
...I THINK YOU LOOK REALLY NICE AND, UM...

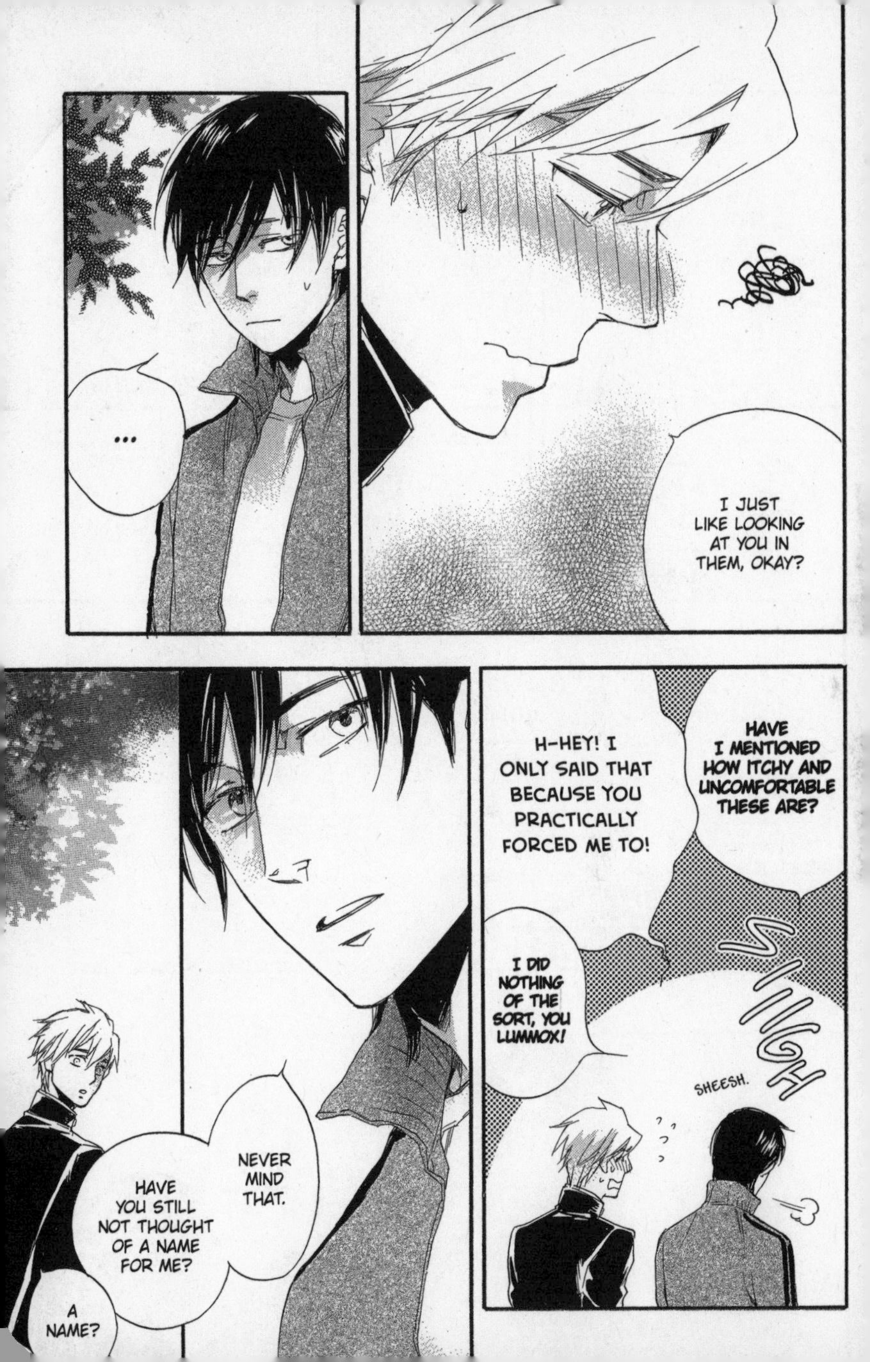
I JUST LIKE LOOKING AT YOU IN THEM, OKAY?
...
HAVE I MENTIONED HOW ITCHY AND UNCOMFORTABLE THESE ARE?
H-HEY! I ONLY SAID THAT BECAUSE YOU PRACTICALLY FORCED ME TO!
I DID NOTHING OF THE SORT, YOU LUMMOX!
SIGH
SHEESH.
NEVER MIND THAT.
HAVE YOU STILL NOT THOUGHT OF A NAME FOR ME?
A NAME?

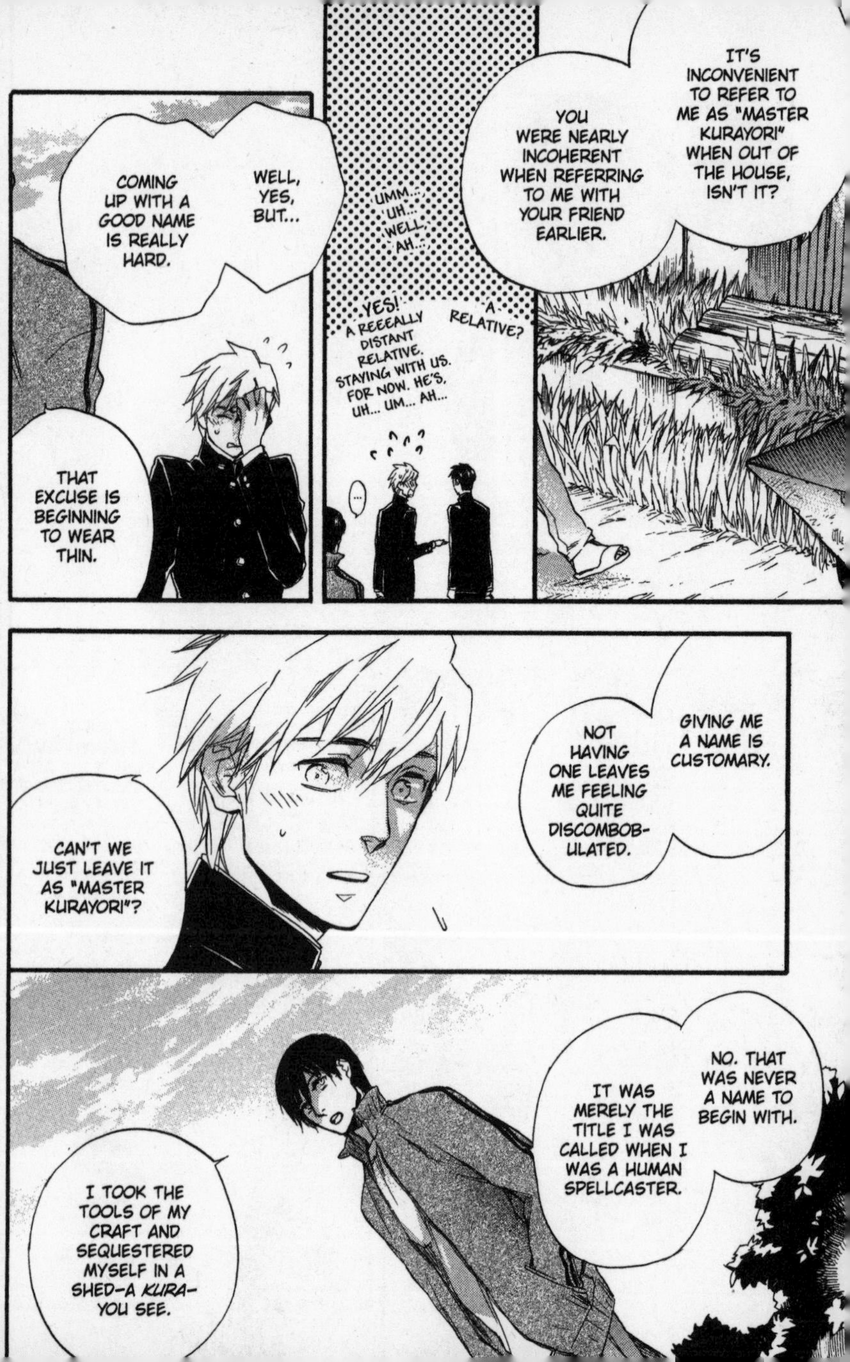
IT'S INCONVENIENT TO REFER TO ME AS "MASTER KURAYORI" WHEN OUT OF THE HOUSE, ISN'T IT?
YOU WERE NEARLY INCOHERENT WHEN REFERRING TO ME WITH YOUR FRIEND EARLIER.
UMM... UH... WELL, AH...
A RELATIVE?
YES! A REEEALLY DISTANT RELATIVE. STAYING WITH US. FOR NOW. HE'S, UH... UM... AH...
...
WELL, YES, BUT...
COMING UP WITH A GOOD NAME IS REALLY HARD.
THAT EXCUSE IS BEGINNING TO WEAR THIN.
GIVING ME A NAME IS CUSTOMARY.
NOT HAVING ONE LEAVES ME FEELING QUITE DISCOMBOB-ULATED.
CAN'T WE JUST LEAVE IT AS "MASTER KURAYORI"?
NO. THAT WAS NEVER A NAME TO BEGIN WITH.
IT WAS MERELY THE TITLE I WAS CALLED WHEN I WAS A HUMAN SPELLCASTER.
I TOOK THE TOOLS OF MY CRAFT AND SEQUESTERED MYSELF IN A SHED—A *KURA*—YOU SEE.

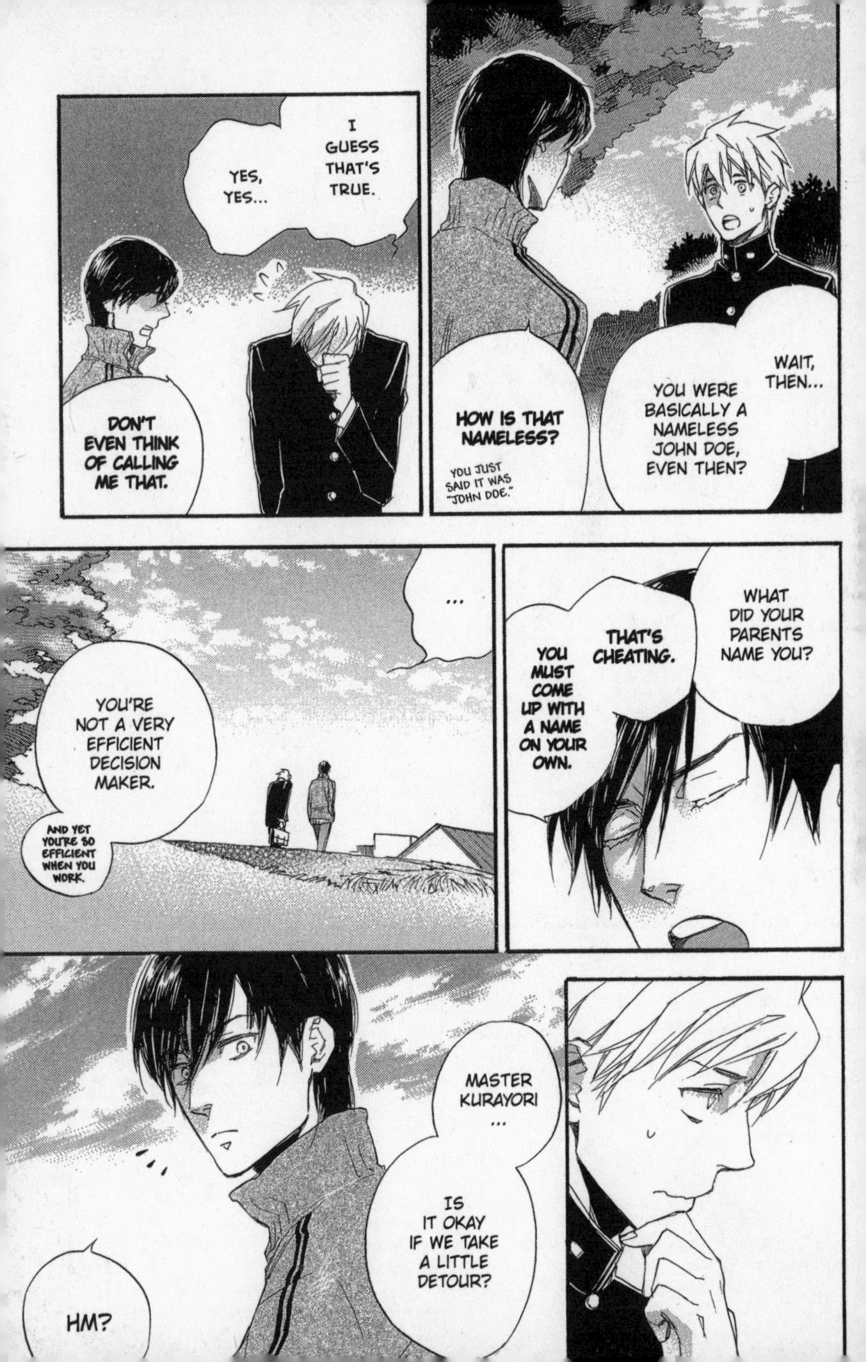
WAIT, THEN... YOU WERE BASICALLY A NAMELESS JOHN DOE, EVEN THEN?
HOW IS THAT NAMELESS?
YOU JUST SAID IT WAS "JOHN DOE."
YES, YES... I GUESS THAT'S TRUE.
DON'T EVEN THINK OF CALLING ME THAT.
WHAT DID YOUR PARENTS NAME YOU?
THAT'S CHEATING. YOU MUST COME UP WITH A NAME ON YOUR OWN.
...
YOU'RE NOT A VERY EFFICIENT DECISION MAKER.
AND YET YOU'RE SO EFFICIENT WHEN YOU WORK.
MASTER KURAYORI ...
IS IT OKAY IF WE TAKE A LITTLE DETOUR?
HM?

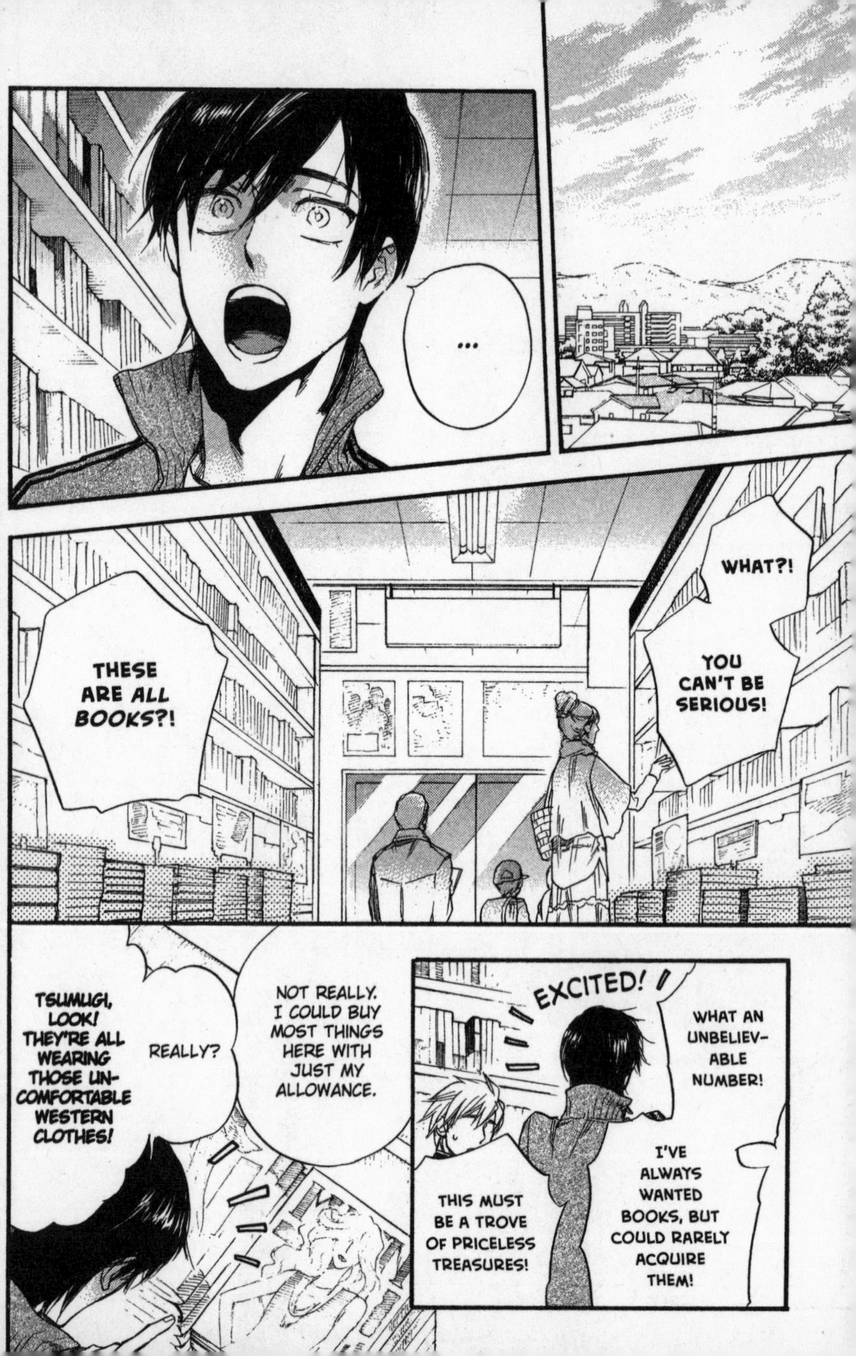
...
WHAT?!
YOU CAN'T BE SERIOUS!
THESE ARE ALL BOOKS?!
EXCITED!
WHAT AN UNBELIEV-ABLE NUMBER!
I'VE ALWAYS WANTED BOOKS, BUT COULD RARELY ACQUIRE THEM!
THIS MUST BE A TROVE OF PRICELESS TREASURES!
NOT REALLY. I COULD BUY MOST THINGS HERE WITH JUST MY ALLOWANCE.
REALLY?
TSUMUGI, LOOK! THEY'RE ALL WEARING THOSE UN-COMFORTABLE WESTERN CLOTHES!

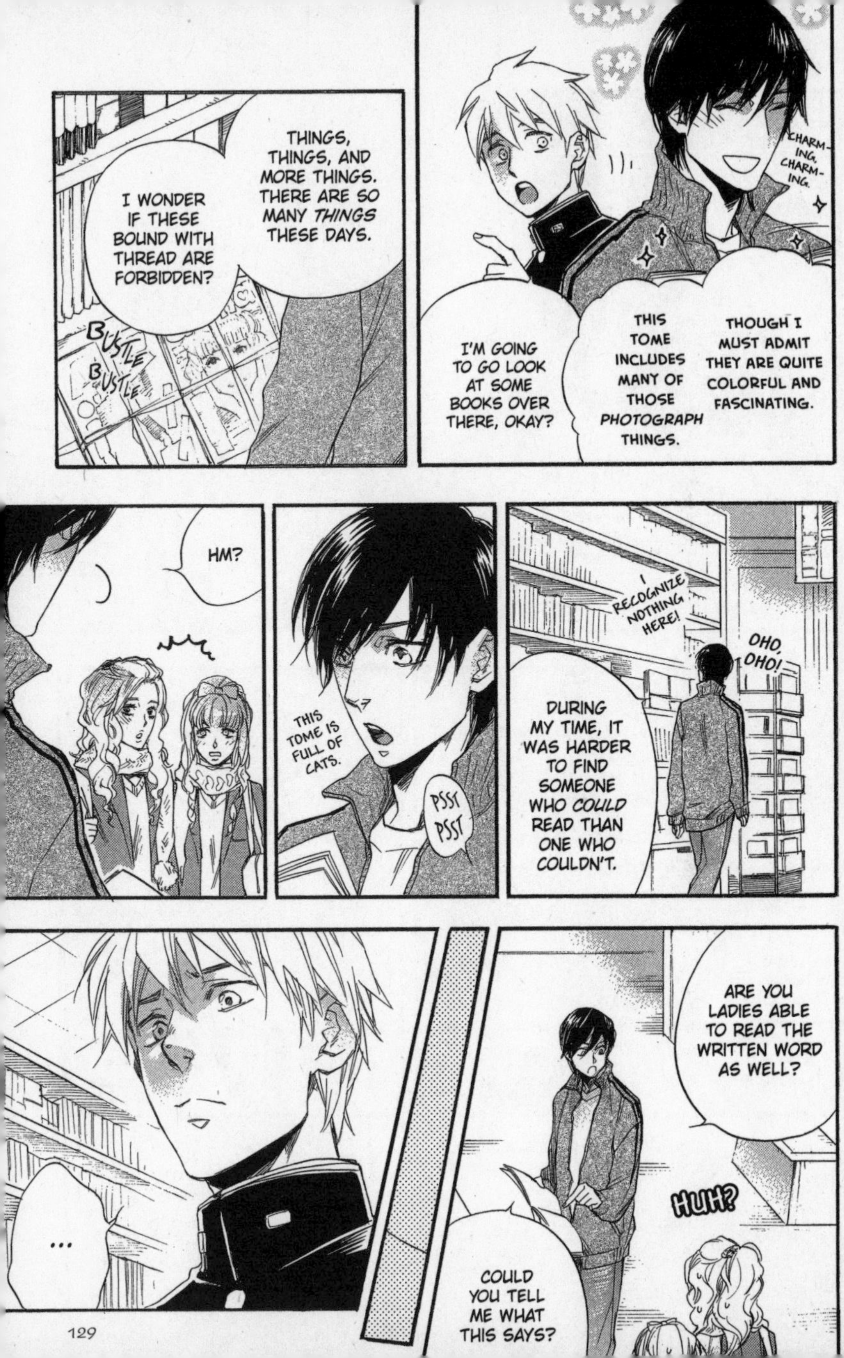
CHARMING, CHARMING.
THOUGH I MUST ADMIT THEY ARE QUITE COLORFUL AND FASCINATING.
THIS TOME INCLUDES MANY OF THOSE *PHOTOGRAPH* THINGS.
I'M GOING TO GO LOOK AT SOME BOOKS OVER THERE, OKAY?
THINGS, THINGS, AND MORE THINGS. THERE ARE SO MANY *THINGS* THESE DAYS.
I WONDER IF THESE BOUND WITH THREAD ARE FORBIDDEN?
BUSTLE BUSTLE
I RECOGNIZE NOTHING HERE!
OHO, OHO!
DURING MY TIME, IT WAS HARDER TO FIND SOMEONE WHO *COULD* READ THAN ONE WHO COULDN'T.
THIS TOME IS FULL OF CATS.
PSST PSST
HM?
ARE YOU LADIES ABLE TO READ THE WRITTEN WORD AS WELL?
HUH?
COULD YOU TELL ME WHAT THIS SAYS?
...

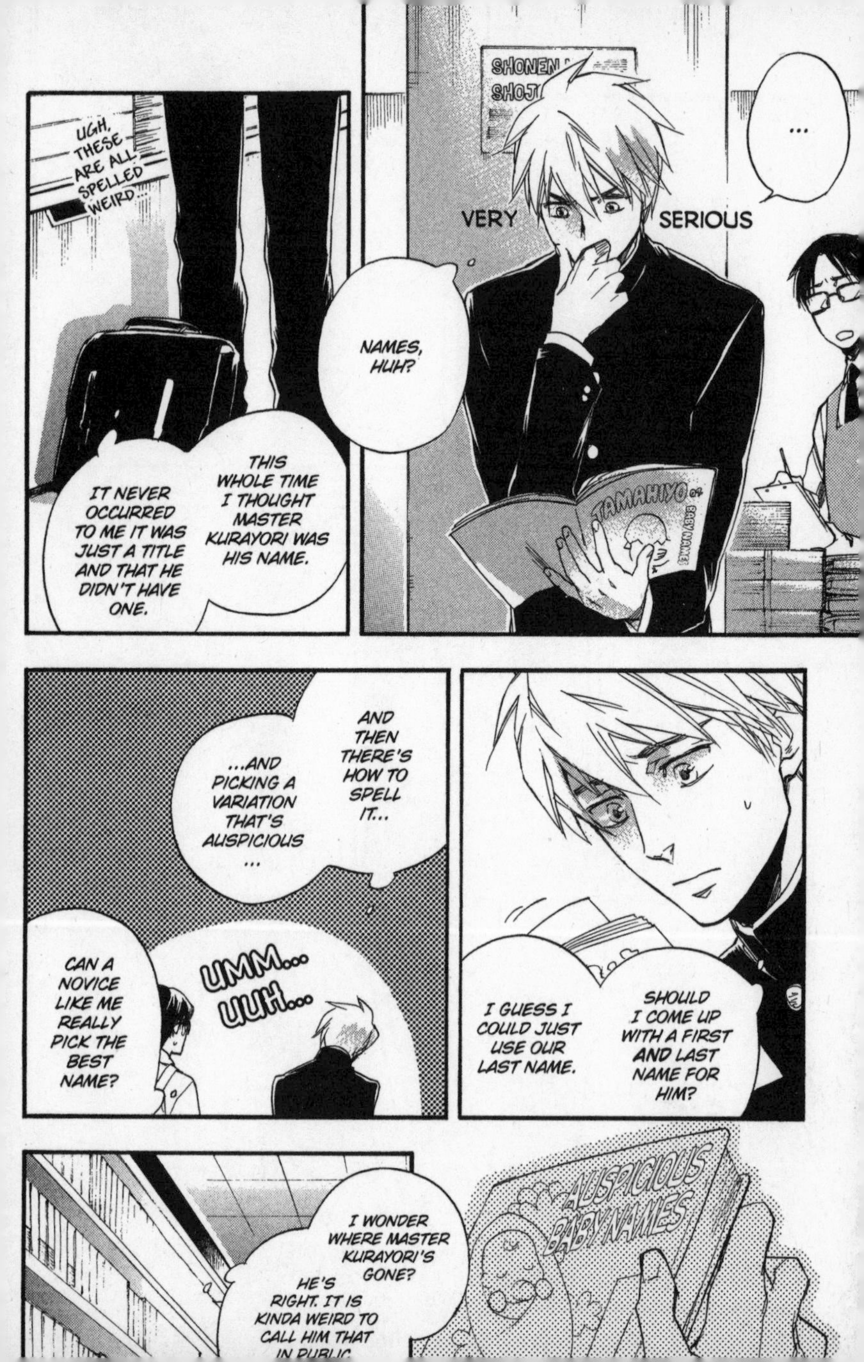

SHONEN
...
VERY SERIOUS
NAMES, HUH?
UGH, THESE ARE ALL SPELLED WEIRD...
THIS WHOLE TIME I THOUGHT MASTER KURAYORI WAS HIS NAME.
IT NEVER OCCURRED TO ME IT WAS JUST A TITLE AND THAT HE DIDN'T HAVE ONE.
SHOULD I COME UP WITH A FIRST AND LAST NAME FOR HIM?
I GUESS I COULD JUST USE OUR LAST NAME.
AND THEN THERE'S HOW TO SPELL IT...
...AND PICKING A VARIATION THAT'S AUSPICIOUS ...
UMM... UUH...
CAN A NOVICE LIKE ME REALLY PICK THE BEST NAME?
AUSPICIOUS BABY NAMES
I WONDER WHERE MASTER KURAYORI'S GONE?
HE'S RIGHT. IT IS KINDA WEIRD TO CALL HIM THAT IN PUBLIC

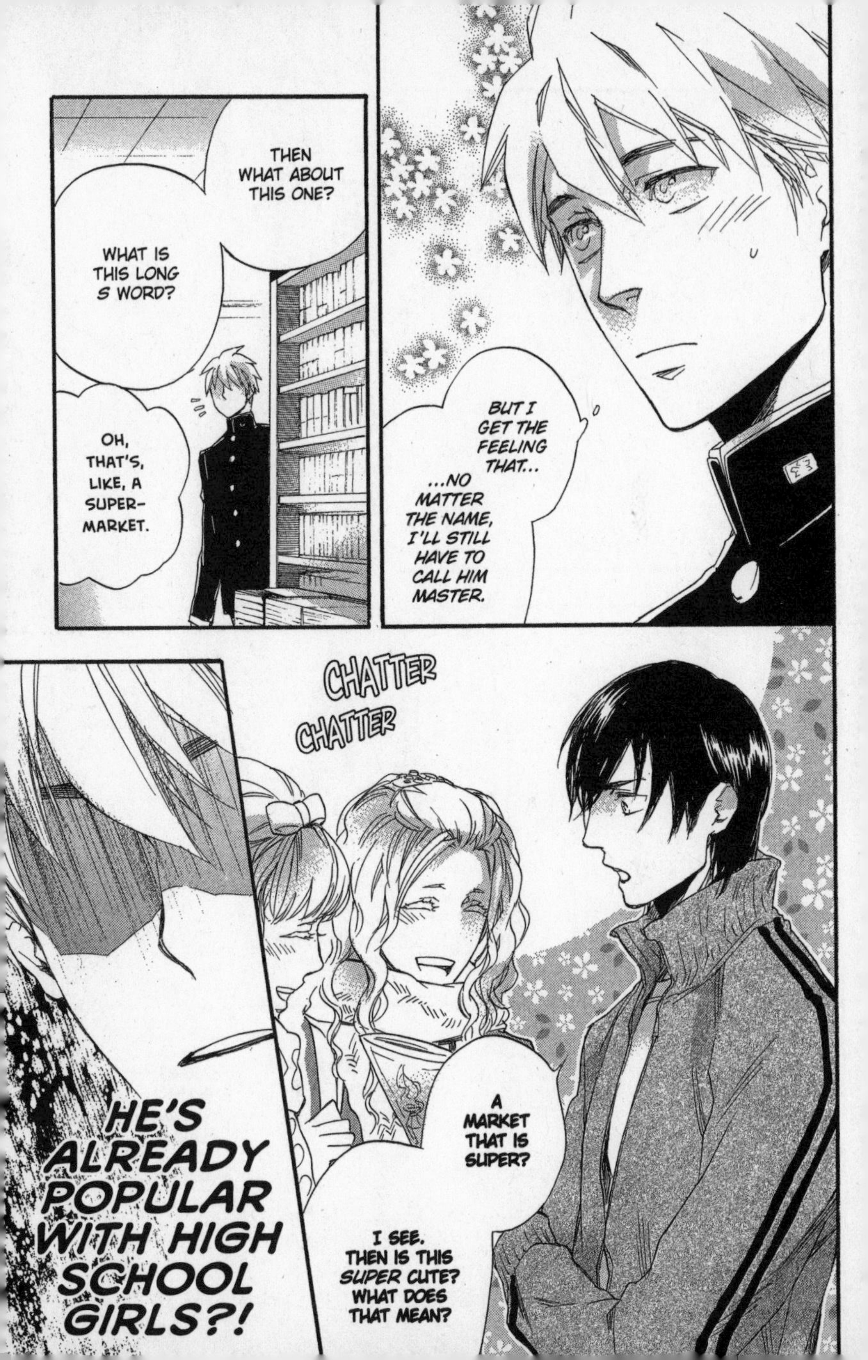
BUT I GET THE FEELING THAT...
...NO MATTER THE NAME, I'LL STILL HAVE TO CALL HIM MASTER.
THEN WHAT ABOUT THIS ONE?
WHAT IS THIS LONG S WORD?
OH, THAT'S, LIKE, A SUPER-MARKET.
CHATTER
CHATTER
A MARKET THAT IS SUPER?
I SEE. THEN IS THIS *SUPER CUTE?* WHAT DOES THAT MEAN?
HE'S ALREADY POPULAR WITH HIGH SCHOOL GIRLS?!

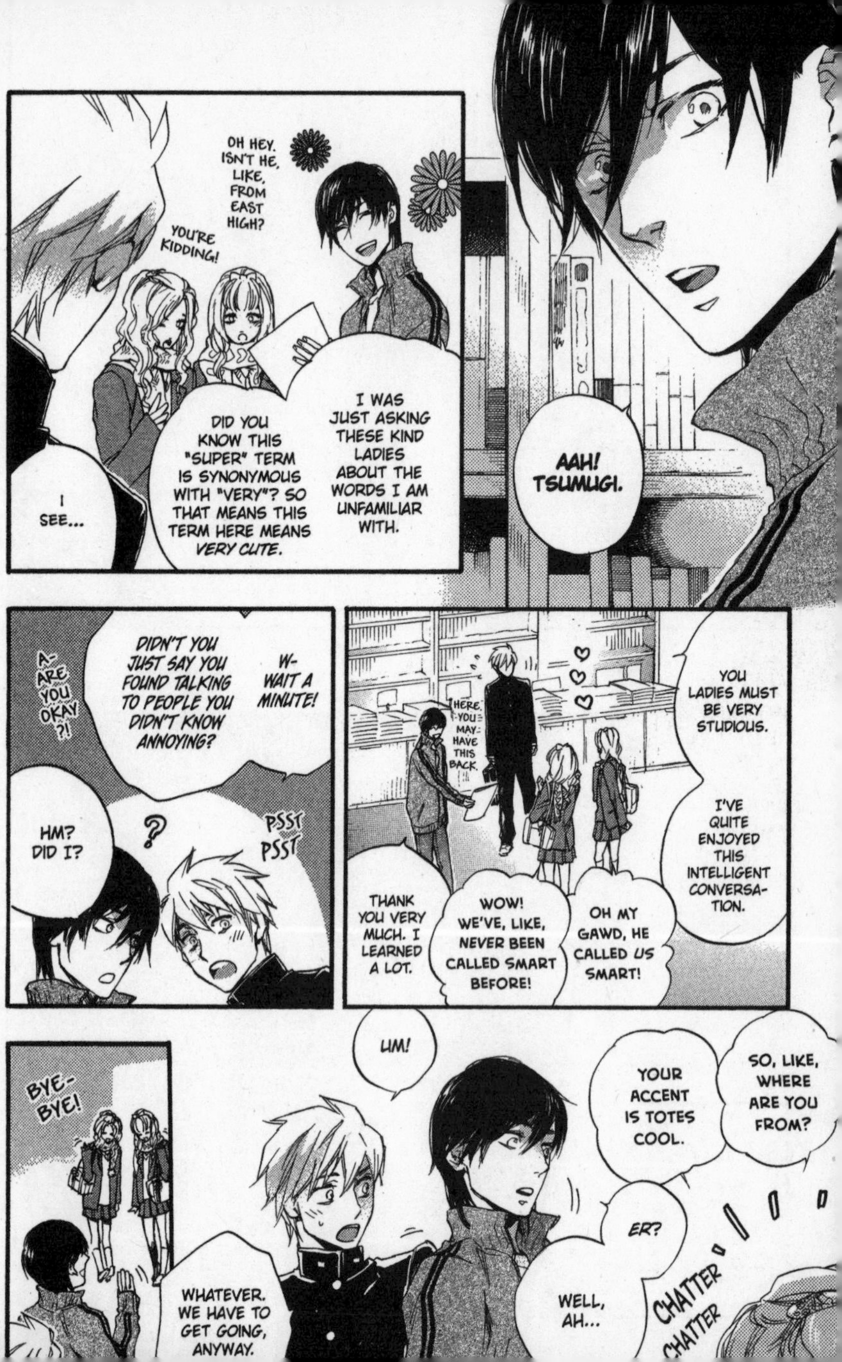
AAH! TSUMUGI.
OH HEY. ISN'T HE, LIKE, FROM EAST HIGH?
YOU'RE KIDDING!
I WAS JUST ASKING THESE KIND LADIES ABOUT THE WORDS I AM UNFAMILIAR WITH.
DID YOU KNOW THIS "SUPER" TERM IS SYNONYMOUS WITH "VERY"? SO THAT MEANS THIS TERM HERE MEANS *VERY CUTE.*
I SEE...
YOU LADIES MUST BE VERY STUDIOUS.
I'VE QUITE ENJOYED THIS INTELLIGENT CONVERSA-TION.
HERE. YOU MAY HAVE THIS BACK.
OH MY GAWD, HE CALLED *US* SMART!
WOW! WE'VE, LIKE, NEVER BEEN CALLED SMART BEFORE!
THANK YOU VERY MUCH. I LEARNED A LOT.
W- WAIT A MINUTE!
DIDN'T YOU JUST SAY YOU FOUND TALKING TO PEOPLE YOU DIDN'T KNOW ANNOYING?
A- ARE YOU OKAY ?!
PSST PSST
HM? DID I?
SO, LIKE, WHERE ARE YOU FROM?
YOUR ACCENT IS TOTES COOL.
UM!
ER?
CHATTER CHATTER
WELL, AH...
WHATEVER. WE HAVE TO GET GOING, ANYWAY.
BYE-BYE!

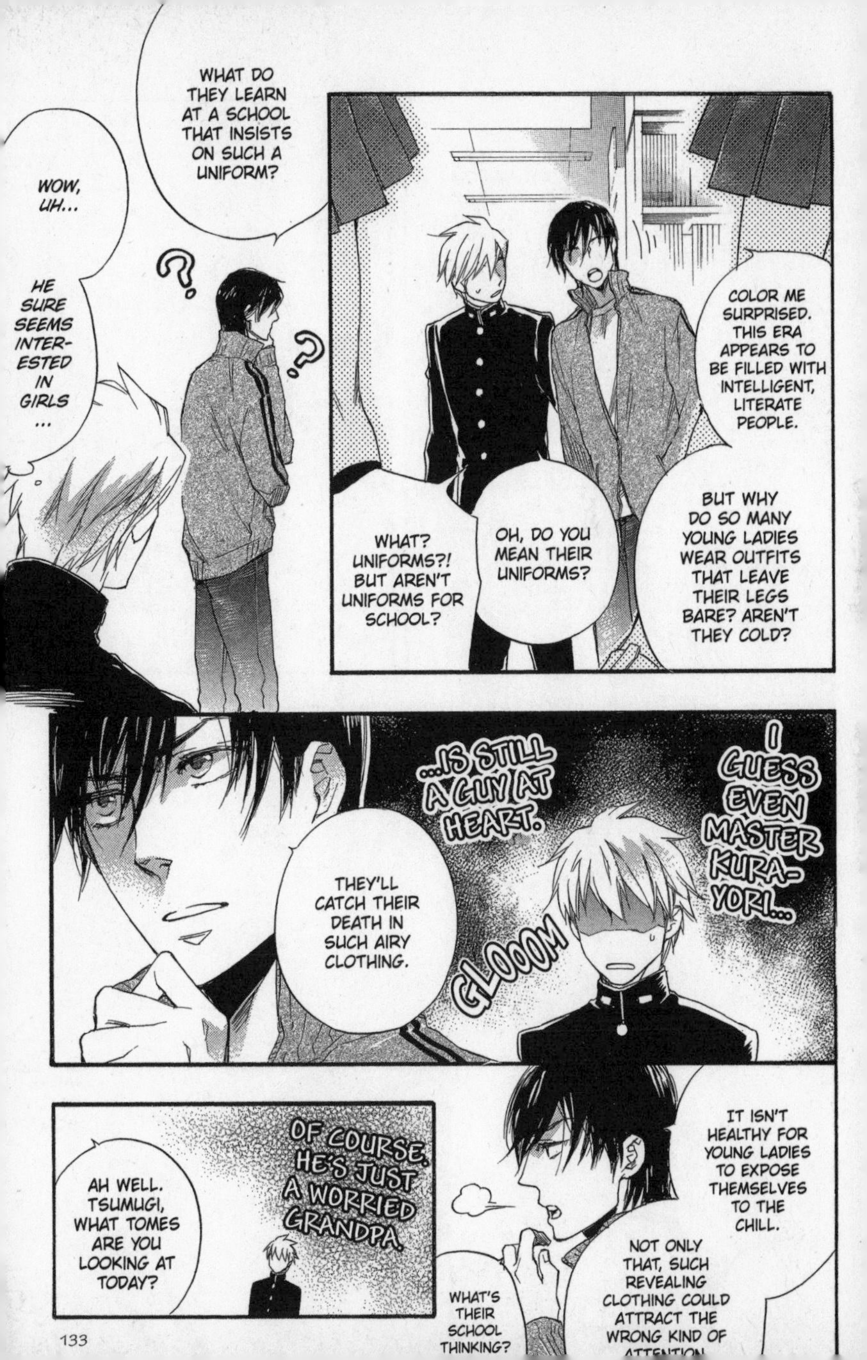
COLOR ME SURPRISED. THIS ERA APPEARS TO BE FILLED WITH INTELLIGENT, LITERATE PEOPLE.
BUT WHY DO SO MANY YOUNG LADIES WEAR OUTFITS THAT LEAVE THEIR LEGS BARE? AREN'T THEY COLD?
OH, DO YOU MEAN THEIR UNIFORMS?
WHAT? UNIFORMS?! BUT AREN'T UNIFORMS FOR SCHOOL?
WHAT DO THEY LEARN AT A SCHOOL THAT INSISTS ON SUCH A UNIFORM?
WOW, UH...
HE SURE SEEMS INTER-ESTED IN GIRLS ...
I GUESS EVEN MASTER KURA-YORI...
...IS STILL A GUY AT HEART.
GLOOOM
THEY'LL CATCH THEIR DEATH IN SUCH AIRY CLOTHING.
IT ISN'T HEALTHY FOR YOUNG LADIES TO EXPOSE THEMSELVES TO THE CHILL.
NOT ONLY THAT, SUCH REVEALING CLOTHING COULD ATTRACT THE WRONG KIND OF ATTENTION
WHAT'S THEIR SCHOOL THINKING?
OF COURSE. HE'S JUST A WORRIED GRANDPA.
AH WELL. TSUMUGI, WHAT TOMES ARE YOU LOOKING AT TODAY?

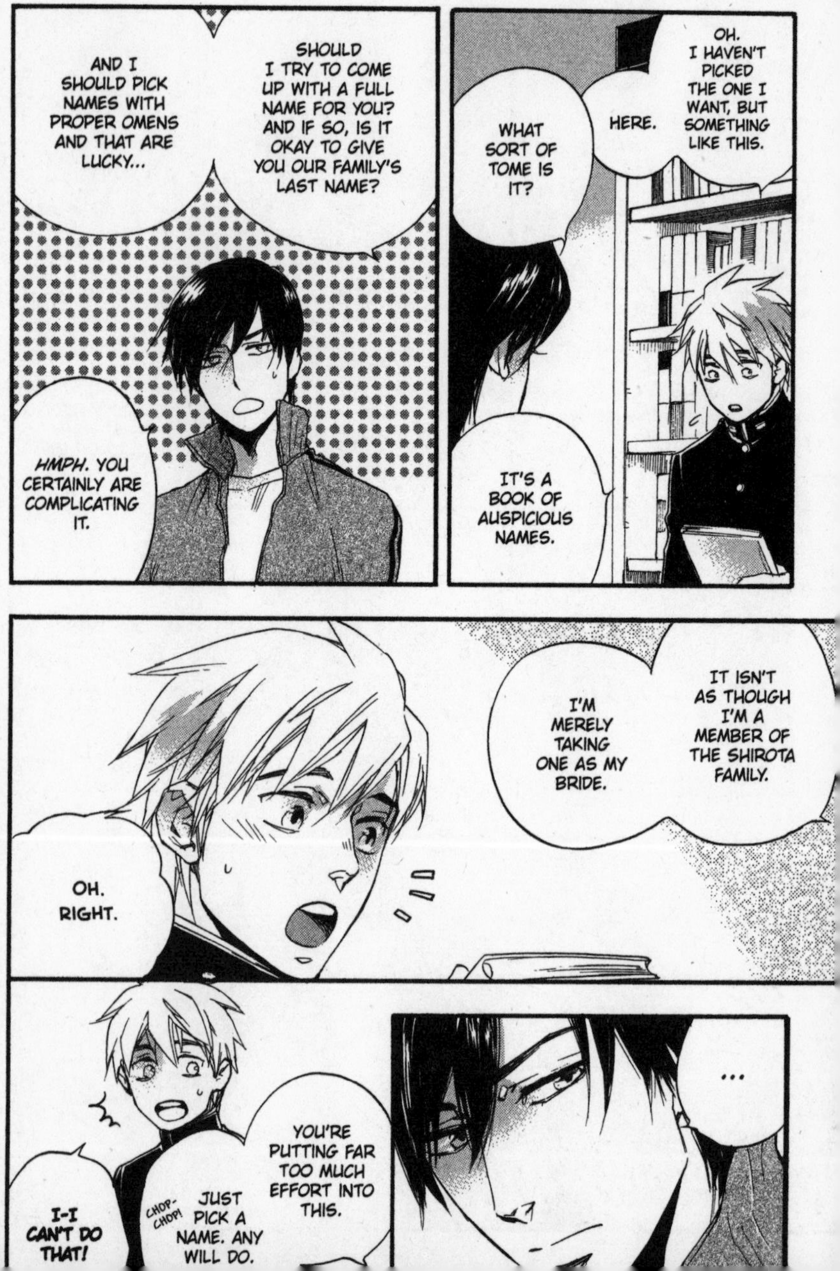
OH. I HAVEN'T PICKED THE ONE I WANT, BUT SOMETHING LIKE THIS.
HERE.
WHAT SORT OF TOME IS IT?
IT'S A BOOK OF AUSPICIOUS NAMES.
SHOULD I TRY TO COME UP WITH A FULL NAME FOR YOU? AND IF SO, IS IT OKAY TO GIVE YOU OUR FAMILY'S LAST NAME?
AND I SHOULD PICK NAMES WITH PROPER OMENS AND THAT ARE LUCKY...
HMPH. YOU CERTAINLY ARE COMPLICATING IT.
IT ISN'T AS THOUGH I'M A MEMBER OF THE SHIROTA FAMILY.
I'M MERELY TAKING ONE AS MY BRIDE.
OH. RIGHT.
...
YOU'RE PUTTING FAR TOO MUCH EFFORT INTO THIS.
JUST PICK A NAME. ANY WILL DO.
CHOP-CHOP!
I-I CAN'T DO THAT!

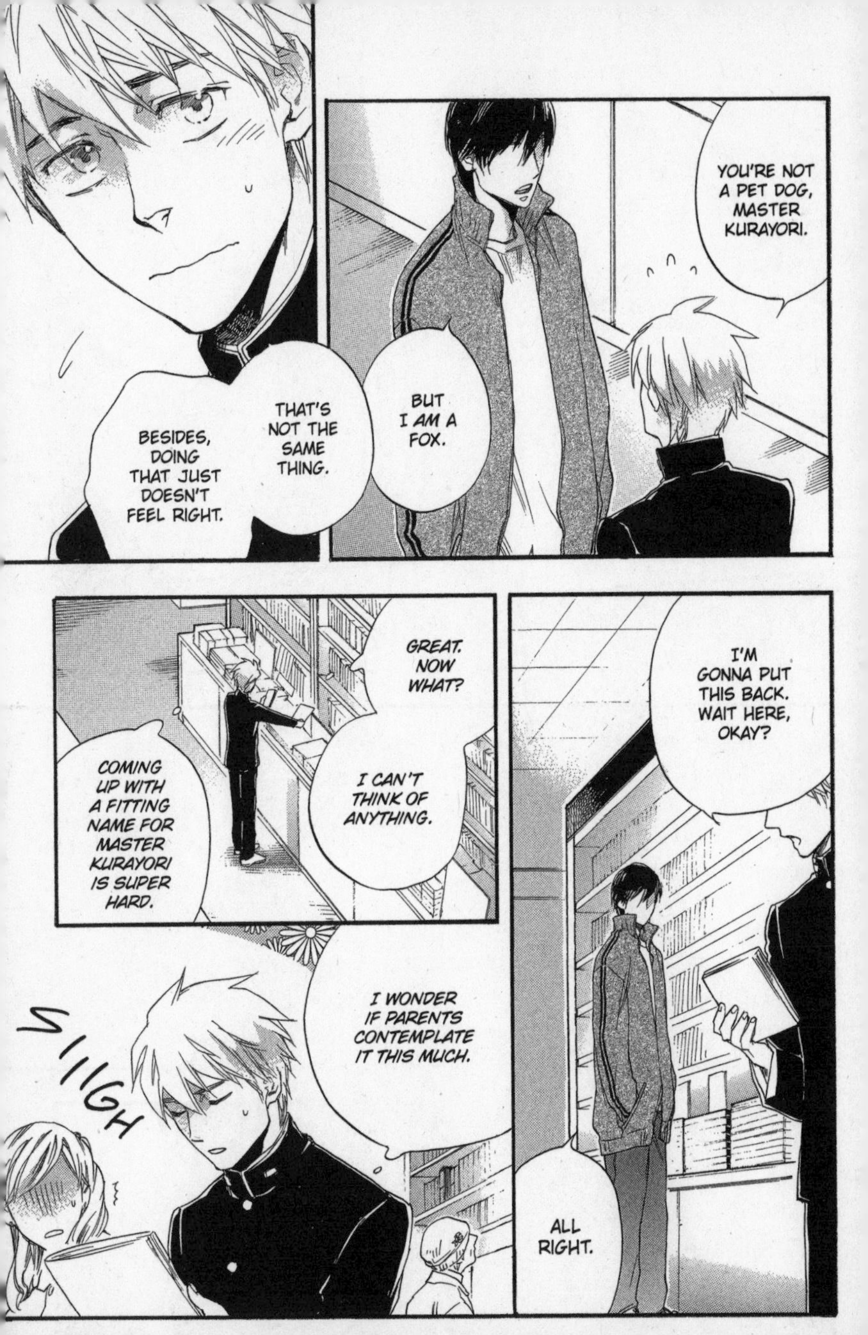
YOU'RE NOT A PET DOG, MASTER KURAYORI.
BUT I AM A FOX.
THAT'S NOT THE SAME THING.
BESIDES, DOING THAT JUST DOESN'T FEEL RIGHT.
I'M GONNA PUT THIS BACK. WAIT HERE, OKAY?
ALL RIGHT.
GREAT. NOW WHAT?
I CAN'T THINK OF ANYTHING.
COMING UP WITH A FITTING NAME FOR MASTER KURAYORI IS SUPER HARD.
SIIIGH
I WONDER IF PARENTS CONTEMPLATE IT THIS MUCH.

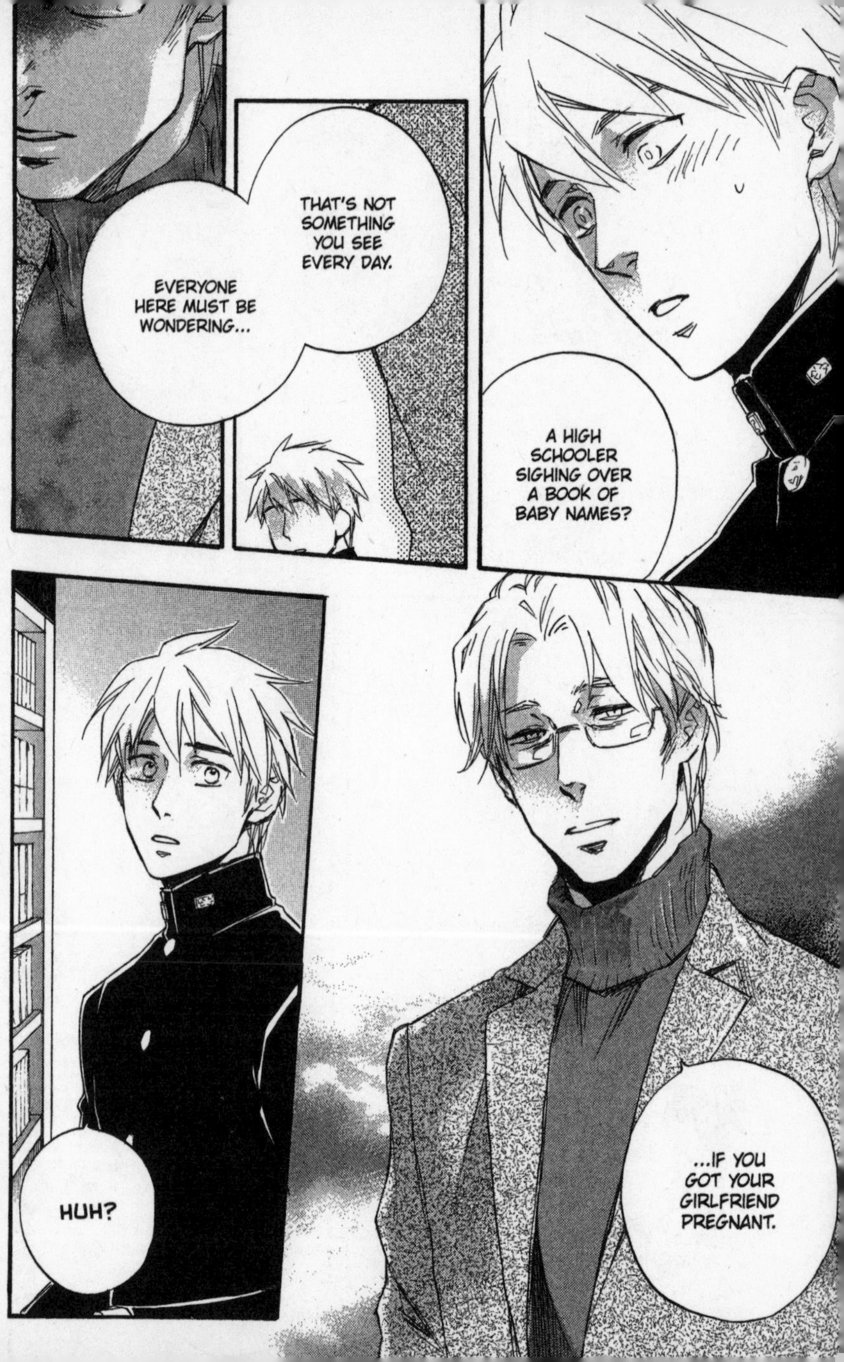
A HIGH SCHOOLER SIGHING OVER A BOOK OF BABY NAMES?
THAT'S NOT SOMETHING YOU SEE EVERY DAY.
EVERYONE HERE MUST BE WONDERING...
...IF YOU GOT YOUR GIRLFRIEND PREGNANT.
HUH?

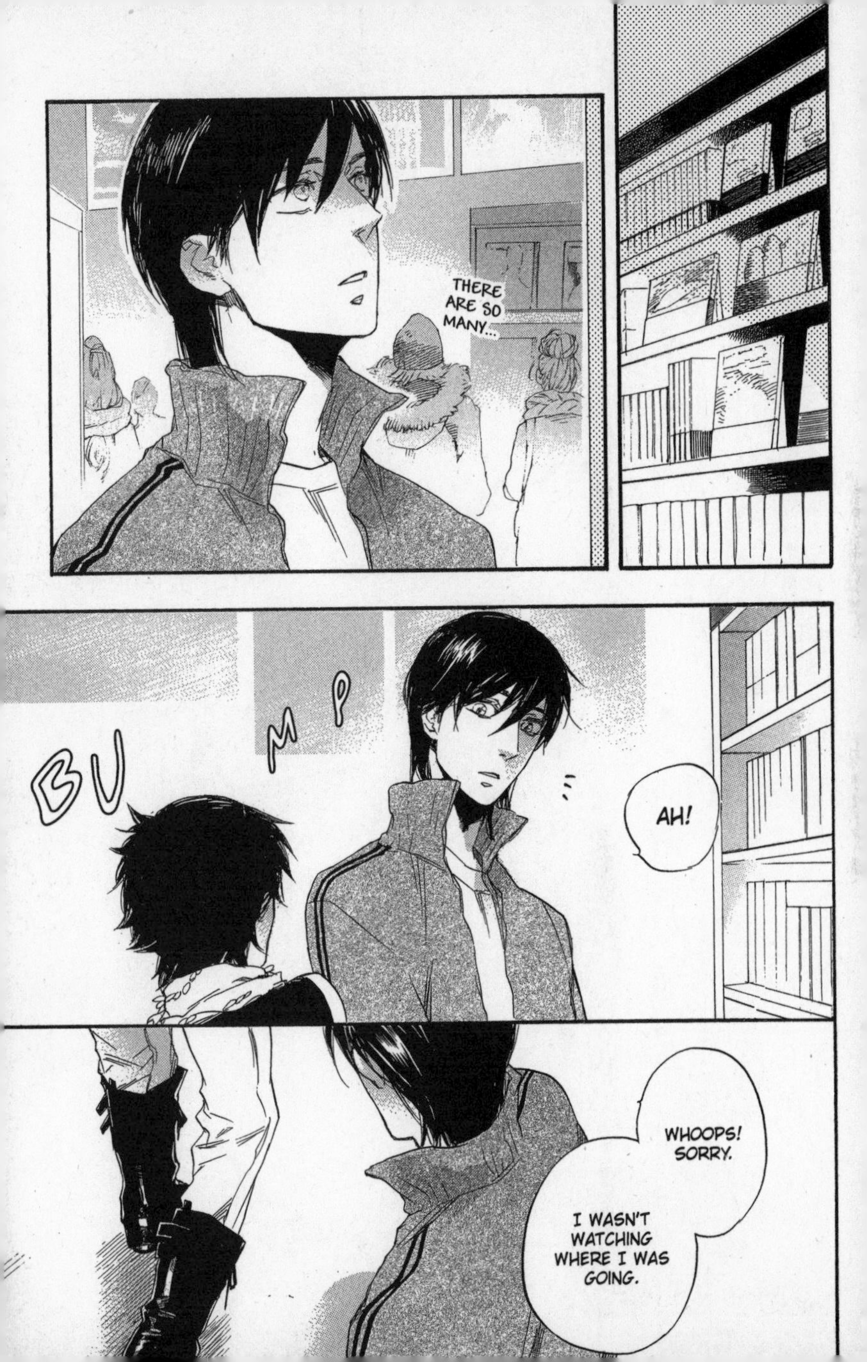
THERE ARE SO MANY...
BUMP
AH!
WHOOPS! SORRY.
I WASN'T WATCHING WHERE I WAS GOING.

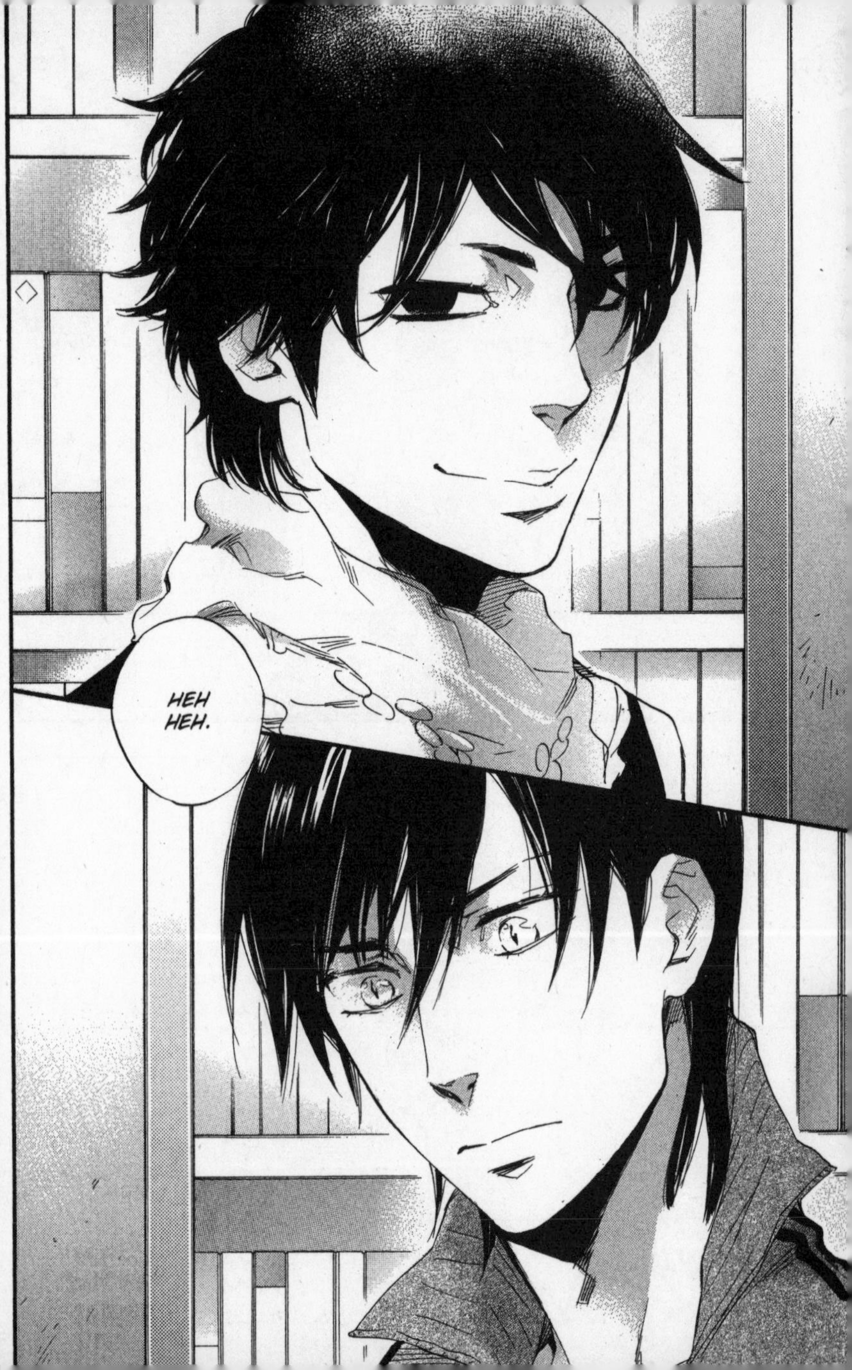
HEH HEH.

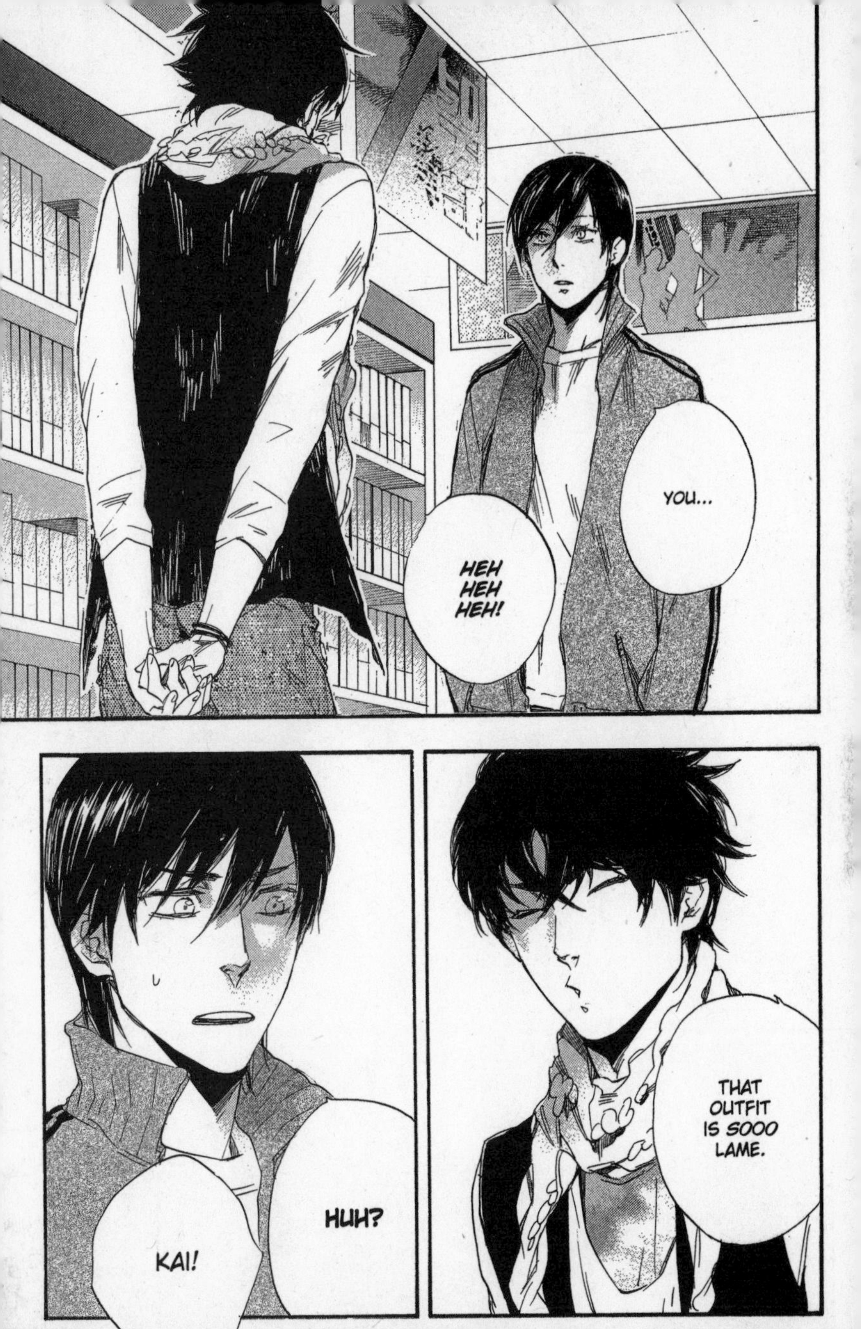
YOU...
HEH HEH HEH!
THAT OUTFIT IS SOOO LAME.
HUH?
KAI!

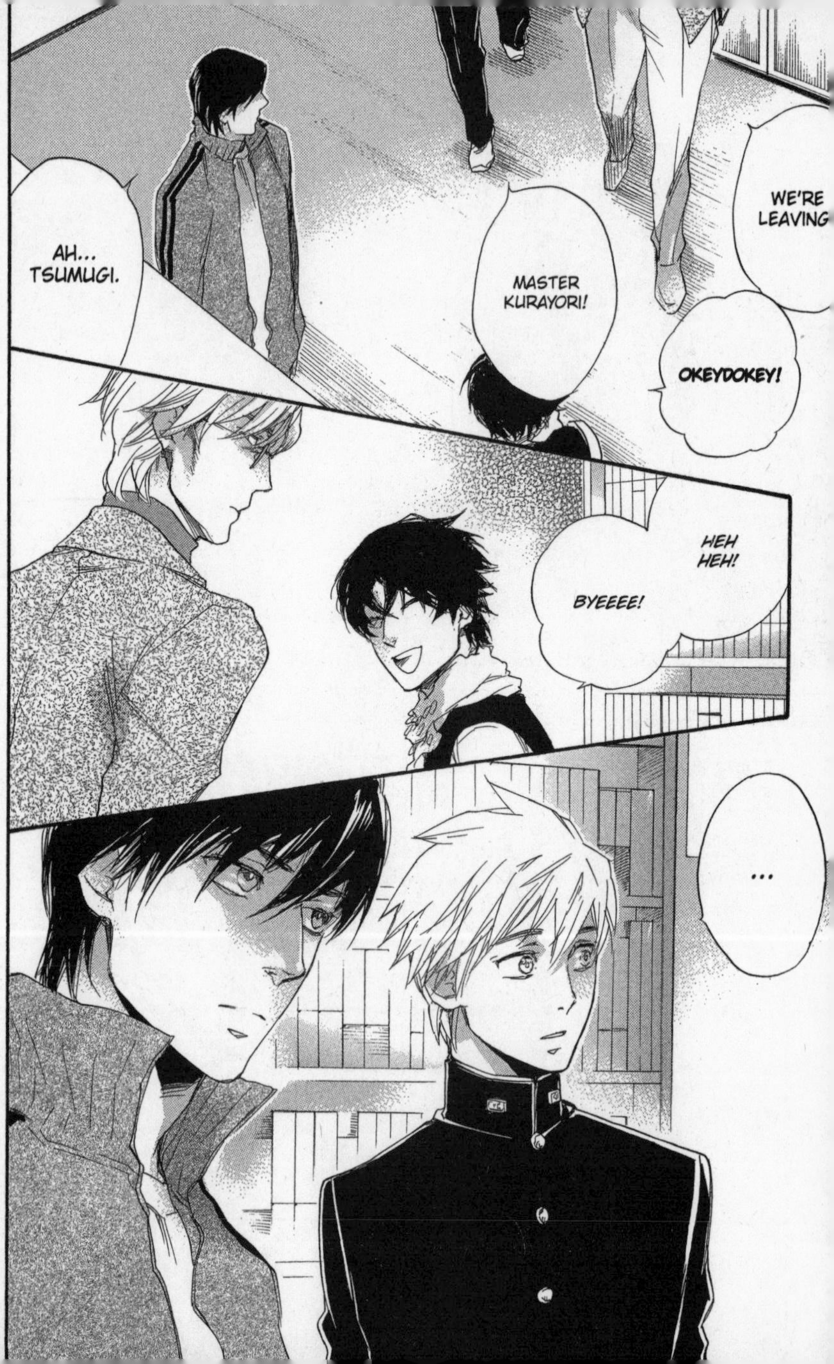
WE'RE LEAVING
OKEYDOKEY!
MASTER KURAYORI!
AH... TSUMUGI.
HEH HEH!
BYEEEE!
...

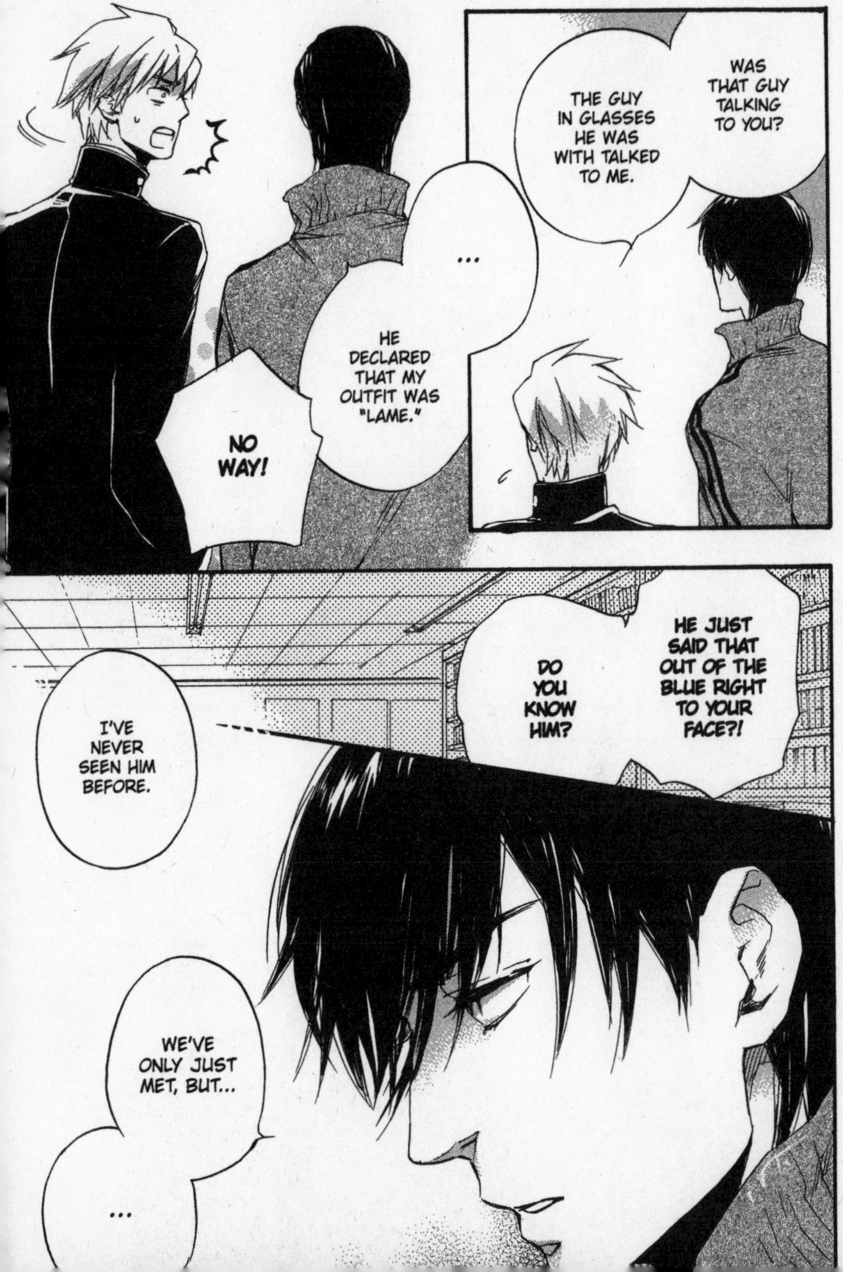
WAS THAT GUY TALKING TO YOU?
THE GUY IN GLASSES HE WAS WITH TALKED TO ME.
...
HE DECLARED THAT MY OUTFIT WAS "LAME."
NO WAY!
HE JUST SAID THAT OUT OF THE BLUE RIGHT TO YOUR FACE?!
DO YOU KNOW HIM?
I'VE NEVER SEEN HIM BEFORE.
WE'VE ONLY JUST MET, BUT...
...

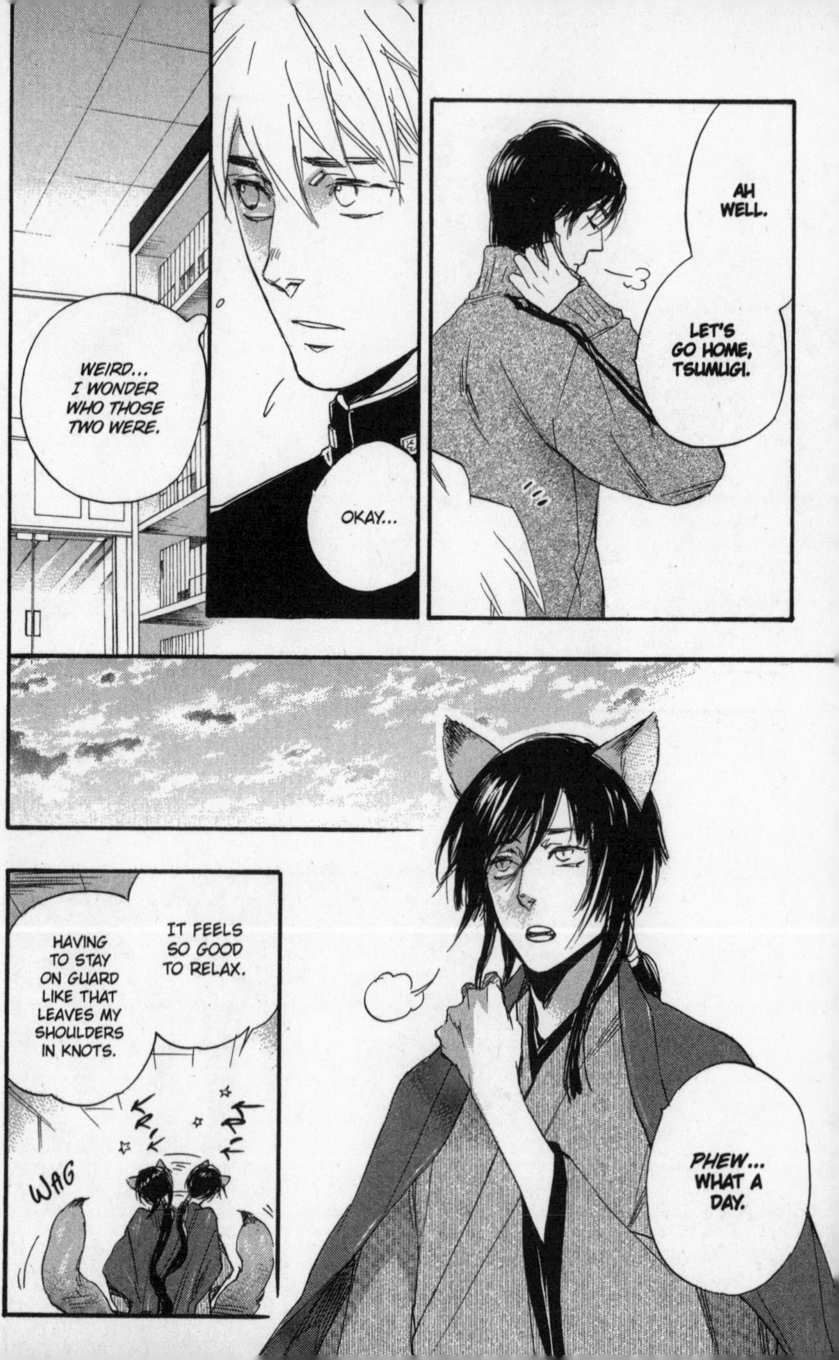
AH WELL.
LET'S GO HOME, TSUMUGI.
OKAY...
WEIRD... I WONDER WHO THOSE TWO WERE.
PHEW... WHAT A DAY.
IT FEELS SO GOOD TO RELAX.
HAVING TO STAY ON GUARD LIKE THAT LEAVES MY SHOULDERS IN KNOTS.
KRIK
KRIK
WAG

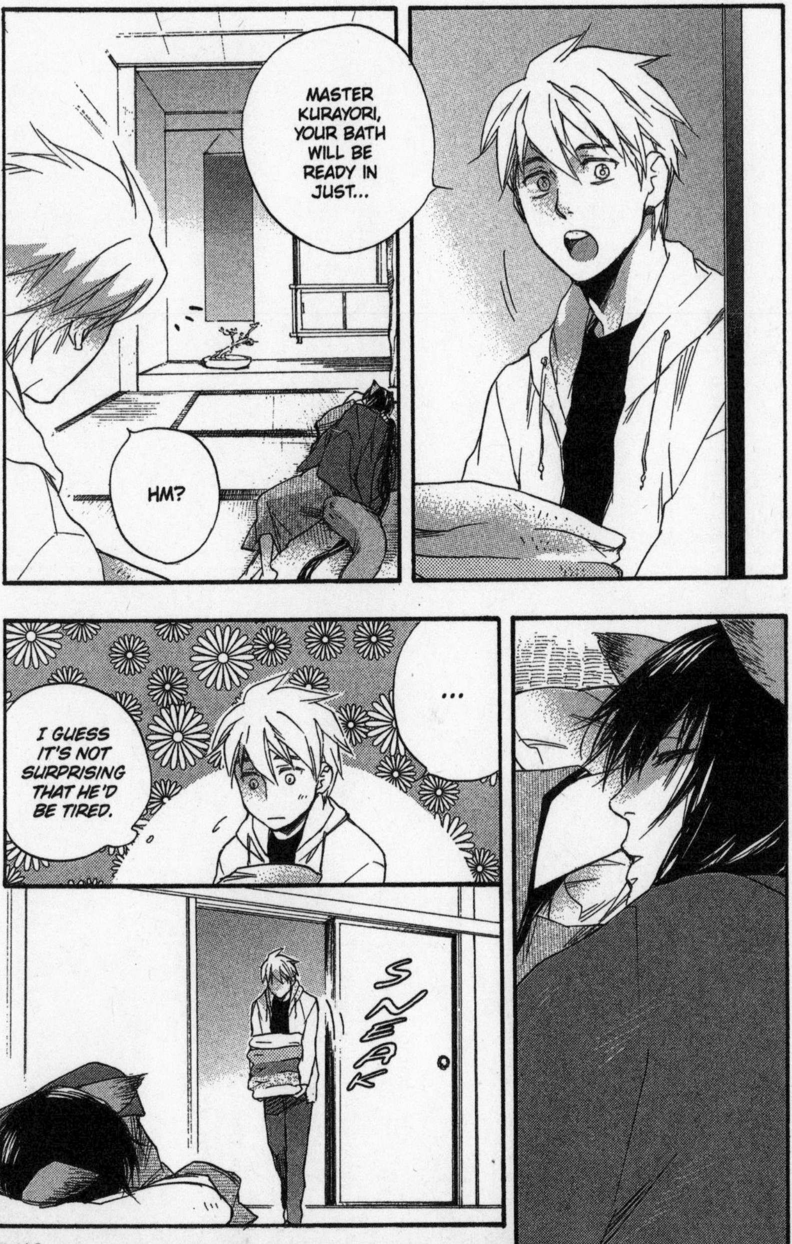
MASTER KURAYORI, YOUR BATH WILL BE READY IN JUST...
HM?
...
I GUESS IT'S NOT SURPRISING THAT HE'D BE TIRED.
SNEAK

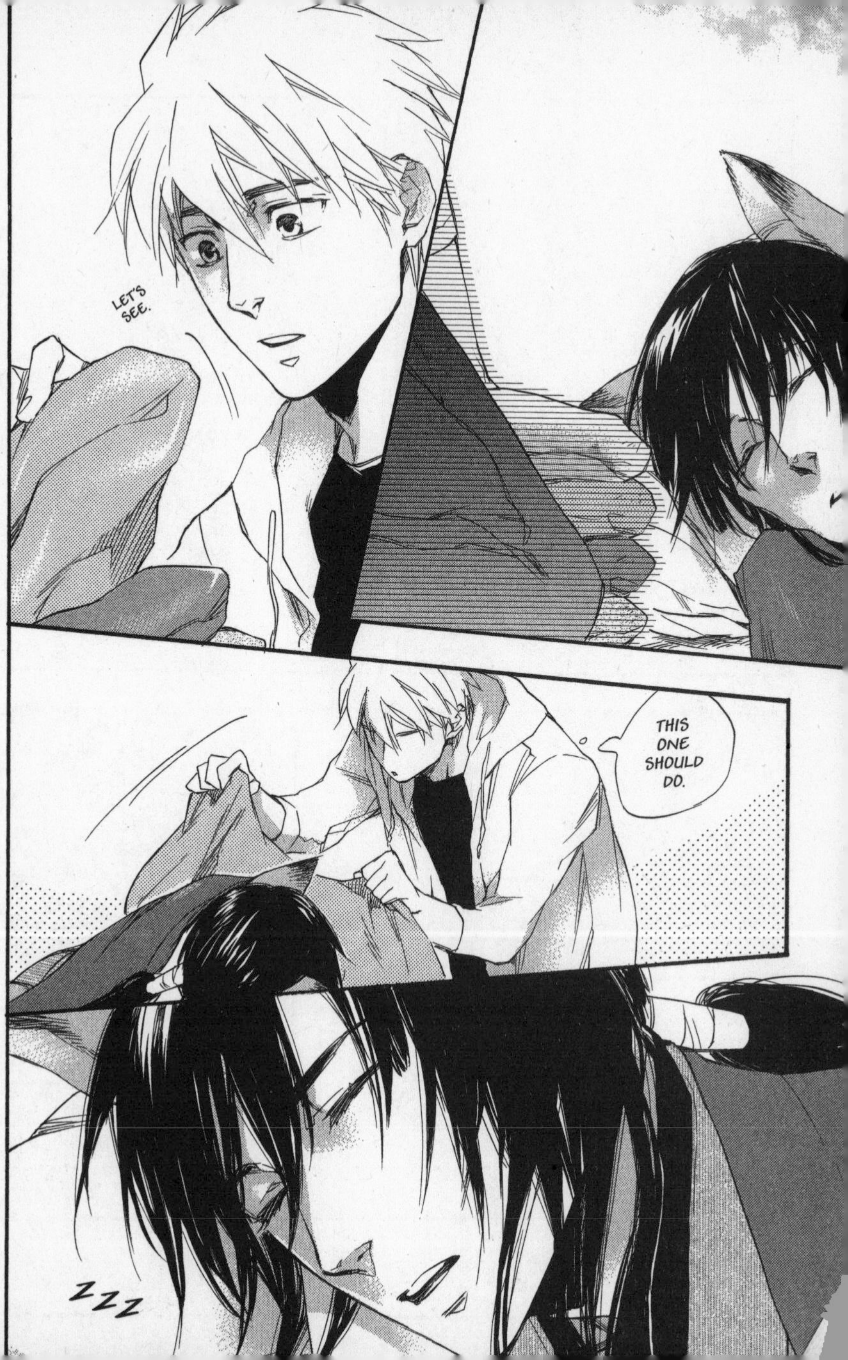
LET'S SEE.
THIS ONE SHOULD DO.
ZZZ

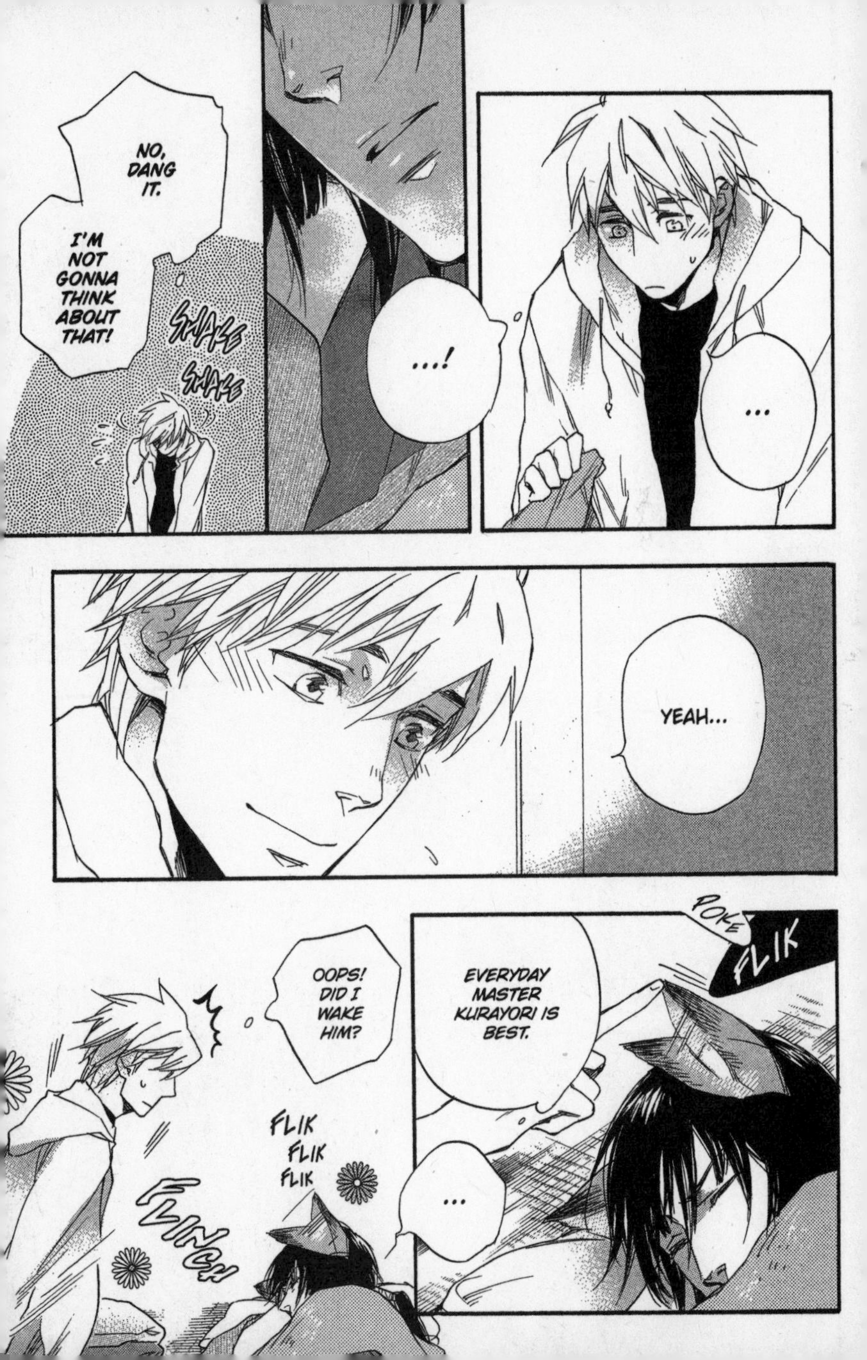
...
...!
NO, DANG IT.
I'M NOT GONNA THINK ABOUT THAT!
SHAKE
SHAKE
YEAH...
POKE
FLIK
EVERYDAY MASTER KURAYORI IS BEST.
...
OOPS! DID I WAKE HIM?
FLIK FLIK FLIK
FLINCH

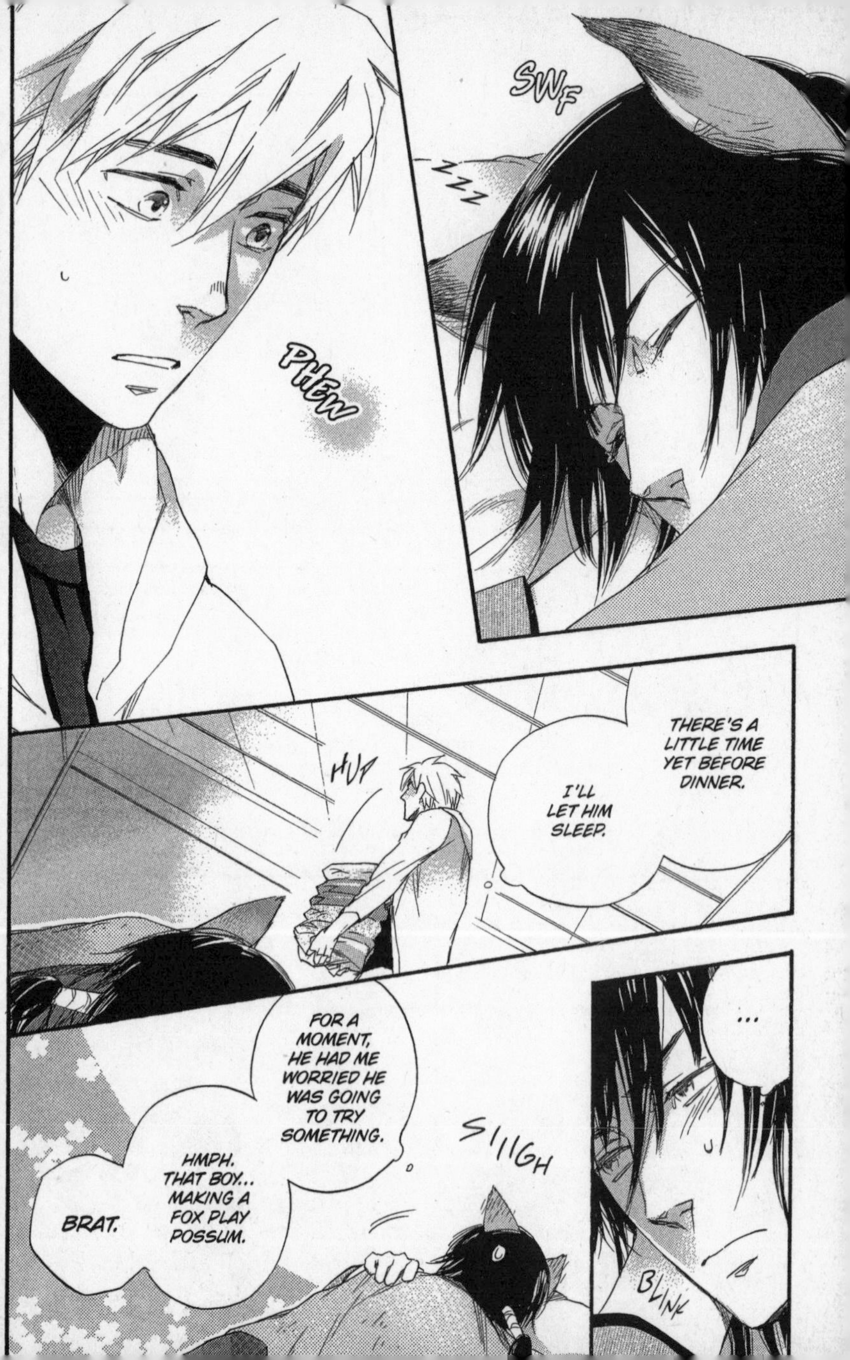
SWF
ZZZZ
PHEW
THERE'S A LITTLE TIME YET BEFORE DINNER.
I'LL LET HIM SLEEP.
HUP
...
BLINK
SIIIGH
FOR A MOMENT, HE HAD ME WORRIED HE WAS GOING TO TRY SOMETHING.
HMPH. THAT BOY... MAKING A FOX PLAY POSSUM.
BRAT.

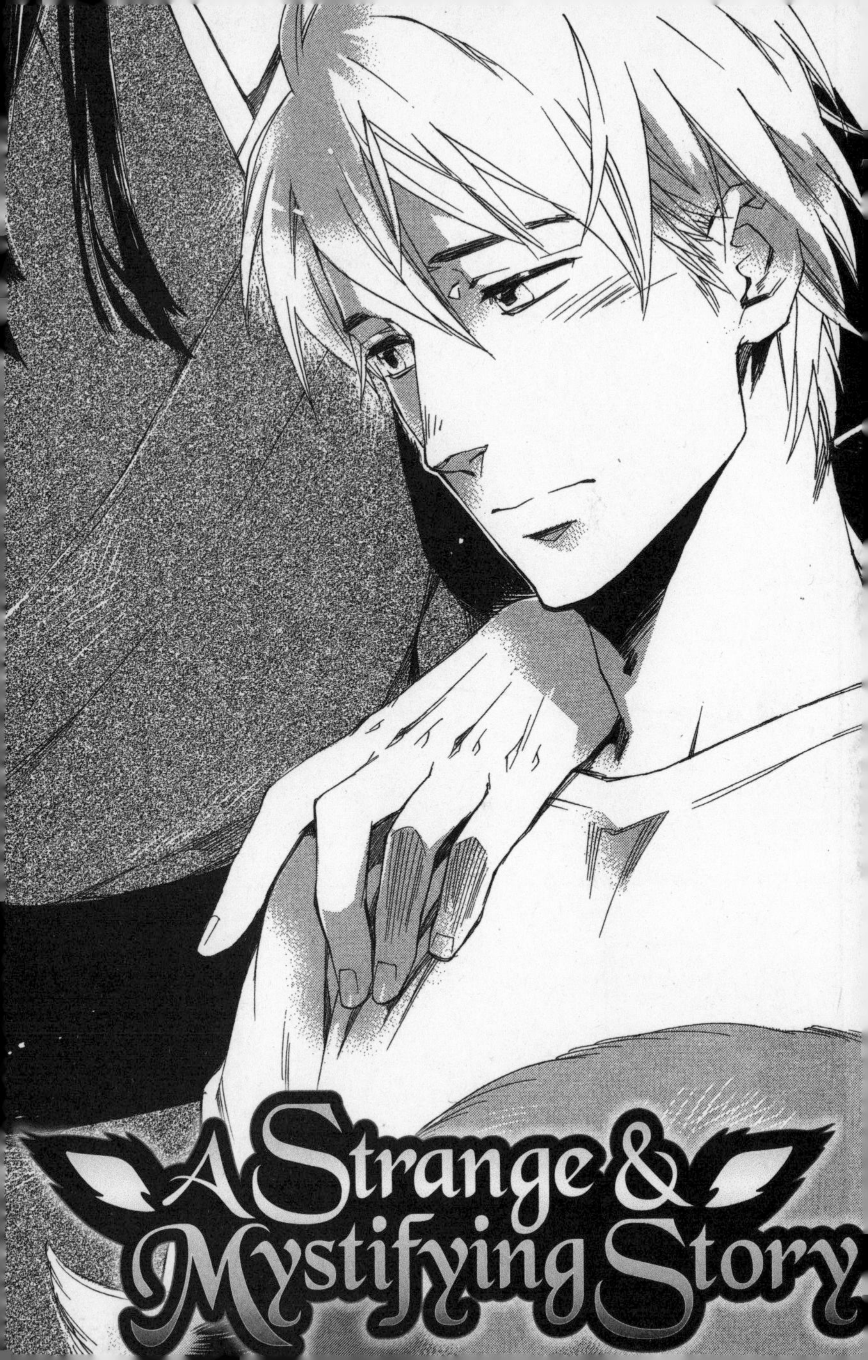
A Strange & Mystifying Story

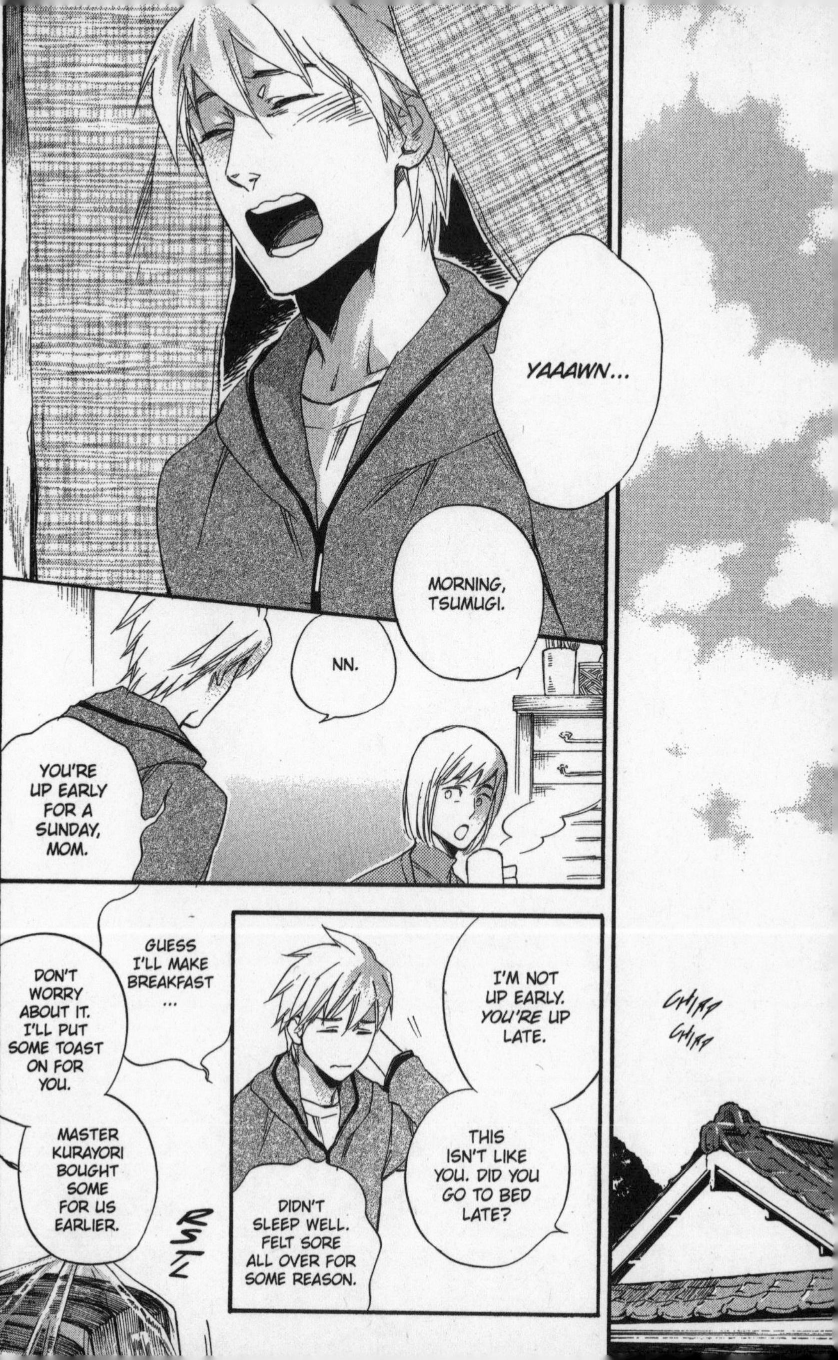
CHIRP
CHIRP
YAAAWN...
MORNING, TSUMUGI.
NN.
YOU'RE UP EARLY FOR A SUNDAY, MOM.
I'M NOT UP EARLY. *YOU'RE* UP LATE.
THIS ISN'T LIKE YOU. DID YOU GO TO BED LATE?
DIDN'T SLEEP WELL. FELT SORE ALL OVER FOR SOME REASON.
GUESS I'LL MAKE BREAKFAST ...
DON'T WORRY ABOUT IT. I'LL PUT SOME TOAST ON FOR YOU.
MASTER KURAYORI BOUGHT SOME FOR US EARLIER.
RSTL

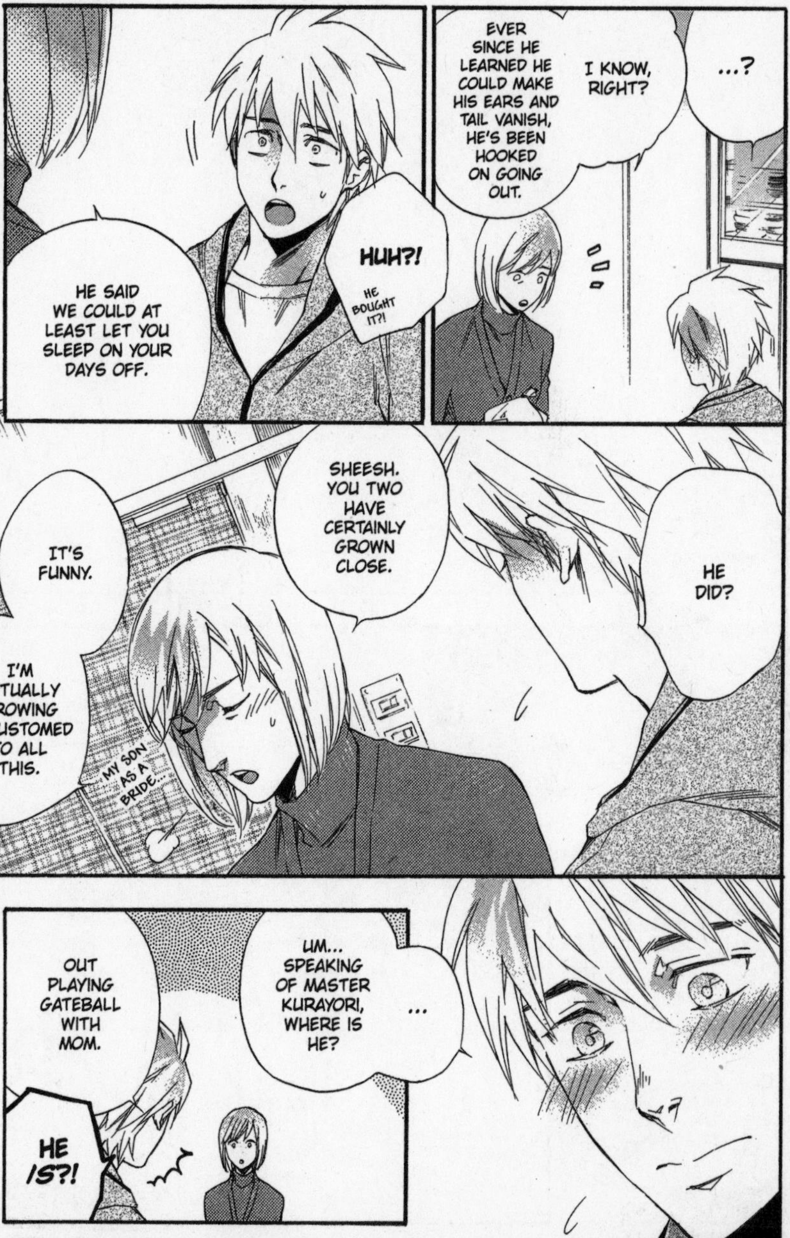
...?
I KNOW, RIGHT?
EVER SINCE HE LEARNED HE COULD MAKE HIS EARS AND TAIL VANISH, HE'S BEEN HOOKED ON GOING OUT.
HUH?!
HE BOUGHT IT?!
HE SAID WE COULD AT LEAST LET YOU SLEEP ON YOUR DAYS OFF.
HE DID?
SHEESH. YOU TWO HAVE CERTAINLY GROWN CLOSE.
IT'S FUNNY.
I'M ACTUALLY GROWING ACCUSTOMED TO ALL THIS.
MY SON AS A BRIDE...
...
UM... SPEAKING OF MASTER KURAYORI, WHERE IS HE?
OUT PLAYING GATEBALL WITH MOM.
HE IS?!

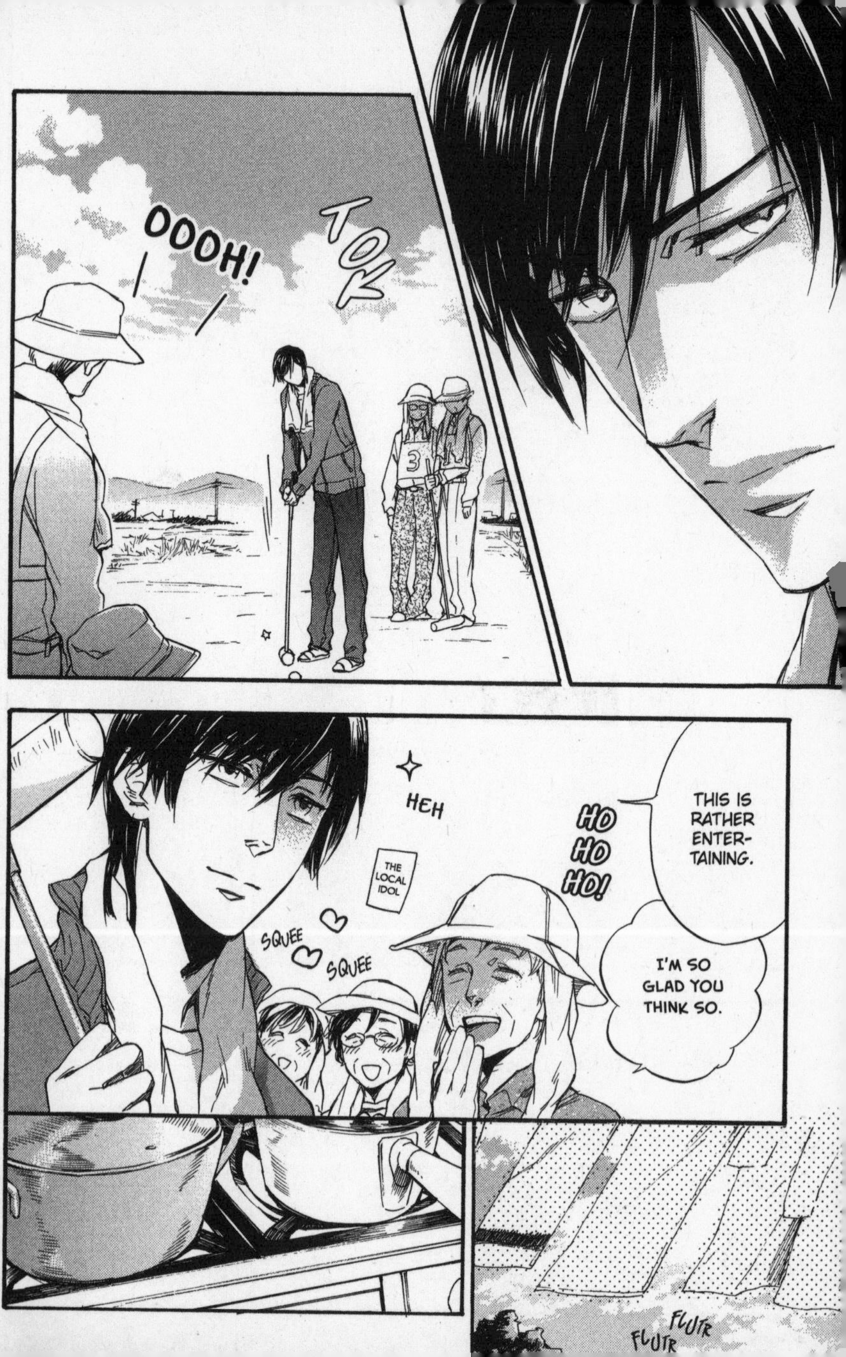
TOK
OOOH!
THIS IS RATHER ENTERTAINING.
HO HO HO!
I'M SO GLAD YOU THINK SO.
HEH
THE LOCAL IDOL
SQUEE
SQUEE
FLUTR
FLUTR

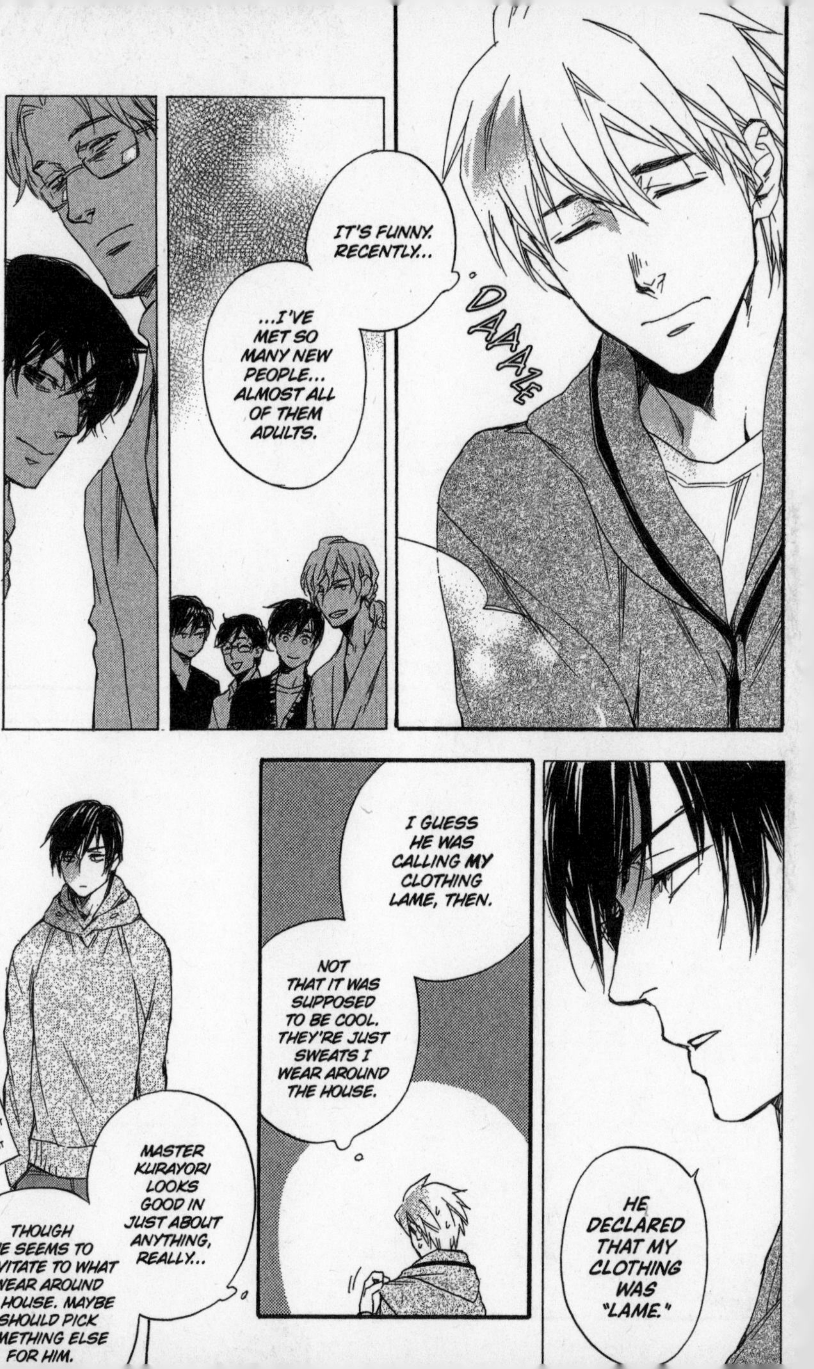
IT'S FUNNY. RECENTLY...
...I'VE MET SO MANY NEW PEOPLE... ALMOST ALL OF THEM ADULTS.
DAAAZE
HE DECLARED THAT MY CLOTHING WAS "LAME."
I GUESS HE WAS CALLING MY CLOTHING LAME, THEN.
NOT THAT IT WAS SUPPOSED TO BE COOL. THEY'RE JUST SWEATS I WEAR AROUND THE HOUSE.
MASTER KURAYORI LOOKS GOOD IN JUST ABOUT ANYTHING, REALLY...
THOUGH HE SEEMS TO GRAVITATE TO WHAT I WEAR AROUND THE HOUSE. MAYBE I SHOULD PICK SOMETHING ELSE FOR HIM.
STILL DOESN'T FEEL RIGHT

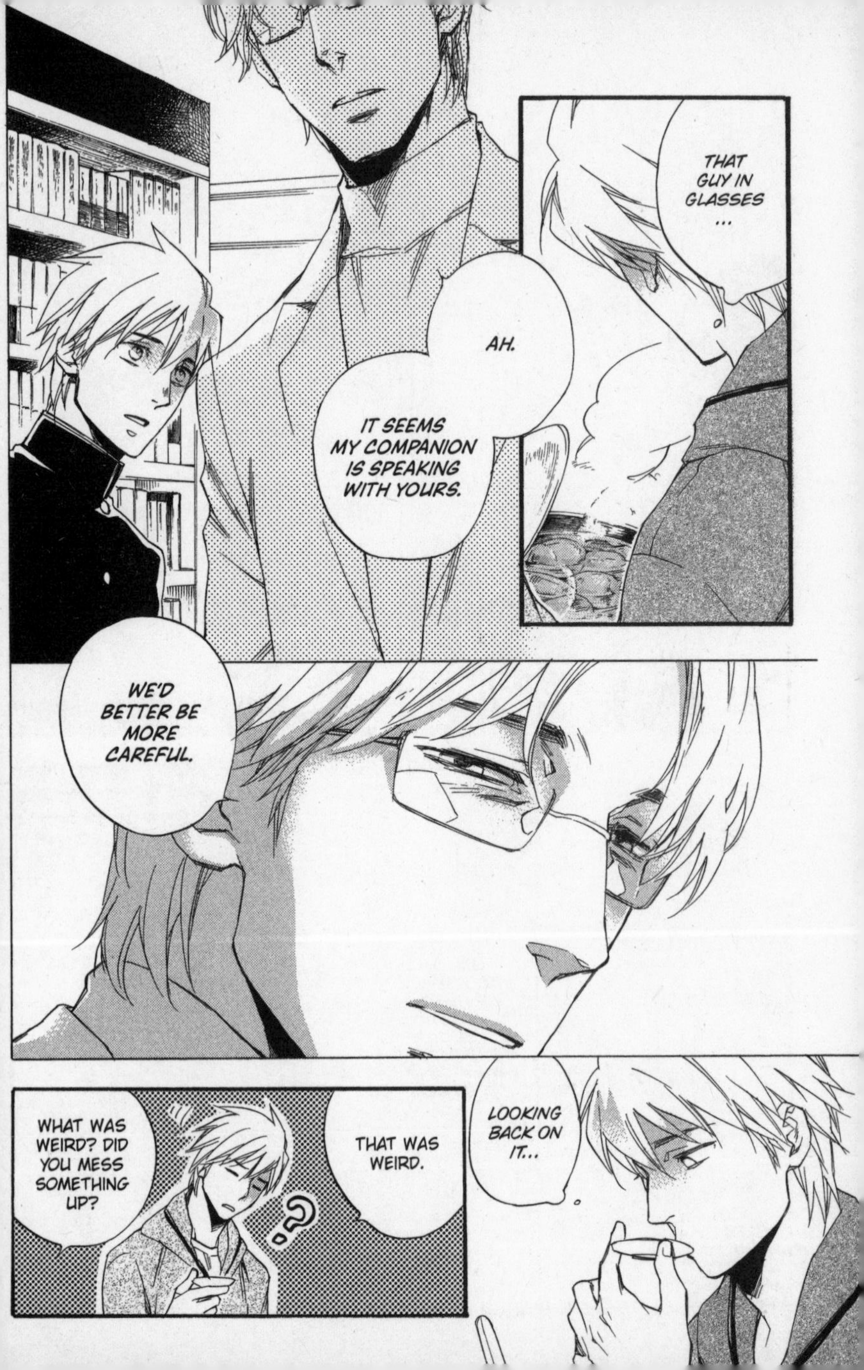
THAT GUY IN GLASSES ...
AH.
IT SEEMS MY COMPANION IS SPEAKING WITH YOURS.
WE'D BETTER BE MORE CAREFUL.
LOOKING BACK ON IT...
THAT WAS WEIRD.
WHAT WAS WEIRD? DID YOU MESS SOMETHING UP?

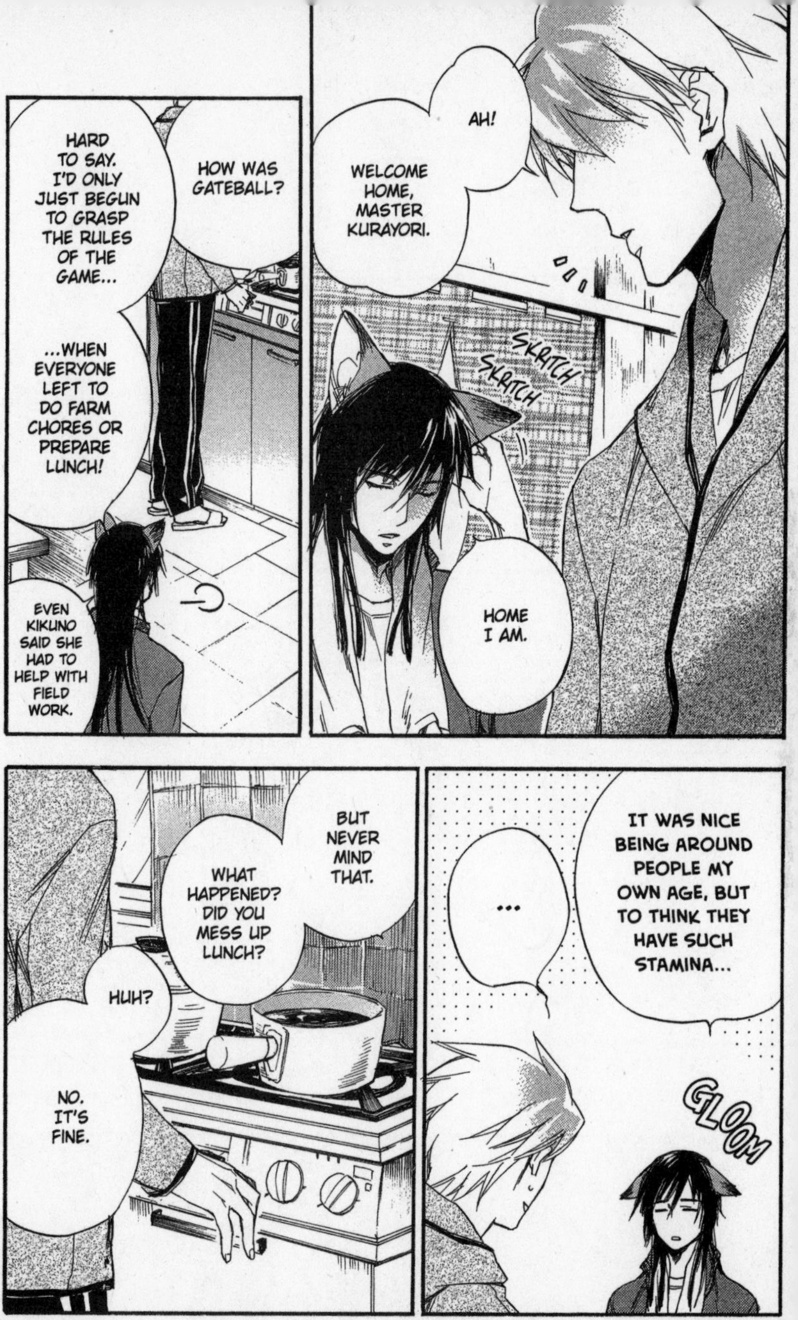
AH!
WELCOME HOME, MASTER KURAYORI.
SKRITCH SKRITCH
HOME I AM.
HOW WAS GATEBALL?
HARD TO SAY. I'D ONLY JUST BEGUN TO GRASP THE RULES OF THE GAME...
...WHEN EVERYONE LEFT TO DO FARM CHORES OR PREPARE LUNCH!
EVEN KIKUNO SAID SHE HAD TO HELP WITH FIELD WORK.
IT WAS NICE BEING AROUND PEOPLE MY OWN AGE, BUT TO THINK THEY HAVE SUCH STAMINA...
...
GLOOM
BUT NEVER MIND THAT.
WHAT HAPPENED? DID YOU MESS UP LUNCH?
HUH?
NO. IT'S FINE.

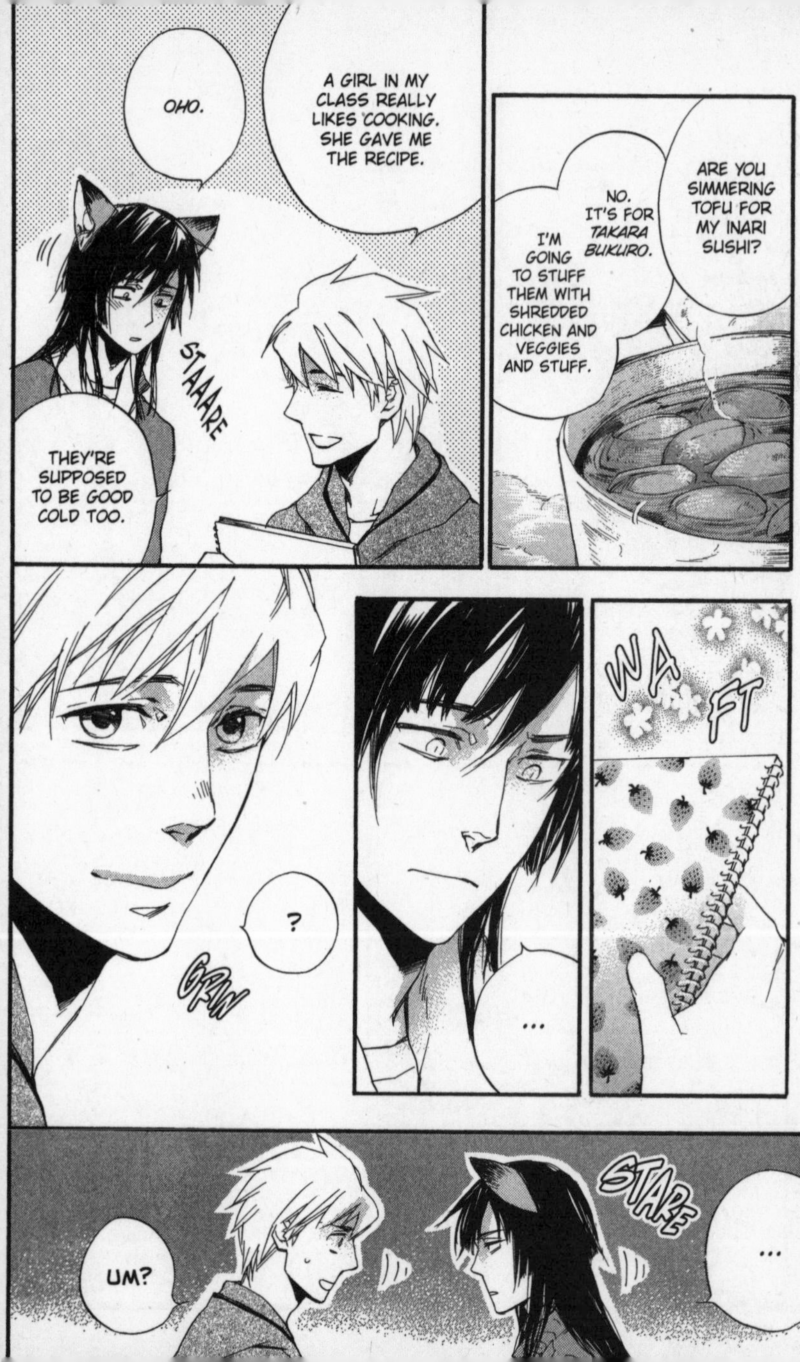
ARE YOU SIMMERING TOFU FOR MY INARI SUSHI?
NO. IT'S FOR *TAKARA BUKURO.*
I'M GOING TO STUFF THEM WITH SHREDDED CHICKEN AND VEGGIES AND STUFF.
A GIRL IN MY CLASS REALLY LIKES COOKING. SHE GAVE ME THE RECIPE.
OHO.
STAAARE
THEY'RE SUPPOSED TO BE GOOD COLD TOO.
WAFT
...
?
GRIN
STARE
...
UM?

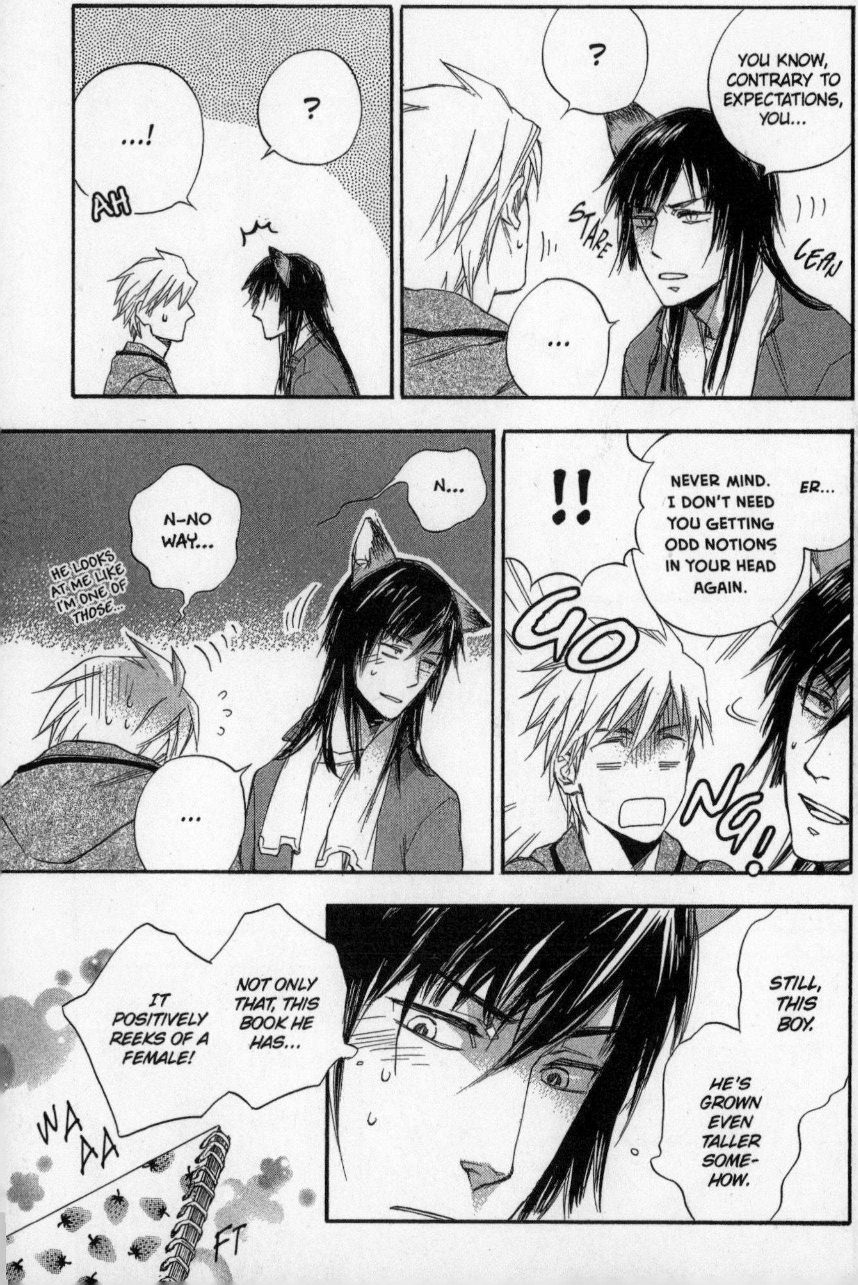
YOU KNOW, CONTRARY TO EXPECTATIONS, YOU...
?
STARE
LEAN
...
?
...!
AH
ER...
NEVER MIND. I DON'T NEED YOU GETTING ODD NOTIONS IN YOUR HEAD AGAIN.
!!
GONG!
N...
N-NO WAY...
HE LOOKS AT ME LIKE I'M ONE OF THOSE...
...
STILL, THIS BOY.
HE'S GROWN EVEN TALLER SOME-HOW.
NOT ONLY THAT, THIS BOOK HE HAS...
IT POSITIVELY REEKS OF A FEMALE!
WAAA
FT

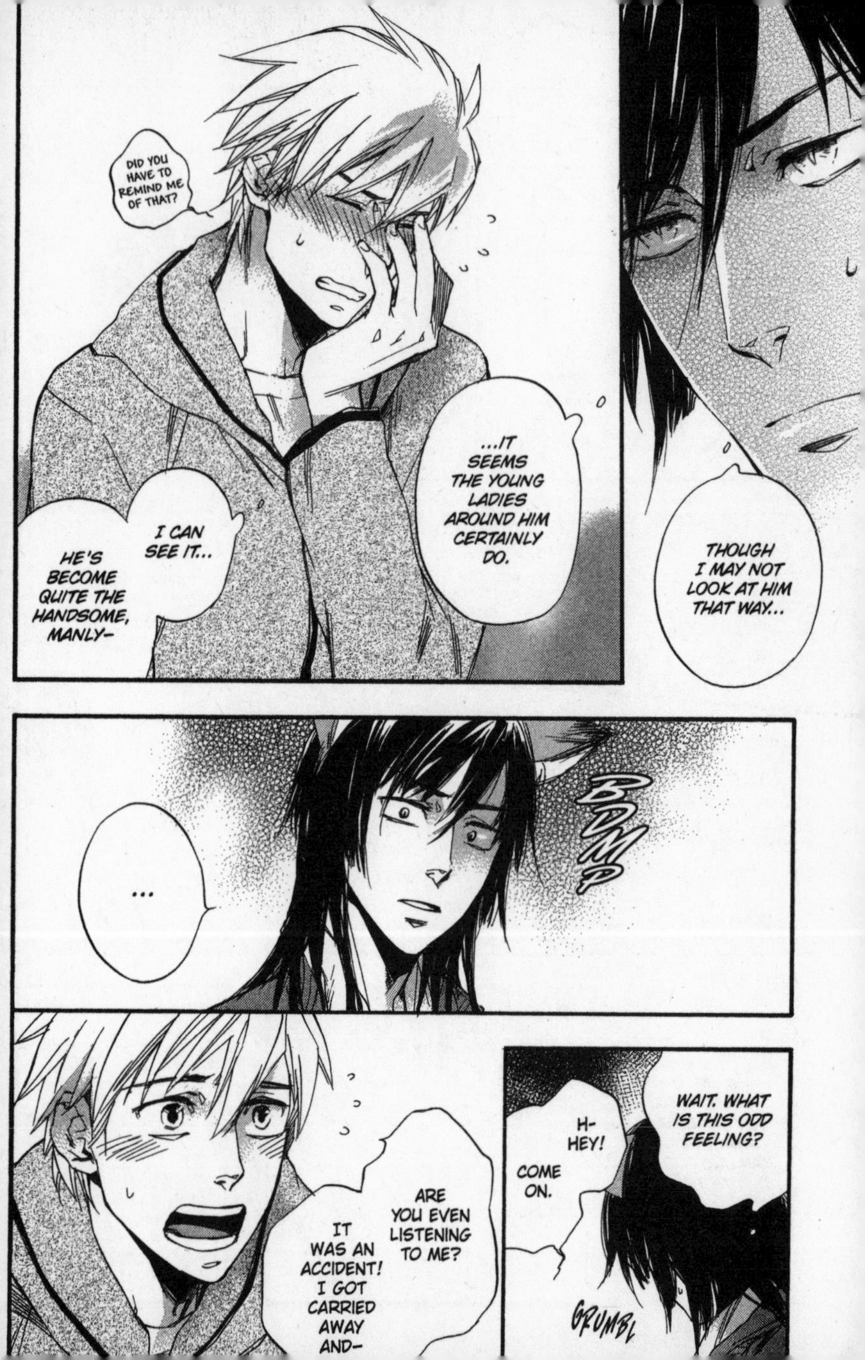
THOUGH I MAY NOT LOOK AT HIM THAT WAY...
...IT SEEMS THE YOUNG LADIES AROUND HIM CERTAINLY DO.
DID YOU HAVE TO REMIND ME OF THAT?
I CAN SEE IT...
HE'S BECOME QUITE THE HANDSOME, MANLY-
...
BDMP
WAIT. WHAT IS THIS ODD FEELING?
H-HEY!
COME ON.
GRUMBL
ARE YOU EVEN LISTENING TO ME?
IT WAS AN ACCIDENT! I GOT CARRIED AWAY AND-

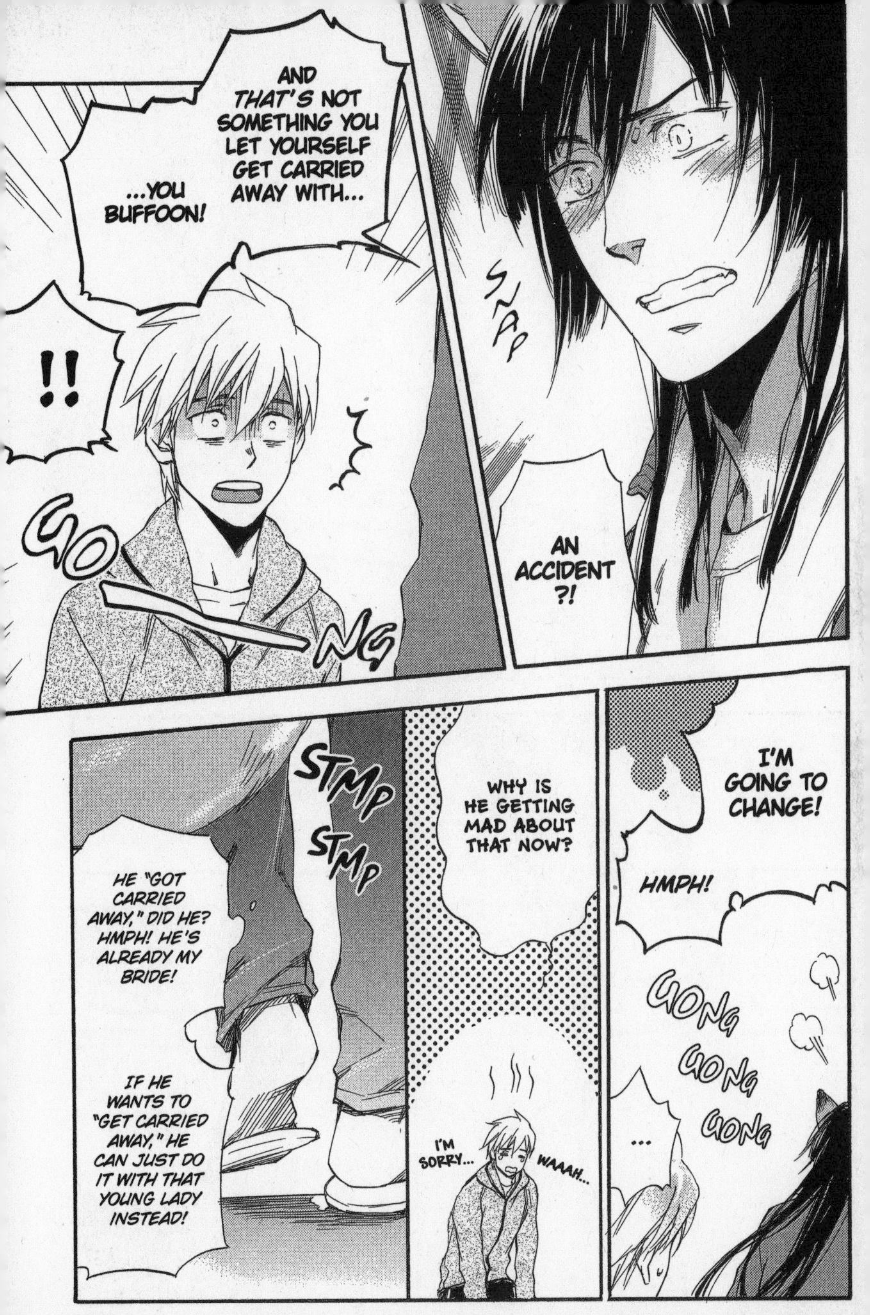
SNAP
AN ACCIDENT ?!
AND THAT'S NOT SOMETHING YOU LET YOURSELF GET CARRIED AWAY WITH...
...YOU BUFFOON!
!!
GONG
I'M GOING TO CHANGE!
HMPH!
GONG GONG GONG
...
WHY IS HE GETTING MAD ABOUT THAT NOW?
WAAAH...
I'M SORRY...
STMP STMP
HE "GOT CARRIED AWAY," DID HE? HMPH! HE'S ALREADY MY BRIDE!
IF HE WANTS TO "GET CARRIED AWAY," HE CAN JUST DO IT WITH THAT YOUNG LADY INSTEAD!

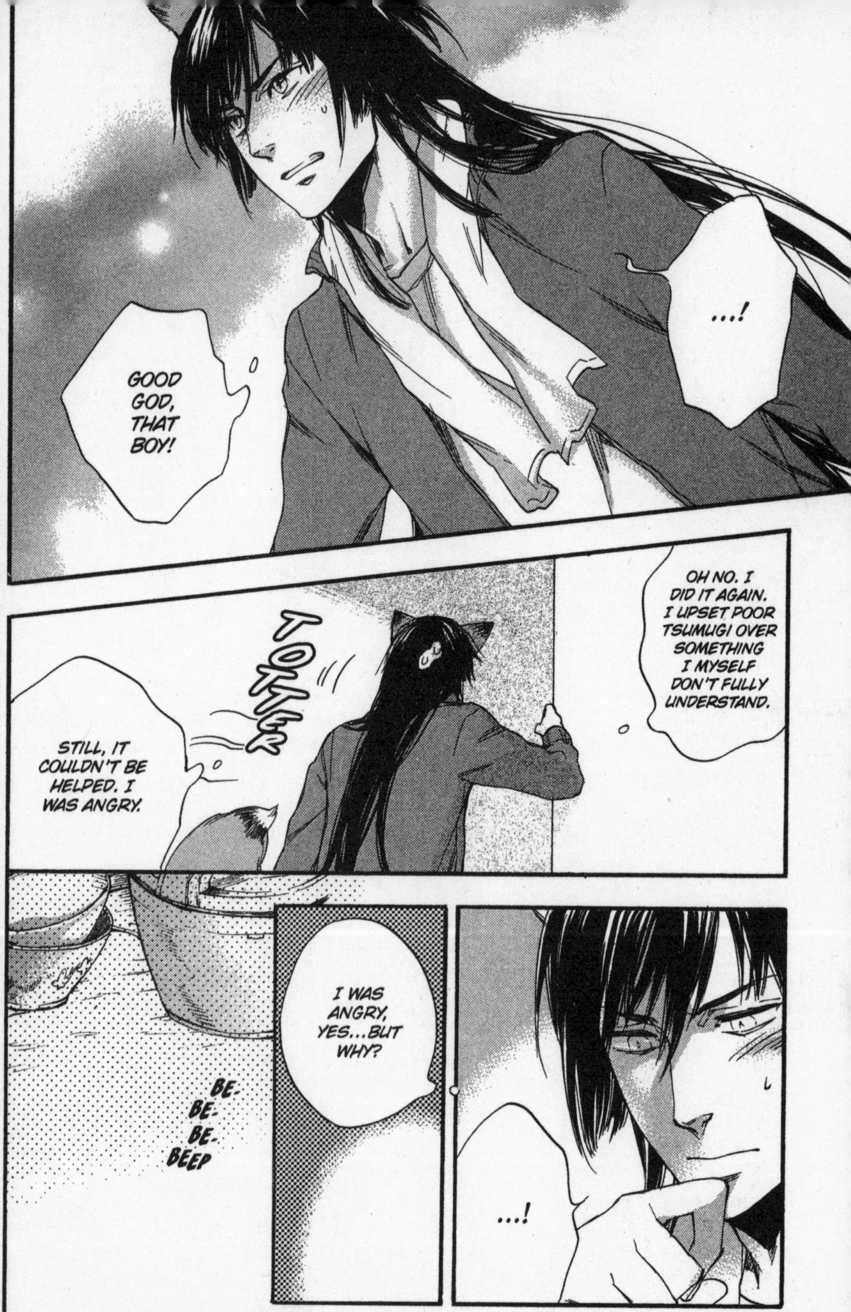
...!
GOOD GOD, THAT BOY!
OH NO. I DID IT AGAIN. I UPSET POOR TSUMUGI OVER SOMETHING I MYSELF DON'T FULLY UNDERSTAND.
TOTTER
STILL, IT COULDN'T BE HELPED. I WAS ANGRY.
...!
I WAS ANGRY, YES...BUT WHY?
BE-BE-BE-BEEP

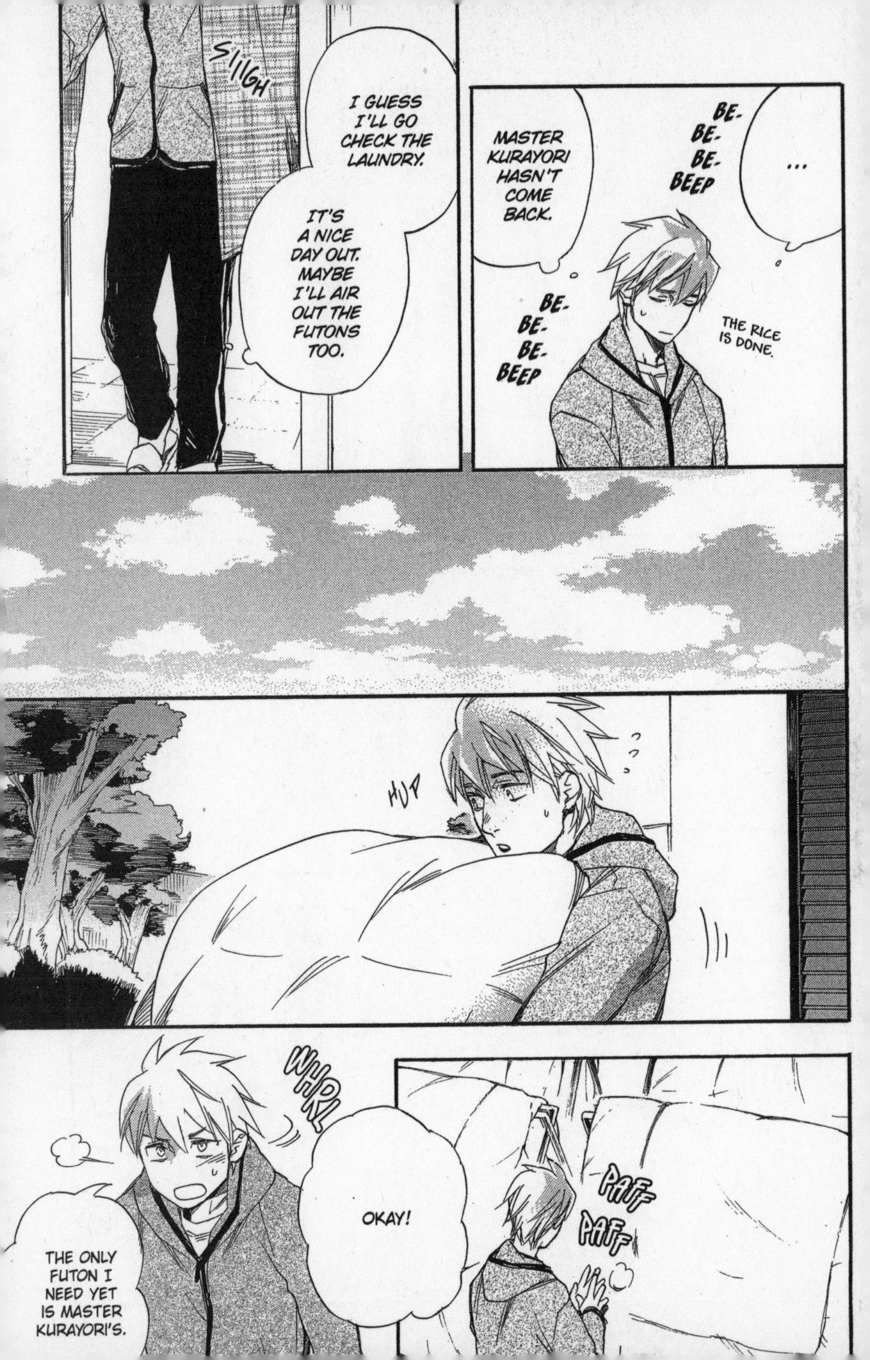
...
BE-BE-BE-BEEP
MASTER KURAYORI HASN'T COME BACK.
THE RICE IS DONE.
BE-BE-BE-BEEP
I GUESS I'LL GO CHECK THE LAUNDRY.
SIIIGH
IT'S A NICE DAY OUT. MAYBE I'LL AIR OUT THE FUTONS TOO.
HUP
PAFF
PAFF
WHRL
OKAY!
THE ONLY FUTON I NEED YET IS MASTER KURAYORI'S.

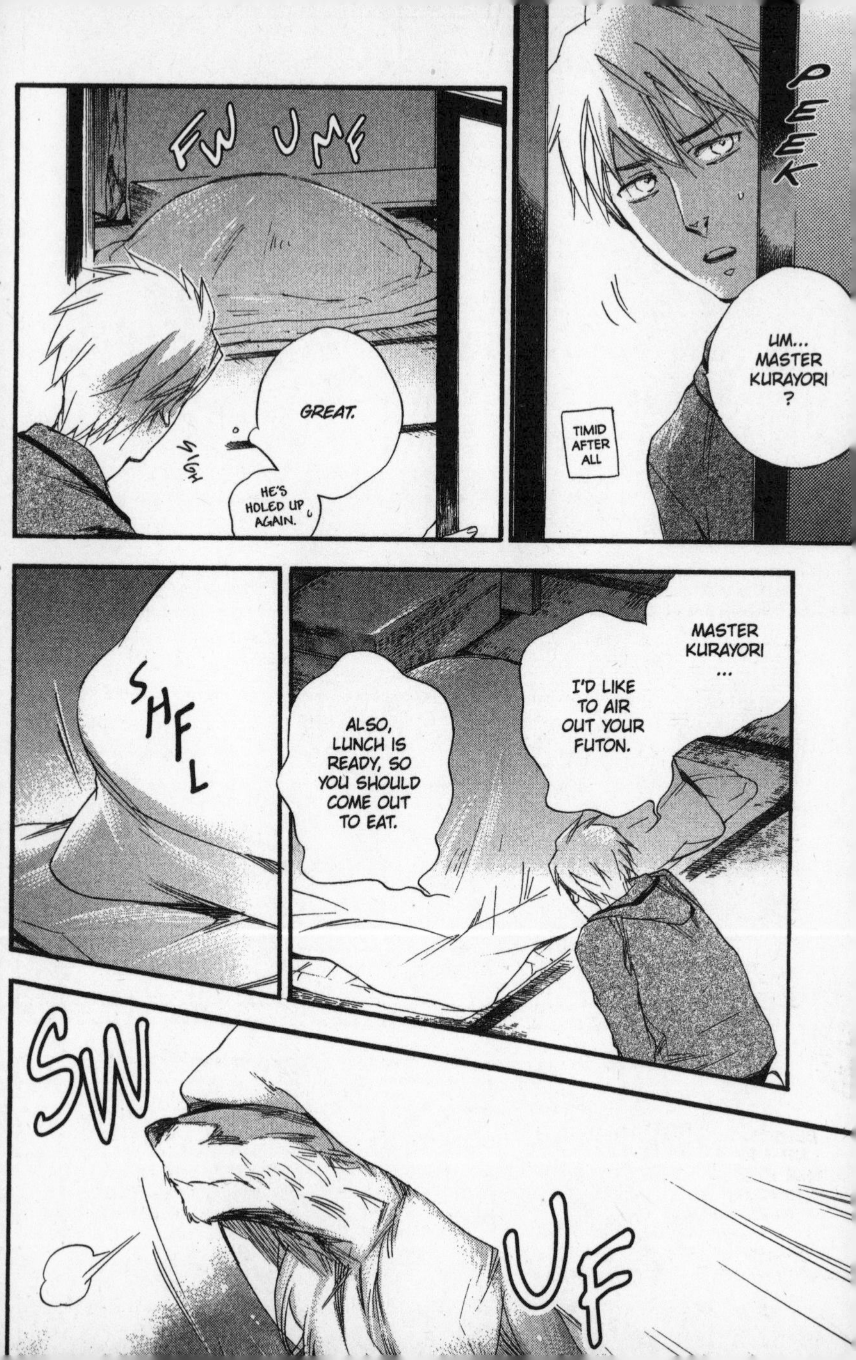
PEEK
UM... MASTER KURAYORI ?
TIMID AFTER ALL
FWUMF
GREAT.
SIGH
HE'S HOLED UP AGAIN.
MASTER KURAYORI ...
I'D LIKE TO AIR OUT YOUR FUTON.
ALSO, LUNCH IS READY, SO YOU SHOULD COME OUT TO EAT.
SHFL
SWUF

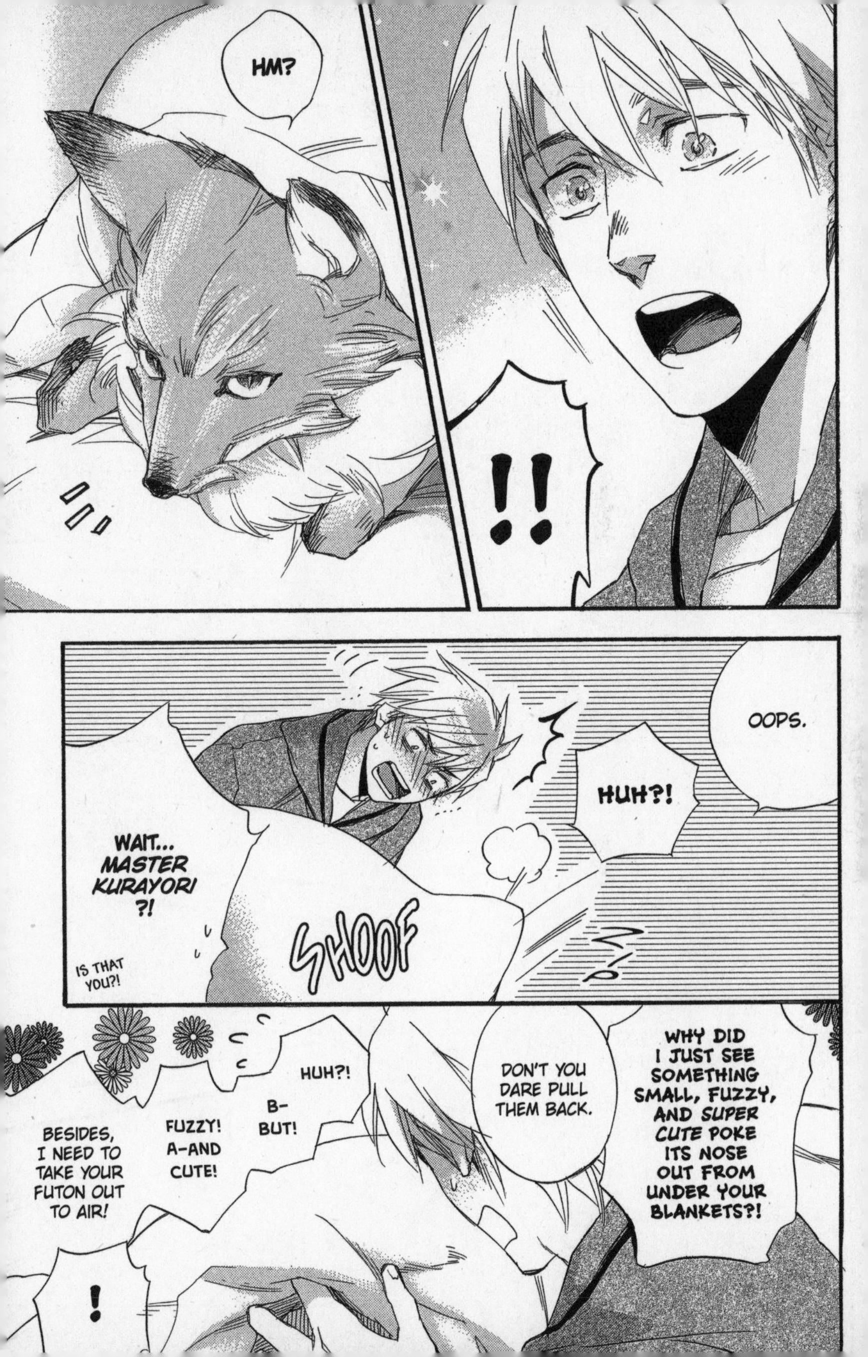
!!
HM?
OOPS.
HUH?!
WAIT... MASTER KURAYORI ?!
IS THAT YOU?!
SHOOF
WHY DID I JUST SEE SOMETHING SMALL, FUZZY, AND SUPER CUTE POKE ITS NOSE OUT FROM UNDER YOUR BLANKETS?!
DON'T YOU DARE PULL THEM BACK.
HUH?!
B- BUT!
FUZZY! A-AND CUTE!
BESIDES, I NEED TO TAKE YOUR FUTON OUT TO AIR!
!

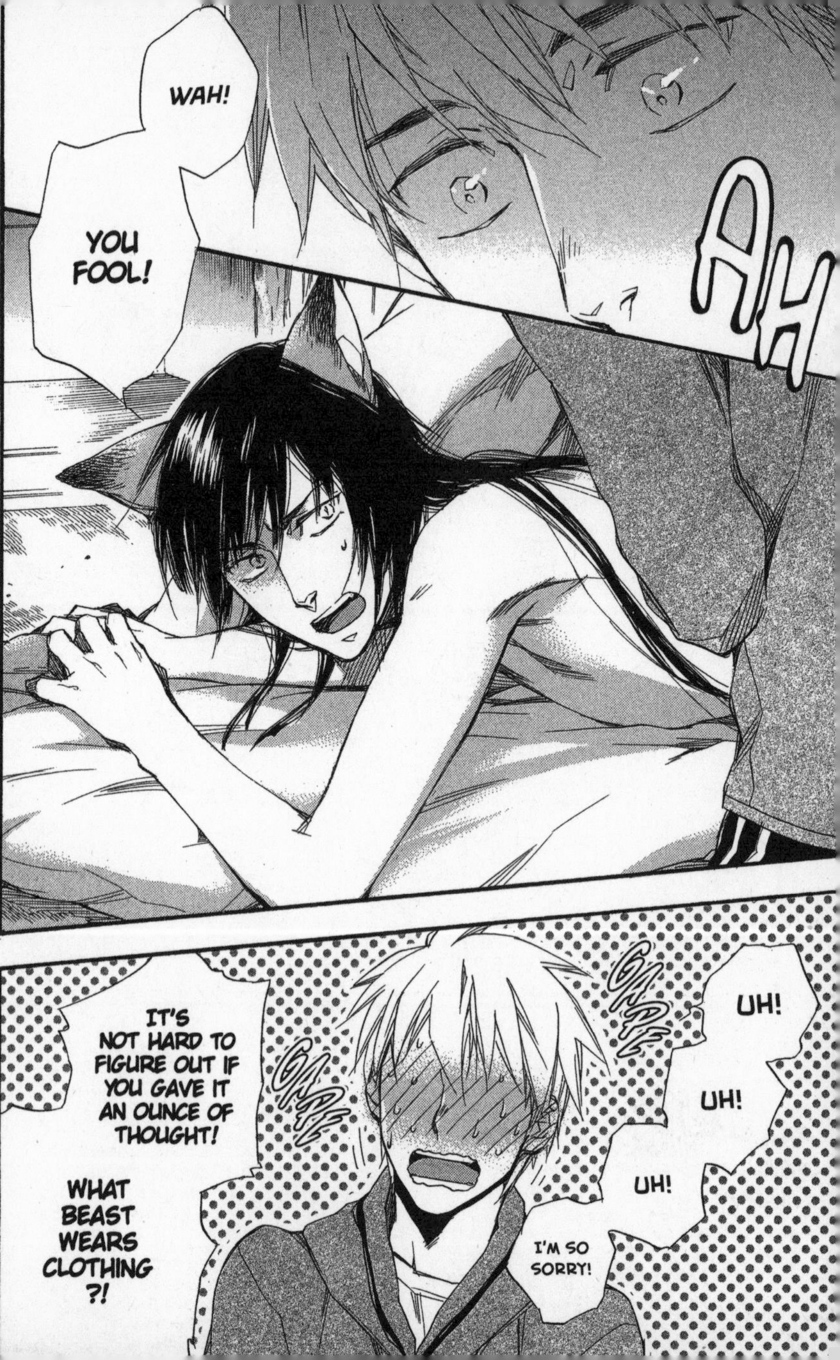
AH
WAH!
YOU FOOL!
UH!
UH!
UH!
I'M SO SORRY!
IT'S NOT HARD TO FIGURE OUT IF YOU GAVE IT AN OUNCE OF THOUGHT!
WHAT BEAST WEARS CLOTHING?!

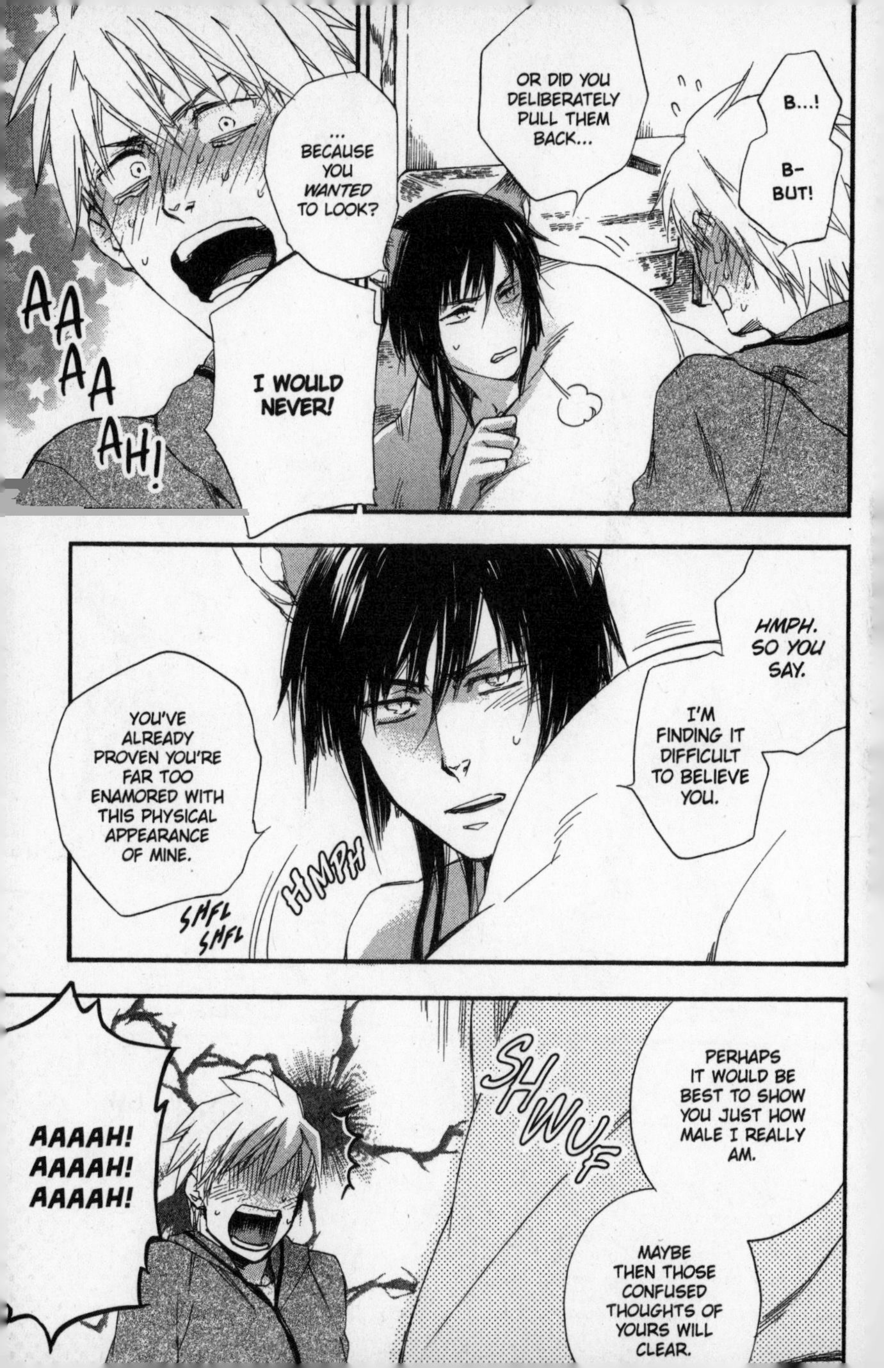
B...!
B- BUT!
OR DID YOU DELIBERATELY PULL THEM BACK...
... BECAUSE YOU WANTED TO LOOK?
I WOULD NEVER!
AAAAH!
HMPH. SO YOU SAY.
I'M FINDING IT DIFFICULT TO BELIEVE YOU.
YOU'VE ALREADY PROVEN YOU'RE FAR TOO ENAMORED WITH THIS PHYSICAL APPEARANCE OF MINE.
HMPH
SMFL SMFL
PERHAPS IT WOULD BE BEST TO SHOW YOU JUST HOW MALE I REALLY AM.
SHWUF
MAYBE THEN THOSE CONFUSED THOUGHTS OF YOURS WILL CLEAR.
AAAAH! AAAAH! AAAAH!

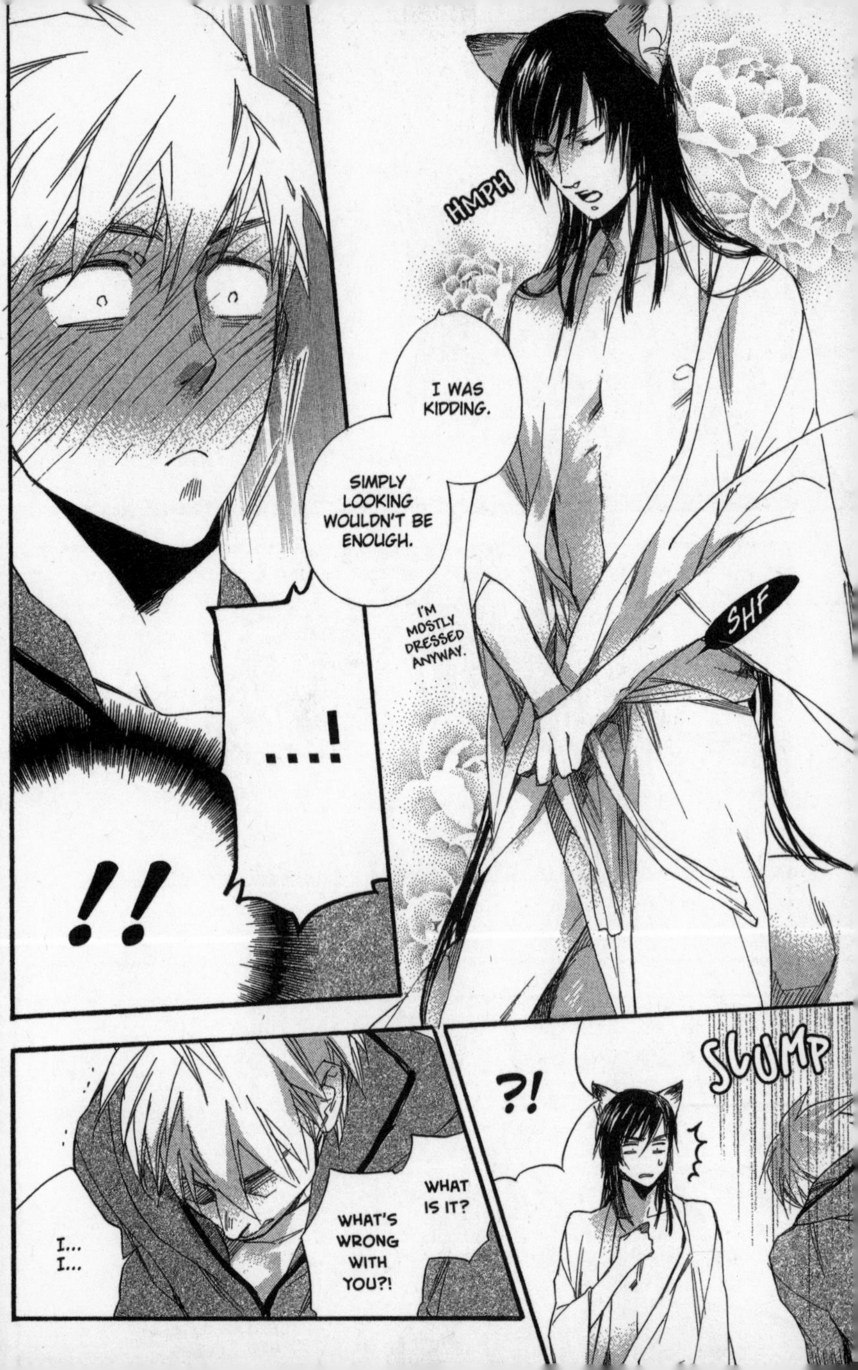
HMPH
I WAS KIDDING.
SIMPLY LOOKING WOULDN'T BE ENOUGH.
I'M MOSTLY DRESSED ANYWAY.
SHF
...!
!!
SLUMP
?!
WHAT IS IT?
WHAT'S WRONG WITH YOU?!
I... I...

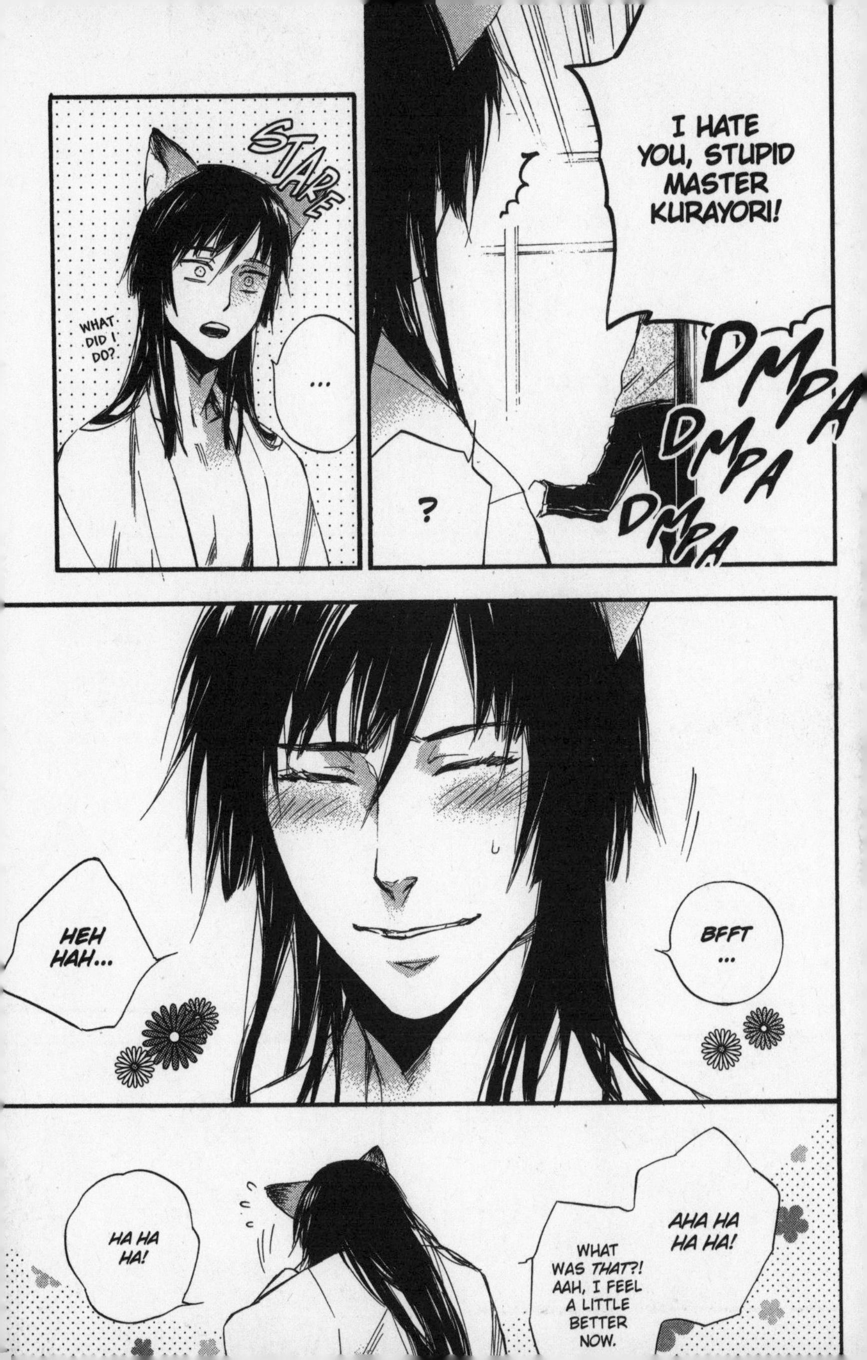
I HATE YOU, STUPID MASTER KURAYORI!
DMPA DMPA DMPA
?
STARE
...
WHAT DID I DO?
BFFT ...
HEH HAH...
AHA HA HA HA!
WHAT WAS THAT?! AAH, I FEEL A LITTLE BETTER NOW.
HA HA HA!

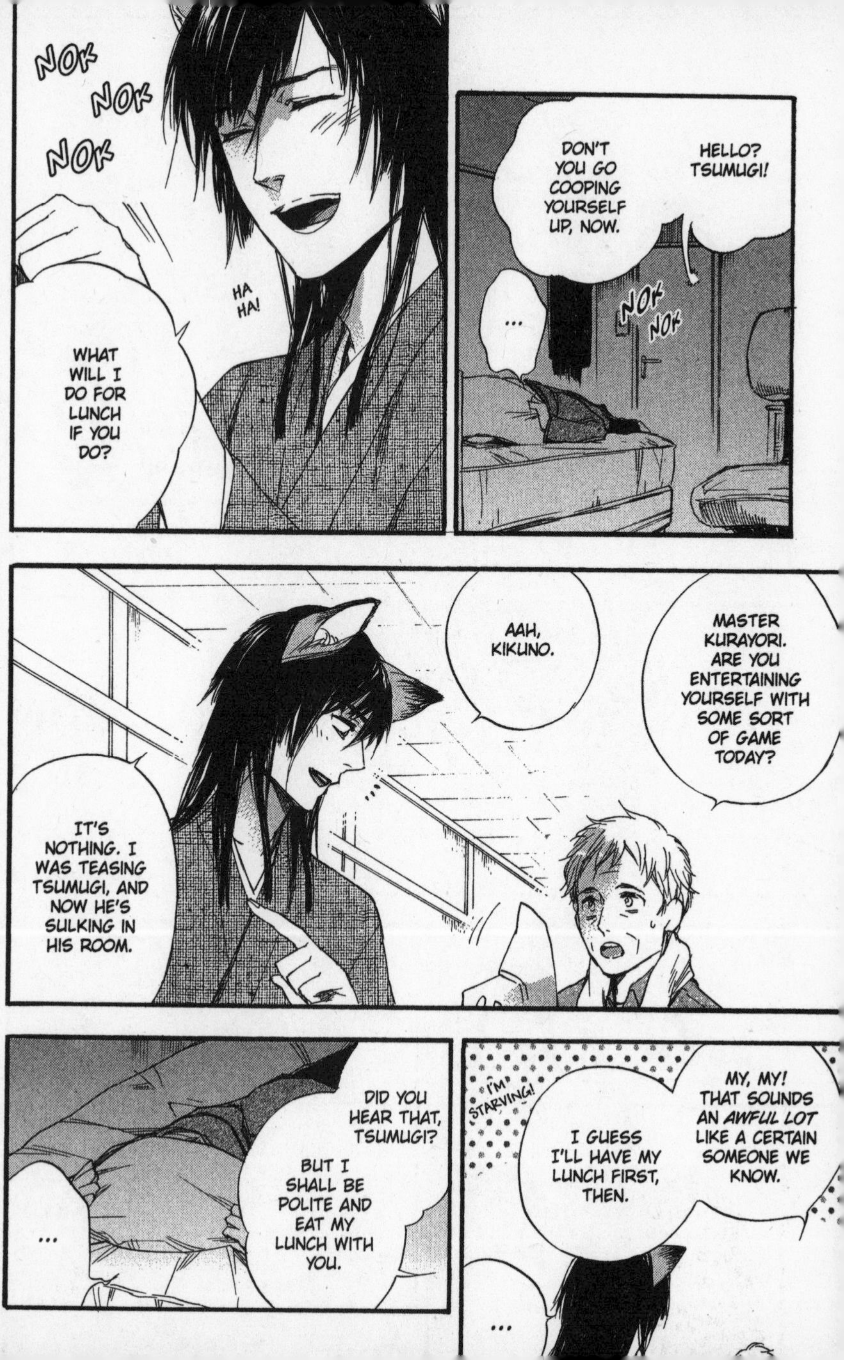
HELLO? TSUMUGI!
DON'T YOU GO COOPING YOURSELF UP, NOW.
NOK NOK
...
NOK NOK NOK
HA HA!
WHAT WILL I DO FOR LUNCH IF YOU DO?
MASTER KURAYORI. ARE YOU ENTERTAINING YOURSELF WITH SOME SORT OF GAME TODAY?
AAH, KIKUNO.
IT'S NOTHING. I WAS TEASING TSUMUGI, AND NOW HE'S SULKING IN HIS ROOM.
MY, MY! THAT SOUNDS AN *AWFUL LOT* LIKE A CERTAIN SOMEONE WE KNOW.
I GUESS I'LL HAVE MY LUNCH FIRST, THEN.
I'M STARVING!
...
DID YOU HEAR THAT, TSUMUGI?
BUT I SHALL BE POLITE AND EAT MY LUNCH WITH YOU.
...

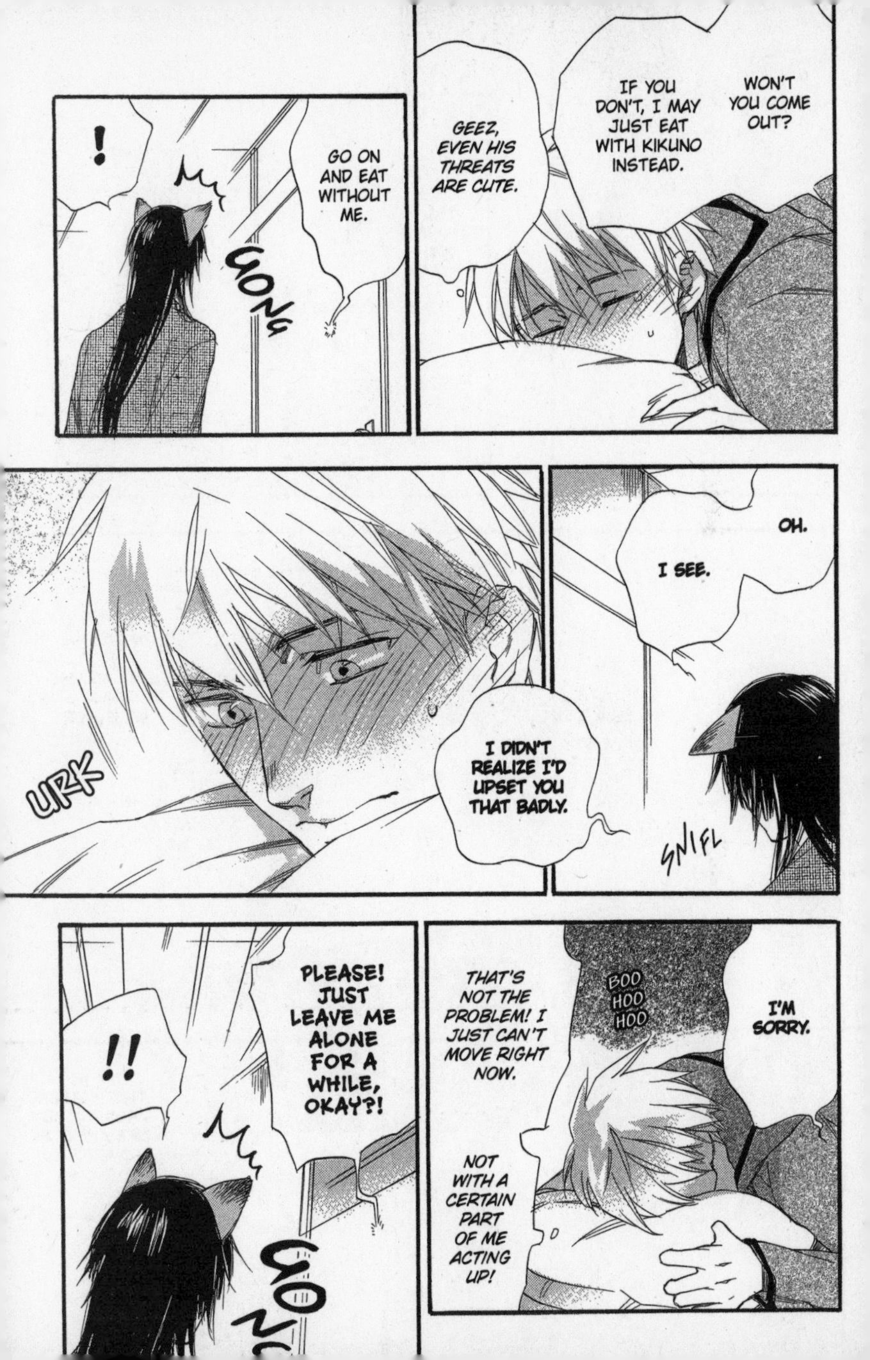
WON'T YOU COME OUT?
IF YOU DON'T, I MAY JUST EAT WITH KIKUNO INSTEAD.
GEEZ, EVEN HIS THREATS ARE CUTE.
GO ON AND EAT WITHOUT ME.
!
OH.
I SEE.
I DIDN'T REALIZE I'D UPSET YOU THAT BADLY.
SNIFL
URK
I'M SORRY.
BOO HOO HOO
THAT'S NOT THE PROBLEM! I JUST CAN'T MOVE RIGHT NOW.
NOT WITH A CERTAIN PART OF ME ACTING UP!
PLEASE! JUST LEAVE ME ALONE FOR A WHILE, OKAY?!
!!

SHFL

SHEESH.

WHAT'S THIS? WHERE'S TSUMUGI?

HE SAID HE DOESN'T WANT TO EAT WITH ME.

I'LL EAT WITH YOU INSTEAD.

GLOOM

MMM.

WHENEVER I'M AROUND MASTER KURAYORI...

...I CAN'T HELP BUT REALIZE THAT I REALLY AM A TEENAGED GUY.

I'VE GOT MORE GOING ON AT HOME THAN AT SCHOOL.

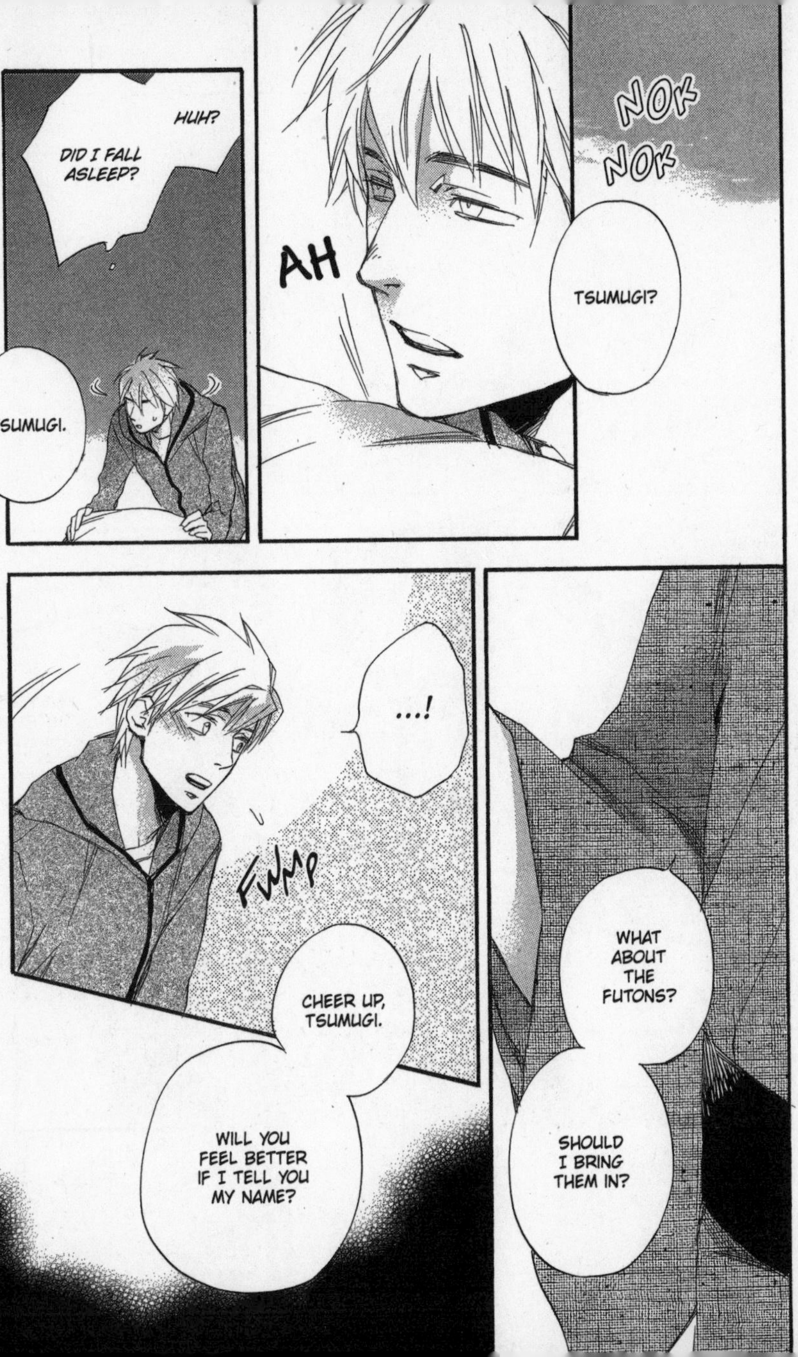
NOK NOK
TSUMUGI?
AH
HUH?
DID I FALL ASLEEP?
TSUMUGI.
WHAT ABOUT THE FUTONS?
SHOULD I BRING THEM IN?
...!
FWMP
CHEER UP, TSUMUGI.
WILL YOU FEEL BETTER IF I TELL YOU MY NAME?

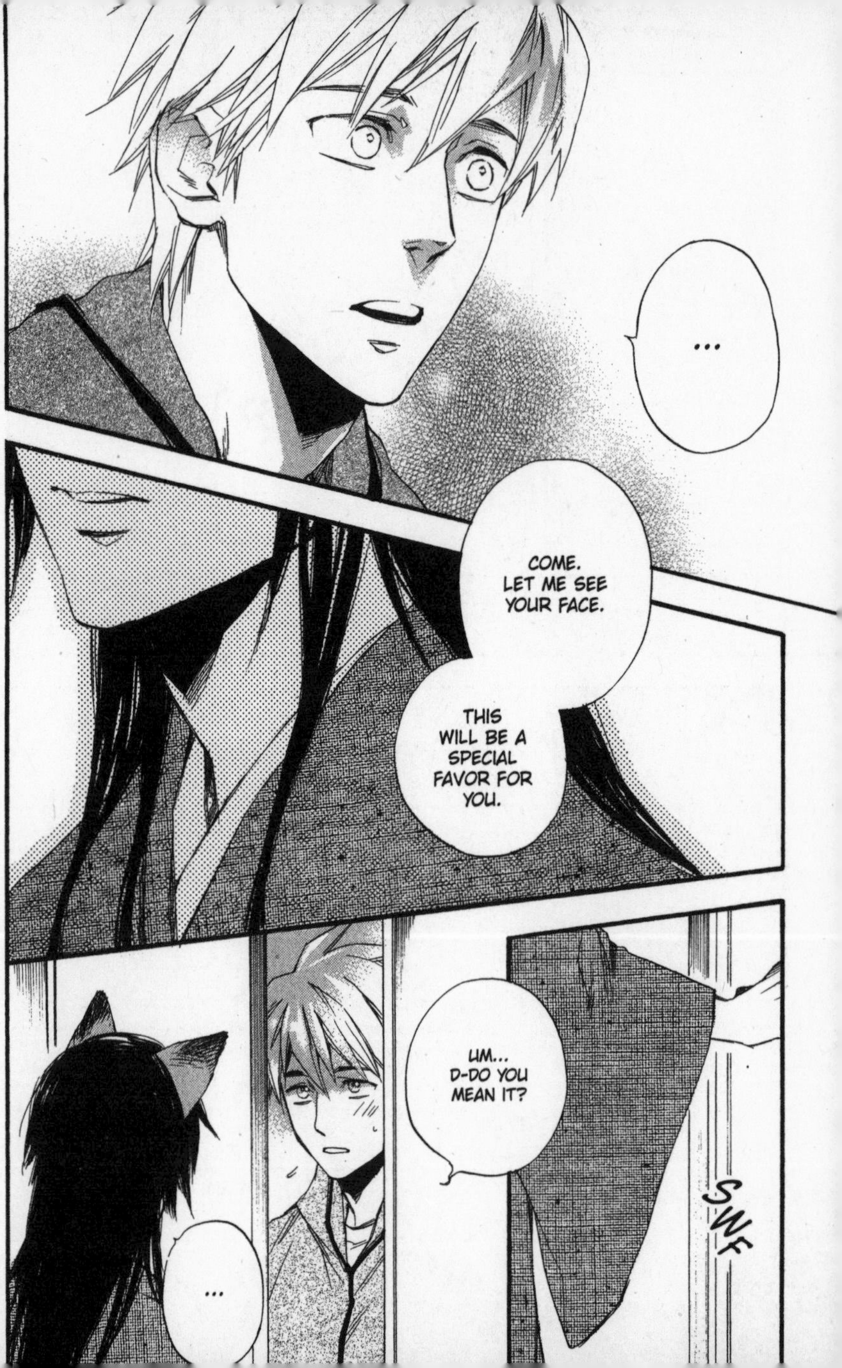
...
COME. LET ME SEE YOUR FACE.
THIS WILL BE A SPECIAL FAVOR FOR YOU.
SWF
UM... D-DO YOU MEAN IT?
...

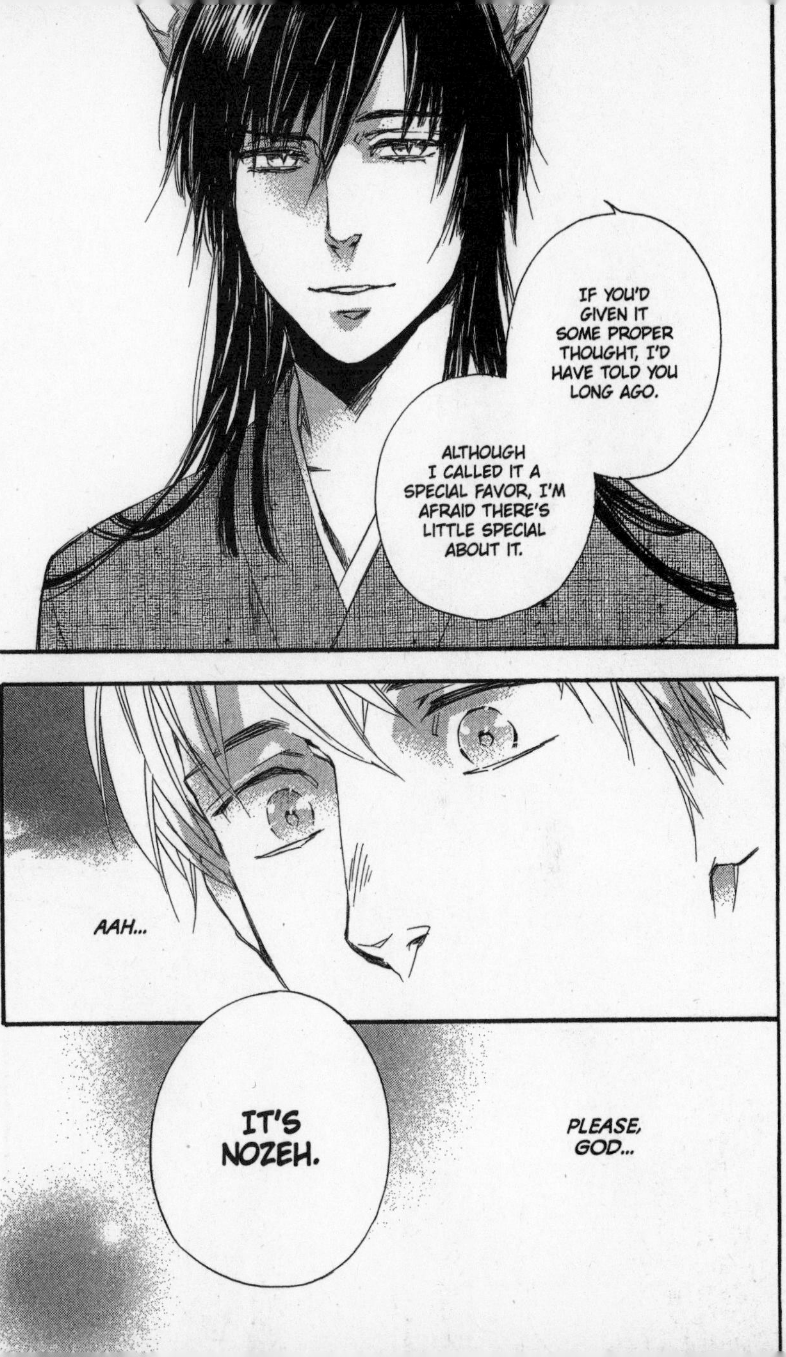
IF YOU'D GIVEN IT SOME PROPER THOUGHT, I'D HAVE TOLD YOU LONG AGO.
ALTHOUGH I CALLED IT A SPECIAL FAVOR, I'M AFRAID THERE'S LITTLE SPECIAL ABOUT IT.
AAH...
PLEASE, GOD...
IT'S NOZEH.

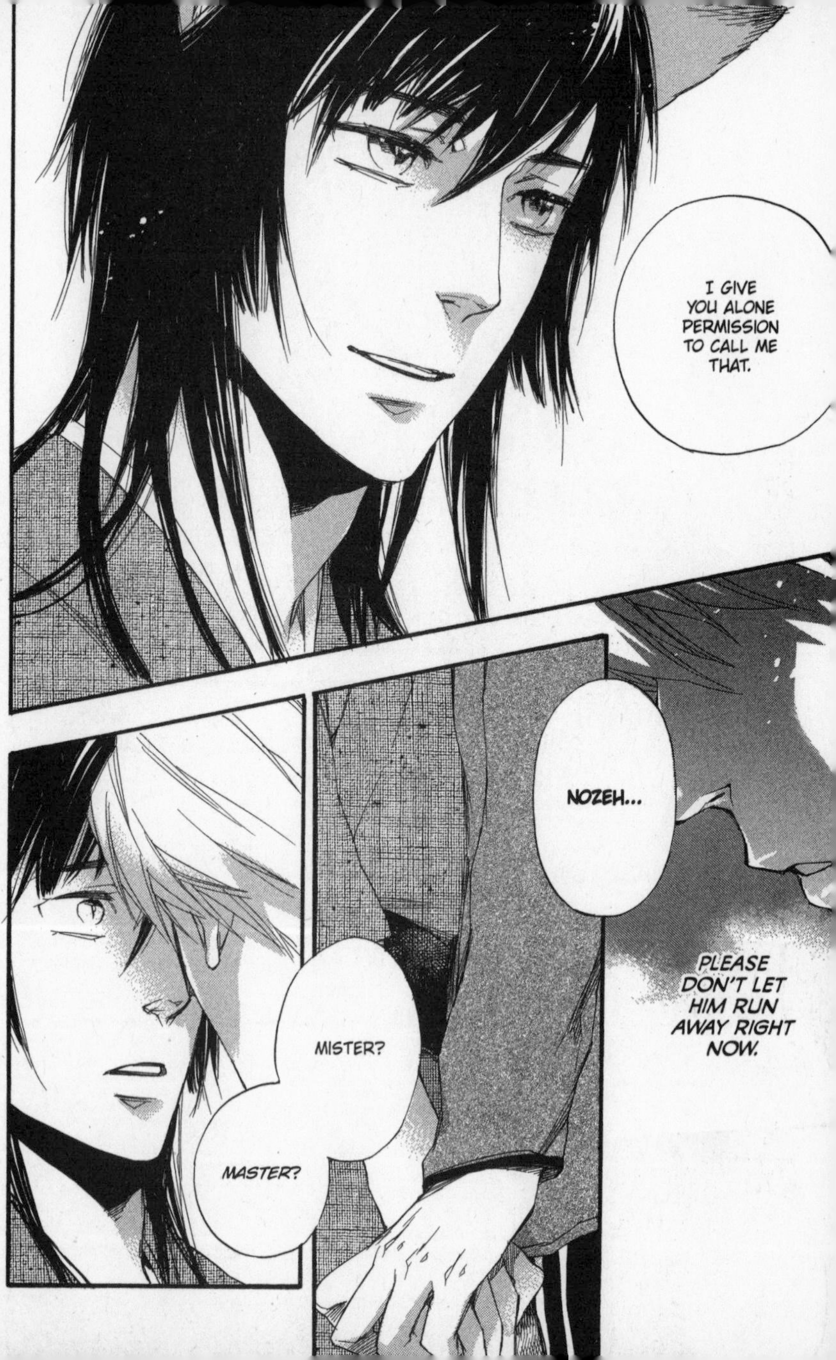
I GIVE YOU ALONE PERMISSION TO CALL ME THAT.
NOZEH...
PLEASE DON'T LET HIM RUN AWAY RIGHT NOW.
MISTER?
MASTER?

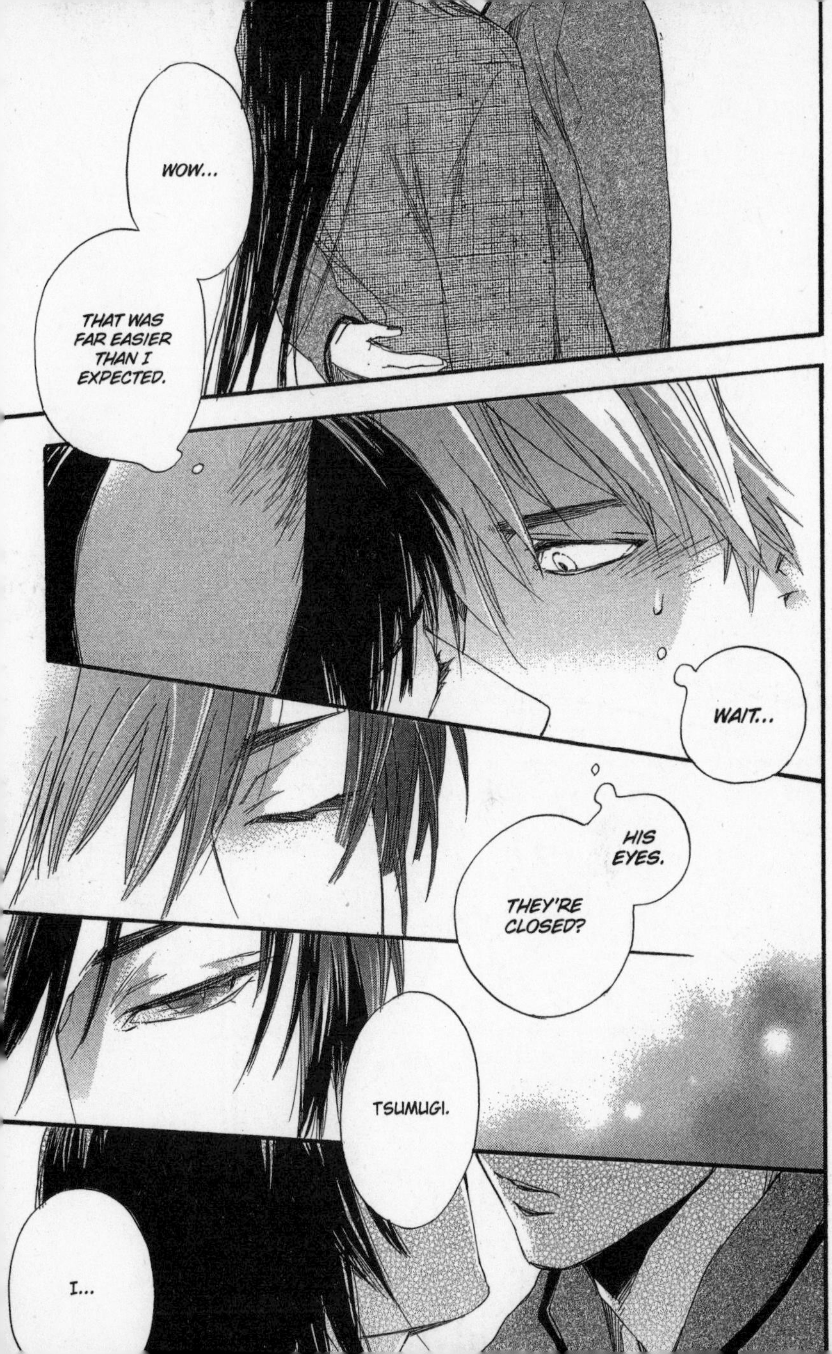
WOW...
THAT WAS FAR EASIER THAN I EXPECTED.
WAIT...
HIS EYES. THEY'RE CLOSED?
TSUMUGI.
I...

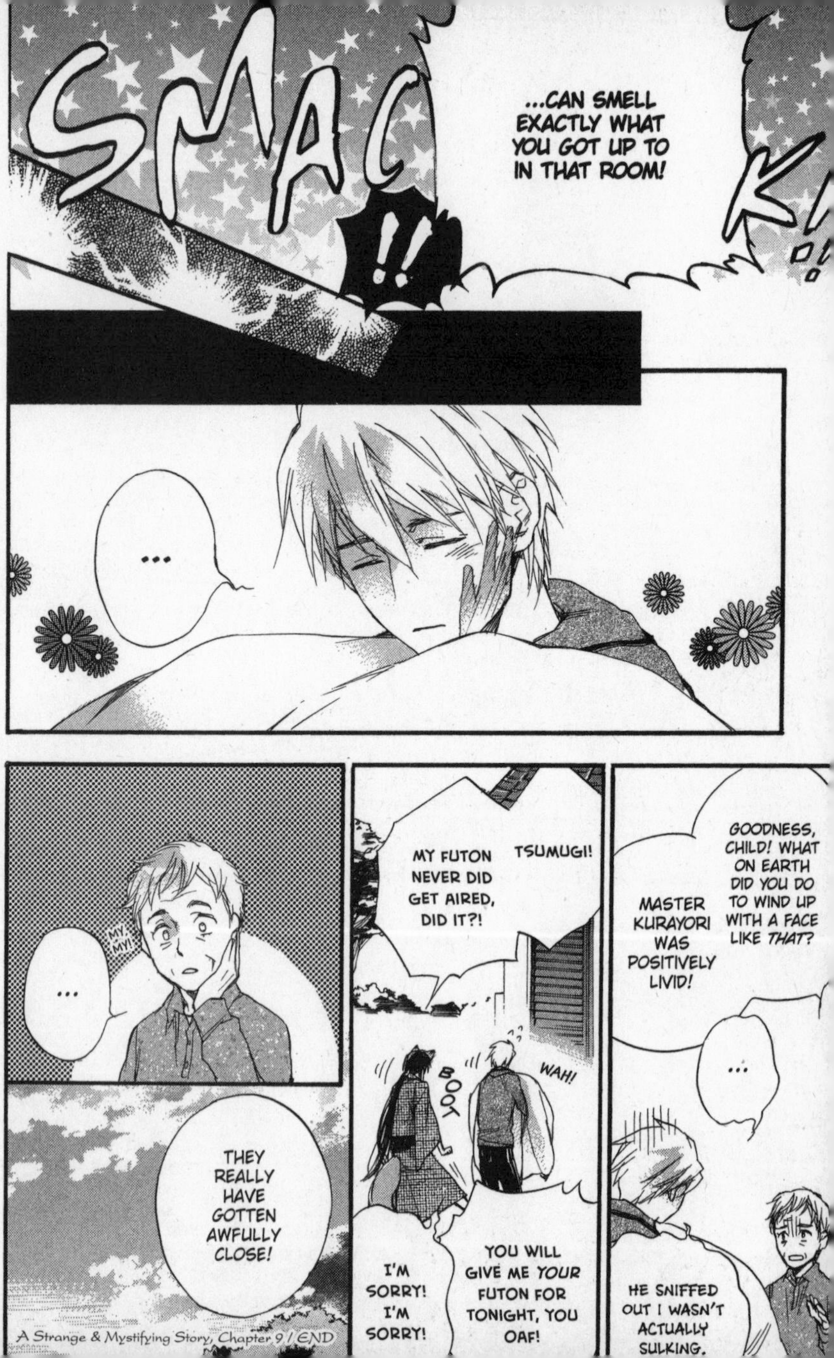
...CAN SMELL EXACTLY WHAT YOU GOT UP TO IN THAT ROOM!
SMACK!!
...
GOODNESS, CHILD! WHAT ON EARTH DID YOU DO TO WIND UP WITH A FACE LIKE *THAT*?
MASTER KURAYORI WAS POSITIVELY LIVID!
...
HE SNIFFED OUT I WASN'T ACTUALLY SULKING.
TSUMUGI!
MY FUTON NEVER DID GET AIRED, DID IT?!
WAH!
BOOT
YOU WILL GIVE ME *YOUR* FUTON FOR TONIGHT, YOU OAF!
I'M SORRY! I'M SORRY!
MY, MY!
...
THEY REALLY HAVE GOTTEN AWFULLY CLOSE!
A Strange & Mystifying Story, Chapter 9 / END

A Strange & Mystifying Story

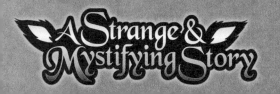

A Strange & Mystifying Story

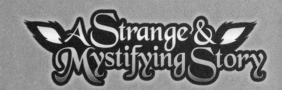

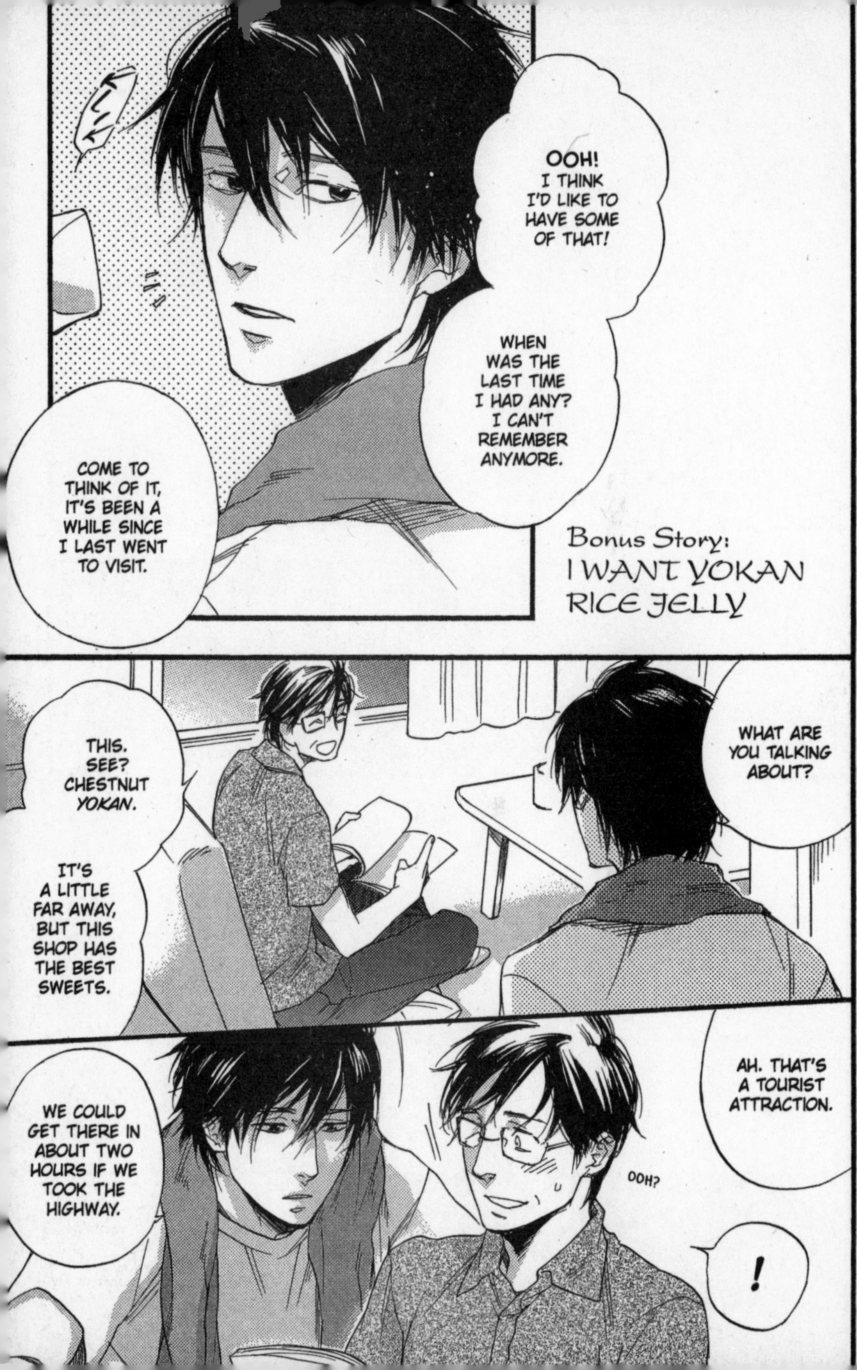
Bonus Story:
I WANT YOKAN RICE JELLY
OOH! I THINK I'D LIKE TO HAVE SOME OF THAT!
WHEN WAS THE LAST TIME I HAD ANY? I CAN'T REMEMBER ANYMORE.
COME TO THINK OF IT, IT'S BEEN A WHILE SINCE I LAST WENT TO VISIT.
WHAT ARE YOU TALKING ABOUT?
THIS. SEE? CHESTNUT *YOKAN*.
IT'S A LITTLE FAR AWAY, BUT THIS SHOP HAS THE BEST SWEETS.
AH. THAT'S A TOURIST ATTRACTION.
!
OOH?
WE COULD GET THERE IN ABOUT TWO HOURS IF WE TOOK THE HIGHWAY.

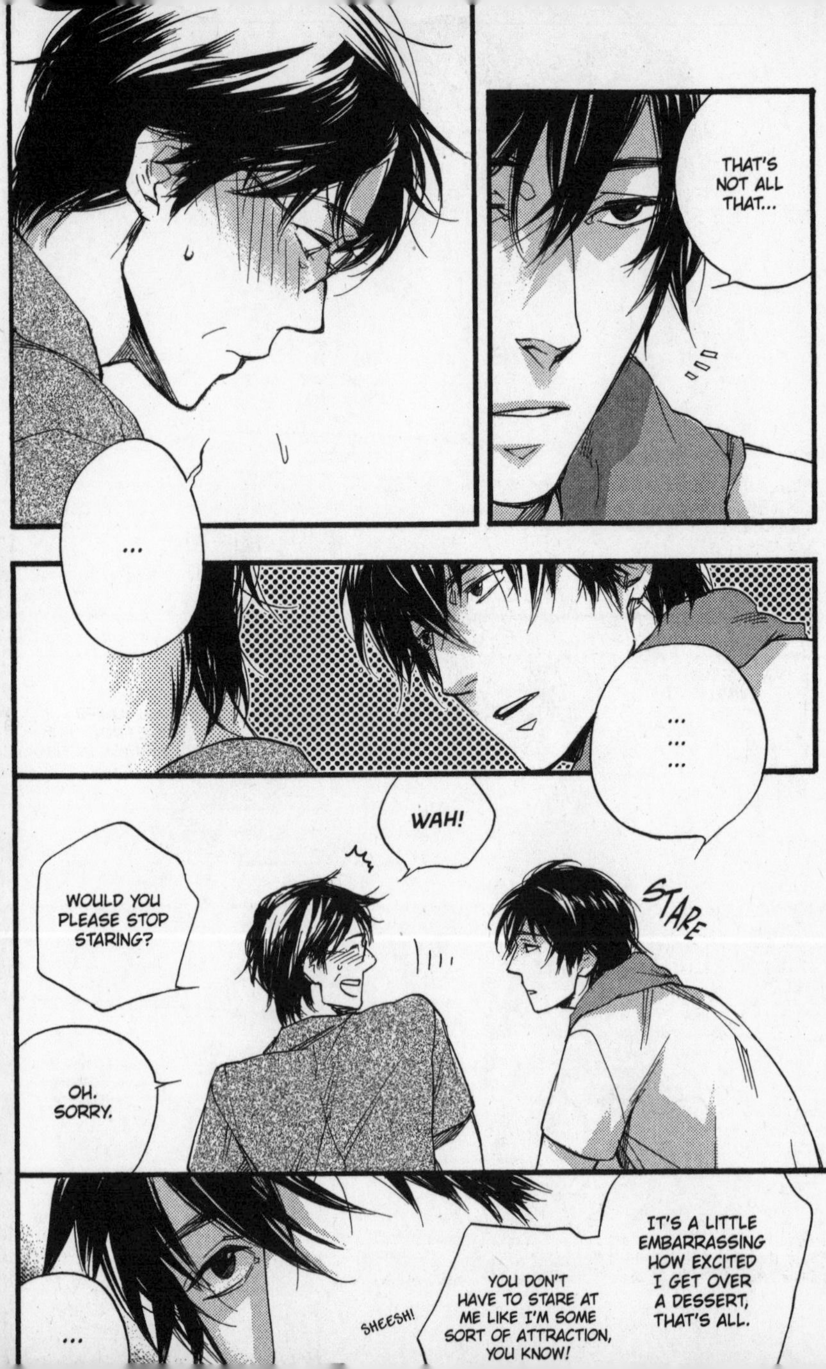
THAT'S NOT ALL THAT...
...
...
...
...
WAH!
STARE
WOULD YOU PLEASE STOP STARING?
OH. SORRY.
IT'S A LITTLE EMBARRASSING HOW EXCITED I GET OVER A DESSERT, THAT'S ALL.
YOU DON'T HAVE TO STARE AT ME LIKE I'M SOME SORT OF ATTRACTION, YOU KNOW!
SHEESH!
...

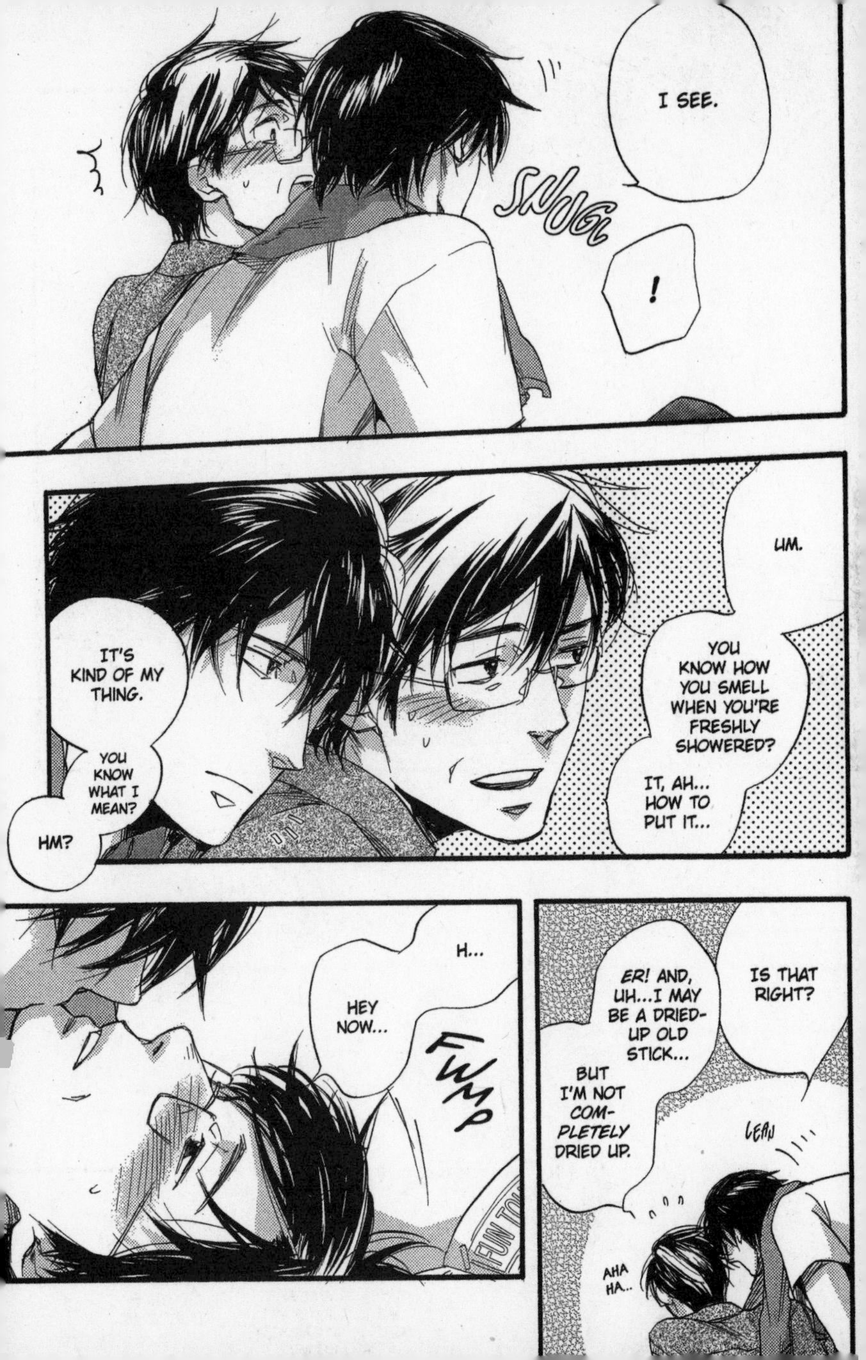
I SEE.
SNUG
!
UM.
YOU KNOW HOW YOU SMELL WHEN YOU'RE FRESHLY SHOWERED?
IT, AH... HOW TO PUT IT...
IT'S KIND OF MY THING.
YOU KNOW WHAT I MEAN?
HM?
IS THAT RIGHT?
ER! AND, UH...I MAY BE A DRIED-UP OLD STICK...
BUT I'M NOT COM-PLETELY DRIED UP.
LEAN
AHA HA...
H...
HEY NOW...
FWMP

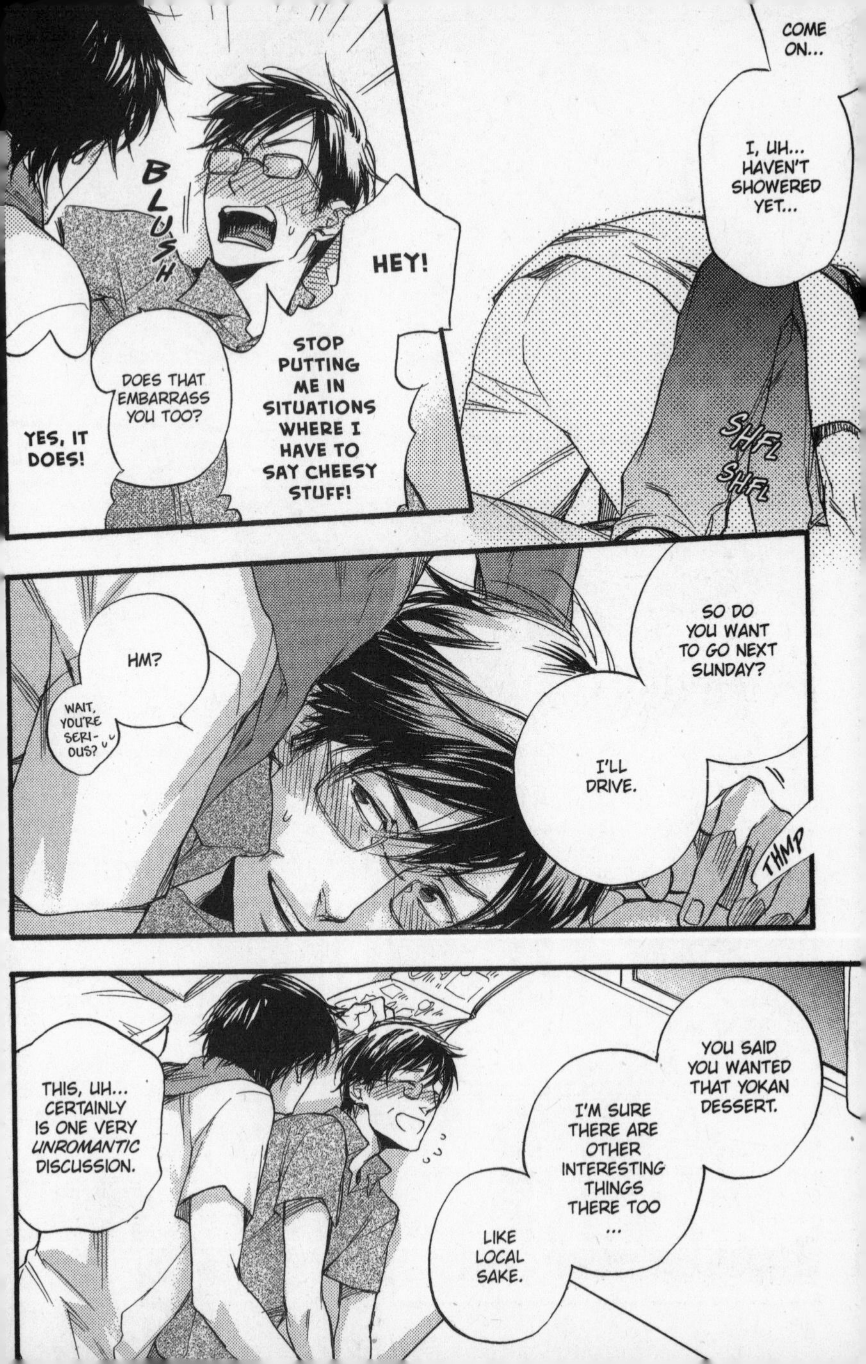
COME ON...
I, UH... HAVEN'T SHOWERED YET...
SHFL SHFL
HEY!
STOP PUTTING ME IN SITUATIONS WHERE I HAVE TO SAY CHEESY STUFF!
BLUSH
DOES THAT EMBARRASS YOU TOO?
YES, IT DOES!
SO DO YOU WANT TO GO NEXT SUNDAY?
I'LL DRIVE.
THMP
HM?
WAIT, YOU'RE SERI-OUS?
YOU SAID YOU WANTED THAT YOKAN DESSERT.
I'M SURE THERE ARE OTHER INTERESTING THINGS THERE TOO ...
LIKE LOCAL SAKE.
THIS, UH... CERTAINLY IS ONE VERY *UNROMANTIC* DISCUSSION.

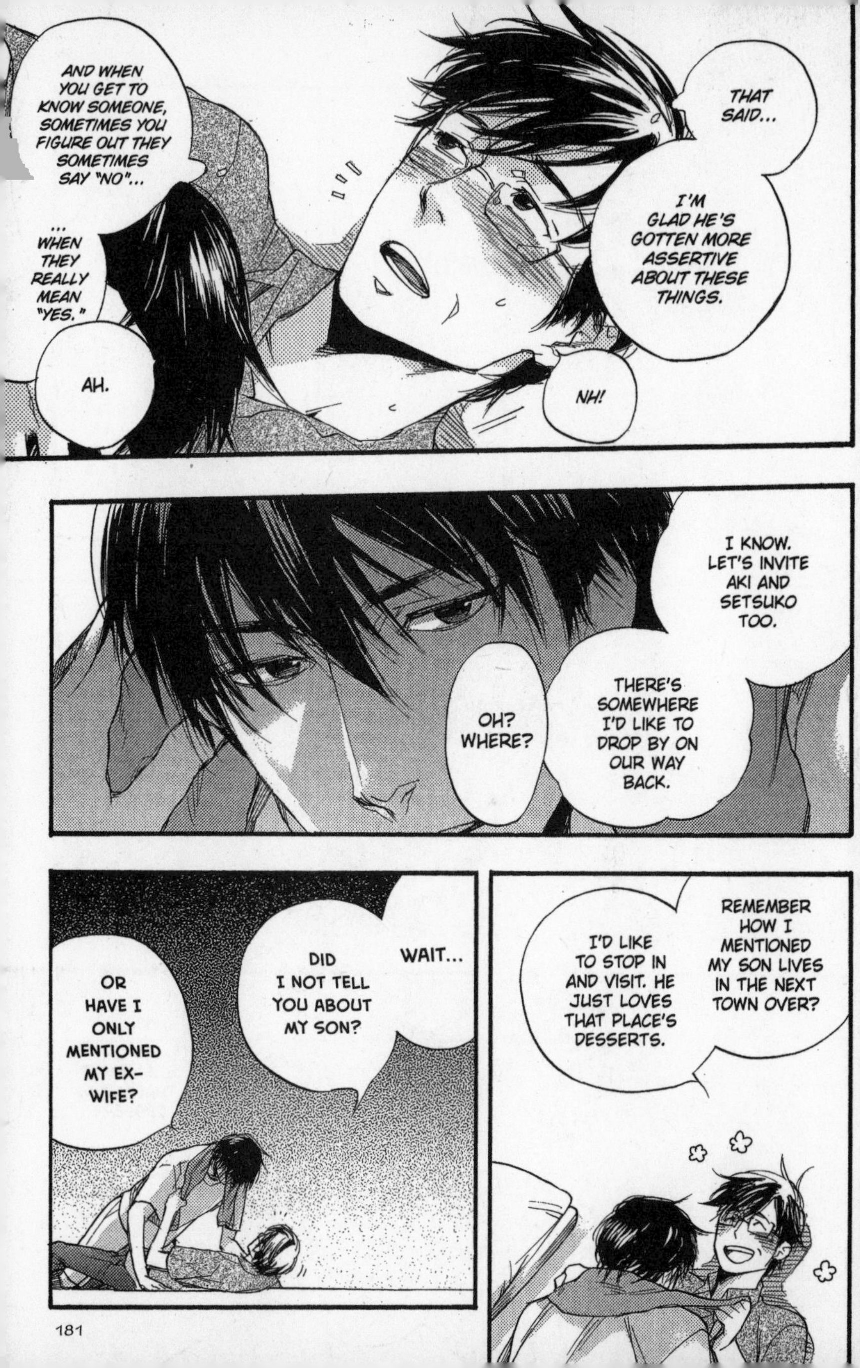
THAT SAID...
I'M GLAD HE'S GOTTEN MORE ASSERTIVE ABOUT THESE THINGS.
NH!
AND WHEN YOU GET TO KNOW SOMEONE, SOMETIMES YOU FIGURE OUT THEY SOMETIMES SAY "NO"...
...WHEN THEY REALLY MEAN "YES."
AH.
I KNOW. LET'S INVITE AKI AND SETSUKO TOO.
THERE'S SOMEWHERE I'D LIKE TO DROP BY ON OUR WAY BACK.
OH? WHERE?
REMEMBER HOW I MENTIONED MY SON LIVES IN THE NEXT TOWN OVER?
I'D LIKE TO STOP IN AND VISIT. HE JUST LOVES THAT PLACE'S DESSERTS.
WAIT...
DID I NOT TELL YOU ABOUT MY SON?
OR HAVE I ONLY MENTIONED MY EX-WIFE?

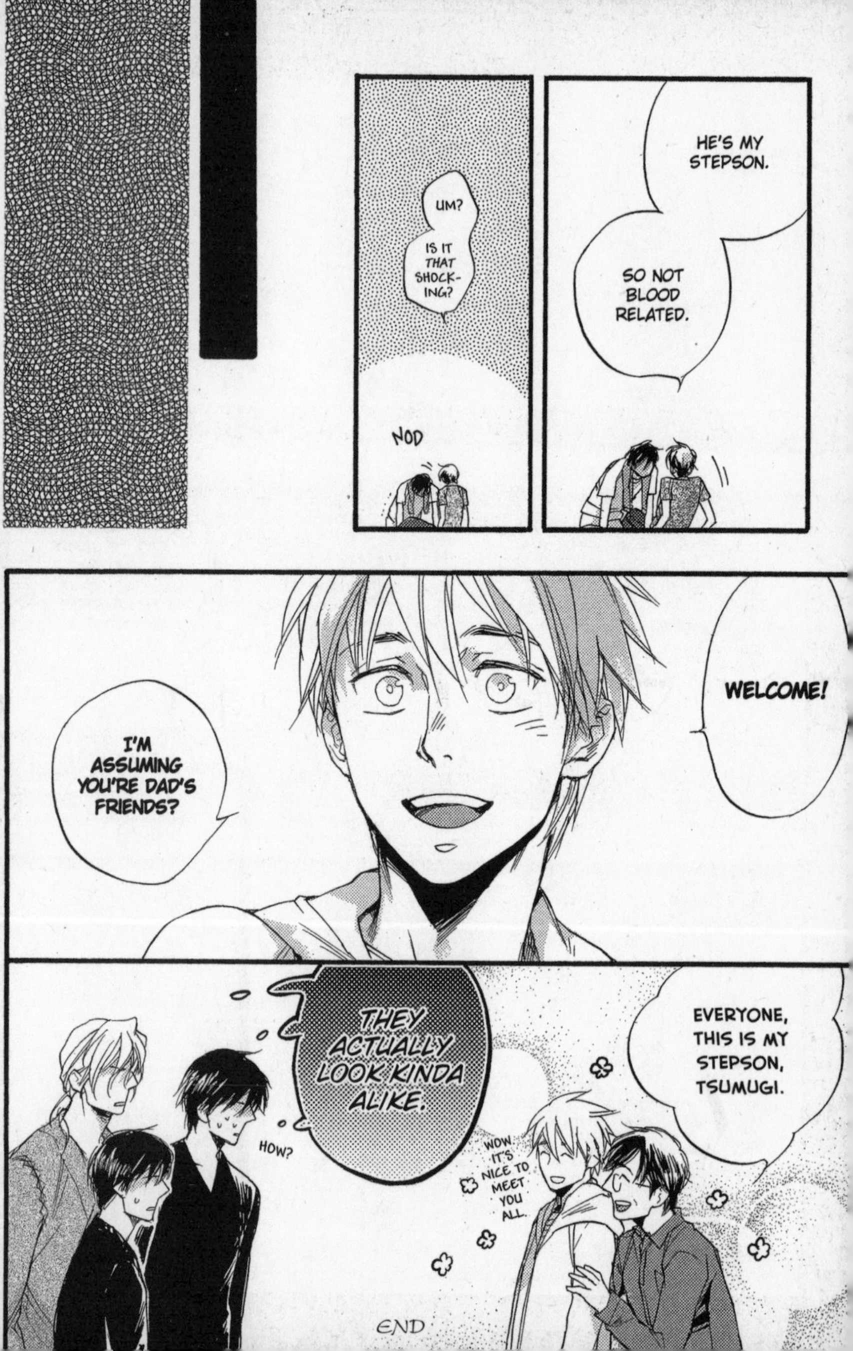
HE'S MY STEPSON.
SO NOT BLOOD RELATED.
UM?
IS IT THAT SHOCKING?
NOD
WELCOME!
I'M ASSUMING YOU'RE DAD'S FRIENDS?
EVERYONE, THIS IS MY STEPSON, TSUMUGI.
WOW IT'S NICE TO MEET YOU ALL.
THEY ACTUALLY LOOK KINDA ALIKE.
HOW?
END

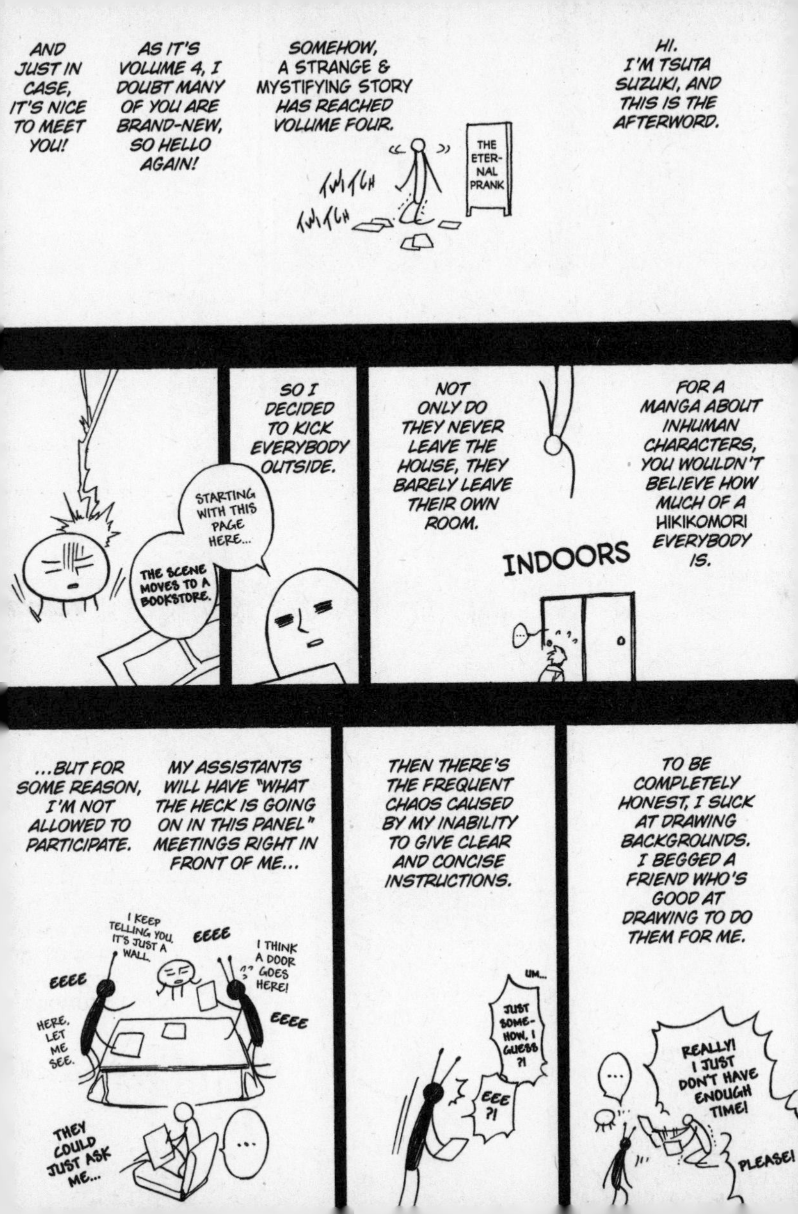
HI. I'M TSUTA SUZUKI, AND THIS IS THE AFTERWORD.
SOMEHOW, A STRANGE & MYSTIFYING STORY HAS REACHED VOLUME FOUR.
THE ETERNAL PRANK
TWITCH
TWITCH
AS IT'S VOLUME 4, I DOUBT MANY OF YOU ARE BRAND-NEW, SO HELLO AGAIN!
AND JUST IN CASE, IT'S NICE TO MEET YOU!
FOR A MANGA ABOUT INHUMAN CHARACTERS, YOU WOULDN'T BELIEVE HOW MUCH OF A HIKIKOMORI EVERYBODY IS.
NOT ONLY DO THEY NEVER LEAVE THE HOUSE, THEY BARELY LEAVE THEIR OWN ROOM.
INDOORS
...
SO I DECIDED TO KICK EVERYBODY OUTSIDE.
STARTING WITH THIS PAGE HERE...
THE SCENE MOVES TO A BOOKSTORE.
TO BE COMPLETELY HONEST, I SUCK AT DRAWING BACKGROUNDS. I BEGGED A FRIEND WHO'S GOOD AT DRAWING TO DO THEM FOR ME.
REALLY! I JUST DON'T HAVE ENOUGH TIME!
...
PLEASE!
THEN THERE'S THE FREQUENT CHAOS CAUSED BY MY INABILITY TO GIVE CLEAR AND CONCISE INSTRUCTIONS.
UM...
JUST SOMEHOW, I GUESS ?!
EEE ?!
MY ASSISTANTS WILL HAVE "WHAT THE HECK IS GOING ON IN THIS PANEL" MEETINGS RIGHT IN FRONT OF ME...
...BUT FOR SOME REASON, I'M NOT ALLOWED TO PARTICIPATE.
I THINK A DOOR GOES HERE!
EEEE
I KEEP TELLING YOU, IT'S JUST A WALL.
EEEE
EEEE
HERE, LET ME SEE.
THEY COULD JUST ASK ME...
...

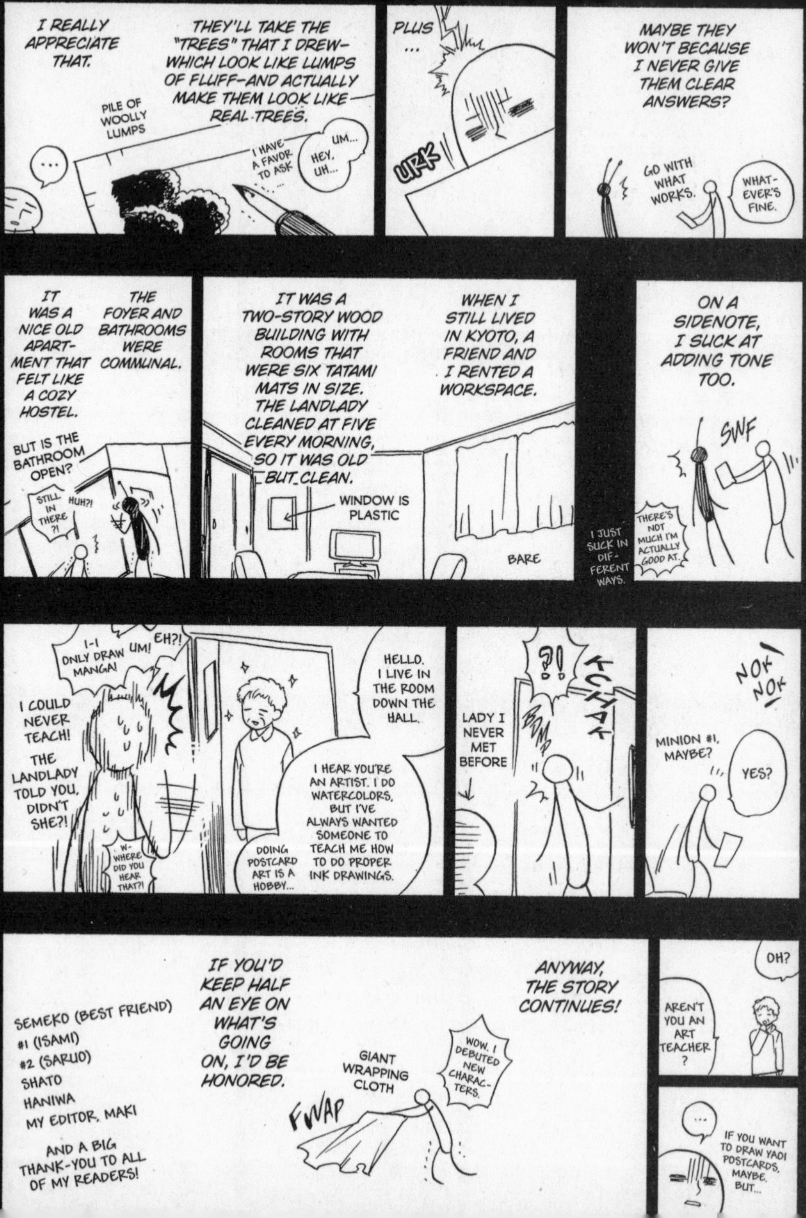

MAYBE THEY WON'T BECAUSE I NEVER GIVE THEM CLEAR ANSWERS?
WHAT-EVER'S FINE.
GO WITH WHAT WORKS.
PLUS...
URK
THEY'LL TAKE THE "TREES" THAT I DREW—WHICH LOOK LIKE LUMPS OF FLUFF—AND ACTUALLY MAKE THEM LOOK LIKE REAL TREES.
I REALLY APPRECIATE THAT.
UM... HEY, UH...
I HAVE A FAVOR TO ASK
PILE OF WOOLLY LUMPS
...
ON A SIDENOTE, I SUCK AT ADDING TONE TOO.
SWF
THERE'S NOT MUCH I'M ACTUALLY GOOD AT.
I JUST SUCK IN DIF-FERENT WAYS.
WHEN I STILL LIVED IN KYOTO, A FRIEND AND I RENTED A WORKSPACE.
IT WAS A TWO-STORY WOOD BUILDING WITH ROOMS THAT WERE SIX TATAMI MATS IN SIZE. THE LANDLADY CLEANED AT FIVE EVERY MORNING, SO IT WAS OLD BUT CLEAN.
WINDOW IS PLASTIC
BARE
THE FOYER AND BATHROOMS WERE COMMUNAL.
IT WAS A NICE OLD APART-MENT THAT FELT LIKE A COZY HOSTEL.
BUT IS THE BATHROOM OPEN?
HUH?!
STILL IN THERE ?!
NOK NOK
MINION #1, MAYBE?
YES?
?!
KCHAK
LADY I NEVER MET BEFORE
BOMP
HELLO. I LIVE IN THE ROOM DOWN THE HALL.
I HEAR YOU'RE AN ARTIST. I DO WATERCOLORS, BUT I'VE ALWAYS WANTED SOMEONE TO TEACH ME HOW TO DO PROPER INK DRAWINGS.
DOING POSTCARD ART IS A HOBBY...
EH?!
UM!
I-I ONLY DRAW MANGA!
I COULD NEVER TEACH!
THE LANDLADY TOLD YOU, DIDN'T SHE?!
W-WHERE DID YOU HEAR THAT?!
OH?
AREN'T YOU AN ART TEACHER ?
...
IF YOU WANT TO DRAW YAOI POSTCARDS, MAYBE, BUT...
ANYWAY, THE STORY CONTINUES!
IF YOU'D KEEP HALF AN EYE ON WHAT'S GOING ON, I'D BE HONORED.
WOW. I DEBUTED NEW CHARAC-TERS.
GIANT WRAPPING CLOTH
FWAP
SEMEKO (BEST FRIEND)
#1 (ISAMI)
#2 (SARUO)
SHATO
HANIWA
MY EDITOR, MAKI
AND A BIG THANK-YOU TO ALL OF MY READERS!

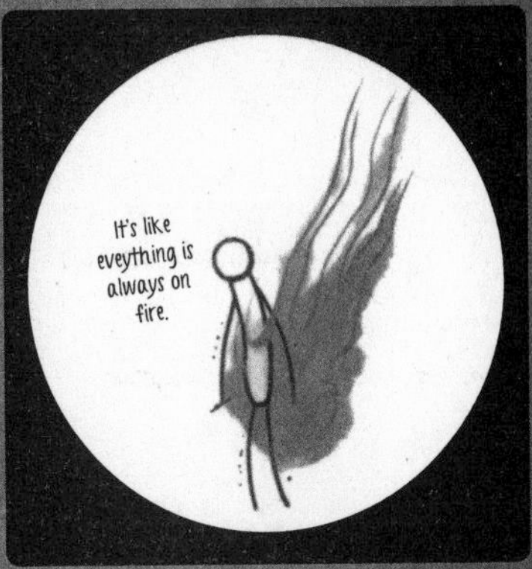
It's like eveything is always on fire.

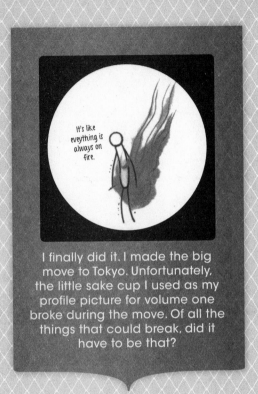

I finally did it. I made the big move to Tokyo. Unfortunately, the little sake cup I used as my profile picture for volume one broke during the move. Of all the things that could break, did it have to be that?

About the Author

This is **Tsuta Suzuki's** second English-language release, with her first being *Your Story I've Known*. Formerly working under the name "Yogore," she has also published *doujinshi* (independent comics) under the circle name "Muddy Pool." Born a Sagittarius in Shikoku, Japan on December 3rd, she has an A blood type and currently resides in Kyoto.

A Strange & Mystifying Story
Volume 4
SuBLime Manga Edition

Story and Art by **Tsuta Suzuki**

Translation—**Adrienne Beck**
Touch-Up Art and Lettering—**Bianca Pistillo**
Cover and Graphic Design—**Julian [JR] Robinson**
Editor—**Jennifer LeBlanc**

libre

Printed in the U.S.A.

Published by SuBLime Manga
P.O. Box 77010
San Francisco, CA 94107

10 9 8 7 6 5 4 3 2 1
First printing, August 2018

M
MATURE

PARENTAL ADVISORY
A STRANGE & MYSTIFYING STORY is rated M for Mature and is recommended for mature readers. This volume contains graphic imagery and mature themes.

SUBLIME
www.SuBLimeManga.com

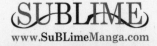